READING, TRANSLATING, REWRITING

SERIES IN FAIRY-TALE STUDIES

General Editor
Donald Haase, Wayne State University

Advisory Editors
Cristina Bacchilega, University of Hawai`i, Mānoa
Stephen Benson, University of East Anglia
Nancy L. Canepa, Dartmouth College
Anne E. Duggan, Wayne State University
Pauline Greenhill, University of Winnipeg
Christine A. Jones, University of Utah
Janet Langlois, Wayne State University
Ulrich Marzolph, University of Göttingen
Carolina Fernández Rodríguez, University of Oviedo
Maria Tatar, Harvard University
Jack Zipes, University of Minnesota

*A complete listing of the books in this series
can be found online at wsupress.wayne.edu*

Reading, Translating, Rewriting
ANGELA CARTER'S TRANSLATIONAL POETICS

Martine Hennard Dutheil de la Rochère

WAYNE STATE UNIVERSITY PRESS   DETROIT

© 2013 by Wayne State University Press, Detroit, Michigan 48201.
All rights reserved. No part of this book may be reproduced without formal permission.

17 16 15 14 13   5 4 3 2 1

LIBRARY OF CONGRESS CATALOGING-IN-PUBLICATION DATA
Dutheil de la Rochère, Martine Hennard.
Reading, Translating, Rewriting : Angela Carter's Translational Poetics / Martine Hennard Dutheil de la Rochère.
pages cm. — (Series in Fairy-Tale Studies)
Includes bibliographical references and index.
ISBN 978-0-8143-3634-2 (pbk. : alk. paper) —
ISBN 978-0-8143-3635-9 (e-book)
1. Carter, Angela, 1940–1992—Criticism and interpretation. 2. Translating and interpreting—History. 3. Fairy tales—History and criticism. 4. Perrault, Charles, 1628–1703—Translations into English—History and criticism. 5. Women in literature. I. Title.
PR6053.A73Z596 2013
823'.914—dc23
2013015474

Grateful acknowledgment is made to the University of Lausanne for the generous support of the publication of this volume.

Quotations from *The Classic Fairy Tales* by Iona and Peter Opie (1974) reproduced by permission of Oxford University Press.

Quotations from Angela Carter's *Bloody Chamber*, copyright © Angela Carter 1979. Reproduced by permission of the author, c/o Rogers, Coleridge & White Ltd., 20 Powis Mews, London W11 1JN.

Quotations from Angela Carter's *Fairy Tales of Charles Perrault*, copyright © Angela Carter 1977. Reproduced by permission of the author, c/o Rogers, Coleridge & White Ltd., 20 Powis Mews, London W11 1JN.

Quotations from Angela Carter's papers held in the British Library, copyright © Angela Carter. Reproduced by permission of the author, c/o Rogers, Coleridge & White Ltd., 20 Powis Mews, London W11 1JN.

Adapted from a design by Chang Jae Lee
Composed in Fournier MT

Contents

Acknowledgments VII

Introduction: Angela Carter's French Connections   1

1. Tracing Editorial Metamorphoses: *The Fairy Tales of Charles Perrault* from 1977 to the Present Day   33

2. Updating the Politics of Experience: From "Le Petit Chaperon rouge" to "Little Red Riding Hood" and "The Company of Wolves"   71

3. Looking Through the Keyhole of Culture, or the Moral Function of Curiosity: From "La Barbe bleue" to "Bluebeard" and "The Bloody Chamber"   109

4. Doing the Somersault of Love: From "Le Chat botté" to "Puss in Boots" and "Puss-in-Boots"   157

5. Revamping Sleeping Beauty: From "La Belle au bois dormant" to "The Sleeping Beauty in the Wood" and "The Lady of the House of Love"   189

6. Recovering a Female Tradition: From "La Belle et la Bête" to "Beauty and the Beast" and "The Tiger's Bride"   227

7. Giving Up the Ghost: From "Cendrillon ou la petite pantoufle de verre" to "Cinderella: or, The Little Glass Slipper" and "Ashputtle *or* The Mother's Ghost"   263

Conclusion: The Poetics and Politics of Translation   299

Notes   303
Bibliography   349
Index   363

Acknowledgments

As Angela Carter knew well, writing is a dialogic activity and every book a collective adventure. I am deeply grateful to my teacher, mentor, colleague, and friend Neil Forsyth for introducing me to Angela Carter's fiction many years ago and sharing his memories of Carter in Japan. Neil patiently read and reread versions of the book in progress with his usual generosity and critical acumen. I am also indebted to Donald Haase for his lasting interest in my research on the fairy tale and encouragements to carry out the projected book, and to the two anonymous readers at Wayne State University Press for their helpful feedback. Recently, Marina Warner kindly read two chapters of the book, and I have benefited from her invaluable insights into Carter's work in context. Over the years, I have had stimulating conversations and friendly exchanges with several members of the fairy-tale community aside from the eminent scholars just mentioned, including Cristina Bacchilega, Stephen Benson, Sue Bottigheimer, Judith Buchanan, Sarah Gamble, Bill Gray, Pauline Greenhill, Elizabeth Wanning Harries, Vanessa Joosen, Anna Kérchy, Gillian Lathey, Ulrich Marzolf, Mayako Murai, Michelle Ryan-Sautour, Monika Wozniak, and Jack Zipes. My debt also extends to close colleagues for their support, advice, and friendship, especially Valérie Cossy, Rachel Falconer, Irene Kacandes, Nidesh Lawtoo, Brigitte Maire, Roelof Overmeer, Christine Raguet, Denis Renevey, and Kirsten Stirling.

Many thanks, too, are due to graduate students who provided valuable research assistance, first and foremost Marie Walz, but also Cyrille François, Olivier Knechciak, and Ashley Riggs, all of them promising researchers in their own right. Michaël Krieger kindly scanned the images. I am also grateful to the many students who have followed my advanced fairy-tale-related classes over the years; they are far too many to name, but I am particularly indebted to Mercedes Gulin, Celia Mehou-Loko, Magali Monnier, Annick Panchaud, Glen Regard, and Geraldine Viret for their contributions and enthusiasm.

I wish to extend my gratitude to Martin Ware for our correspondence and for his permission to reproduce his artwork from *The Fairy Tales of Charles Perrault*. I hope that the present study will contribute to the rediscovery of his unique fairy-tale illustrations. Michael Foreman also gave permission to reproduce the cover of the second edition of *Sleeping Beauty and Other Fairy Tales*. I am grateful for having been granted access to the Angela Carter Papers at the British Library and thank the efficient and helpful librarians of the manuscript section. I would also like to thank Carter's agent and friend, Deborah Rogers, and her team at Rogers, Coleridge & White Ltd. for giving me permission to use unpublished material from this invaluable archive. This also extends to the Penguin Group and Oxford University Press for permission to reproduce textual and visual material.

To finish the manuscript, I have benefited from a semester-long reduction of my teaching duties granted by the Dean's Office; and the Publication Commission of the Humanities Faculty at the University of Lausanne generously covered copyright-related costs and indexing. Many thanks also to the highly professional team at Wayne State University Press, especially Annie Martin for supervising the publication process, Kristina E. Stonehill for her help with the rights, and Mimi Braverman for her efficient and rigorous editing of the manuscript.

Some portions of the book have appeared in a different form in several journals and edited books. I would like to thank the editors for granting permission to reprint extended and revised versions of the following essays: "Modelling for Bluebeard: Visual and Narrative Art in Angela Carter's 'The Bloody Chamber,'" in *The Seeming and the Seen: Essays in Modern Visual and Literary Culture*, ed. Beverly Maeder, Jürg Schwyter, Ilona Sigrist, and Boris Vejdovsky (New York: Peter Lang, 2006), 183–208; "New Wine in Old Bottles: Angela Carter's Translation of Charles Perrault's 'La Barbe bleue'" (co-authored with Ute Heidmann), *Marvels & Tales* 23.1 (2009): 40–58; "Updating the Politics of Experience: Angela Carter's Translation of Charles Perrault's 'Le Petit Chaperon Rouge,'" *Palimpsestes* 22 (2009): 187–204; "'But Marriage Itself Is No Party': Angela Carter's Translation of Charles Perrault's 'La Belle au bois dormant,'" *Marvels &*

Tales 24.1 (2010): 131–51; "Conjuring the Curse of Repetition or 'Sleeping Beauty' Revamped: Angela Carter's *Vampirella* and 'The Lady of the House of Love,'" in *Des Fata aux fées: regards croisés de l'Antiquité à nos jours,* ed. Martine Hennard Dutheil de la Rochère and Véronique Dasen (special issue of Etudes de Lettres 289.3–4 [2011]), 333–54; "From Translation to Rewriting: The Interplay of Text and Image in *The Fairy Tales of Charles Perrault* and *The Bloody Chamber and Other Stories,*" *Journal of the Short Story in English* 56 (2011): 93–108; and "Les métamorphoses de Cendrillon: analyse comparée de deux traductions anglaises du conte de Perrault," in *Autour de la retraduction,* ed. Enrico Monti and Peter Schnyder (Paris: Orizons, 2011), 157–79.

Last but not least, Pascal Dutheil de la Rochère helped me throughout the entire process, not only by dealing with copyright matters but also in many other ways. His and Alexis's love, patience, and good humor have sustained me for even longer than it took to write this book. I am therefore dedicating it to "the boys" (as Carter would say).

Introduction

ANGELA CARTER'S FRENCH CONNECTIONS

Each reading is a translation.

—OCTAVIO PAZ, "TRANSLATION: LITERATURE AND LETTERS," 159

Translation is a little explored facet of Angela Carter's rich creativity, even though it formed the background for and counterpoint to her fairy-tale rewritings in *The Bloody Chamber and Other Stories* (1979). Always a curious traveler, Carter liked to move between continents, cultures, languages, literatures, genres, and media, and this gave her writing its distinctive experimental edge, adventurous spirit, and provocative force. Deliberate decentering through linguistic and cultural translation characterizes her life and her work. This probably began when she "ran away" to Japan in 1969, as Neil Forsyth, who first met her in Tokyo, confirms: "Her brilliant essay on the Japanese tattoo is an obvious instance of this fascination. She did not know Japanese, so could not 'translate' exactly, but the power of the images around her was already a powerful stimulus."[1] Carter's experience of Japan echoes that of Roland Barthes in his 1970 essay, *L'empire des signes* (*The Empire of Signs*), as Lorna Sage has aptly noted. Barthes, like Carter, considered the encounter with a radically different environment and the resistance to translation as a unique occasion to think, write, and create. Carter even combined several forms of linguistic and cultural displacement during her stay in Japan when she translated Xavière Gauthier's *Surréalisme et sexualité* into English while working on *The Infernal Desire Machines of Doctor Hoffman* (1972).[2]

A few years later, Carter seized an opportunity to brush up her French when she was commissioned to retranslate Charles Perrault's *Histoires ou contes du temps passé, avec des Moralités* (1697) into English for Victor Gollancz.[3] She deliberately modernized their language and message in *The Fairy Tales of Charles Perrault* before rewriting them for adults in *The Bloody Chamber and Other Stories*. Despite the linguistic, historical, and cultural gap, Carter found in Perrault's *contes* a type of imaginative literature compatible with her own "demythologizing" project. Their worldly morals in particular chimed in with the idea that "*this* world is all that there is" ("Notes from the Front Line," 38), and lent themselves to Carter's materialist, socialist, and feminist standpoint.[4] Not only did Carter become closely familiar with Perrault's collection on this occasion, but she also immersed herself in the international fairy-tale tradition. Although her translation for children foregrounds Perrault's teaching of down-to-earth lessons about life, against standard commonplaces about the genre as escapist, Carter's self-styled "book of stories about fairy stories" ("Notes from the Front Line," 38) explores the potential for re-creation and alternative retellings, inviting us to rediscover the tales anew, just as she did herself in the hot summer of 1976.

In "Notes from the Front Line" Carter encourages "the reader to construct *her* own fiction for *herself* from the elements of my fictions" (37). She memorably adds, if only parenthetically: "Reading is just as creative an activity as writing and most intellectual development depends upon *new readings of old texts*. I am all for putting new wine in old bottles, especially if the pressure of the new wine makes the old bottles explode" (37; italics mine).[5] I propose to examine some of the forms that this kind of active reading takes in Carter's work both as a translator from the French and as an author in her own right.

Further, in this study I argue that Carter's view of creation as stemming from the dynamic interplay of reading and writing was intimately connected to, and perhaps even originated in, her experience as a translator. To do so, I trace the interrelationship between reading, translating, and fiction writing as continuous and intricately related activities that reflect a coherent aesthetic and pragmatic project. In other words, translation *was* for Carter the laboratory of creation in which she conducted her literary experiments, and it gave a new impulse and direction to her writing.

In *The Fairy Tales of Charles Perrault* (1977) Carter tried to recover a sense of the French author's original project (as she saw it), which paradoxically entailed adapting and reformulating the seventeenth-century *contes* for young readers steeped in a completely different context. The work of translation brought an awareness of the agency of the translator as mediator and re-creator, and Carter simultaneously discovered the historical thickness, textual density, and dual mode of address (children and adults) of Perrault's deceptively simple tales. She could not convey all this complexity in her translation but would explore it more fully in her rewritings. *The Bloody Chamber* can therefore be seen as the continuation of and counterpoint to *The Fairy Tales of Charles Perrault*, all the more so because the two projects were carried out more or less simultaneously. Jack Zipes remarks in his introduction to the recent paperback reissue that "as she began her work on Perrault, [Carter] also started writing her own original stories that formed the basis of *The Bloody Chamber*."[6]

Even though the critical consensus reads into Carter a feminist imperative to subvert classic fairy tales, my aim is to show that she valued Perrault as a practical educator, a proto-folklorist, and an accomplished storyteller. She went on to respond to more hidden aspects of his texts and recover a lesser known folktale tradition associated with the Grimms in her rewritings while opening up the fairy tale to many other genres and media. Carter's twofold project therefore reflects an ongoing dialogue with Perrault as a fellow writer who used his art to communicate useful knowledge and develop reading skills for different categories of readers. Thus Carter's interest in this distinguished civil servant and member of the Académie française is not as surprising as it may first seem.

Translating and/as Rewriting: Angela Carter and the Creative Turn of Translation Studies

Moreover, critics are not merely the alchemical translators of texts into circumstantial reality of worldliness; for they too are subject to and producers of circumstances. . . . The point is that texts have ways of existing that even in their most rarefied form are always enmeshed in circumstances, time, place, and society—in short, they are in the world, and hence worldly.

—EDWARD SAID, *THE WORLD, THE TEXT, AND THE CRITIC*, 35

It is absurd to see translation as anything other than a creative literary activity, for translators are all the time engaging with texts first as readers and then as rewriters, as recreators of that text in another language.

—SUSAN BASSNETT, "WRITING AND TRANSLATING," 174

The development of translation studies in the second half of the twentieth century was an occasion to reappraise the role of translation in literary history and to discover—or rediscover—key figures who contributed to the circulation of texts, genres, and ideas that had a significant impact on the receiving culture. Angela Carter is a good case in point. Heralded as one of the major writers of the twentieth century, Carter revived the fairy tale as a genre for adults in *The Bloody Chamber*, even starting a fashion that lasts to this day. And yet her activity as a translator has been almost completely ignored, although its links with her literary practice reflect an understanding of the profoundly *transformative* nature of translation. This coincides with the creative turn in translation studies, which challenges widespread notions of translation as derivative and debased, marginal and mechanical, and draws attention to the complex processes involved in this intimate and productive form of close reading.

Against long-standing notions of equivalence that led to endless debates about the relative faithfulness of individual translations, the most significant contemporary theories of translation have followed up on Walter Benjamin's epochal essay "Die Aufgabe des Übersetzers" (1923), which rethinks translation as a form that ensures the afterlife of a literary work.[7] For Benjamin the original text and its translation, although different in status and nature, are mutually dependent insofar as each version of the source is unique, constituting "another stage in the evolution of the original since a text bears in itself all possible translations and gets all the richer with each additional reading-rewriting."[8] The time of a book is not located in the moment of writing but in the open, future-oriented, and limitless temporality of reading and memory. Meaning is not contained within the text but is produced in the act of reading, as in the theories of reception propounded by Hans Robert Jauss and Wolfgang Iser.

After Benjamin, Jacques Derrida's deconstruction of the hierarchy between source and target texts has also contributed to the rethinking of translation as process and supplement, repetition with productive difference. Instead of considering translation as the mere reproduction of a text in another language, an apparently neutral "transaction," Derrida reconceptualizes it as a "transferential and transformational" act.[9] In his turn, Lawrence Venuti calls for a translation practice and ethics that self-consciously inscribes and valorizes difference in order to make the translator visible and to recognize his or her cultural role and creative intervention.[10]

In this study I also extend the meaning of translation to encompass the various forms of creative transposition identified by Roman Jakobson in "On Linguistic Aspects of Translation"; these transpositions occur "either [as] intralingual transposition—from one poetic shape into another (or rewording in a different form or genre), or [as] interlingual transposition—from one language into another, or finally [as] intersemiotic transposition—from one system of signs into another, e.g. from verbal art into music, dance, cinema or painting."[11] Carter's work illustrates the three types of transposition outlined by Jakobson. Specifically, "intersemiotic transposition" is a shaping force of literature that is often neglected, as Liliane Louvel observes, when texts are examined in isolation from their material reality and broader cultural context. Louvel suggests that the interplay of text and image implies operations akin to translation, and she describes the modalities of this dialogue in *Texte/Image: Images à lire, textes à voir* (2002), where she argues that "the term of *translation* is flexible enough to describe what happens when we move from image to text and vice versa within a dialogic system of response, an operation of translation or interpretation" (148). After Derrida, Louvel sees the interplay of text and image in terms of a differential structure of analogy and difference (or, rather, *différance*) that arises from their tension, so that "the passage between the two semiotic codes is to be read in-between" (149).[12] The dynamic process of intersemiotic (or intermedial) translation therefore requires a form of active reading on the part of the reader or viewer, who is made to move to and fro (Louvel uses the term *oscillation*) between text and image. This model is particularly relevant for the fairy tale as a genre associated with storytelling and dramatic performance but also illustrated books, films, and other mixed modes of cultural expression. My contention is that the interplay of French and English, of the literary fairy tale and the oral folktale, and of text, voice, and image, informs the creative dynamic that brings together *The Fairy Tales of Charles Perrault* and *The Bloody Chamber*.

Carter's experiments with the fairy tale in her short stories and in her radio plays exemplify this process. The radio plays were meant to recreate the aural experience of storytelling and explore "the atavistic lure, the atavistic power, of voices in the dark," with sound effects designed to stimulate the listener's imagination (or inner eye).[13] The scripts were published in book form in *Come unto These Yellow Sands* (1985), with paintings by Richard Dadd. Three of Carter's radio plays offer variations on "Puss in Boots," "Little Red Riding Hood," and "Sleeping Beauty" and hence rework the same fairy-tale material used in *The Bloody Chamber*. Each time the story is transposed into another medium, it produces an altogether different experience, whether as oral performance or written text.[14] Intermedial transposition, therefore, was a mainspring of Carter's creative enterprise not only because the writer experimented with her own work and the idea of the multiple, multidimensional, and open-ended text, but also because she had a strongly visual imagination and a long-standing interest in the interrelationship between text, voice, and image.

Apart from discussing Martin Ware's original artwork for *The Fairy Tales of Charles Perrault*, I will show that Iona and Peter Opie's *Classic Fairy Tales*, which contains many illustrations, also found its way into Carter's own collection of fairy-tale rewritings. The notion of the dialogic, hybrid, metamorphic text that is so central to Carter's literary practice therefore escapes easy categories, for it cuts across traditional boundaries between the arts on the one hand and linguistic, cultural, and national frontiers on the other. What I propose to call the *translational poetics* at the heart of Carter's work thus brings together aesthetics and politics as it tirelessly interrogates and subverts naturalized divisions, oppositions, and hierarchies and draws its creative energy from productive differences.[15]

Rethinking translation after the cultural turn also means that both source and target texts must be apprehended in context to recognize their status as unique productions embedded in a particular social, economic, and cultural reality; studying them together highlights their differences as pointing to a genuine process of re-creation. It also draws attention to the importance of translation in the evolution and interaction of literature and culture. According to André Lefevere and Susan Bassnett, "Translation is, of course, the rewriting of an original text. All rewritings, whatever their intention, reflect a certain ideology and a poetics and as such manipulate literature to function in a given society in a given way."[16] From the perspective of postcolonial studies, Homi K. Bhabha, in *The Location of Culture*, theorizes the concept of "cultural translation" as a defining feature of contemporary cultural exchanges that destabilizes the claims of authority of the original text and moves beyond the fraught binaries of authentic and inauthentic, original and copy, source and target. Instead, Bhabha focuses on the *movement* of translation as an ongoing, complex, and dynamic process that takes place *in-between* cultures.[17] Inasmuch as Bhabha's model challenges fixed oppositions, naturalized categories, and artificial hierarchies in order to foreground the constitutive hybridity and in-betweenness of culture(s), it also provides a useful way to highlight the cross-linguistic and cross-cultural dimension of Carter's work as a major source of creativity. Drawing on these new paradigms of translation, in this study I seek to capture the dynamics of creation in Carter's work within the framework of translation.

Angela Carter's Translational Poetics, or the Magic of Foreign Words

> Better—than Music! For I—who heard it—
>
> I was used—to the Birds—before—
>
> This—was different—'Twas Translation—
>
> Of all tunes I knew—and more—
>
> —EMILY DICKINSON, "BETTER—THAN MUSIC! FOR I—WHO HEARD IT"

The international fairy-tale tradition gave Angela Carter a unique playground to experiment with literary and cultural translation. Perrault's late-seventeenth-century *contes*, with their obsolete turns of phrase and vocabulary, ironic asides, ambiguous language, and veiled allusions to the author's own time and milieu, went against commonplaces about the alleged simplicity of the fairy tale. The translation for children glosses over these difficulties, but the rewriting often takes up aspects of the text that resisted translation or were left unexplored in *The Fairy Tales of Charles Perrault*. It also revisits a tradition of "folk-tales" that Carter read or heard in childhood from the perspective of adulthood. Carter's *translational poetics* not only links the translation and the rewriting but also characterizes *The Bloody Chamber* itself, as the presence of foreign words and recurrent situations of cross-cultural encounters confirm. Thus Carter's Transylvanian Beauty chatters away in "heavily accented French" in "The Lady of the House of Love" (*Bloody Chamber*, 100, 103; also 102, 104, 105). In "Puss-in-Boots" the worldly-wise Puss speaks his native Bergamasque with a touch of French "since that is the only language in which you can purr" (68). The necrophagous Duke in "Wolf-Alice" eats his corpses "provençale," that is, stuffed with garlic (121), in a gruesomely comic mix of ghoulish horror associated with Central Europe spiced with southern French cuisine.[18] In "The Erl-King" the young woman ensnared by the earl-king cries "Ach!" in German when his kisses turn into a bite (88), probably in homage to Goethe's ballad. In "The Tiger's Bride" a Dostoyevskian Russian gambler traveling with his young and beautiful daughter loses her at cards to the Beast in Italy. Formerly titled "La Bestia," this tale places various cross-cultural encounters at the heart of the narrative: The landlady refers to the Beast in Italian as "la Bestia," and she exclaims "Che bella!" when she sees the young woman (52). In the Beast's castle a monkey acts as an interpreter between the man-tiger and his bride, hinting at even more outlandish experiences of interspecies encounters and the challenges they pose to communication. Some form of mutual understanding will nevertheless be reached by the two protagonists beyond the language barrier.[19] Carter's rewritings therefore inscribe linguistic difference as they thematize and enact situations of cross-cultural confrontation, negotiation, and exchange and explore their transformative effects.

Retranslating French fairy tales into English in the second half of the twentieth century also required finding a suitable form to communicate relevant knowledge to children. Just as translation is necessarily concerned with issues of transmission and reception, fairy tales have long had a sociocultural and communicative function. They even acquired an explicitly pedagogical role when seventeenth-century literary tales were adapted for child readers in England. Gillian Lathey traces this rich history in *The Role of Translators in Children's Literature*. She shows how the strategies and aims of the translators roughly follow the contours of changing perceptions of childhood and of children's needs, interests, and abilities. Not unlike Mary Wollstonecraft, "who chose to translate Christian Gotthilf Salzmann's stories of everyday life in the late eighteenth century because their moral message matched those in her own publication for children" (Lathey, *Role of Translators*, 6–7), Carter contributes to a long-standing tradition of translators of moral (or moralized) tales for children at a time when it is no longer fashionable to do so, as she wryly observes in "The Better to Eat You With." Carter's recuperation of the moral may have been in part a reaction against Disney's exploitation of the fairy tale as safe, fun, family entertainment devoid of the sharp life lessons that made the storytelling tradition meaningful and socially relevant. Unsurprisingly, however, Carter goes on to redefine the "moral tale" through Perrault and the idea of "moral literature" itself.

Although *The Fairy Tales of Charles Perrault* conforms to modern-day ideas of the fairy tale and adapts Perrault accordingly, Carter also reassesses the nature, value, and significance of his work.[20] As Sherry Simon observes:

> Translators contribute to cultural debates and create new lines of cultural communication. [They] are necessarily involved in a politics of transmission, in perpetuating or contesting the values which sustain our literary culture. It should be stressed, however, that it is not the gendered identity of the translator as such which influences the politics of transmission as much as the *project* which the translator is promoting. Feminism, in its diverse forms, has become the powerful basis of many such projects. (*Gender in Translation*, x–xi)[21]

A self-declared feminist, Carter was concerned with education as a key to emancipation, hence her interest in children's literature. She found Perrault's *contes* congenial to her own project, and the choices that she made in her translation further enabled her to reclaim the genre at a time when the fairy tale was a hotly debated subject in feminist circles. Because language does not simply mirror but also shapes reality, literature can help bring about social change. According to Helen Simpson, Carter was using the fairy tale with a deliberate radical intent: she even declared in a letter to Robert Coover that she believed "that a fiction absolutely self-conscious of itself as a different form of human experience than reality (that is, not a logbook of events) can help to transform reality itself."[22]

Carter's view of the fairy tale, then, reflects the socially progressive and utopian drive that Jack Zipes sees as an essential component of the genre. It is also consistent with the traditional role of storytelling documented by Marina Warner in *From the Beast to the Blonde: On Fairy Tales and Their Tellers*: a domestic art that enchants and delights but also serves to transmit useful knowledge and experience as well as subversive social comment. Carter indeed saw Perrault as the mediator of a popular tradition of storytelling by nurses and old wives that could be endlessly adapted for new audiences and purposes. As a translator of Perrault, Carter in turn participated in this chain of transmitters, whose activity was consistent with her own idea of a responsible and meaningful feminist practice. As an author in her own right, Carter could more fully and self-consciously celebrate the fairy tale as a literary art. The translation-rewriting dynamic can thus be seen as an invitation to read on different levels and for different publics. Even though Carter took Perrault's claims and intentions at face value, stressing the popular origin and educational value of the fairy tales as stories for children, her rewritings develop the more advanced skills that the French author asked of his older, more sophisticated and experienced readers.

The Fairy Tales of Charles Perrault belongs to a long history of translation and reception of fairy tales as assimilated to children's literature since the eighteenth century. The formation of a canon of English-language children's books through the circulation, translation, and adaptation of a body of texts aimed at young readers in Europe has been well documented in recent years.[23] The history of this changing corpus echoes current debates about education, morality, and the role of imaginative literature. Unsurprisingly, a comparative analysis of Perrault's texts and Carter's translation nearly 300 years later reveals profound transformations of the genre as the fashionable salon entertainment became modern bedtime stories for children. Aside from significant changes in form, language, tone, style, meaning, and audience, in this study I examine the construction of a child reader in Carter's translation, the reorientation of didacticism and moralizing in favor of emancipation, the manipulation of generic conventions and expectations, the pressure of the Grimms' *Kinder- und Hausmärchen*, the introduction of new cultural references and intertextual echoes, the interplay of text and image in the editions under scrutiny, and the rediscovery of a female fairy-tale tradition.

Another modality of boundary crossing that I address in this study is the interplay of creative and critical literature in Carter's fairy-tale-inspired fiction. *The Bloody Chamber* is a volume of "stories *about* fairy stories" (Carter, "Notes from the Front Line," 38; italics mine). As Carter herself admitted, albeit with some misgivings, fiction was for her a means to work out ideas and develop arguments.[24] The dense intertextuality characteristic of her writing style accordingly reflects her engagement not only with her literary and visual sources but also with the reception of the fairy tale in psychoanalytical, formalist, and feminist criticism. As Stephen Benson and Vanessa Joosen convincingly argue, fairy-tale studies have come to prominence in close interaction with the phenomenon of fairy-tale rewritings.[25] Carter notoriously plays a central role in this debate, both directly through her own work as a translator, commentator, editor, and writer of fairy tales and indirectly through the polarized critical reception of her own writings in the 1980s. A detailed examination of the translation-rewriting dynamic brings a fuller understanding of Carter's position in this debate and sheds light on the impact of her intervention in fairy-tale discourse. Carter actively participated in the development of fairy-tale studies and even joined the editorial board of *Merveilles & Contes* (now *Marvels & Tales*), founded by Jacques Barchilon in 1987 at the University of Colorado.[26] She also had close contacts and exchanged ideas with two of the most influential and productive fairy-tale scholars today: Jack Zipes, whose work as a critic, translator, and editor of fairy tales has played a crucial role in renewing interest in fairy-tale study and criticism, and Marina Warner, writer of fiction, criticism, and cultural history, including the seminal *From the Beast to the Blonde*; both Zipes and Warner have paid tribute to Carter.[27]

Reassessing the Role of Translation in Angela Carter's Work

A folktale is a poetic text that carries some of its cultural contexts within it; it is also a travelling metaphor that finds a new meaning with every telling.

—A. K. RAMANUJAN, *FOLKTALES FROM INDIA*, 1

In her 1990 introduction to *The Virago Book of Fairy Tales* Carter explains that she is using the term *fairy tale* "loosely," "as a figure of speech" to refer to a vast body of diverse narratives passed on "by word of mouth" (*Angela Carter's Book of Fairy Tales*, xi). This broad understanding of the genre reconciles the literary fairy tale with folklore, in which Carter professed an even greater interest in than myth in "Notes from the Front Line." A close examination of the translation-rewriting dynamic nevertheless reveals productive tensions between the literary and the folk heritage. Broadly, the translation seeks to restore a socially critical edge and progressive pedagogical role to the familiar stories of "Bluebeard," "Little Red Riding Hood," or "Sleeping Beauty" as retold by Perrault, whereas the rewritings collected in *The Bloody Chamber* imaginatively uncover a tradition of folktales obscured by the fairy-tale canon, albeit in the highly literary style favored by the French seventeenth-century female fairy-tale authors with whom Carter implicitly aligned herself as a self-proclaimed mannerist. As several critics have shown, the folktale played a crucial role in Carter's writing, and it even constituted, to quote Stephen Benson, "a seam through her output from the early novels to one of her last published volumes, *The Second Virago Book of Fairy Tales*."[28] I would be prepared to argue, however, that the literary fairy tale also contributed to Carter's aesthetics and signature style.

Carter's fairy-tale-inspired fiction has been amply documented in monographs, collections of essays, and individual articles, with particular emphasis on *The Bloody Chamber*.[29] Some critics have broadened the scope of inquiry to consider Carter's children's books (Jack Zipes), her work for radio, film, and television (Charlotte Crofts), and edited collections of fairy tales for Virago (Mayako Murai), let alone the reception of her work in literature, film, and other media.[30] Carter's translations from the French, however, have received only scant attention. In the short homage "Remembering Angela Carter" published in Danielle Roemer and Cristina Bacchilega's pioneering *Angela Carter and the Fairy Tale*, originally published as a special issue of *Marvels & Tales* in 1998, Jacques Barchilon praises Carter's translation for its exactness but rapidly moves on to her "beautiful literary echoes of classical folktales"[31] and their ensuing correspondence and collaboration. More recently, Ute Heidmann and Jean-Michel Adam briefly refer to Carter's "The Fairies" and "Bluebeard" as reflecting a generic shift in their contribution to *Language and Verbal Art Revisited* (2006).[32] The most extensive discussion so far is Jack Zipes's introduction to the Penguin reissue of *The Fairy Tales of Charles Perrault* (2008), which underlines the importance of translating Perrault in the development of Carter's career and stresses its innovative nature as a "remake."

My own work started with an examination of the interplay of text and image in "The Bloody Chamber" in *The Seeming and the Seen* (2006) and was pursued in comparative analyses of Carter's translations of "Bluebeard" (2009), "Little Red Riding Hood" (2009), "Sleeping Beauty" (2010), and "Cinderella" (2011).[33] In the present study I extend the scope of the inquiry to the rewriting process. I also respond to Zipes's perplexity at Carter's decision to translate Perrault "at the height of the feminist movement" (*Fairy Tales*, xix) and to his claim that "she definitely had to 'misinterpret' him" (xix).

Zipes rightly observes that "very few critics realize that Perrault played a highly significant role in Angela Carter's development as a fairy-tale writer."[34] He even speculates that "if it were not for the fact that she was commissioned to translate Perrault's *Histoires ou contes du temps passé avec des moralités* (1697) in 1976, she would probably not have conceived her unique, ground-breaking collection of feminist fairy tales."[35] Sharing Zipes's call for a reassessment of the role of translation in Carter's oeuvre, if not his vision of Carter's perception of Perrault as a conservative writer, I offer a critical complement to his timely reissue of *The Fairy Tales of Charles Perrault*, long out of print. By situating the translations in the broader context of Carter's literary development, I hope to show that her masterpiece, *The Bloody Chamber*, in fact originated in Perrault's *Contes de ma mère l'Oye*, to cite the title of the 1695 manuscript edition (echoed on the frontispiece, which features a female storyteller surrounded by young people). What is more, this collection of "New Mother Goose Tales," as Carter called them, reflects the background research that she carried out for her translation. Her rediscovery of the international fairy-tale tradition even shaped her understanding of the dialogic nature of fiction itself, reflected in the interplay of (re)reading and (re)writing as the generating principle for creation.

The Fairy Tales of Charles Perrault testifies to Carter's deep knowledge of French and full investment in the task. Jacques Barchilon praises the "accuracy and imagination"[36] of her modern retranslation, which he contrasts with Marianne Moore's "inaccurate" one. Because reading played such a central role in Carter's literary practice, it is interesting to reconstitute her personal library. As the "Selected Bibliography" appended to *The Fairy Tales of Charles Perrault* (1977) indicates, when she undertook the task of translation, Carter familiarized herself with fairy-tale scholarship and with the European fairy-tale tradition as steeped in cross-cultural exchanges inseparable from translations and adaptations. She immersed herself in the study of Perrault's *contes*, including the life of their author, the larger social and discursive contexts in which they were embedded, and their early reception in England. Because she consulted various editions of Perrault's famous collection in French and in English, including Iona and Peter Opie's *Classic Fairy Tales* (1974), which reproduces the first English translation of the familiar tales and outlines their textual development, Carter could not ignore the complex editorial history of Perrault's collection, especially in translation. Moreover, having read Jacques Barchilon's 1975 study *Le conte merveilleux français de 1690 à 1790*, Carter was aware of the social and literary environment in which the French *conteurs* and *conteuses* operated and knew how they transformed a popular tradition of folktales into mock naive, subtly ironic, and sophisticated literary fairy tales.

In fact, Carter shared Barchilon's call to rehabilitate the fairy tale not only as a literary genre but also as *authored* texts at a time when the names of Perrault, d'Aulnoy, and others were little known in the English-speaking world.[37] In *The Authentic Mother Goose Fairy Tales and Nursery Rhymes*, Barchilon pays tribute to the "distinguished authors" (8) behind the mythic figure of "Mother Goose." An important section of the introduction, significantly titled "The Mother Goose Tales as Literature" (16–29), stresses the importance of recovering the author behind the beloved fairy tales.

Barchilon also points out that, although rooted in folklore, Perrault's *contes* are situated in a specific historical and aesthetic context, "the Baroque Period" (*Authentic Mother Goose Fairy Tales*, 18), and are "told on two levels" (21) so that they "artfully juxtapose the wonderful and real" (25); their artfulness, humor, veiled allusions to sexuality and social mores, however, are often lost in translation.[38] Although fairy tales tend to be dehistoricized and universalized, modern-day scholars insist, following Barchilon, on the necessity to read them in context. Carter's decision to work from the first editions of Perrault's *contes* testifies to the importance she gave to a text-based approach to literary tales and her awareness of their sociocultural significance, political subtext, and ideological implications; consequently, she contributed to this major methodological shift in fairy-tale studies.[39] The quality of Carter's translation and detailed introduction to the 1977 edition of *The Fairy Tales of Charles Perrault* also reflects a high idea of the task of the translator and a desire to live up to the combined "challenge and pleasure" of making the tales "seem as fresh as they must have seemed to the first readers," to quote the dust jacket of the first edition.

Retelling Fairy Tales for All Ages: Carter's Contrapuntal Project

> As we look back at the cultural archive, we begin to reread it not univocally but contrapuntally, with a simultaneous awareness both of the metropolitan history that is narrated and of those other histories against which (and together with which) the dominating discourse acts.
>
> —EDWARD SAID, *CULTURE AND IMPERIALISM*, 59

Translation, as we have seen, is a form of rewriting. I conversely propose to consider rewriting as a form of translation, based on contrapuntal analyses of Carter's twofold project as translator and author. Edward Said uses the term *counterpoint* as a critical and methodological tool in *Culture and Imperialism* (1993). Said famously defines the term in relation to the composition of Western classical music, where various themes play off one another to create music (if not harmony) within a polyphonic system. The idea of counterpoint captures Said's linking of critical discourse and artistic expression, intellectual inquiry and social responsibility, which Carter was also concerned with. Counterpoint, then, emphasizes that each voice (or retelling, as I use it here) is unique but it also depends on the other voices which it responds to. In my opinion, then, a contrapuntal reading sheds light on Carter's double project of translation and rewriting as interconnected and yet distinct and mutually illuminating reformulations of a familiar story for different kinds of readers.[40]

Thinking of the translation-rewriting dynamic in terms of the concept of counterpoint also hints at Carter's lifelong interest in the interplay of language and music. This is nowhere more apparent than in her comic version of "Puss in Boots" for radio and her libretto for an *opera* of Virginia Woolf's *Orlando*, let alone the numerous references to music (Wagner, Debussy, etc.) in *The Bloody Chamber*. Carter often conveys this interest in mixed visual and musical images in relation to her own work, as in her conversation with Helen Simpson, where she expresses her preference for short fiction as follows: "The short story is not minimalist, it is rococo. I feel in absolute control. It is like writing chamber music rather than symphonies."

A study of the dynamics of creation in Angela Carter's work confirms Jack Zipes's claim in the introduction to *The Fairy Tales of Charles Perrault* that translation was a "remaking" of Perrault's tales that Carter would pursue in *The Bloody Chamber*: "This was typical of Carter, a very independent and original thinker, who rebelled against classical tradition while absorbing and recreating it in her own distinct down-to-earth, baroque manner."[41] Interestingly, "independent thinking," "rebellion against a classic tradition," and even "down-to-earth" and "baroque manner" apply equally well to Perrault. I therefore propose to qualify the notion of "subversion" of Perrault that characterizes the critical consensus in Carter criticism in favor of "reclamation." For one thing, translating is a fundamentally ambivalent gesture because it involves appropriation and re-creation, but it also contributes to the canonization of its source. Moreover, in the case at hand, Carter explicitly aligns herself with Perrault's project, and like him she rehabilitates the fairy tale as a modern genre par excellence. Far from underestimating the originality and boldness of Carter's endeavor or the changes introduced by the modern translator, internal and paratextual evidence (essays, prefaces, interviews, etc.) confirms that Carter's response to Perrault was overwhelmingly positive and sympathetic. She approved of his rebellious spirit and his siding with the Moderns in the famous quarrel, repeatedly expressed admiration for the artful simplicity of his tales, recognized the importance of the morals, and reactivated their socially critical edge. Moreover, Carter made Perrault into a child-friendly figure who played a key role in recovering a neglected or despised storytelling tradition. In short, Carter strove to communicate the spirit, vision, and wisdom of the familiar tales popularized by Perrault against the Disneyfication of the genre. Angela Carter's conscious endorsement of the role of empathetic cultural mediator of Perrault's *contes* in English therefore encourages us to reconsider his contribution to the fairy-tale tradition. Both the title of *The Fairy Tales of Charles Perrault* and the lengthy preface detailing the author's life and work indicate that Carter wanted to give visibility to the author and his didactic project as much as to his *contes*. She believed that Perrault's distinct intervention had been forgotten, misunderstood, or assimilated to the escapist tradition that she disapproved of. *The Fairy Tales of Charles Perrault* even stresses the continuity between Perrault's *contes*, Carter's translations, and her own rewritings in its very structure.

The Fairy Tales of Charles Perrault closes with a translation of "Peau d'Ane" (Donkey-Skin), which originally belonged to Perrault's earlier volume of verse tales. Carter's translation is in fact based on the more popular anonymous prose version of 1781 (not on the original verse text published in Perrault's 1694 collection). Carter nevertheless retains Perrault's playful moral and uses it as an occasion for pointed social commentary and metafictional comment.

> The story of Donkey-Skin is not something you might read every day in the morning papers. But as long as there are children, mothers, grandmothers and Mother Goose, it will always seem new. (*Fairy Tales*, 157)

> Le Conte de Peau d'Âne est difficile à croire,
> Mais tant que dans le Monde on aura des Enfants,
> Des Mères et des Mères-grands,
> On en gardera la mémoire.
> (Perrault, *Contes*, 115)

Thus Carter chooses to end *The Fairy Tales of Charles Perrault* with a story of incest broaching the theme of devious sexuality that opens *The Bloody Chamber*, a collection in which Carter notoriously explores the sexual subtext of the familiar tales.

The connection between Perrault's literary *contes* and Carter's own fairy-tale rewritings is made through Perrault's tribute to mothers and grandmothers telling the age-old story of "Peau d'Ane" to children. This stresses the role of an oral female fairy-tale tradition with which Carter affiliated herself. She even refers to the mythical figure of Mother Goose, which Perrault's text does not mention here, but which connects his own *Contes de ma Mère l'Oye* to her own project as a collection of *new* Mother Goose tales.[42] Tellingly, Carter translates Perrault's future-oriented "On en gardera la mémoire" as "It will always seem new," which projects the fairy tale into her own present.

The concluding words of *The Fairy Tales of Charles Perrault* thus echo the working title of her own collection of *new* Mother Goose tales that happily mix oral and literary sources, high art and popular culture, but this time with special attention paid to the obscured tradition of the folktale and neglected female voices. Carter's contrapuntal project thus hinges on Mother Goose as the pivotal figure between the translation and the rewritings, as the provisional title and working plan of the volume sketched out in Carter's journal for 1977 confirm.

Plan: *The Bloody Chamber, or, New Mother Goose Tales*

a) The Bloody Chamber—(Bluebeard)
b) (Red Riding Hood)
    i. The Werewolf
    ii. Old Count story (rococo, untitled, unfinished)
    iii. The Company of Wolves
c) The Snow Queen (lyrical, unfinished)—(Sleeping Beauty)
Another Sleeping Beauty; when he touches her, she dissolves into powder? A beautiful girl asleep in an attic, in her wedding dress, in a trunk.
"Old houses keep their secrets" W. De la Mare style.
d) Cinderella story—very primitive, very archaic; the ash-girl.
e) Beauty & the Beast
f) Puss-in-Boots, à la Beaumarchais; the feline factotum. Figaro, here! Figaro, there![43]

Carter's collection is organized around several tales inspired by Perrault: one on "Bluebeard," three on "Little Red Riding Hood," two on "Sleeping Beauty," one on "Cinderella," and one on "Puss in Boots." The fifth tale in the plan, which is not from Perrault, is a reworking of "Beauty and the Beast" inspired by Jeanne Marie Leprince de Beaumont's classic fairy tale, which Carter also translated. Because, as we know, *The Bloody Chamber* eventually included two distinct retellings of the tale placed immediately after the title story, Carter's interest in a female fairy-tale tradition apparently grew during those years. In December 1978 she even planned a sequel to *The Bloody Chamber*: "Stories for fairy tale book 2" comprises Beaumont's "Beauty and the Beast" and four of Marie-Catherine d'Aulnoy's *contes de fées*, including "The Blue Bird," "The White Cat," "The Yellow Dwarf," and "The Wonderful Sheep" (with a question mark), although it is uncertain whether Carter had a volume of translations or rewritings in mind.[44]

It is of course hazardous to reconstitute a precise chronology in the development of Carter's work, and yet it is tempting to imagine that being commissioned to translate Perrault led to a rediscovery of female authors such as Beaumont and d'Aulnoy.[45] Beaumont, in particular, embodies even better than Perrault the cross-cultural exchanges between France and England and the reorientation of the fairy tale as a genre for children. This probably impelled Carter to translate two of her fairy tales (published in *Sleeping Beauty and Other Favourite Fairy Tales* in 1982) and include two retellings of "Beauty and the Beast" in *The Bloody Chamber* ("The Courtship of Mr. Lyon" and "The Tiger's Bride"), for she admired the literary qualities of Beaumont's prose. Even at this early stage in the composition of these "new Mother Goose tales," the titles of the rubrics reflect multiple influences, including French and German tales, Walter de la Mare's ghost stories (de la Mare himself revisited fairy tales in *Told Again* [1927]), and Beaumarchais's satirical comedy. Carter's abundant notes reveal a wealth of other eclectic sources, from poetry (often quoted in the original French, English, or German) to songs and films, cookbooks, bird manuals, Gilles Deleuze, Roland Barthes, Walter Benjamin, and Tristan Tzara, to name a few.

Rewriting classic fairy tales for *The Bloody Chamber* also gave Carter an opportunity to pursue her dialogue with Perrault by exploiting what she had found in the French texts but had to leave out in her translations for children: their mock naïveté and misleading simplicity; hidden sexual subtext and social critique; adult humor, wit, and irony; literary self-consciousness and allusions; playful references to the author's own time and milieu underneath fairy-tale timelessness; and the interplay of text and image that would become a staple feature of fairy-tale books. Indeed, as Perrault scholars have shown, his *contes* are highly elaborate cultural productions whose message is by no means univocal. Marc Escola even ends his illuminating study of the famous collection by stressing how the *contes* create a reading experience that puts meaning into play and simultaneously invites and resists interpretation; each tale, he argues, contains the material that serves to create another. Like Carter, Escola also observes that every reader becomes a potential author who re-creates the story in his or her own way, so that nobody can claim possession of their "true" meaning. There, he concludes, surely lies the most compelling and truly modern lesson of Perrault's tales.[46]

Carter's anticonformist spirit and feminist sensibility impelled her to recover a female storytelling tradition, then, but it did not lead her to reject or condemn Perrault, unlike many of her contemporaries who objected to the fairy tale as an inherently sexist genre. Reading Perrault in the original language and in scholarly editions enabled her to discover a much more complex reality than the stereotyping attached to the genre. After Simone de Beauvoir's critique of fairy-tale heroines in *Le deuxième sexe* (1949) (*The Second Sex*), some feminist thinkers and writers were understandably eager to challenge, contest, and displace the cultural authority of the powerful social fictions propounded by the fairy tale. Although Perrault came to represent the dominant literary tradition complicit with patriarchal norms and values, Carter preferred to judge for herself and returned to the texts. This made her aware of the need to distinguish between the cultural myth of Sleeping Beauty, Cinderella, and other fairy-tale heroines on the one hand and the actual texts on the other. Just as she would use Sade to intervene in the feminist debate on pornography by polemically presenting him as a "moral pornographer" in *The Sadeian Woman: An Exercise in Cultural History* (1979), Carter rehabilitates Perrault as a kindred free spirit, a worldly ironist, and a practical moralist. She even implicitly connects Perrault and Sade, on whose works she was also working at the time, when she describes *Justine, or the Misfortunes of Virtue* as "a black, inverted fairytale" (*Sadeian Woman*, 39); in the story of Justine, innocence, ignorance, and virtue are punished, and vice and aggressive sexuality are rewarded. Carter explicitly compares Justine to a Cinderella figure who rejects the help of a fairy godmother on moral grounds and falls in love with the wrong man—and justly suffers for it.[47] Gamble notes that Carter herself thought of "The Bloody Chamber" as a supplement to her investigation of sexual politics and power relations in *The Sadeian Woman*, and so both texts can be read contrapuntally as a prime instance of the interplay of cultural criticism and fiction in Carter's work.

Always inclined to read texts and genres against received ideas about them, Carter perceived the worldliness hiding behind fairy-tale magic and was alert to the social role of the form. This echoes her famous formulation of the function of art as a means of "knowing the world" in *The Sadeian Woman*: "Fine art, that exists for itself alone, is art in a final state of impotence. If nobody, including the artist, acknowledges art as a means of knowing the world, then art is relegated to a kind of rumpus room of the mind and the irresponsibility of the artist and the irrelevance of art to actual living becomes part and parcel of the practice of art" (13). In this study I therefore draw a more nuanced and complex picture of Carter's long-standing interest in Perrault.

The Fairy Tales of Charles Perrault indeed turns Perrault's sophisticated *contes* for adults into fairy tales for children that reflect Carter's political, aesthetic, and pedagogical project. Working from Jacques Barchilon's two-volume critical edition of the dedication manuscript of 1695, published in 1956, and Andrew Lang's scholarly edition of the 1697 *Histoires ou contes du temps passé* in *Perrault's Popular Tales* (1888), Carter rediscovered the *moralités* (morals) that are often cut in fairy-tale collections, including Lang's immensely successful "coloured" fairy books (1889–1910) and, more surprisingly, Iona and Peter Opie's *Classic Fairy Tales* (1974), all listed at the end of *The Fairy Tales of Charles Perrault*. This rediscovery was to change Carter's understanding of the nature of Perrault's *contes* and orient her translation project. On the dustcover for *The Fairy Tales of Charles Perrault* she explains that her main aim was to "freshen up" his tales for children: "Perrault wrote down his fairy tales in a style of absolute simplicity and perfect charm and it seemed to me both a challenge and a pleasure to translate them in a manner which makes them seem as fresh as they must have seemed to the first readers in the time of Louis XIV." The "simplicity" and "charm" that Carter praises in Perrault make the tales good carriers of useful advice and empowering knowledge as lively, entertaining educational texts for the nursery. In "The Better to Eat You With" (1976), she opposes Perrault's practical tales to the work of irresponsible "nutters, regressives and the unbalanced" (451) who have colonized the field of children's literature.

> The notion of the fairy-tale as a vehicle for moral instruction is not a fashionable one. I sweated out the heatwave browsing through Perrault's *Contes du temps passé* on the pretext of improving my French. What an unexpected treat to find that in this great Ur-collection— whence sprang the Sleeping Beauty, Puss in Boots, Little Red Riding Hood, Cinderella, Tom Thumb, all the heroes of pantomime—all the nursery tales are purposely dressed up as fables of the politics of experience. (452)

Although this statement reflects misguided—if widespread—notions about the original readership ("nursery tales") and nature ("simple") of Perrault's *Histoires ou contes du temps passé*, Carter draws attention to the importance of the morals and the significance of the tales as "fables of the politics of experience." Through Perrault the translator strives to revive the French *contes* against the English tradition of fantasy and imaginative literature for children. In this, Carter is following the storytellers of old, as well as the first translator of Perrault into English, Robert Samber, whose aim was to transmit the "Wisdom and Virtue" of Perrault's "Fables," as he called them in the dedication to his 1729 edition *Histories, or Tales of Past Times, with Morals*, with the express purpose of entertaining and instructing his dedicatee's children.

Carter was familiar with Samber's early translation through Iona and Peter Opie's *Classic Fairy Tales* (1974), but she also owned a reprint of "G. M."'s "Englished" edition of the tales. The quotations in this book are from Carter's own inscribed edition of *Histories or Tales of Past Times told by Mother Goose, with Morals*, published in London by the Fortune Press in 1928 and based on an earlier edition (see "Note on the Text," 106). Although far less famous than Samber's "classic" edition, "G. M."'s is remarkably similar, except for a few minor details.

The authorship of the first English translation of Perrault's *contes* is a complex and debated issue, although the critical consensus today is in favor of Robert Samber. Samber was a prolific "Grub street" writer who translated miscellaneous texts and also published (and even plagiarized) others under his own name.[48] When an earlier edition of *Histories, or Tales of Past Times*, dated 1719 (in roman numerals), was discovered (the "G. M. Gent." translation), it was claimed that the initials on the cover were those of a lexicographer of Swiss origin, Guy Miège (1644–1718?) ("Gent." standing for "Gentleman"). Miège, who taught languages in London at the time, translated from the French, and made several French and English dictionaries, might have authored the translation attributed to Samber. Iona and Peter Opie, however, were able to demonstrate that the date was a misprint and reclaimed Samber as the first translator of Perrault's tales.

Nearly 250 years later, Carter reintroduced into English a perception of the fairy tale as a carrier of useful knowledge about life and the world, and this is consistent with her lifelong "dedicat[ion] to the idea that the role of literature was to instruct and well as to divert," to quote Sarah Gamble.[49]

The Fairy Tales of Charles Perrault also questions a static, ahistorical, universal, and stereotypical understanding of the genre by stressing the unique nature of Perrault's endeavor. By using the translating process to freshen up the text and update its meaning to make it relevant for young readers, Carter also recuperates the "moral intentions" and hidden political critique contained in Perrault's morals. The didactic mode, which is seldom associated with Carter's fiction, was in fact a key element of her translation *and* her rewritings as (more or less complex) "reading lessons."

Reading Lessons: From Bottled Message to Exploding Meaning

I do put everything in a novel to be read—read in the way allegory was intended to be read . . .—on as many levels as you can comfortably cope with at the time.

—JOHN HAFFENDEN, "ANGELA CARTER," 86

Carter's fiction draws on romance, Gothic, sci-fi, and other "mythologizing" genres, to which the author self-consciously opposes the fairy tale as a pedagogical tool. Against the moralistic, edifying, and preachy literature for children that used to dominate the reception of the fairy tale in England, Carter aligns herself with an alternative, French, *moraliste* tradition, to which Jean de La Fontaine's *fables* and Perrault's *contes* are affiliated, to teach about the ways of the world.[50] The fact that Carter glosses Perrault's *contes* as "*fables* of the politics of experience" indicates that she made the connection herself, possibly by way of Samber. This, I would be prepared to argue, is what she discovered in the morals of Perrault's *contes* and in his invitation to read closely in his dedicatory preface to *Histoires ou contes du temps passé*.[51] In her turn, Carter strove to teach a thing or two to her young readers and to develop more sophisticated reading skills in her older readers as part of an educational effort toward liberation and emancipation from oppressive cultural myths. The translation-rewriting dynamic can therefore be seen as a two-step reading lesson for young and more advanced readers and as a reflection on the different modes (or regimes) of reading outlined by Barchilon.

Against the critical stereotype of Carter as a riotous, rebellious, and subversive writer, an examination of the translation-rewriting dynamic therefore suggests that she affiliated herself with fabulist writers who instructed their readers in the ways of the world by developing their ability to think for themselves. Both in the form of the tales (including a story and its moral) and in the proclaimed intentions stated in the prefaces (especially when they pertained to the reading experience), Carter found in Perrault a reflection on the nature and effects of reading akin to her wish to promote the active reader. Carter's double project of translating for children and rewriting for adults can thus be seen as two *reading lessons* that emphasize the value of fairy tales as stories to think with.[52] The translations form the basis for the development of more sophisticated interpretative skills through a dense, allusive, and self-conscious writing style designed to fashion an intellectual habit in readers, who learn to decipher the world in which they live. This, I believe, is how Carter reinterprets the didactic intent of Perrault's *contes* in *The Bloody Chamber*. Whereas the first reading lesson formulated in *The Fairy Tales of Charles Perrault* communicates a useful message in a straightforward fashion, the rewritings foster a reading experience that does not take signs at face value but confronts the reader with complexity, ambiguity, allusion, and textual density and therefore invites active reading—including reading between the lines and even reading against the grain of the text.

Developing critical faculties is an essential tool for emancipation, as the heroine of the programmatic tale, "The Bloody Chamber," learns the hard way. Like the moralists of old, Carter pursues an ethical imperative as she anchors her discourse in the real, concrete, material world *not* in order to promote conformity to the norm but to convey human experience. Unlike the moralistic or moralizing writers distributing "moraline," to borrow Nietzsche's word, the French moralist authors of the seventeenth and eighteenth centuries were lucid and distanced observers of human behavior whose body of work served to teach their readers about social reality and convey some truth about human character, based on the exercise of reason and the intellect rather than Christian morality.[53] In this sense Carter was the true inheritor of La Fontaine and Perrault: a contemporary moralist with a feminist and socialist twist.

What Carter found in Perrault, then, beneath the surface of the *merveilleux*, was a way of using the fairy tale compatible with her own view of literature as an occasion for knowledge, practical instruction, and intellectual development. For Perrault and Carter alike, the fairy tale is no mere fiction or fantasy disconnected from reality; rather, it gives clues to decipher it in the sensible moral hiding between its lines. As Perrault memorably puts it in his preface to *Histoires ou contes du temps passé* (1697), "A Mademoiselle": "Ils renferment tous une Morale très sensée, et qui se découvre plus ou moins, selon le degré de pénétration de ceux qui les lisent" (*Contes*, 127) (They all contain a very sensible Moral, which reveals itself to a greater or lesser degree, depending on the intellectual abilities of the readers).

In "The Better to Eat You With," a lively and provocative essay in which Carter praises the moral tales of Perrault over fantasy, Carter contrasts prevalent notions of the fairy tale in England with an alternative French tradition of the *conte*. She warmly approves of Perrault's use of the genre as a means to instruct children about the dangers of the world and to help them develop qualities and strategies to survive them and even turn them to their advantage. More profoundly, perhaps, Carter sensed a commonality of worldview in their shared curiosity for all aspects of life, their taste for intellectual debate and polemic, their manipulation of literary conventions and rhetorical masks, their interest in children and educational matters, their unsentimental treatment of social and gender relations, their concern with the condition of women (including marital policy and access to knowledge), and the wry, elegant humor and playful, ironic distance that characterizes their fiction. These two writers had in fact much more in common than we might think. To be sure, both centrally contributed to the development of the fairy tale as a self-consciously "modern" genre in their own time and culture.

Studying the intricate and complex connections that link Carter's translations to her rewritings demonstrates that "reading a book is like re-writing it for yourself. And I think that all fiction should be open-ended. You bring to a novel, anything you read, all your experience of the world. You bring your history and you read it in your own terms."[54] The creative dimension of reading that, according to Derrida and others, is realized in its highest and most intense form in translation, is a key to Carter's fiction. The continuum of reading, translation, and rewriting is itself related to fairy tales as stories passed on from one generation to the next and endlessly reinvented as they are retold.⁵⁵ Discarding any simple idea of authorship, authority, and original creation, Carter promotes the active engagement with the texts of the past, because every reader is a potential author who can tease out new meanings in old texts. Carter thus represents literary practice as a bold gesture of appropriation and transformation, noting that the ferment of the new wine will in some cases liberate energies that will shatter the container itself. Her approval of the explosive effects of the decanting experiments carried out in the laboratory of fiction draws attention to the profoundly transformative effect of the translating and rewriting process as it frees up anticonventional readings of old texts and challenges expectations, certainties, and comfortable beliefs, undermining all efforts to contain meaning and creativity.

From *The Fairy Tales of Charles Perrault* to *The Bloody Chamber*

Do not despise popular culture. It is the matrix of all art.

—ANGELA CARTER, "MISCELLANEOUS FAIRY TALE MATERIAL" FILE,

ANGELA CARTER PAPERS, BRITISH LIBRARY, 1/82

But I realize that I tend to use other people's books, European literature,

as though it were a kind of folklore. Our literary heritage is a kind of

folklore.

—JOHN HAFFENDEN, "ANGELA CARTER," 82

In *The Fairy Tales of Charles Perrault* Angela Carter emulates the alleged simplicity of fairy tales as stories for children, whereas in *The Bloody Chamber* she uncovers an alternative tradition of folktales that bear witness to the ancient origins, social role, and international scope of the fairy-tale genre. The focus of this study is mainly on the French sources, although I occasionally refer to the Grimms' famous collection of *Kinder- und Hausmärchen*. I concentrate on the tales that Carter chose to translate *and* rewrite for *The Bloody Chamber*, with the sole exception of "Ashputtle *or* The Mother's Ghost," which was published later.

In Chapter 1 I document the making and reception of *The Fairy Tales of Charles Perrault* and trace its publication history from its first edition to its recent paperback reissue, including *Sleeping Beauty and Other Fairy Tales*. In Chapter 2 I analyze Carter's "Little Red Riding Hood" in conjunction with the radio play *The Company of Wolves* and three stories included in *The Bloody Chamber* ("The Werewolf," "The Company of Wolves," and "Wolf-Alice"). In Chapter 3 I examine "Bluebeard" in counterpoint to "The Bloody Chamber," with a focus on vision and visual culture. In Chapter 4 I focus on "Puss in Boots," the eponymous radio play, and its hyphenated prose variation "Puss-in-Boots." In Chapter 5 I consider "The Sleeping Beauty in the Woods" together with "The Lady of the House of Love" and the radio play *Vampirella*. In Chapter 6 I focus on Carter's translation of Beaumont's "La Belle et la Bête" (Beauty and the Beast) and "Le Prince Chéri" (Sweetheart) alongside "The Courtship of Mr. Lyon" and "The Tiger's Bride." Finally, in Chapter 7 I examine Carter's "Cinderella: or, The Little Glass Slipper" in counterpoint to "Ashputtle *or* The Mother's Ghost," which I read as Carter's most accomplished reflection on the creative process and as a poignant farewell to her readers.

I have not treated the tales that Carter translated but did not rewrite as such, namely, Perrault's "Les Fées" (The Fairies), "Riquet à la Houppe" (Ricky with the Tuft), "Le Petit Poucet" (Hop o' My Thumb), "Les Souhaits ridicules" (The Foolish Wishes), and "Peau d'Ane" (Donkey-Skin).[56] Although we can only speculate on Carter's reasons for choosing some tales rather than others to rework, her choices may have had something to do with the status of these tales in the fairy-tale canon.

Perrault's earlier *contes en vers* are unambiguously of literary origin. "Griselidis" is based on a story by Giovanni Boccaccio in the *Decameron*, which Petrarch translated into Latin.[57] Perrault's self-styled *nouvelle* is distinct from his *contes*, and furthermore the story does not belong to the fairy-tale canon, as Carter herself points out in the introduction to *The Fairy Tales of Charles Perrault*. Not quite suitable as a children's story, "Griselidis" tells about the sufferings of a peasant girl who marries a wealthy and tyrannical noble named le Prince, who tests her obedience and patience through increasingly cruel trials. The tale ends with praise for wifely patience, in spite of the husband's cruelty and abuse. Although Carter chose not to translate it, the story of an aristocratic husband's domination, manipulation and cruelty toward his young wife is reminiscent of Carter's variation on

"Bluebeard" in "The Bloody Chamber" as cautioning against the seductive dangers of submitting to a perverse husband.

Another verse tale, "Les Souhaits ridicules," which Carter did translate in a prose version, reworks a fable by Jean de La Fontaine included in his 1678 famous collection *Fables*. This comic tale mocks a peasant couple who squander their good fortune.[58] The tale is not part of the modern fairy-tale canon, so Carter's decision to translate it can be seen as a confirmation of her wider interest in the narrative tradition of comic and bawdy tales.

In all her translations Carter stresses the homey message of the tales: the positive impact of kind words in "The Fairies," the transformative power of love in "Ricky with the Tuft" ("This is not a fairy tale but the plain, unvarnished truth," *Fairy Tales*, 110), the defense of the underdog in "Hop o' My Thumb" ("The runt of the litter ends up making the family's fortune," 129), and the human comedy of "The Foolish Wishes," where natural gifts are misused. Jacques Barchilon and Henry Pettit say of "Les Fées" that "it is the least known of the Perrault collection" (*Authentic Mother Goose*, 14), although it circulated in English as "Diamonds and Toads." Similarly, they observe that "Le Petit Poucet" is often confused with the more ancient English story of "Tom Thumb" (15). Carter did not seem to find enough inspiration in these stories to rewrite them, perhaps because of their proximity to an English tradition.

I make scant reference to two stories included in *The Bloody Chamber* that are not based on Carter's translation of Perrault, namely, "The Snow Child" and "The Erl-King," although both stories reference fairy-tale-related genres. "The Snow Child" is based on a variant of "Snow White" collected by the Grimms, and "The Erl-King" harks back to folklore as transmuted by German and English romantic poetry.[59] "The Erl-King" weaves together references to the bird-like heroine of the Grimms' "Fitchers Vogel" and the mysterious forest spirit feared by the child of Goethe's ballad "Der Erlkönig," which Schubert put into music in 1815. In March 1977 Carter even quoted Goethe, mixing German and English, in view of a project titled "The garden of talking beasts & flowers." The poem begins:

> Kennst dü das land where the wise beasts speak;
> there is a garden there of talking beasts & flowers.
> The leaves shudder at the noble sonorities of the lions....
> In the land where the lemon trees grow

Several elements from this early draft (of which there are two variations in the notebook) found their way into *The Bloody Chamber*, including the key motif of the "tiger-lilies" in "The Bloody Chamber" and the "grunting Adam" "picking the thick lice from his mate's brown pelt" in "Wolf-Alice." The first two drafts are interspersed with notes on Jacob Boëhme's Adamic language of the senses, which restores communication between beasts and men, as a kind of prelapsarian (and pre-Babelian) utopia ironized by Carter.

The Goethe reference also applies to Carter's "Beauty and the Beast" retellings, especially "The Tiger's Bride," set as it is in Italy (Venice and Mantua are mentioned as alternative locations). On the fourth page of the notebook, Carter sketches out the opening of this story, also laid out as a poem. Further on, she quotes the opening of Christina Rossetti's "The Dead City," a poem about getting lost in a labyrinthlike, entangling, wood peopled by birds, and she even mentions Rossetti's famous fairy-tale poem "Goblin Market." She also cites a line from Baudelaire (in French) and observes that "The Erl-King" is a "kind of Beauty and the Beast." This weaving together of German, English, and French sources further confirms the translational dynamics of Carter's writing. Although separate, all the stories included in *The Bloody Chamber* collection thus "segue into [one] another" (*Angela Carter's Book of Fairy Tales*, xxii).

Primarily text-based, my contrapuntal analysis of Carter's translations and rewritings also situates them in their literary and cultural context. To do so, I have drawn on the Carter archive at the British Library, which helps elucidate the author's working method. As Carter's friend and literary executor Susannah Clapp points out in *A Card from Angela Carter* (2012), Carter's journals

> were partly working notes and partly casual jottings, roughly arranged so that the two kinds of entry were on opposite pages. They were stacked in the study: lined exercise books in which she had started to write during the 60s and which covered nearly 30 years of her life. She decorated their covers as girls used to decorate their school books, with cut-out labels (the Player's cigarette sailor was one), paintings of cherubs and flowers and patterns of leaves.[60]

The rediscovery of this material gives us invaluable insights into Carter's creative method, background reading, and diverse sources.

Because illustration is an integral part of Carter's inspiration, and of the fairy-tale tradition generally—from the frontispiece and vignettes of Perrault's original collection to picture books for children and fairy-tale films—I include a number of illustrations that Carter was familiar with, from the richly illustrated *Classic Fairy Tales* to Martin Ware's etchings for *The Fairy Tales of Charles Perrault*, which Carter reworked in her own stories. I also include Michael Foreman's cover for Carter's *Sleeping Beauty and Other Favourite Fairy Tales*. As her preparatory notes show, Carter was quite knowledgeable about fairy-tale literature and iconography. This, I argue, sheds light on the complex interplay of visual, textual, and musical imagination displayed in Carter's work during this period.[61] Carter also revised and reworked her own texts at each stage of the editorial process, as the handwritten, typewritten, and printed drafts testify. The multiple drafts were almost always annotated and they draw attention to the many forms that translation took in the course of the creative process.

Provisional Conclusion

Perrault belonged to a circle of mostly female writers who used the *conte de fées* as a subtly ironic and erudite game in the ancien régime salons to address social and gender issues (in a veiled and subtly humorous fashion) and to debate the role of art and literature. When Carter (re)translated Perrault into English, she self-consciously followed the work of translators, adaptors (including Beaumont), and editors who democratized and popularized the genre by opening it up to all ages and classes of readers, as though in response to Benjamin's mourning of the disappearance of the "art of storytelling" and with it "the ability to exchange experiences."[62] Carter's translations carry a straightforward message articulated in the moral, whereas her rewritings for adults destabilize authorship and open up textuality and meaning, and thus capture the hidden complexity of Perrault's deceptively simple and pseudo-naive *contes*.

But if the age-old storytelling tradition shapes Carter's translation project, a more writerly understanding of the fairy tale informs *The Bloody Chamber*. "Translation is the most intimate act of reading," says Gayatri Chakravorti Spivak.[63] Rereading Perrault's *contes* in the original French and in scholarly editions reproducing the full text (including the morals) made Carter aware of the gap between the actual texts and their modern reception. She understood the need to distinguish Perrault's ironic and worldly *contes* from their Disneyfied stereotype. This enabled Carter to reconsider the poetics and politics of the fairy tale against the grain of preconceived ideas about the genre. In turn, she revived the fairy tale from her own perspective and in her own time as a fundamentally modern genre from which all kinds of readers can learn.

Far from subverting Perrault, then, Carter reclaimed his contribution to fairy-tale literature against a modern understanding of the genre as synonymous with fairyland. In the rewritings the didactic mode of narration is obviously complicated by the dense intertextuality and postmodern poetics deployed by the author as she addresses more sophisticated readers. But even then, Carter returns and reclaims an understanding of the fairy tale that predates its confinement to the nursery; its aesthetics and subversive gender politics are in fact reminiscent of the French wonder tales of the late seventeenth and early eighteenth century, with their varied, baroque, allusive styles, knowing, ironic tone, and veiled social critique. In my opinion the didactic intent is still present in Carter's rewritings, but this time it is to stimulate readers' intellectual curiosity and interpretative skills and to activate or enlarge their cultural baggage. Carter's fiction notoriously resists single and simple interpretations, and this helps her audience become better, more creative, and critical readers.

I

Tracing Editorial Metamorphoses

THE FAIRY TALES OF CHARLES PERRAULT
FROM 1977 TO THE PRESENT DAY

Angela Carter's Translation Today: Perrault's Sp(l)itting Image in Paperback

The making of a book is notoriously influenced by powerful intermediaries and prescriptors—commissioners, editors, publishers, booksellers—quite apart from the author. Their influence is not always easy to assess, and this may be even more true in the case of a translation, where there is often a further layer of external interference. Translators' choices are usually constrained by what Basil Hatim and Ian Mason call the brief for the job that they have to perform. This brief includes "the purpose and status of the translation, the likely readership and so on.... Thus one key element of the *skopos* [the purpose of translating] is the specification of the task to be performed, as stipulated by the initiator of the translation (employer, commissioner, publisher, etc.)."[1] Material evidence of the specific conditions and circumstances of Angela Carter's translation of Charles Perrault's *contes* for Victor Gollancz is lacking (brief, contract, etc.), as far as I know, apart from the general context outlined in the Introduction; but one can nonetheless learn a lot from the editorial history of the publication, reception, and reprints of *The Fairy Tales of Charles Perrault* (1977). In this chapter I trace subtle but significant shifts in modern authorial constructions of Perrault and his *Histoires ou contes du temps passé* in English, which Carter's (re) translation helped to shape from the late 1970s to the present day.[2]

The recent Penguin paperback reissue of *The Fairy Tales of Charles Perrault* marks yet another stage in the reception of Perrault's *contes* in English and gives visibility to Carter's output as a translator. The two covers used for the paperback edition draw on distinct images of Perrault: one as a children's author and the other as a writer of *contes* for grown-ups (as it is now widely admitted) filtered through Carter's own fairy-tale rewritings. Jack Zipes's informative introduction also helps to establish Carter as a gifted translator aside from her status as a "modern classic" author in her own right. The two paperbacks reproduce Carter's foreword to the 1977 edition as an afterword, but they do not include Martin Ware's original illustrations.

The first reissue was published as *Little Red Riding Hood, Cinderella, and Other Classic Fairy Tales of Charles Perrault* in the Penguin Classics series in 2008. The new title echoes those of the 1977 and 1982 editions, namely, *The Fairy Tales of Charles Perrault* and *Sleeping Beauty and Other Favourite Fairy Tales*. It stresses Perrault's version of the tales as *classics* and gives pride of place to two of the most popular stories in the fairy-tale canon, "Little Red Riding Hood" and "Cinderella." The disappearance of "Sleeping Beauty" may indicate a heightened awareness of feminist criticism of the tale, especially when it is associated with Angela Carter. Another possible reason is that a sentimental romance would be considered maudlin today or even as going against the spirit of Perrault's *contes*.

The cover of Penguin's *Little Red Riding Hood* reproduces a classic example of fairy-tale imagery with John Hassal's Art Nouveau illustration of "Little Red Riding Hood" among the poppies (c. 1898), where the colors red and black dominate (Figure 1.1). The scene depicts the little girl picking up flowers, unaware that she is being watched by the wolf in the background. In her blood-red cloak she looks like a pretty poppy soon to be plucked herself, and her bell-shaped cloak (with one button undone) reinforces the link between the girl and the flowers. The tension between the moment of innocent childhood play and the presence of the unseen predator (except by the viewer) creates suspense and dramatic irony, especially for readers aware of Perrault's dramatic ending to the tale. The book seems to be targeting grown-up readers eager to rediscover Perrault's version of the familiar tales and recover a sense of childhood from the perspective of adulthood. The choice of red lettering for the translator's name subtly hints at the connection between the bloody ending of "Little Red Riding Hood" and the title of Carter's own collection of fairy-tale rewritings.[3]

The other reprint is identical except for its cover and title. Appearing in Penguin's Modern Classics series, which publishes works by "the great

Figure 1.1. Cover of the 2008 paperback Penguin Classics edition of Little Red Riding Hood, Cinderella, and Other Classic Fairy Tales of Charles Perrault. *Courtesy of Penguin Books Ltd.*

authors of the twentieth century," it places the emphasis on the translator rather than the original author of the tales (Figure 1.2).[4] *The Fairy Tales of Charles Perrault* is in fact the first title in a series of reprints of Carter's fiction with new introductions by contemporary writers. It was followed by *Heroes and Villains*, with an introduction by Robert L. Coover, and *The Infernal Desire Machines of Doctor Hoffman*, introduced by Ali Smith, in 2011. The grouping of these texts associates the fairy tale with Carter's particular brand of speculative fantasy. *Heroes and Villains* (1969) is a dystopian novel written in the aftermath of the sexual revolution, and *Infernal Desire Machines* (1972) is a picaresque, Swiftian journey about the war between desire and reality inspired by Surrealism and informed by Xavière Gauthier's feminist response to its sexual iconography.[5] The cover illustrations are all by the controversial visual artist Marilyn Minter.

The Modern Classics paperback edition reproduces the title of the 1977 edition of *The Fairy Tales of Charles Perrault*. Carter's name stands out in white—and in bigger letters than Perrault's—on a black, silver, and pinkish mauve background. The cover presents a photograph by Minter, an American visual artist of Carter's generation known for her daring and provocative pictures that play with the codes of advertising and pornography.[6] Titled "Stepping Up" (2005), the piece belongs to a series of four huge photographs that Minter presented on four billboards, sponsored by the public arts organization Creative Time, for a happening in Manhattan's Chelsea district in March 2006. The conjunction with Perrault's worldly fairy tales mediated by Carter is particularly felicitous.

The photo (Figure 1.2) characteristically combines glamour and squalor, fairy-tale romance and rough trade. This close-up of two slippered feet plays with the glam trash iconography of a modern-day Cinderella wearing a high-heeled strass Dior slipper, slick and shiny, in which black, dirty pink, and silver dominate. The sexual identity of the "Cinderella" figure is ambiguous, and the focus is on the sexy pale pink shoe and blackened foot, smeared with mud, dirt, or grease, caught as she is climbing a metal staircase. The steps, like the heel and ankle, are wet, as if sprinkled with drops of water or dew, and they look glazed over, at once earthbound and unreal. The association with Cinderella is made through the slipper but also through the glassy or icelike bottom step that metonymically displaces the magical fabric of the fairy-tale slipper onto the slippery steps. The slipper/slipping connection, however, casts an ironic light on the photo's title

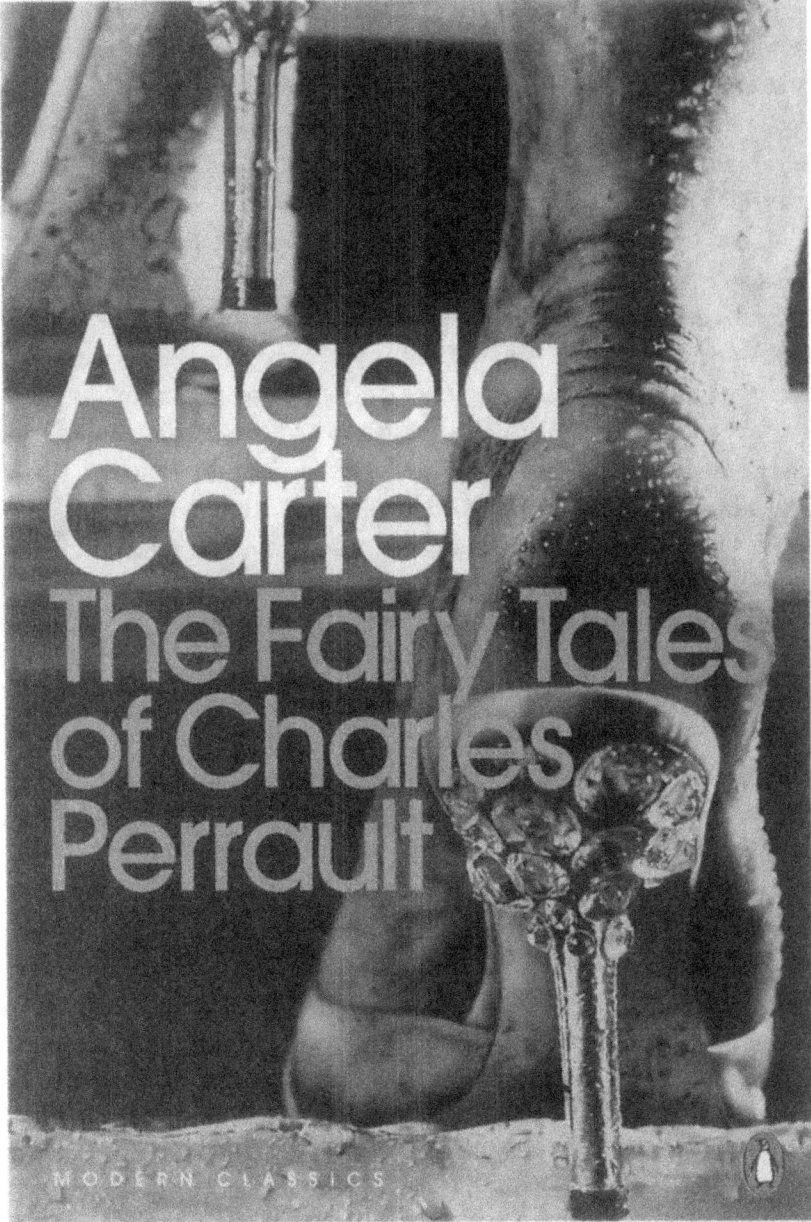

Figure 1.2. Cover of the 2008 paperback Penguin Modern Classics edition of The Fairy Tales of Charles Perrault. *Courtesy of Penguin Books Ltd.*

("Stepping Up"). It suggests that the steps may provoke a fall and therefore ironize the fairy-tale allusion to Cinderella as the ultimate wish-fulfillment tale of social climbing (materialized in the woman's arrested movement) as today's real magic. The combination of glamorous high fashion and smut also hints at morning-after partying and nightclubbing that Minter documented in the 1980s.

Minter's artwork is postmodern in the sense of being ambiguously complicit with what she critiques (to borrow Hutcheon's definition of postmodernism). Also known for her work on pornography, Minter's visual art focuses on a consumer society that turns people into objects in its parody of the eroticized ads of glossy magazines. In challenging cultural myths based on fairy-tale imagery, like Carter, Minter, with her mock-fashion, porno-chic photography and shoe fetishism, cleverly updates the "Cinderella" tale for adult readers familiar with Carter's sexually candid rewritings of classic tales. Although Carter's own take on "Cinderella" in the translation is, of course, quite different from Minter's, the book cover plays on their shared interest in sexuality, cross-dressing, pointed social critique, and devastating (if often misunderstood) humor.

In short, the two covers of the Penguin paperback editions target quite different publics, thereby drawing attention to the dual reception of Perrault's *contes* in the twenty-first century as a "classic" author of children's stories but also as an author of coded tales for adults. Minter's image owes much to *The Bloody Chamber*, which took the fairy tale out of the nursery. By returning to pre-eighteenth-century conceptions of the fairy tale, Carter initiated a veritable fashion for "adult fairy tales" in the twentieth century that anticipated Minter's celebration of a contemporary Cinderella, half fashion victim, half liberated girl, climbing the steps to fame and success (or just to bed to sleep off a rough night).

Jack Zipes's introduction to the recent paperback edition of *The Fairy Tales of Charles Perrault*, titled "The Remaking of Charles Perrault and His Fairy Tales" (vii–xxvii), is followed by a list of "Suggestions for Further Reading" on Angela Carter and Charles Perrault, including selected modern editions of Perrault's *contes* in French. After Carter, and in dialogue with her, Zipes has contributed to a large extent to the renewal of academic interest in the fairy tale, and his *Fairy Tales and the Art of Subversion* (first published in 1983) has greatly influenced contemporary understandings of the genre. In Zipes's characteristic style the introduction is both scholarly and highly readable, and it establishes Carter as a gifted translator and a renowned fiction writer and editor of fairy tales. Zipes observes that "very few critics realize that Charles Perrault played a highly significant role in Angela Carter's development as a fairy-tale writer" (vii), and he goes on to establish a connection between Carter's translations and *The Bloody Chamber*. Carter is seen as a modern-day Cinderella who was no "docile and obedient goddaughter" content with simply receiving Perrault's gifts. Rather, her translations are "an unusual brazen appropriation of [Perrault's] works" that "remade Perrault and his tales into something different from what they were" (vii). This study of the interplay of Carter's translations and rewritings, based as it is on close textual analysis and careful documentation, bears out Zipes's claim but complicates it as well, in the sense that Carter's relation to and understanding of Perrault is less unruly than Zipes (or we) may think. To some extent, Carter's project of rehabilitation of Perrault is even bolder than a mere appropriation or subversion, especially when we consider it against its broader historical and critical context dominated by feminist criticism of classic fairy tales.

Zipes structures his introduction so as to give equal attention to Perrault and his modern translator, although Carter is given pride of place. His account of Carter's life and literary career covers her work as a fiction writer, essayist, journalist, children's author, editor, and translator, and it also includes her teaching activities and projects that her early death prevented her from completing. Zipes's portrait ends on a more personal note, expressing his perplexity at "Carter's attraction to Charles Perrault, a well-born, conservative writer at Louis XIV's court" whose "understanding of women and their social roles was very limited, to say the least" ("Remaking of Charles Perrault," xii). Carter's interest in Perrault, however, becomes less "strange" (xii), I believe, if we consider that she responded to his double affiliation with the folktale and the literary fairy-tale tradition.

Zipes spends the next few pages of his introduction outlining Perrault's life, work, and broader context, including a corrective as to the nature of his *contes*, which, contrary to what most people believe, were *not* written for children ("Remaking of Charles Perrault," xi–xvi). The individual tales and their "cultural ramifications up to the present" (xvi) are briefly presented, with a focus on their sexual politics and recent critical reception. Zipes is troubled by Carter's choice to translate Perrault at the height of the feminist movement, despite his alleged "patriarchal attitude regarding gender roles, social codes of courting, hierarchical familial and political relations, inheritance, and government," and he attributes it to Carter's odd "weakness" for "conservative gentlemen" (xix). Carter, he argues, remakes Perrault's tales into an "earthy" project "more in tune with [her] radical vision of aesthetics and the efficacy of storytelling" (xix). The question that puzzles Zipes, then, is how to reconcile Carter's interest in Perrault with her commitment to feminism and socialism, which translated into a desire to revive a popular tradition of female storytelling.

The last section of Zipes's introduction is devoted to readings of the moral of "Cinderella" and "Sleeping Beauty" that illustrate Carter's "br[inging] down to earth" ("Remaking of Charles Perrault," xx) of Perrault's sophisticated tales. Zipes identifies two main tendencies in Carter's translation.

> First, she turned all the verse morals at the end of each tale into prosaic folksy proverbs that often contradict what Perrault endeavoured to communicate. Second, she added numerous phrases to the tales to give them a more "folk" atmosphere consistent with the oral tradition, and she transformed longer sentences into succinct, paratactic phrases reminiscent of simple storytelling. (xx)

Of course Zipes is right in observing that "Perrault's morals are much more complex, ironic, delicate, and ambivalent than Carter's frank messages to readers, whom she wants to advise in a blunt and succinct manner" (xxii), but a comparative analysis nevertheless shows that she closely followed her source. Although it is true that Carter adopts a "contemporary English idiom and cadence" (xxiv) and "sympathizes with many of the persecuted or oppressed protagonists" (xxiv), she also conveys some of the social critique and humor of her source. Zipes's conclusion echoes Carter's observation that translation is a re-creation in a different period and culture. His affirmation that "Perrault inspired Carter to delve more deeply into the origins and meanings of fairy tales" (xxv) is borne out by a contrapuntal analysis of the more radical revisionary enterprise of *The Bloody Chamber*. Far from "misread[ing]" Perrault, however, Carter perceived the emancipating potential of Perrault's *contes*, which she would respond to more fully in her rewriting.

Editing, Illustrating, Framing:
The Role of the Paratext in Fairy-Tale Collections

Before we explore the translation-rewriting dynamic, in this section I outline Carter's translation project as formulated in the foreword to the first edition of *The Fairy Tales of Charles Perrault* (1977) and in an earlier article for *New Society*, "The Better to Eat You With" (1976), where Carter explained what she found in Perrault that she sought to communicate through her translation.

Ever since the invention of the printing press, Gérard Genette remarks, texts have presented themselves through a frame that shapes reception and interpretation, even though individual readers may not always be aware of its influence. Genette sees the role of the *paratext* as essential for a full understanding of the nature and purpose of a text published in book form; the paratext shapes the reading experience by raising expectations about genre and audience. The liminal space of the paratext is "the means by which a text makes a book of itself and proposes itself as such to its readers, and more generally to the public. Rather than with a limit or a sealed frontier, we are dealing in this case with a *threshold*."[7] This threshold corresponds to the editorial presentation of a text, which comprises the name of the author, title, cover, dedication, epigraph, preface, introduction, notes, quotes on the dust jacket, blurb—in short, any visual or textual inscription that does not belong to the main body of the work.

Charles Perrault's *contes* are a good case in point. They are usually read in isolation from their original context of publication and regardless of the author's intentions and statement of purpose expressed in the programmatic prefaces of the 1695 and 1697 editions. Partly because the literary fairy tales of France have been assimilated to children's literature, these productions have undergone radical editorial changes, especially in translation. As a result, the reception of Perrault's *contes* is marked by significant paratextual and textual changes that conditioned their reception in England and abroad. These manipulations both ensured the popularity of the tales and led to misunderstandings about their original nature and purpose through decontextualization, anonymization, and reworking.[8]

It is now widely known that Perrault wrote in the fashionable genre of the *conte merveilleux*, which was the favorite mode of salon writing and *mondain* literary culture in France at the turn of the seventeenth century, led by such figures as Marie-Catherine d'Aulnoy.[9] Often exhibiting the culture of women in witty or ironic ways, this literature of imagination served to criticize social mores and institutions, such as courtship and marriage, in a seemingly innocuous fashion and provided courtly entertainment within an adult setting. Like the literary productions of his contemporaries, however, Perrault's *contes* were gradually detached from their author and his social and discursive environment. This phenomenon was facilitated by the author's claim that they were inspired by old wives' tales (*contes de nourrice*), by their compact form and deceptively simple style, and by the debated authorship of his *Histoires ou contes du temps passé* (1697), whose preface is signed with his son's name, P. Darmancour.[10] This led to Perrault's *contes* being assimilated to folk culture, often symbolized by the mythical figure of Mother Goose.[11]

This phenomenon becomes all the more important when we consider how the *mise en livre* was an essential aspect of the *conte de fées* that emerged in late-seventeenth-century France.[12] In the first issue of *Féeries*, titled *Le recueil* (2004), Jean-Paul Sermain comments on the importance of the composition, framing, and elaborate discursive strategies of fairy-tale collections in establishing the *conte de fées* as a literary genre. He convincingly argues that the programmatic prefaces and complex framing devices (textual as well as visual) were originally designed to mark a deliberate rupture from oral practices and traditional culture in order to affirm the literariness of the author's project. The *conte de fées* was institutionalized as a literary genre that reclaimed and yet profoundly transformed an oral heritage. Angela Carter's twofold project reflects this double legacy and emerges out of their productive tensions; whereas the Perrault-based translation gives an oral "touch" to the written text, *The Bloody Chamber* is a self-consciously literary endeavor that pays tribute to the folklore that inspired the classic tales. Carter was also acutely aware of her role as a modern mediator and interpreter influenced by her own times and context. A close examination of the paratext of *The Fairy Tales of Charles Perrault* is revealing in this regard.[13]

Carter presents Perrault's *contes* somewhat anachronistically as children's literature and challenges received ideas about the fairy tale as an authorless, universal, and timeless genre. Familiar with the work of such folklorists as Andrew Lang and literary scholars such as Jacques Barchilon, she stresses the popular origin of Perrault's tales but also the originality of his endeavor and the artistry of his rendering of the old stories. Although Carter does not translate the programmatic prefaces of the 1695 or 1697 editions, her introduction to *The Fairy Tales of Charles Perrault* outlines the historical context, biographical circumstances, and intentions of the author (as she saw them) that are often missing from fairy-tale collections and anthologies, especially children's books. Influenced by her interest in popular culture and folklore, then, Carter's vision of Perrault's literary tales is nevertheless mostly positive and empathetic; she praises the man and his work, celebrating the aesthetic qualities of his *contes* and stressing the role of the morals, which are often neglected or altogether omitted.[14] Indeed, for Carter the value of these stories lies in their being tales of instruction that stress the worldliness of literature that she in turn seeks to transmit to her modern readers.

One cannot underestimate the importance of Carter's discovery of the bipartite structure of Perrault's *contes*. Each tale is composed of a short narrative followed by one or two *moralités* in verse that comment on the tale's message or lesson. The translator or writer perceived that the decision to add a moral is a complex gesture that inscribes the storyteller's subjectivity and interpretative activity within the structure of the text while drawing attention to the significance of storytelling as meaningful social practice and commentary. As we know, Perrault's morals both imitate and parody the form of the fable. But whereas the moral of a fable spells out the meaning of the story in allegorical fashion, Perrault's double morals in the 1697 edition subtly ironize the idea of a single and simple message to be drawn from the tale, as they often contradict each other or bear little relevance to the story itself. To quote Marc Escola, "The morals are not meant to induce a moralizing reading; they rather invite a distanced, self-conscious and erudite play with itself that does not directly elicit a moral from the fictional text."[15] The *contes* of Perrault therefore both imitate and gently mock the fable genre revived by La Fontaine, inasmuch as they ironize the convention of the moral.[16]

The disappearance of the morals in several editions of fairy tales that Carter was familiar with, including Iona and Peter Opie's *Classic Fairy Tales* (1974), which proclaims itself to be text based, did not escape Carter's notice. By contrast, scholarly editions such as Andrew Lang's *Perrault's Popular Tales* (1888) and Jacques Barchilon's *Perrault's Tales of Mother Goose* (1956) changed Carter's perception of the nature and function of Perrault's tales and significantly influenced her work as a translator and author in her own right.

In "The Better to Eat You With" Carter makes a strong case against "fairyland" and escapist fantasies to which she opposes the practical politics of Perrault's tales, based on their morals: "The notion of the fairy tale as a vehicle for *moral instruction* is not a fashionable one" (452; italics mine). She nevertheless goes on to reclaim Perrault's *"project for worldly instruction"* (453; italics mine). If the moral is a manner of interpretative supplement built into the source text, the translator in turn proposes a new interpretation of the story articulated most forcefully in the moral.

The illustrator further underlines the separation of the story from its moral in *The Fairy Tales of Charles Perrault*. Martin Ware inserts a lizard, which materializes the textual transformation effected in the shift from the story to its commentary (because the lizard is derived from the famous scene of magical transformation in "Cinderella"). The lizard even suggests the animal metamorphosis of the sinuous typographical sign that is conventionally used to mark a separation.[17] What is more, it inevitably suggests a pun on the moral as a twist in the tail/tale, thereby playfully uniting word and image.

Angela Carter's Personal Library: Textual Sources and Background Reading

When Angela Carter read Charles Perrault's *contes* in the original French in 1976, this truly defamiliarizing experience was an eye-opener that radically transformed her perception of the genre. She rediscovered the fairy tale from a new perspective, and this firsthand experience of Perrault's texts enabled her to distinguish the tales from "fairyland" as a sinister realm invested by "nutters, regressives and the unbalanced, as though a potential audience of children granted absolute licence" ("The Better to Eat You With," 451), as she put it with her customary mordant wit. Carter recorded the experience in an enthusiastic article for *New Society* in which she praises Perrault's *contes* not only for their narrative effectiveness and stylistic economy but also for their pedagogical force and worldly wisdom.

> I sweated out the heatwave browsing through Perrault's *Contes du temps passé* on the pretext of improving my French. What an unexpected treat to find that in this great Ur-collection—whence sprang the Sleeping Beauty, Puss in Boots, Little Red Riding Hood, Cinderella, Tom Thumb, all the heroes of pantomime—all these nurs-

ery tales are purposely dressed up as fables of the politics of experience.[18] ("The Better to Eat You With," 452–53)

At first Carter associated Perrault's stories with "nursery tales" (452) and the modern canon of "Children's Classics" (452). But in the course of her research she quickly worked out that far from being confined to the nursery, the *contes de fées* were addressed to a sophisticated, adult, and predominantly female audience. Although the reputation of Perrault as an author for children and the editorial constraints of the series compelled Carter to downplay the tales' textual and semantic complexity to make them amenable and accessible to a young audience, rewriting them in *The Bloody Chamber* would offer her the freedom to continue Perrault's project in her own remarkably inventive and knowing stories, complete with intertextual allusions and a sharper socially critical edge.

Apart from Barchilon's *Perrault's Tales of Mother Goose*, Carter's main source of information was Lang's erudite edition of Perrault's *contes en vers* and *contes en prose* in *Perrault's Popular Tales*. Lang's introduction even formed the basis of her own foreword to *The Fairy Tales of Charles Perrault*, and his abundant "Notes on the Several Tales by Perrault and Their Variants" provided her with material for *The Bloody Chamber*. In addition to these firsthand sources, Carter lists Barchilon's study of the French literary fairy tale at the time of Louis XIV, *Le conte merveilleux français de 1690 à 1760* (1975) and Iona and Peter Opie's lavishly illustrated *Classic Fairy Tales* (1974). In the course of her reading Carter became aware of the narrative potential of Perrault's *contes* and of the antiquity, richness, and variety of the fairy-tale and folktale tradition. Carter rediscovered a wealth of alternative versions of the stories that would feed into her fairy-tale rewritings. She learned that fairy tales have always been (re)made to speak of contemporary realities, as the example of Perrault had shown, and when working on her own re-creations, she self-consciously situated herself in a long chain of storytellers and adapters.

Rediscovering Perrault's "Fables of Experience": *The Fairy Tales of Charles Perrault* (1977)

Like many other collections of fairy tales for children, the first edition of *The Fairy Tales of Charles Perrault* (1977) does not reproduce the dedicatory preface of Charles Perrault's *Histoires ou contes du temps passé*; it is replaced by a fairly detailed and informative introduction. Likewise, the frontispiece and gouache vignettes of the original edition and the woodcuts of the second edition are replaced by Martin Ware's black and white etchings.

Carter's choice to translate the *contes en prose* alongside some *contes en vers* is significant. Although she does not include "Griselidis," an early *nouvelle en vers* ("La Marquise de Salusses ou la Patience de Griselidis," 1691) for reasons that she explains in the foreword, she bases her translation of "Les Souhaits ridicules" (The Foolish Wishes) and "Peau d'Ane" (Donkey-Skin) on prose versions that she probably found in the *Cabinet des fées*. Moreover, Carter reorganizes the sequence of the texts by giving pride of place to "Little Red Riding Hood," as in the early translation edited by Robert Samber.[19] However, *The Fairy Tales of Charles Perrault* distinguishes itself from most modern editions by its mention of the author's name in the title, a detailed introduction, the inclusion of the morals (and the recognition of their importance), and a select bibliography—all of which signal a pedagogical intention and an effort to convey a sense of Perrault's original project.

Most editions of Perrault's *contes* for children indeed adapt the tales freely and sometimes even contain tales by other authors. Thus Marie-Jeanne L'Héritier de Villandon's *"L'Adroite Princesse ou les aventures de Finette"* was often attributed to Perrault, as in Samber's early-eighteenth-century edition of *Histories or Tales of Past Times, with Morals*. The fact that Carter owned a copy of a reprint of the twelfth edition dated 1802 and published in London by the Fortune Press in 1928, testifies to her bibliophile interests. Similarly, Marie-Catherine d'Aulnoy's and Jeanne-Marie Leprince de Beaumont's *contes de fées* were sometimes published under Perrault's name, as Carter herself noted in the foreword to *The Fairy Tales of Charles Perrault*.[20] The emphasis placed on the classic tales as authored texts also goes against the assimilation of the genre to an English tradition, as in Joseph Jacobs's *English Fairy Tales*, illustrated by John D. Batten, of which Carter held a rather dilapidated copy in an original edition (including crayon marks by a young child).

Whereas Perrault's *contes en vers* and *contes en prose* were originally published in separate volumes, *The Fairy Tales of Charles Perrault* unifies them in a single book whose title is modeled on older collections of translated fairy tales by French authors, such as *The Fairy Tales of Madame d'Aulnoy* (1892).[21] This tends to homogenize what Perrault had conceived as two distinct projects. As Sermain observes, Perrault's earlier collection was a heterogeneous mix including a prototypical *conte de fées*, "Peau d'Ane" (the generic label *conte de Peau d'âne* already existed at the time of Perrault); a tale based on a novella by Giovanni Boccaccio, "Grisélidis"; and a comic tale in the manner of *fabliaux*, "Les Souhaits ridicules." The subsequent collection of *Histoires ou contes du temps passé, avec des moralités*, on the other hand, stressed the ancient origin of the tales, the educational function of the morals, and the scene of storytelling.[22] This suggests that nobody can claim ownership of the fairy tale; editorial transformations are an inherent property of the genre, as the familiar stories circulate and are translated, appropriated, and adapted in turn.

The presence of the author's name as part of the title of *The Fairy Tales of Charles Perrault* and the mention of the names of the translator and illustrator on the dust jacket, however, reinstate a form of collective authorship to the familiar stories (Figure 1.3). The indication "newly translated by Angela Carter" also explicitly designates the book as a *re*translation. Perrault is remade into a modern figure through the joint intervention of the translator and the visual artist, against the anonymous tradition associated with the mythical figure of Mother Goose; the presence and agency of the modern mediators is recognized.

The illustration on the dust cover (also reproduced on the inside cover page), by Martin Ware, features six of the most well-known fairy-tale characters in a style that combines realism and fantasy. The characters pose as though for a family picture on a background of shaded tones of blue (top) and yellow (bottom). Carefully composed to create a sense of symmetry, the scene represents Donkey-Skin on the far left, almost completely hidden underneath her animal disguise, a diminutive and elderly Hop o' My Thumb standing in front of her. This dwarflike figure wearing a striped sweater, buckled boots, and a black top-hat, could also be the good fairy's messenger wearing seven-league boots in "The Sleeping Beauty in the Wood." Next to them, a ginger Puss in Boots stands upright in the forefront, his head turned to look straight at the viewer. Occupying the middle ground, a wolf wearing the grandmother's bedtime bonnet lies in profile. On the right, Ware's visualization of the ogre from "Puss in Boots" as a strange, hybrid figure with closed eyes, a still face, and peaked ears, radiant mane, and feline body (including a curling tail mirroring the cat's), stands upright and in profile.[23] Illuminating the scene, an anthropomorphized sun borrowed from "The Foolish Wishes" casts lightning down on the wolf and

Figure 1.3. Cover of the 1977 edition of The Fairy Tales of Charles Perrault. *Courtesy of Martin Ware.*

therefore restores poetic justice (in the manner of the Grimms) to the wolf who goes unpunished in Perrault's version of "Little Red Riding Hood."

The unusual treatment of this gathering of fairy-tale characters is not only perceptible in the realistic style in which these hybrid characters (most of them half-human and half-animal) are represented but also in the visual echoes that link them. Ironically, the dwarf and the sun look like versions of the Prince Charming figure from "The Sleeping Beauty in the Wood" (*Fairy Tales*, 65), and the cunning Puss wears a striped pajama evoking a convict's uniform, just like the dwarf (looking like Stan Laurel in *The Second Hundred Years*, 1927, perhaps a nod to Maurice Sendak).[24] The suggested rapprochements between these fairy-tale characters thus provide a visual equivalent of the dynamics of repetition with variation, modernization, combination, and condensation characteristic of Carter's retellings of the familiar tales in *The Bloody Chamber*.

The image on the back cover shows a larger group of fairy-tale characters huddling around a leafless tree, with a smiling young woman in a white crinoline dress occupying center stage; she could be any of the fairy-tale heroines in a wedding dress. She is flanked by a small lizard metamorphosing into a coachman (from "Cinderella") on the left, along with the incestuous father from "Donkey-Skin" (wearing dark glasses and bringing a dazzling dress "the colour of the sun" [*Fairy Tales*, 144] to seduce his daughter). Next to him, a tall and grim-looking man wearing a beret, an earring, and stubble, evokes the ogre from "Hop o' My Thumb." Four smaller characters, including a Little Red Riding Hood figure, a sour-looking woman with her hair in a bun (one of Cinderella's stepsisters?), and two unidentifiable figures stand in the shadow of the fairy-tale heroine. She is flanked on the right by a short and long-nosed Ricky with the Tuft in profile and a smartly dressed but stern-looking Bluebeard with a monocle and top hat. Separated from Bluebeard by a winged Lilac Fairy (from the prose adaptation of "Donkey-Skin"), who stands arm in arm with the serial killer, the young woman smiles at him. Is he, then, the groom? At any rate, the remains of Bluebeard's murdered wives litter the floor, along with a broken mirror (from "Ricky with the Tuft") and Cinderella's glass shoe on one side and the telltale key to Bluebeard's chamber of horrors on the other. A butterfly associated with Little Red Riding Hood (but also visually with Cinderella) sits on the young woman's dress, in the exact center of the group. The butterfly is a motif that appears flying around the head of Cinderella's Fairy Godmother in the middle of the volume (*Fairy Tales*, 85). She is represented as an elderly and grim-looking woman in a tight, ankle-long printed dress and extravagant hat; the feathers, flowers, and diminutive fruits (including a pumpkin) decorating her hat attract butterflies, suggesting metamorphosis and magic and perhaps also the lure of fake trimmings. This idea is reinforced by the presence of butterflies in Ware's illustration for Little Red Riding Hood "gathering nuts and chasing butterflies" (24) in *The Fairy Tales of Charles Perrault*.

Nearly all the characters and motifs figuring on the dustcover reappear in the etchings inside the book, including the personified sun from "The Foolish Wishes." Whereas masculine power is represented by the sun radiating light on the cover, vignette, and full-page representation of Jupiter, the "king of the gods" (*Fairy Tales*, 133) in "The Foolish Wishes," feminine power is embodied by the Fairy Godmother and her association with speech. Louis XIV had chosen the sun as his emblem and was henceforth known as the Sun King, and he even liked to play Jupiter in spectacles held at Versailles; here, the sun symbolizes a godlike ability to create wonders and fulfill wishes, although it also suggests the tyrannical power of omnipotent monarchs through the link with Louis XIV's absolute rule and the incestuous king of "Donkey-Skin," a connection stressed visually by Ware.

The inside title page of *The Fairy Tales of Charles Perrault* portrays an elderly, bespectacled woman in a feathered hat and long dress printed with roses, taken from Cinderella. This modern-day version of Perrault's Fairy Godmother departs from the traditional iconography of "Mother Goose," who figures in the frontispiece of Perrault's *Contes de ma mère l'Oye* and *Histoires ou contes du temps passé* and subsequently became a staple feature of fairy-tale collections. Ware's mundane fairy, however, is no benevolent peasant woman telling stories to a small captive audience of children in a homey setting. A bourgeois (if slightly eccentric), urbane version of the archetypal storyteller, the woman is standing in profile, and yet her head is turned to face the reader, looking sternly at him or her through her spectacles. The storyteller of old is now probably a reader (she's wearing glasses) and even a schoolmarmish figure. She seems to be pointing at the ground (a gesture that we can interpret as signaling the worldliness of Perrault's *contes* and even more so Carter's retranslations for a modern audience) or perhaps at the flowers decorating her dress, which are associated with the power of speech in the volume. The foreword to the 1977 edition is indeed framed by an open rose, as is the select bibliography. This contemporary equivalent of Perrault's vignettes evokes the "two roses, two pearls and two fat diamonds" (*Fairy Tales*, 76) that drop from the mouth of the polite daughter in "The Fairies" (illustrated on page 77) and therefore associates the gift of language with magic, wealth, and success.[25]

The popularity of Mother Goose (and to a lesser extent, Mother Bunch) in England is reflected in Carter's reference to this emblematic figure in the opening paragraph of her foreword, as an embodiment of the origin and source of the fairy-tale tradition itself. And yet, as the translator takes pains to explain in the introduction, "Mother Goose herself bore no relation to any real person, but was a collective name for every granny, nanny or old wife who ever kept children content with stories about unfortunate princesses, talking beasts or seven-league boots" (*Fairy Tales*, 9).[26] Carter attributes to Perrault the revival of the folk tradition represented by the mythical female storyteller. She goes on to challenge commonplaces about Perrault's *contes* as escapist fantasies, stressing their actuality instead. Through her translation she gives them renewed life and edge by updating their discourse on manners and morals, which modern readers have often misconstrued as a pressure to conform to dominant norms and values.

Carter's foreword is mainly based on Andrew Lang's introduction to *Perrault's Popular Tales*, "edited from the original editions" of Perrault's *contes en prose* and *contes en vers*. This scholarly edition established by a leading folklorist is preceded by a preface and a detailed introduction. Carter summarizes and adapts the information contained in the first part of Lang's introduction, composed of a short biographical sketch, information on the circumstances of the writing and publication of Perrault's tales, and a concluding section on the genre titled "Fairies and Ogres" (xxxv–xli), which purports to document the origin and spread of the tale. As Lang puts it in the preface, "Each prose story has also been made the subject of a special comparative research; its wanderings and changes of form have been observed, and it is hoped that this part of the work may be serviceable to students of Folk Lore and Mythology" (vi). This introductory part is followed by "Notes on the Several Tales by Perrault, and Their Variants" (xlii–cxv). Lang's enthusiasm for Perrault and for the fairy tale in general as well as his fondness for anecdotes about Perrault's life are also found in Carter. More surprisingly, perhaps, she adopts the Victorian scholar's assumptions about Perrault's *contes* as belonging to folklore and children's literature, although this is in contradiction to Barchilon's observations in *Perrault's Tales of Mother Goose* and *Le conte merveilleux français de 1690 à 1760*.

Following Lang in *Perrault's Popular Tales*, Carter asserts that Perrault's *contes* derive from "the unwritten tradition of folk-lore handed down by word of mouth from one generation to another" (*Fairy Tales*, 9).[27] In the biographical sketch that follows (based on Perrault's *Memoirs*, mediated through Lang), she stresses the strong personality of the author, his rebellious and independent spirit, and his extraordinary polyvalence; she also repeats that he was a loving husband and father who allegedly wrote fairy tales to entertain and educate children. For example, the anecdote of Perrault's argument with a philosophy teacher when he was still a pupil, which led to his leaving school with a friend to embark on a course of self-study, clearly amuses and delights the anti-authoritarian and mostly self-taught Carter. Perrault's early defense of novelty and independent thinking also captures something of his strong personality and position on the side of the Moderns against the conservative (and misogynist) defenders of the Ancients.

Carter's lively portrait of Perrault presents him in fairy-tale terms as a resourceful Hop o' My Thumb, or even Puss in Boots figure—a gifted dilettante who "was always to do those things best that he had not been trained for" and who achieved literary fame on the basis of a volume of fairy tales that "he did not even publish under his own name . . . , one of the fortunate accidents with which his life abounded" (*Fairy Tales*, 10).[28] Likewise, the paragraph devoted to Perrault's career as a civil servant ends with a praise of "the healthy opportunism with which [Perrault] was to dower Puss in Boots" (10). This allows Carter to drive home the message she wants to communicate to her readers, namely, that Perrault's life can be read as a real-life equivalent of the prototypical fairy tale that rewards qualities dear to Carter: independence of mind and intelligence, anticonformism, polyvalence and curiosity, kindness and affection toward one's wife and children, and social responsibility combined with a dose of worldly wisdom and "healthy opportunism," which earned Perrault a rich and diverse career, harmonious family life, and literary reputation that continues to this day.

Perrault's official career as a member of the prestigious Académie française is mentioned, but the emphasis is on his love match with 19-year-old Marie Guichon "against the advice of his influential patron, Colbert" (*Fairy Tales*, 10) and the birth of their three children (including the youngest, Pierre). Carter comments that "Perrault was now a very rich bourgeois indeed, as rich as Bluebeard" (11). His fortunes took a downward turn with his wife's and Colbert's deaths but, never defeated by adversity, he turned to his children's education and defense of the Moderns. Carter suggests that during his long retirement, Perrault kept himself busy by "tinkering with the tales that he probably first found in the popular form of the blue paper-covered chap-books called *La Bibliothèque Bleue*" (11).²⁹ According to Carter, then, Perrault is not so much the author as the adapter of existing fairy tales circulating in popular culture.

Carter's brief account of Perrault's *contes en vers* begins chronologically with "The Marquise de Salusses, or the Patience of Griselda," written in the style of La Fontaine. Carter explains that she has not included a translation of the tale because "it is neither a popular tale nor a folk tale" (*Fairy Tales*, 12). Another reason for Carter's rejection of "Griselidis" may be its alleged praise of female forbearance and patience, which probably irked the feminist translator. Carter's description of the tale as being about "the abuse of his wife by a psychopathic aristocrat" (11), however, echoes her own Bluebeard-based "Bloody Chamber."

Carter also mentions "The Ridiculous Wishes" (first published in *Le Mercure Galant* in 1693) and "Donkey-Skin," which sparked a controversy with "the great pedant and classicist" (*Fairy Tales*, 12) Nicolas Boileau. Once more, Perrault's energy and wit are stressed in the famous battle when he championed popular tales, declaring "that the true inheritors of Boileau's classic Homer were those who delighted in fancies such as ogres with seven-league boots" (12). The translator's project thus continues Perrault's rehabilitation of a popular tradition of great storytellers as truly modern.

Carter also mentions Perrault's reference to children and goes on to speculate about the authorship and origin of the prose tales. She voices the hypothesis that the nursery stories that Pierre Perrault heard in childhood were told to his father, who put them down on paper, and she even muses on the collective authorship of the tales, recognizing that the published collection "bear[s] all the marks of a sophisticated hand" (*Fairy Tales*, 13). Although Carter is aware that Perrault's *contes* are not the simple and naive stories that readers take them to be, she wants to believe that they are the result of collaborative work, in keeping with her understanding of the popular origins of the genre and her desire to stress the role of women, servants, and children.

Against prevailing assumptions, however, Carter also underlines the artistic nature of the *contes* and attributes the popularity of Perrault's versions to their form and style, and therefore their literary merit: "The style in which these familiar, popular themes were re-created suited them so well that Perrault's versions of the seven stories became the standard ones and, through translation and continuous reprintings and retellings, entered back again into the oral tradition of most European countries, especially that of England" (*Fairy Tales*, 13). After Lang, Carter stresses the traffic between the oral and literary traditions on the one hand and the circulation of the tales between France and England on the other. The personal anecdote of being told the story of "Little Red Riding Hood" as a child "in almost Perrault's very words" by her grandmother, "although she never spoke a single word of French in all her life" (*Fairy Tales*, 13) serves to underline this.

Carter also contrasts the apparent simplicity of Perrault's *contes* with the vogue for "ornate, baroque and sometimes monstrous excesses" (*Fairy Tales*, 13–14) in the fairy tales of the eighteenth century.[30] Carter's social consciousness emerges as she puts the emergence of the fairy-tale tradition in context and sets "the extravagance of the court" against the "great hardship[s]," "constant famines," and "continuous economic instability" of the people of France, the only wealth of the illiterate peasantry residing in their "folk-lore of songs, tales, ceremonies and dances" (14). In Carter's understanding, then, Perrault retained the style and spirit of folk culture, even though he belonged to the privileged class that used fairy tales as entertainment for the leisurely members of the aristocracy. She briefly mentions "Ladies and gentlemen of rank and fortune" (14), such as Madame d'Aulnoy, le Chevalier de Mailly, Antoine Galland, and even Voltaire. She also refers to Madame de Beaumont and *Le cabinet des fées*, the anthology put together by Charles-Joseph de Mayer, before concluding this first section with a reference to the French Revolution, which put an abrupt end to the fairy-tale fashion.

Carter recognizes that Perrault's *contes* invite a double reading. Although they seem straightforward and simple, they are "told with a great deal of literary art . . . that conceals art" (*Fairy Tales*, 15). Perrault's productions are artful but also folklike, as they retain "the simplicity of form and the narrative directness of the country story-teller" (15); likewise, fairy-tale characters are treated "as abstractions" (15), as in the folktale, which "tends to define identity by role" (15). Carter approves of Perrault's refusal of "affectation" (15) that goes against his "taste, common sense, and, perhaps, sense of fidelity to his sources" (16). Perrault is considered a proto-folklorist who, like Carter herself, paid homage to the popular tradition of the folktale retold in an artistic (though not "affected") fashion. And yet Carter notes that some details (including "the gilded chambers" and "superbly elegant clothes") anchor the tales in "Perrault's own world, the sumptuous court of the Sun-King" (16).

Perrault's *contes* are also situated within the larger context of the European fairy-tale tradition, starting with Giovanni Francesco Straparola's *Piacevoli Notte* and Giambattista Basile's *Lo Cunto de li Cunti* (also known as *Il Pentamerone*). Carter notes parallels between some of these stories and Perrault's tales, though apparently "no direct influence" (*Fairy Tales*, 16) on them.[31] Carter argues that Perrault drew on "the lore of the same kind of country people who told stories to Jacob and Wilhelm Grimm in Germany" (16), which "he extensively rewrote and even, on occasion, censored" (16).[32] Carter will borrow the idea of rewriting in *The Bloody Chamber*, although she will make sure to restore what Perrault allegedly "censored." She concludes by contrasting Perrault's "elegant, witty and sensible pages" with "the savagery and wonder and dark poetry of the Grimms' 'Household Tales'" (17), which would inspire several of her rewritings.

The last section begins with a recognition that "each century tends to create or re-create fairy tales after its own taste" (*Fairy Tales*, 17), which applies to Perrault's *contes* as much as to Carter's translation and rewritings. Perrault's modernity is reasserted, along with the author's refusal to "indulge in excesses of imagination for the imagination's own sake" (17), which echoes Carter's own critique of fantasy in "The Better to Eat You With" and her rejection of art for art's sake in *The Sadeian Woman*. Perrault's *contes*, she notes, prefigure the Enlightenment in their concise style, precise language, irony, and realism (17). There lies their usefulness as "parables of experience" where "the succinct brutality of the traditional tale is modified by the application of rationality" (17). The fairy tale therefore reconciles age-old folk wisdom and modernity.

Taking "Little Red Riding Hood" and "Bluebeard" as prime examples of Perrault's pragmatic pedagogy, Carter defends the author against the psychoanalytical critics (read: Bruno Bettelheim) who have reproached him for integrating the disturbing material of the tales into "a well-mannered schema of good sense" (*Fairy Tales*, 18). This, Carter argues, is for the best, because Perrault not only cautions his readers against the dangers of the world but also neutralizes the horror of the old tales, adding for instance "a comforting footnote" in the second moral of "Bluebeard." She also approves of Perrault's matter-of-fact attention to "worldly security" (18) and progressive sexual politics: Bluebeard's wife cleverly "uses her inheritance to secure for herself another, better husband" (18). Likewise, Carter stresses Perrault's "humane" treatment of Cinderella's sisters, implicitly contrasting it with the cruelty of the Grimms' version of the story. The French tale condemns their moral defects (redeemable through "moral effort") but neither punishes them physically (as in the German tale) nor depicts them as ugly (as in Disney's film). This allows Carter to reclaim Perrault for the type of materialist feminism that she embodied and defended. Even Perrault's fairies "have rather less the air of supernatural beings derived from pagan legend about them than that of women of independent means, one way or another, and are prepared to help along a little sister who finds herself in difficulties, personages as worldly-wise and self-confident as Mae West" (18–19).

Carter's rapprochement between the fairy godmothers and the "naughty," witty, and voluptuous movie star is exploited in Ware's illustration for the Lilac Fairy, modeled on a photograph of Mae West, down to the shapely figure, confident posture, and design of her dress in "My Old Flame."[33] The fairy is a resourceful, funny, smart, and sexy woman, and she also functions as a delegate of the author in the fiction. Carter thereby aligns herself with a long tradition of female authors who have represented themselves as fairies in the literary tradition, albeit in a modern incarnation that reconciles female solidarity with "badass" femininity.[34]

Carter concludes by deploring that Perrault's "craftsmanship" combined with "his good-natured cynicism" is lacking in twentieth-century children's literature, hence her attempt to rehabilitate his *contes*: "From the work of this humane, tolerant and kind-hearted Frenchman, children can learn enlightened self-interest from Puss; resourcefulness and courage from Hop o' My Thumb; the advantages of patronage from Cinderella; the benefits of long engagements from the Sleeping Beauty; the dangers of heedlessness from Red Riding Hood; and gain much pleasure, besides" (*Fairy Tales*, 19).

Early Reception of *The Fairy Tales of Charles Perrault*

The Fairy Tales of Charles Perrault was well received if we consider the reviews collected in the Angela Carter Papers, with the exception of one mixed review in the *Times Literary Supplement* (London) (*TLS*).[35] Although Carter's translation was generally praised for its energy and wit and Ware's black-and-white illustrations were admired for their force and originality, they also made some reviewers uneasy; the adjective "disturbing" appeared twice to describe their effect on the viewer. In keeping with the information given on the front flap of *The Fairy Tales of Charles Perrault*, the book was marketed as "a collection of fairy tales for children" and was accordingly reviewed in the "children's books" sections of a number of newspapers.

An early review of the book by Angela Burdick appeared in the "Art and Studies" section of the *Irish Times* (September 30, 1977), titled "A New Look at Old Fairy Tales." It reproduces Ware's striking portrayal of the Lilac Fairy as Mae West and of Little Red Riding Hood in a split frame. Burdick praises Carter's "lively and updated translation" for its "wit and clarity." After Carter, she portrays Perrault as a fairy-tale-like character "constantly snapping at convention and authority, an anarchist and pacifist, . . . a man of enormous energy and diverse talents and interests." The debated authorship of the tales is mentioned, although it is the putatively bohemian career of the author that attracts the most attention. Rather anachronistically (and with some twisting of historical fact), Perrault becomes a proto-pacifist and eccentric who declined to go to war and abandoned his official career in order to write fairy tales. He also becomes a figure of identification for children: "Children will be pleased to know that he baulked at his teachers' philosophical tenets, founded on grounds of mere authority and was forced to leave school before completing his education because of this disagreement. He decided that 'novelty was itself a merit.'"

Burdick also comments on Ware's illustrations (indicating that they were then exhibited at the Oxford Gallery), observing that "Perrault inspired many brilliant illustrators, including our very own Harry Clarke." She praises Ware's illustrations, noting that they were his first commission as an illustrator, but she also describes them as "at times grotesque" and "inspired more by a nightmare than a Fairy Tale." Ware's technique, she notes, "makes them very much characters of the 70s too": "Mae West features in much the same way that Dougal from 'The Magic Roundabout' drops into Ralph Steadman's drawings for 'Through the Looking-Glass' and Stan Laurel pounds through Maurice Sendak's 'Mickey in the Night Kitchen.' The intrusion of the character does not imply anything significant and is probably meaningless to the kids, but a sort of joke for the adults." Burdick draws attention to a common strategy of creative and innovative illustrators of children's books who self-consciously addressed both children and adults by alluding to modern culture (such as popular TV programs and movies).[36]

Burdick concludes her review on a celebratory note by describing the stories as "enchanting" and repeats the idea of Perrault as the first author to commit the oral fairy-tale tradition to paper. After Carter, the reviewer sees Perrault's versions of the familiar tales as a more authentic rendering of his folkloric sources than their bowdlerized and moralized adaptations. "But this is the real thing," she notes, "not the ersatz version and Red Riding Hood meets a sticky end when she is gobbled up by the wolf albeit with a certain humour in the moral at the end of each tale." Although she does not explicitly mention Grimm's "Rotkäppchen," Burdick's choice of tale to illustrate the difference between Perrault's versions and the moralized adaptations that had become canonical in England is significant. The review even reproduces the cautionary moral that warns young girls against "talking to strangers" by way of conclusion. Burdick then picks up on Carter's depiction of Perrault as a rebellious figure and implicitly opposes him to the Grimms' subsequent appropriation of the fairy tale to enforce bourgeois values and conformity to the norm.[37] Like Carter, she rejoices in Perrault's anticonformism, though this is of course more retroactive projection than an accurate account of the ups and downs of Perrault's life and career as a civil servant and member of the prestigious Académie française. The review ends with a celebration of the supposed folkloric "authenticity" of Perrault's tales, the phrase "not the ersatz version" being underlined by hand, possibly by Carter herself.

The Fairy Tales of Charles Perrault was reviewed a few days later in the *Evening Standard*, on October 4, 1977 (the mention of Gollancz in handwriting suggests that this review was transmitted to Carter). Ware's illustration for "The Sleeping Beauty in the Wood" is reproduced with the caption "Perrault's wicked fairy." The review is titled "For Older Children," and it expresses a strong sense of surprise at rediscovering the tales anew, away from the romantic stereotypes associated with the genre: "We think we know the story of Sleeping Beauty whose prince turned up after a hundred years to make her happy ever after. But it seems that her marriage brought her a highly unpleasant mother-in-law who liked eating babies. Love prevailed which, said M. Perrault in 1697, shows the advantage of long engagements." Just like "Little Red Riding Hood," "Sleeping Beauty" is usually known in England through the Grimms' "Dornröschen" (often translated as "Briar Rose"). The surprise of the reviewer comes from Perrault's versions not complying with the conventions and values (including the conservative ideology) associated with the genre.[38] Perrault's tales are described as "ironical, witty, direct. Young girls beguiled by strangers are fools, Red Riding Hood deserved to be gobbled up."

The reviewer also describes Ware's illustrations as unusual and striking: "Weird and formal, they show characters dressed as for family charades. Granny has just set aside her knitting to be the Wicked Fairy, Hop o' My Thumb is wearing Uncle's wellingtons and Sleeping Beauty is the star of the local dramatic society. Intriguing, and it reads well aloud." In Ware's illustrations ordinary people are made to impersonate fairy-tale characters in a recognizably modern setting and British cultural context (Wellingtons, pantomime tradition, etc.). The dramatic quality of the etchings and the oralized style of the translation are noted, and the overall effect of book encapsulated in the word "intriguing."

During the same period, Ian Mayes devoted the first (and longest) of six reviews of children's books to *The Fairy Tales of Charles Perrault* in a special selection of books for the *National Children's Book Week*, October 1–8, 1977. Titled "Dark Corners of Childhood," it reproduces Ware's illustration for "Cinderella." Mayes is enthusiastic about the book, declaring that "children who are lucky enough to get this book will treasure it for a lifetime." After a few words about Perrault's life and times, Mayes expresses his surprise and delight at rediscovering these "weary or hackneyed stories" anew and comments on the peculiar mix of humor and horror that Carter manages to convey in her translation. He stresses the role of the morals as "pendants of comic understatement to several of the more horrific happenings" in "Bluebeard" or the casual concluding statement in "The Sleeping Beauty in the Woods."

> Perrault tells us, "The king could not help grieving a little; after all, she was his mother." There is no kiss to awaken the sleeping princess in this version. The prince simply falls upon his knees before her and the spell is broken. And in Cinderella or Cinderbritches the step sisters aren't ugly, they suffer the moral disfigurement of pride. Cinderella forgives them and finds them fine husbands. A splendid book from beginning to end and the illustrations are very good too.

The reviewer insists on the refreshing experience of going back to Perrault's versions whose economy, grace, and subtle humor are praised (probably against Grimm or even Disney). He notices the macabre elements of "Bluebeard" but also the neutralizing effects of the dry humor of the narrator's asides and the matter-of-fact morals, and the civilized ending of "Cinderella" is once again implicitly contrasted with the gory punishment of the stepsisters in the German *Märchen*.

A. J. Krailsheimer's review for the *TLS*, dated October 28, 1977, and titled "Red Riding Hood Rides Again," is more mixed. It is illustrated by Ware's etchings for "Ricky with the Tuft" and "Little Red Riding Hood." An editor of *Three Sixteenth Century Conteurs* (1966)[39] and the translator of several books from the French, Krailsheimer begins by bluntly questioning the appropriateness of Perrault's tales as children's stories, noting the discrepancy between the requirements of the "bedtime story" and the variable length of the *contes*, and the near absence of fairies in them. Although they contain magic and violence (even "actual horror," which he sees as characteristic of the genre and therefore not objectionable as such), the problem for him is that Perrault's French *contes* only partly overlap with the English fairy-tale canon. Thus Krailsheimer reproaches Carter for introducing foreign fairy tales into the homegrown tradition.

> As for familiarity, four are perennial subjects for Christmas pantomime (Red Riding Hood, Sleeping Beauty, Cinderella and Puss in Boots, though the last has become indissolubly linked in English tradition with Dick Whittington) while Bluebeard has inspired more than one play or opera, but the other five, except perhaps Hop o' My Thumb, are by no means well known in English (The Fairies, Ricky with the Tuft, Foolish Wishes and Donkey-Skin).

Not only do the *contes* of Perrault imperfectly fit the generic label of the "fairy tale" in Krailsheimer's understanding of the term, but some of them are not familiar to the readers. What is at stake here, implicitly, is no less than Carter's project as a cultural translator that moves across national frontiers and cross-fertilizes "native" traditions.

Krailsheimer also objects to the literary merits of Perrault's versions of the tales and faults Carter for choosing the anonymous prose adaptation of "Donkey-Skin" for her translation (even implying that she did so out of ignorance). This gives him an occasion to parade his scholarly knowledge of Andrew Lang's edition, which, incidentally, Carter cites in her book. The reviewer clearly disapproves of Carter's privileging of Perrault; he grudgingly admits that the Frenchman authored the first literary version of the familiar tales, but remarks that the Grimms' versions are better known in England. Only in the last paragraph does he discuss the literary merits of the translation ("stylish and lively"), with a focus on Carter's recovery of Perrault's worldly morals and a passing reference to Ware's "original and disturbing illustrations."

The review ends on a rather sour note, doubting the success of Carter's reclamation of Perrault for pedagogical ends and even the popularity of the fairy tale in the present age. Carter's belief in the relevance and topicality of Perrault's tales is naive or misguided, Krailsheimer argues, for fairy tales have been replaced by modern-day consumerism, advertising, and the new "magic" of color TV. At best, Perrault can be "presented as 'the book of the pantomime,' and with any luck Martin Ware's original and disturbing illustrations will tempt children to read these timeless tales on their own merits." Unlike the positive reviews found in mainstream newspapers, Krailsheimer's scholarly article, published in a more highbrow journal, finds fault with Carter's preference for Perrault's *contes* and her project to revisit fairy tales for pedagogical purposes. The impact of Carter's endeavor would prove him wrong.

The subsequent reception of *The Fairy Tales of Charles Perrault* was oriented toward the market of Christmas books. In a short article published in the "stocking fillers" column of *The Catholic Herald*, dated November 25, 1977, Gerard Loughlin briefly presents the book as including "eight of the best known and best loved of all fairy tales" by Charles Perrault "printed here complete with the *Moralités*" and two other tales by Perrault. Carter's translation is praised as "fresh and vivid and altogether delightful." The reviewer follows Carter's line of argument when he celebrates Perrault's tales for their "great artistry," though they "never betray or deny their peasant and age-old origins. They are the 'traditional' tales—'Red Riding Hood,' 'Cinderella'—which, while read to children (and God forbid that this should ever cease!) contain elements and undertones decidedly adult." The reviewer associates the adult, disturbing, and dark dimension of the familiar stories not with Perrault's tales but with Ware's pictures, which he praises for being "precise, unusual, [and] sophisticated." The parenthetical comment signals that the question of the appropriateness of Perrault's tales for children was debated at the time (as though in response to Krailsheimer's criticism) and that the strangeness of the familiar stories was captured by the visual artist, before becoming a staple feature of Carter's rewritings.

Also in the spirit of the fairy-tale gift book, *The Fairy Tales of Charles Perrault* was briefly presented in the "Christmas Book Supplement" of the *Express & News* on December 1, 1977, among other recent publications for children. This magazine stressed the "exoticism" of Perrault's French tales ("Angela Carter takes us to France with her sprightly new translation") and praised Ware's etchings for "catch[ing] the grotesque as well as the charming elements in the stories." Likewise, the book was listed in the "Books for Children" section (under "Older Fiction") of the *Daily Mail* on December 15, 1977, once again emphasizing the quality of the translation that goes back to Perrault's "original" versions and praising Martin Ware's etchings as "elegantly modern."

In some cases Ware's pictures attract even more attention than the translation itself. In the *Hampstead & Highgate Express*, for instance, Ware's caricature of Fanchon from "The Fairies" (known in England as "Toads and Diamonds") is reproduced with the following caption: "Since she can't keep a civil tongue in her head, Fanchon suffers an outpouring of reptiles every time she opens her mouth. She's to be found in *The Fairy Tales of Charles Perrault*, the 17th century French civil servant who gave the world the definitive versions of Little Red Riding Hood, Bluebeard, Cinderella and other stories." The same illustration, described as "striking," "never sentimental and often positively disturbing," was reproduced in the *Times Educational Supplement*, on November 25, 1977. Five drawings by Ware also appeared before Christmas in *Hibernia* (December 16, 1977) under the rubric "Fictionaries" (book reviews).

In sum, *The Fairy Tales of Charles Perrault* was positively reviewed by readers surprised and delighted to rediscover the fairy tale in Carter's translation of a pre-Grimm literary source and similarly intrigued by the modernity of Ware's illustrations. However, the mixed reaction of the *TLS* reviewer shows that the preference for "homegrown" traditions also created some dissatisfaction with the book.

Domesticating Perrault, or the Fairy Tale as Bedtime Story: *Sleeping Beauty and Other Favourite Fairy Tales*

In the aftermath of the success of *The Bloody Chamber*, Victor Gollancz reissued Carter's translations as *Sleeping Beauty and Other Favourite Fairy Tales* (1982). This second edition, which includes two new tales by Jeanne-Marie Leprince de Beaumont (including the popular "Beauty and the Beast" and the lesser known "Sweetheart"), was published in a larger format with a soft cover and color illustrations by the popular and award-winning illustrator of children's books Michael Foreman.[40] The title of the book announces that "Sleeping Beauty" is given pride of place, and the sequence of texts is reorganized accordingly.[41] The 1982 edition is more clearly marketed for children than the original one. The French literary source of the tales (which troubled the *TLS* reviewer) disappears from the cover in favor of the anonymous category of the "favourite fairy tale." Whereas the 1977 book was daring, the 1982 reissue is charming but more conventional in its editorial choices. The 1977 edition challenged received ideas about the nature and function of the fairy tale as imaginative literature, introduced new stories into the British canon, and marked a rupture with traditional fairy-tale iconography. The 1982 edition, less markedly critical of the dominant reception of the genre with its soft colors, dreamlike landscape, and gentle humor, situates the stories within a tradition of medieval and courtly romance reminiscent of late-nineteenth-century fairy-tale illustrations (especially the English tradition exemplified by Richard Doyle, Walter Crane, and Arthur Rakham) and highlights the pursuit of love as the primary theme of the volume (Figure 1.4).[42]

The pastel technique and traditional motifs represented on the cover and the more child-friendly style of the illustrator tend to reinforce conventional ideas about the genre. The cover illustration features dark woods in the background, a high-turreted castle, a Prince Charming portrayed as a knight in armor galloping on his decorated white horse (in a pink, silver, and gold harness dotted with hearts and stars) toward the Sleeping Beauty (represented as a hazy profile above the woods).[43] Mauve, white, and pink dominate on a soft green background, and the sky is a pinkish yellow.

The back cover is more disquieting. A heart-shaped yellow coach travels in a dark forest, observed by a half-grotesque, half-threatening ogre looming over the woods, while a fanged wolf hides in the bushes in the forefront.[44] The good fairy in her dragon-drawn chariot is crossing the

Figure 1.4. Cover of the 1982 edition of Sleeping Beauty and Other Favourite Fairy Tales. *Illustration by Michael Foreman.*

sky in the other direction, leaving the passengers unprotected. The picture emphasizes magical action and supernatural creatures and brings together characters and scenes drawn from several tales; it also plays with the fairy tale's double audience of children and adults. The cover revisits the French fairy tales through the kind of romantic medievalism typical of British fairy-tale imagery but with a touch of humor and fantasy.

Sleeping Beauty and Other Favourite Fairy Tales was probably designed to capitalize on Carter's celebrity in the aftermath of *The Bloody Chamber*, giving adult readers an opportunity to familiarize their children with the French tradition and relying on Foreman's reputation as an illustrator of children's books to grab children's interest. This new edition dispels the objections and general unease expressed by some reviewers upon the publication of the first edition by conforming to the common reader's expectations about the genre.

Relatedly, the introduction is much reduced and relegated to the end of the book, and the bibliography disappears altogether. Some information about Charles Perrault and Jeanne-Marie Leprince de Beaumont is nevertheless given in an afterword, casually titled "About the Stories" (*Sleeping Beauty*, 125–28). Carter distinguishes between two moments in the emergence of children's literature articulated around the fairy tale: Perrault's pragmatic project giving way to Beaumont's concern with moral education at a time when edifying literature "expanded rapidly in Europe" (125). The description of Perrault's work basically sums up the foreword of the first edition, with Beaumont's tales being contrasted for their moral purpose and greater creative freedom. Carter's argument that Perrault's and Beaumont's different uses of the fairy tale reflect a profound change in sociocultural attitudes toward children between the seventeenth and eighteenth centuries is based on Philippe Ariès's *Centuries of Childhood*.[45]

It is noteworthy that Carter locates the origin of Perrault's *contes* in a universal and orally transmitted folklore even more firmly in *Sleeping Beauty and Other Favourite Fairy Tales* than in *The Fairy Tales of Charles Perrault*: "Nor do [Perrault's] stories belong exclusively to France; folklore acknowledges no frontiers" (*Sleeping Beauty*, 125). She makes the same claim about Beaumont's literary *contes de fées* in light of other beast marriage stories throughout the world. Carter here echoes Iona and Peter Opie's *Classic Fairy Tales* (137–38), although she significantly does *not* retain their disquisition on the literary origins of the tale.[46] Carter's somewhat convoluted formulation, however, signals a slight unease, as though she were anticipating possible objections: "And, if Madame de Beaumont, writing rather later, shapes her tales with more glamour and less fidelity to source material, her *Beauty and the Beast* still has its origins deep in the antique, international heritage of the folk-tale" (*Sleeping Beauty*, 125). Both the folktale and the literary tale, Carter asserts, originate in "grannies, nannies and old wives" whose stories "once in print, became 'fixed' in forms that have remained remarkably unaltered until our own day" (126). The staying power of "Beauty and the Beast" is nevertheless attributed to Beaumont's literary merits.

Carter then contrasts Perrault and Beaumont along the lines of a "changing history of taste" (*Sleeping Beauty*, 126). Her insistence on the time gap between the two authors and, with it, of changing ideas about childhood and the role of the fairy tale, goes against common perceptions of the genre as fixed, homogeneous, and unchanging. In the short biographical sketch that Carter devotes to Perrault, she again insists on his rebellious character, retaining the incident of his quarrel with his philosophy teacher that led him to leave school at a young age. She stresses the benefits of self-education, making Perrault into an early proponent of "the emancipation of children" from formal schooling. For the second edition, then, Carter retains the "child" Perrault at the expense of the gifted writer, civil servant, and influential academician caught up in the great aesthetic debate of his time. Likewise, she portrays Perrault as a successful, "self-consciously progressive man, who became a rich and powerful bourgeoise [*sic*] apt to believe, perhaps, that no happy ending comes without the enlightened self-interest with which he credits Puss in Boots" (126). Carter goes on to trace the emergence of the fairy-tale canon, starting with Perrault's "standard versions" (126). She mentions the 1729 English translation, the fashion for "rococo" fairy tales, which "lost all contact with the illiterate peasantry and, indeed, with children" (127), and the publication of Charles-Joseph de Mayer's *Le cabinet des fées* (1789). Carter's celebration of the oral, "folk" tradition associated with old wives, nurses, and children, is perceptible in this passage.

The second half of the afterword presents Jeanne-Marie Leprince de Beaumont's life and times and assesses her contribution to fairy-tale literature. Because it is at once informative and relevant to Carter's project as a translator and writer, I want to analyze it in some detail. Carter begins by stressing Beaumont's role in reviving the fairy tale as a genre for children, after the vogue of sophisticated *contes* for adults (Charles Perrault occupies an ambiguous position, with the studied simplicity of his tales addressed to a mixed audience). Carter notes that Madame de Beaumont "worked exclusively for young people, both as a writer and as a governess" (*Sleeping Beauty*, 127). The figure of the governess immediately suggests the connections with Charlotte Brontë that would be activated in her translation, although Carter unfortunately did not live long enough to rewrite the Victorian novel from the perspective of Adèle Varens (see her preface to the Virago edition of *Jane Eyre*). Further, Carter notes that Beaumont's "talent for the 'literary' fairy tale combined with an enthusiasm for education. She herself was a person who could not have existed before her own time, a respected and respectable woman who earned her own living. Her very existence, and her contemporary fame, is symptomatic of social change" (*Sleeping Beauty*, 127). Once again, Carter's portrayal of a fellow-writer becomes a self-portrait of sorts: an active, gifted woman earning a living by writing and sharing an interest in the fairy tale as a means to combine literary creation and experimentation, entertainment and pedagogy. The decision to include Beaumont in the second edition is also very much in the spirit of what Virginia Woolf and later Elaine Showalter recommended to women eager to create (or recover) a sense of continuity and literary genealogy with like-minded literary "foremothers."[47] In this sense Carter's choice to include two of Beaumont's *contes* in the 1982 edition and to devote half of the afterword to a female predecessor is consistent with second-wave feminist literary scholarship, in that she rediscovers and reclaims a female tradition overshadowed by Perrault.

Carter takes care to present "Beauty and the Beast" in context, signaling that the tale was embedded in a larger volume: "Her [Beaumont's] *Magasin des enfants, ou dialogues entre une sage Gouvernante et plusieurs de ses Elèves*, was printed in London in 1756. The book intended to blend 'the useful' with 'the agreeable' in the form of a collection of moral tales, of which *Beauty and the Beast* is one. It was translated as *The Young Misses Magazine* in 1761" (*Sleeping Beauty*, 127). The title of the book is quoted in full, signaling that the fairy tale was subsequently isolated from its original frame. Carter notes the double aim of the moral tales included in the collection and mentions its early reception in English. She also points out that Beaumont's *conte* is itself a rewriting or shortened version of a literary source, Madame de Villeneuve's *La Jeune Américaine et les contes marins* of 1740 (which appears to contradict what Carter said at the beginning about the folk origin of the tale).

With regard to the origins of "Beauty and the Beast," it is telling that

Carter makes no mention of the literary tradition retraced by the Opies, although she explicitly refers to *The Classic Fairy Tales* as one of her main sources: "Madame de Beaumont's *Beauty and the Beast* is not only the 'classic text,' as Iona and Peter Opie put it, 'of the world-wide beast-marriage story,' but one of the finest, as it is one of the earliest, of all short stories" (*Sleeping Beauty*, 127). The Opies put much emphasis on the parallels and differences with the Latin intertext (and even quote from it in Latin, hinting that the story itself might have come from a Greek source despite its presentation as an old wives' tale in Apuleius's text), but Carter does not retain it, probably because this would be too much in contradiction to her notion of the folk origins of the fairy-tale tradition. Carter admires Beaumont's ability to transform the fairy tale into modern fiction. Her characters have "real inner life" and "Beauty, with her stoicism, courage and kindness, is a fully-realised heroine in the manner of modern fiction rather than in the two-dimensional mode of the fairy tale" (128). Carter thus stresses the importance of Beaumont's contribution to the fairy-tale tradition, but she also suggests that the genre is intimately linked with the rise of the novel.[48]

Unlike "the bright colours, precise outlines and stock adjectives" of Perrault's *contes* that Carter associates with "the old wives' country story telling," Beaumont's prose is "self-conscious, sensuous, evocative" (*Sleeping Beauty*, 128) as well as musical and melancholic. These literary qualities coupled with a preoccupation with virtue indicate a shift from "the Age of Reason" to "the Cult of Sensibility."

> Beauty's happiness is founded on her abstract quality of virtue; Prince Sweetheart can only be happy if he is good and is saved by the love of a good woman. Seventy or eighty years before the "sage gouvernante" discussed virtue with her pupils in a manner, perhaps, not unlike that of the Fairy Candida in prince Sweetheart—that is, "being good" is "doing what you're told"—Perrault added an ad hoc collection of morals to his tales, from which his readers could choose the one they liked best. (128)

The end of the afterword marks a significant "return to Perrault," a move away from moralizing to individual choice. Carter even reiterates the analogy between the young Perrault and Puss: "He applauded the ingenuity of a quick-witted con man like Puss in Boots. The boy who ran away from school admired inventiveness. Madame de Beaumont is not like that" (*Sleeping Beauty*, 128). Carter concludes: "In her lovely stories, we see the fairy tale melting into both a magical art, and also into the kind of abstract moralising that would dominate nineteenth century stories for children" (128).

2

Updating the Politics of Experience

FROM "LE PETIT CHAPERON ROUGE" TO "LITTLE RED RIDING HOOD" AND "THE COMPANY OF WOLVES"

Old Wine in New Bottles: Blood Connections in "Little Red Riding Hood"

For me, writing for radio involves a kind of three-dimensional storytelling.

—ANGELA CARTER, PREFACE TO *COME UNTO THESE YELLOW SANDS*, 7

"Little Red Riding Hood," Angela Carter's translation of Charles Perrault's "Le Petit Chaperon rouge," is given pride of place in *The Fairy Tales of Charles Perrault*. This reflects both the preeminence of the story in the modern fairy-tale canon and its central role in Carter's body of work. Sandra Beckett has extensively documented how, from Perrault onward, the story of the little girl in red has become a paradigmatic crossover text that appeals to children and adults alike.[1] Carter was very much aware of this double audience, and she returned to the story repeatedly to explore how its basic conflict, dramatic plot, memorable dialogue, and striking images can be reconfigured anew for different purposes. Mostly known through Perrault's and the Grimms' classic—and distinct—versions of the story, "Little Red Riding Hood" is also a palimpsest text with ramifications in folklore and werewolf stories, and a rich cultural legacy in different genres and media.

Carter took the familiar tale as the basis for three short stories, a radio play, and a film script, which enabled her to experiment with different styles, settings, endings, generic combinations, and narrative perspectives. *The Bloody Chamber* contains three stories grouped at the end of the volume. Carter's initial plan was to place them immediately after the title story, starting with "The Werewolf" in folktale fashion, then the "rococo", "Wolf-Alice," and finally the manifold retellings of "The Company of Wolves."[2] The tale is linked to the title of Carter's collection through the color red associated with blood, and the encounter between a beast (or beastlike) character and a nubile girl constitutes a major structuring device that unifies the volume as a whole.[3] In this sense Carter's variations on Little Red Riding Hood form a continuum with her Bluebeard and Beauty and the Beast stories, and they further complicate the opposition between the two protagonists.[4] The articulation of Carter's translation of Perrault to the multiple retellings therefore hinges on the shift from a two-dimensional text to a multidimensional one: from a short, compact tale presenting a basic conflict, linear story line and straightforward cautionary message to retellings that explore alternative narrative paths, thicken the plot, and make meaning increasingly unstable through proliferating possibilities.

The creative dynamic even extends beyond *The Bloody Chamber* collection to encompass a radio play and a screenplay. Carter would indeed transpose the Chinese box narrative structure of the short story "The Company of Wolves" into a "three-dimensional" radio play bearing the same title, which reframes the bouquet of stories through the paradigmatic scene of storytelling whereby a grandmother tells stories to a Red Riding Hood figure while she is knitting a warm red shawl for her. Eventually, Carter evolved a screenplay from the radio play with help from the director Neil Jordan, expanding it and adding a new layer through the dream sequence of Rosaleen, who plays the Red Riding Hood figure. The first draft was completed by July 1983, and *The Company of Wolves* was released in 1984. Transposing and adapting the radio play into a predominantly visual medium obviously involved further transformations and new possibilities. To quote Jordan: "The visual design was an integral part of the script. It was written and imagined with a heightened sense of reality in mind." He added that Carter "was thrilled with the process, because she loved films."[5] Jordan and Carter were even considering adapting another radio play, *Vampirella*, for the screen when she fell ill.

The embedded narratives and interlocking frames of the various adaptations of "The Company of Wolves" as text, sound, and image turn a linear story into a multifaceted object that can be experienced and understood on many levels. Its complex structure creates an effect of perspective or depth that also brings to the fore the palimpsestic history of the tale and its shifting meaning. In other words, whereas in her translation of Perrault's tale Carter seeks to warn children against predators in a plain and simple manner, "The Company of Wolves" toys with the idea of the indirect, winding path through its digressive structure, and, as a "deviant" narrative, suggests alternative possibilities to the predictable outcome.

Carter saw in Perrault's *conte* "the succinct brutality of the folktale modified by the first stirrings of the Age of Reason" ("The Better to Eat You With," 453). The tale carries a worldly message that children can learn from, and this is what the translator wants to convey. Carter even describes the story of Red Riding Hood in her course notes as "the child of a single parent whose most significant relative is her grandmother."[6] In her own variations on the story collected in *The Bloody Chamber*, however, Carter would conduct more daring and sophisticated experiments. She would return to the folktale tradition and engage with anthropological, symbolic, and psychoanalytical interpretations that read "archaic patterns of ritual initiation; forbidden thresholds; invitatory incantations to pubertal rites" into the story. These elements that "our more barbarous times rejoice in for their own sakes" (453) would feed into her *new* Mother Goose tales. Carter's view of creation as stemming from the dynamic interplay of reading, translating, and (re)writing is therefore inseparable from changing perceptions and understandings of the tale reflected in her multiple and interlocking retellings of the story.

Carter also responds to feminist critics who accused Perrault of disempowering the female heroine by making her a naive and passive victim of the wolf and to Bruno Bettelheim, who in *The Uses of Enchantment* (1976) found the tragic ending inappropriate for children and favored the Grimms' version instead.[7] The probable influence of Erich Fromm's *Forgotten Language: An Introduction to the Understanding of Dreams, Fairy Tales, and Myths* (1951) can also be perceived in Carter's association of the red hood as symbolizing menstruation and approaching puberty with her reading of the tale as a rite of passage (both social or sexual) in "The Company of Wolves." Carter also seems to be drawing on the work of the folklorists Andrew Lang and Paul Delarue. Because she is ignorant of danger, the girl is unable to rescue herself in Perrault's tale, unlike her folk counterpart in "The Story of Grandmother," who tricks her powerful opponent. This inflects all three of Carter's rewritings, where the girl has greater agency;

she is either armed, fearless and prepared to confront the wolf, or playful and knowing in the game of seduction with her male counterpart, or even a hybrid wolf-girl who instinctively ministers to a beastly Count wounded by gunshot. The centerpiece, "The Company of Wolves," openly addresses and tackles the sexual subtext of the tale. However, instead of blaming the girl's behavior or even indicting predatory masculinity, the story becomes an occasion to explore female sexual desire and beastly attraction.[8] The devouring of the grandmother and Little Red Riding Hood has often been seen as a metaphor for rape in fairy-tale criticism, and this interpretation dominates many retellings in fiction, film, and children's books.[9] And yet Carter was more interested in complicating the prey-predator opposition, in keeping with her unorthodox feminist standpoint.[10]

In "Notes from the Front Line" (1983) Carter declares that she is a feminist writer "because I'm a feminist in everything else and one can't compartmentalize these things in one's life" (37). She also posits a gendered reader for her fiction that presents "a number of propositions in a variety of different ways" that leave the reader free "to construct her own fiction for herself from the elements of my fictions" (37). She goes on to add that reading old texts anew is analogous to "putting new wine in old bottles, especially if the pressure of the new wine makes the old bottles explode" (37). The reverse image of "old wine in new bottles" suggests a link to a particularly macabre version of "Little Red Riding Hood" that Carter was familiar with: "The Story of Grandmother." The ambiguous title of the folktale (is it by or about the grandmother?), shocking images of endogamous anthropophagy, positive outcome (for the girl if not for the grandmother), and metafictional implications provided Carter with food for thought regarding issues of intergenerational transmission, gender roles, and the presence of the other within the self. This folktale, in which the girl is made to eat her grandmother's flesh and drink her blood before sleeping with the wolf and saving her own life, can indeed be related to storytelling itself, whereby old stories are constantly retold in new forms and live on in new bottles—or bodies.

Carter's work derived a new energy from revisiting the fairy-tale tradition in the wake of the feminist movement's second wave.[11] Because the reader is a potential author who can make old stories anew, the translation-rewriting dynamic becomes a bold gesture of incorporation, assimilation, and re-creation of the stories from the past. In "The Story of Grandmother" the archaic motif of feeding on powerful ancestors can even be seen to symbolize the folk tradition that forms the underbelly of the fairy-tale canon. In contrast to the classic versions that were long used as a "quintessential moral primer,"[12] the folktale does not enforce conformity with the norm but rather suggests more disturbing possibilities for survival. Intellectual development, Carter argues, is bound up with rereading old texts against the grain of received ideas and dominant ideologies, and it also implies exploring new paths and directions. Perrault's tale serves to teach young readers to distinguish between words and intentions, appearance and reality, literal and figurative meaning, as the moral indeed encourages them to do, but Carter's detour through the "wild philology" of the Grimms suggests even more complex options. In her own rewritings she confronts readers with multilayered, open-ended narratives that thwart expectations and "expose or upset the paradigms of authority inherent in the texts they appropriate";[13] their notoriously intricate, allusive, palimpsestic style and metamorphic structure require the reader's active participation in the endless deconstruction and reconstruction of meaning.

Examining Carter's translation of "Le Petit Chaperon rouge" in *The Fairy Tales of Charles Perrault* in counterpoint with its retellings in *The Bloody Chamber* sheds light on the author's view of the interrelationship between reading, translating, and (re)writing as continuous and inseparable activities. Carter's extension of translation into a new writing project was not unlike Barbara Godard's decision to write a translation diary "to explore the interdiscursive production of meaning that is translation.... Both re/writings came together: the essay on the process and the translation itself."[14] The translation becomes a means to reinstate Perrault's "project for worldly instruction" ("The Better to Eat You With," 453) *against* common conceptions of the fairy tale as imaginative literature divorced from reality. Carter indeed aligned herself with Perrault when she realized that, far from being escapist, the tale was an occasion to discuss the real-life dangers and dilemmas of the author's own time and milieu.

Perrault explains in the dedicatory preface "A Mademoiselle" that unlike the fables of antiquity, his *contes* all contain a useful moral. It is therefore tempting to relate Perrault's image of the tale as a text that encapsulates a sensible message in the moral to Carter's bottles metaphor. The containment of meaning serves a clear pedagogical purpose for both writers, who share a common goal to teach and instruct their readers, as stated in the prefaces of their respective fairy-tale collections.¹⁵ Whereas Perrault may be tongue-in-cheek in his insistence on the moral import of his tales, Carter chooses to take his declared intentions at face value in the translation. But in her rewritings of the tale for *The Bloody Chamber*, she works in an altogether different textual space to explore more explosive strategies. Taken together, the two projects gradually sensitize readers to the art of engaging with textual complexity and variability and take an active part in interpretation and re-creation. Perrault himself of course had already pointed out that readers are key agents in the production of meaning, because meaning reveals itself according to the readers' degree of intelligence or perceptiveness.¹⁶

Carter's rewritings are therefore best understood in counterpoint to her translation, insofar as "Little Red Riding Hood" lays the ground for several variations or, to borrow her own words, "a number of propositions" on the familiar story. "The Werewolf," "The Company of Wolves," and "Wolf-Alice" as well as the radio play and the film script show that Carter pursued her critical and creative engagement with Perrault's *conte* well beyond *The Bloody Chamber*.¹⁷ The pedagogical intentions of the translation are carried over in the rewritings, although in a different form and for a different public, thereby forming a progressive reading course that teaches life lessons in the dangers of the world and how to face up to them before introducing the reader to the headier pleasures of textuality.¹⁸

In the essay "The Better to Eat You With" (1976), whose very title hints at the importance of "Little Red Riding Hood," Carter enthuses on discovering Perrault's "healthily abrasive attitude to his material" (453). Perrault's "abrasive" version of the story is implicitly set against the "smooth-talking" wolves of the moral that use language to delude and devour (or abuse) young girls.

An examination of seventeenth-century texts shows that Perrault's "Le Petit Chaperon rouge" is centrally concerned with gender issues, although this dimension has often been misunderstood in the critical reception of the tale. In his preface to the *Contes en vers* (1695), Perrault explicitly defines his own project against the fables of the Ancients. In contrast to the tale of Psyche, which was merely designed to entertain, his *contes* all contain a useful and modern moral, which makes them better suited for storytelling. Accordingly, "Le Petit Chaperon rouge" teaches a cruel but useful lesson, as it wryly comments on the failure of mothers and grandmothers to caution their daughters against the threat represented by seducers, embodied in the story by a deceitful wolf. The comparison that Perrault's educated readers would no doubt spontaneously make between the ancient *fabella* and the story of "Le Petit Chaperon rouge" highlights the responsibility of the mother in the girl's tragic fate. The older women have left the younger one in ignorance of the presence of sexual predators, especially those inevitably attracted by a girl going out alone and wearing a small and brightly colored *chaperon* that sets off her youthful beauty, instead of a *grand chaperon* (i.e., a chaperone) who would have protected her honor and her life. The pun would not have escaped Perrault's contemporary readers.

In keeping with the modern reception of Perrault's *contes*, *The Fairy Tales of Charles Perrault* is aimed at children. What that means for Carter is that they are cautionary tales or "little parables of experience" (*Fairy Tales*, 17) that help children cope with the trials of life and the real enough dangers of the world. Although Carter translates Perrault partly to restore a pre-Romantic tradition that goes against the Grimms' Biedermeier, moralistic version of the story, her rendering of the tale nevertheless reflects the subtle influence of "Rotkäppchen." In the French *conte* the mother simply instructs the young girl to take goodies to her grandmother, but it is the Grimm brothers who turn the tale into a Christian parable that promotes obedience to the mother and the need to follow the "straight path" of virtue and escape the "old sinner" (*alter Sünder*) Wolf.[19] Another crucial difference is that in Grimm the two women are rescued from the wolf's belly thanks to the intervention of hunters, who represent male strength and authority, and the little girl has fully integrated the moral admonition or injunction when she declares that never again will she ignore her mother's advice.

Although Carter deliberately writes against the Grimms' moralizing *Märchen* and favors Perrault's version instead because it carries useful, practical advice about the world, her translation nevertheless bears subtle traces of the German text in its depiction of a young girl who becomes an unwitting accomplice in her tragic fate. Carter indeed modernizes the content of Perrault's *conte*; the libertines haunting young ladies' bedchambers at the Court of Louis XIV become pedophiles hunting down children in the streets, although the threat of sexual abuse is perceptible only by an adult reader. Carter thus updates the cautionary moral when she addresses young readers, but also (more indirectly) the grown women who pass on fairy tales to the next generation and therefore play a role in preserving the integrity of children.

Angela Carter's Scholarly Sources, or Grandma's Blood in a Bottle

> In the popular versions, in Brittany and the Nièvre, the wolf puts the grandmother in the pot, and her blood in bottles, and makes the unconscious child eat and drink her ancestress!
>
> —ANDREW LANG, *PERRAULT'S POPULAR TALES*, LV

Andrew Lang's *Perrault's Popular Tales* was mainly intended as "an introduction to the study of Popular Tales in general" (v). Lang admits that he had never seen "the Paris editions of 1694 and 1695" (v); the publication of Jacques Barchilon's scholarly edition of the manuscript copy of the *Contes de Ma Mère l'Oye* created quite a stir when it came out in 1956. For obvious reasons, then, Lang's edition contains only the text of Perrault's 1697 edition, framed by an introduction presenting the author's life and work and a brief section devoted to each tale: "Each prose story has also been made the subject of a special comparative research; its wanderings and changes of form have been observed, and it is hoped that this part of the work may be serviceable to students of Folk Lore and Mythology" (vi). Lang considered fairy tales a minor genre ("little thing," xvi) and Charles Perrault's collection as the quirk of a gifted and slightly eccentric gentleman, who became part of the family through the alleged universality of his tales ("Every generation listens in its turn to this old family friend of all the world," xvi).

In the section titled "Perrault's Popular Tales," Perrault's *contes* are favorably contrasted with the fashion for sophisticated fairy tales "to amuse the ladies with at Versailles" (*Perrault's Popular Tales*, xvii). For Lang, "our Mother Goose's Tales" (xvii), as he calls them, "must have resembled the arrival of the Goose Girl, in her raiment, at the King's Palace. The stories came in their rustic weeds, they wandered out of the cabins of the charcoal burners, out of the farmers' cottages, and after many adventures, reached that enchanted castle of Versailles" (xvii). The author of the *contes* conveniently disappears in this section, where in fairy-tale fashion agency is given to the tales themselves as they travel to court to get recognition. Significantly, their beauty is not associated with Perrault's heroine in "Peau d'Ane" but with the Grimms' "Goose Girl" instead, possibly through an association with "Mother Goose," which facilitates the appropriation of

Perrault's *contes* as "*our* Mother Goose's Tales" (italics mine) in England. According to Lang, then, Perrault is not so much the author as the transmitter of a folk tradition of "old wives' fables" (xxii) through which he achieved "immortality," even though the fairy-tale scholar was aware of the tales' literary sources and classical or mythical resonances.

To further support the idea of a popular origin for the tales, Lang hypothesizes that the "naïveté, and popular traditional manner of their telling" results from the collaboration of Perrault's son and, through him, "his Nurse" (*Perrault's Popular Tales*, xxix): "Contrast with these refinements, these superfluities, and incoherences, the brevity, directness, and simplicity of *Histoires et Contes du Temps passé*. They have the touch of an intelligent child, writing down what he has heard told in plain language by plain people" (xxx). Lang also praises the "little grain of French commonsense" (xxxii) that characterizes Perrault's own version of "fairy-land" as "he tames the wild *fée* into the Fairy Godmother" (xxxii). Lang's account of the authorship of the tales is thus split into a positive portrayal of Perrault and a claim that he was a mere transmitter of folklore. Lang's influence on Carter's views of the origin and nature of Perrault's tales thus becomes obvious.

Lang starts the section devoted to "Le Petit Chaperon rouge" with the moral that, he argues, reflects Perrault's own understanding of the tale, unlike the nurses who allegedly transmitted the story to the writer through his son. He speculates that "they *may* have hinted at the undesirable practice of loitering when one is sent on an errand, but the punishment is out of proportion to the offence. As it stands, the tale is merely meant to waken a child's terror and pity, and probably the narrator ends it by making a pounce, in the character of Wolf, *c'est pour te manger*, at the little listener" (*Perrault's Popular Tales*, lv–lvi). The scene of storytelling that Lang evokes probably alludes to Perrault's (apparently apocryphal) marginal note inviting the teller to raise her voice when she utters the last line of the dialogue for greater impact on the child listener. The notion of performance attached to the tale, relying as it does on multiple role playing, would be echoed directly in Carter's evocation of a similar childhood memory and more indirectly in her multiple retellings of the story.

The folklorist even goes so far as to speculate that the happy ending of the Grimms' "Rotkäppchen" "may either have been the original end, omitted by Perrault because it was too wildly impossible for the nurseries of the time of Louis XIV, or children may have insisted on having the story 'turn out well'" (*Perrault's Popular Tales*, lvi). Making the connection between folktale and myth, Lang goes on to give numerous examples of this ending and the allegorical interpretations to which it has given rise: "In either case the German *Märchen* preserves one of the most widely spread mythical incidents in the world,—the reappearance of living people out of the monster that has devoured them" (lvi–lvii).

The wealth of related myths enumerated by Lang may have stimulated Carter (an ever curious reader and born comparatist) to create her own variations on the tale and to play with what Lang aptly calls "the *machinery* of the story" (*Perrault's Popular Tales*, lvi). This emphasis on the formal aspect of the tale (its working parts, plot elements, images) as a system of related elements that operate to produce specific effects anticipates the structuralist bent of the 1970s that also forms the critical backdrop for Carter's rewriting experiments aside from anthropology, psychoanalysis, and feminism.[20]

In their introduction to *The Classic Fairy Tales* the Opies observe that fairy tales have more to do with wisdom (in the sense of philosophy of life) than magic and that upon close scrutiny the tales are quite different from "the popular conception of them" (12).[21] This is also how Carter understood them. The Opies note that "Little Red Riding Hood" has nothing magical about it, "other than that the animals behave to a greater or lesser degree like human beings, and are able to speak, an accomplishment which comes as no surprise to students of Aesop" (12). The ancient fabulistic tradition that Perrault's *contes* is closely related to has a strong didactic element, inasmuch as it teaches a useful lesson about the ways of the world (its power relations, deceptions, hypocrisies, vanities, etc.), distinct from the moralized fairy tales of the later period. Recovering this tradition could not but appeal to someone of Carter's temperament, her libertarian and materialist convictions, and her strong sense of social responsibility and political commitment.

The Opies begin their introduction to "Little Red Riding Hood" by stressing the popularity of the tale and "the fact that no version of the story has been found prior to Perrault's manuscript of 1695, and its subsequent publication in *Histoires ou Contes du temps passé*" (*Classic Fairy Tales*, 93). This contradicts the hypothesis of Andrew Lang and other folklorists who believe "The Story of Grandmother" to be "the original folktale from which they [i.e., Perrault's and Grimms' versions] surely derive."[22] The major differences between the oral tale reconstructed by Paul Delarue (on the basis of several similar stories collected by A. Millien in the late nineteenth century) and Perrault's literary version are the preeminence of dramatic dialogue, the presence of a *bzou* (i.e., werewolf), and the fact that the girl is made to drink her grandmother's blood and eat her flesh, a disturbing archaic motif that allegedly appears "in all of the folk versions with variations in detail."[23] The girl also throws her garments in the fire when asked to undress, and she deceives the werewolf by pretending that she needs to relieve herself outside; she then ties the woolen thread that binds her foot to a tree and, thanks to this trick, safely returns home.[24] The reconstructed folktale has no explicit moral, but it nevertheless stresses the need to develop survival skills and learn to trick a powerful opponent.

Delarue argues that the elements of cruelty, oddity (what he terms "puerility," i.e., the roads of needles and the road of pins), and impropriety (the hairy body of the "grandmother") could not be included in Perrault's literary tale because they were too shocking for his time and milieu, although his version kept "a folk flavor and freshness which make of it an imperishable masterpiece."[25] After Delarue, Carter invented her own ur-version of the tale in "The Werewolf," and she recycled several elements of the reconstructed folktale in "The Company of Wolves."[26] "Wolf-Alice," however, explores another path, because it moves away from the fairy-tale tradition to imagine a case similar to that of the wolf-child Kaspar Hauser.

In "Animals in the Nursery," an article published in *New Society* in 1976, Carter elaborates on these real-life cases as an opportunity to rethink the distinction between nature and culture, animality and humanity, and she quotes from Lucien Malson's *Les enfants sauvages* (1964), which argues that human nature is primarily a cultural process.[27] Carter criticizes children's literature as a "Garden of Eden world of wise, talking beasts, sentient flowers, sermonizing stones" ("Animals in the Nursery," 298) and proposes to recover a sense of the wilderness of the wild world instead: "Real wolves and panthers," she observes in relation to the anthropocentric dimension of Kipling's *Jungle Books*, "do not venerate us at all. All fictional animals are imaginary animals. Adult writers take unfair advantage of child/beast solidarity to perpetuate animal fables that are really systems of moral instruction" (300). Although Carter's translation follows the conventions of the animal fable, the rewritings stage encounters between human beings and wolves that acknowledge a shared wildness.[28]

The Opies observe that the early reception of "Little Red Riding Hood" and the popularity of the tale in England were facilitated by its omnipresence in children's culture, including picture books and toy books, illustrations (notably by famous artists such as Thomas Bewick), and pantomimes. Charles Dickens memorably acknowledged that Little Red Riding Hood was his first love, and his entire literary output bears the trace of the influence of his childhood reading and listening to his nurse's scary stories. The Opies happily dismiss the conjectures of the mythologists evoked by Lang and argue instead that "the final dialogue alone, between the wolf and the little heroine, is what raises the story to the classic level" (*Classic Fairy Tales*, 93). The most famous line of the exchange, we remember, is echoed in the title of Carter's 1976 essay ("The Better to Eat You With"). The Opies also comment on the dramatic dénouement of Perrault's tale, which "ends with unsentimental abruptness" (94).

Unlike the translation, which follows Perrault closely, "The Company of Wolves" explores the utopian possibility of reconciling (wo)man and beast, in keeping with Carter's observation in "Animals in the Nursery" that the humanization of animals in children's books "obliterates the fact that man himself is only another animal with particularly complex social institutions" (301). This idea also informs "The Tiger's Bride," a retelling of "Beauty of the Beast" in which Beauty chooses to embrace beastliness instead of domesticating and humanizing the tiger, which shows that the various bodies of tales are interconnected.

The Opies go on to list alternative endings to the tale in various renderings by nineteenth-century editors and authors of children's books. They allude to "The Story of Grandmother" when they mention the particularly "nasty" Breton folktale in which "the wolf puts the grandmother's blood in bottles, and induces the unsuspecting heroine to drink her ancestress" (*Classic Fairy Tales*, 94), before summarizing the plot of the Grimms' "Rotkäppchen." They conclude with references to children's games involving wolves and the associated meaning of "wolf" as woman-hunter, probably deriving from Perrault's *conte*. Significantly, an illustration from a pop-up scene of the little girl and the wolf from the *Theatrical Picture-book* (c. 1870) is reproduced in *The Classic Fairy Tales* (39) (Figure 2.1). The caption, "Too much talking is hurtful," echoes Carter's own reading of Perrault in her translation, but the pop-up picture book evokes the structural devices used in the rewritings and their three-dimensional effects.

The nineteenth-century toy book for children, with its layered background of dense forests and thatched cottage (more reminiscent of "Rotkäppchen" than "Le Petit Chaperon rouge"), creates an effect of perspective that reproduces the idea of the girl's journey deep into the woods. It also evokes Carter's threefold retelling of the tale in *The Bloody Chamber* and her concern with depth in the radio play. Carter would even adopt the device (*dispositif*) of the pop-up book (as a childlike, comic version of the popping new wine in old bottles image, with subversive possibilities) in her last work for television, the controversial and little-known *Holy Family Album* (1991), which features various animation mechanisms, including "real curtains opening on a renaissance painting and the most disturbing cut from a pop-up Christmas card to a baby's head emerging from a vagina . . . to highlight the fact that the birth of Christ is rarely, if ever, portrayed as a real, physical birth."[29]

From "Le Petit Chaperon rouge" to "Little Red Riding Hood": Keeping the Wolf from the Door

Perrault's literary *contes* are both like and unlike the wolf: falsely naive, childlike, and mischievously playful but not to be taken at face value. They

Figure 2.1. A pop-up scene from the Theatrical Picture-book, *c. 1870, reproduced in* The Classic Fairy Tales *by Iona and Peter Opie.*

speak with a forked tongue not to deceive, like the wolf, but to warn the reader as a potential victim of real-life predators. The structure of the text reflects this duality in the short narrative and its separate moral. Notoriously allusive and subtly ironic, the meaning of the *conte* is (at least) double, divided, and thereby invites reading on more than one level.[30]

By contrast, Carter's translation adapts the text to make it easily accessible to young readers. She unifies the meaning of the text and the moral, simplifies the message (encapsulated in one sentence), and emphasizes the dialogic dimension of the story instead. The paragraph divisions facilitate reading by a child, and the short sentences and simple syntax, familiar vocabulary and active verbs, racy dialogue, and emphatic punctuation anticipate its *oral* delivery by an adult. The famous final dialogue is a favorite passage for tellers and listeners alike. The exchange creates anticipation and suspense and provokes a mix of horror and thrill in the young audience when the girl gradually discovers the bodily features of the disguised wolf and realizes that she is not talking to her grandmother. The funny game between storyteller and audience then gives way to the sobering moral. Carter simultaneously addresses a child reader or listener and an older, experienced female reader who acts as storyteller. This echoes Carter's vivid childhood memory of hearing the story of "Little Red Riding Hood" from her own grandmother "in almost Perrault's very words." In her preface to *The Fairy Tales of Charles Perrault*, Carter fondly recalls, "She liked, especially, to pounce on me, roaring, in personation of the wolf's pounce in "Red Riding Hood" at the end of the story, although she could not have known that Perrault himself suggests this acting-out of the story to the narrator in a note in the margin of the manuscript" (13).[31]

When she translates the tale, Carter seeks to recapture this moment through markers of orality and presence that foreground the dramatic nature of Perrault's text and even more so of the versions recorded by Delarue. In early editions of Perrault's text, the dialogue is integrated within the narrative. In Samber's 1729 translation, the lines spoken by Little Red Riding Hood are italicized. In Carter's modern translation, they are laid out as dramatic dialogue; and in the previous exchange, when the talking wolf proposes a game to the girl on the way to her grandmother's house, "*this* road" and "*that* road" are italicized. The translator is clearly imagining the story in performance by stressing voice and intonation. Carter does not foreground the confusion between the grandmother (as storyteller) and the wolf in the translation. The theme of disguise and role playing is nevertheless stressed by lexical choices; for example, "The wolf *disguised* his voice" (*Fairy Tales*, 26; italics mine) (to convey "Le Loup lui cria en adoucissant sa voix," *Contes*, 144), and in the bed scene the little girl "was surprised to see how odd her grandmother *looked*" (*Fairy Tales*, 26; italics mine) (for "elle fut bien étonnée de voir comment sa Mère-grand était faite en son déshabillé," *Contes*, 144).[32] The complication of clear-cut oppositions and well-defined roles allowed by impersonation draws attention to the situation presented in the tale itself, whereby a mother and a grandmother demonstrate their inadequacy to protect the child they supposedly love so much.[33] The ambivalent role played by parental figures is thus enacted in the scene of storytelling that underlies Carter's text. The possibilities opened up by role switching, substitutions, and shifting identities become a central strategy in the retellings of the story published in *The Bloody Chamber*, as they explore the narrative paths not taken in the classic versions.

Carter's translation for children reflects the reception of Perrault's *conte* and the pressure of the Grimms' moralizing version of the story in "Rotkäppchen" as a disobedience and punishment tale. In the opening sentence Perrault's "Il était une fois une petite fille de Village" (*Contes*, 143) is conveyed by "Deep in the heart of the country, there lived a pretty little girl" (*Fairy Tales*, 23), which immediately evokes the fairytale imagery and folk setting of the German *Märchen*. Likewise, Perrault's human type turns into a mere wolf. Perrault indeed capitalizes *Loup*, which suggests personification and allegorical meaning; "compère le Loup" (*Contes*, 143) clearly references La Fontaine's fables, where *compère* (companion or accomplice) is used in connection with animals such as the fox or the wolf to underline their lack of scruples and guileful character. In "Rotkäppchen" the Wolf begins its process of naturalization, although the biblical resonances also invite a reading of the tale as a Christian parable. In Carter's modern fairy tale for children, however, the literalization of the tale is complete.[34]

The translator expressed her admiration for the economy and force of Perrault's tale in "The Better to Eat You With."

> And what a craftsman Perrault was! "Little Red Riding Hood" is a classic of narrative form. The plot arises from the interaction of the wolf and his hunger, and the child and her ingenuity. The suspense springs from our knowledge of the predatoriness of wolves and our

perception of Red Riding Hood's ignorance of it. No child reared on these austere and consummately constructed narrative forms is going to be easily fobbed off with slipshod stream-of-consciousness techniques, or overheated poetic diction. (454)

The directness of Perrault's tales contributes to their effectiveness, characterized by "a style marked by concision of narrative (there is not an ounce of flab on any story)" (*Fairy Tales*, 17). This correspondence of style to plot (including its abrupt denouement) becomes a central source of experiment in the rewritings. The metaphor of flab used by Carter in connection with Perrault's writing is suggestive of the possibilities (the Little Red Riding Hood–like text consumed by the wolflike reader, the association of the "lean and mean" style with the wolf, etc.) she explored in the many retellings of the story that compose "The Company of Wolves." There, the narrator is like the wolf trying to lure and catch the reader, who is cast in the role of the prey and addressed as "you."[35] The baroque style (characterized by the fold, according to Gilles Deleuze) suggests a relationship between the wolf's smooth tongue and the seductions of literary language, which can be related to the stylistic excess of "The Bloody Chamber" as playing with the idea of the perverse seductions of art.

In "The Company of Wolves" Carter proposes a series of variations on the basic plot in a complex frame, including one that figures at the center of Neil Jordan's experimental fantasy-horror film *The Company of Wolves* (1984), in which the girl knowingly plays up to the (were)wolf's seduction game and ends up sleeping peacefully in his arms. These new and thought-provoking combinations and complications of the constitutive elements of the tale aim to delight Carter's adult readers but also to develop their interpretative skills and allow them to experience the heady pleasures of much more complex writing styles, circumvoluted syntax, and rich imagery, multiplying narrative structures, and alternatives to the prescribed social script.

Carter, who admired Perrault's tales for being "told with a great deal of literary art but it is the kind that conceals art" (*Fairy Tales*, 15), uses short sentences and avoids subordination in her translation. She opts for active verbs instead of present participles, as in "One day, her mother baked some cakes on the griddle and said to Little Red Riding Hood" (*Fairy Tales*, 23) ("Un jour sa mère, ayant cuit et fait des galettes, lui dit," *Contes*, 143). Similarly, Carter resorts to strong contrastive conjunctions to clarify meaning and reinforce the oppositional logic at work in the tale. She also takes pains to provide explanations to the young reader, especially when the famous *chaperon* is introduced: "This good woman made her a red hood *like the ones that fine ladies wear when they go riding*" (*Fairy Tales*, 23; italics mine). The translator feels the need to gloss the characteristic piece of clothing by which the girl is known in order to bridge the historical gap, but as she does so, she also stresses the difference of social class between the peasant girl and the striking sartorial feature that makes her so conspicuous: This "disguise," which her irresponsible grandmother has made for her (a gift turning into a curse, as it were), masks her origins and flags her beauty, and this will bring about her downfall.

Another problem of course is that the girl is ignorant of danger and of wolves in particular. Whereas in Perrault, "la pauvre enfant . . . ne savait pas qu'il est dangereux de s'arrêter à *écouter* un Loup" (*Contes*, 143; italics mine), in Carter's translation the danger is of a different order: "The poor child did not know how dangerous it is to *chatter away* to wolves" (*Fairy Tales*, 24; italics mine). This emphasis on "Too much talking is hurtful," to quote the toy book reproduced in the Opies' *Classic Fairy Tales*, prepares the reader for Carter's modern moral: "Don't talk to strangers." To reinforce this, Carter adds to the description of the girl playing in the wood the explanation that she was late "because she *dawdled along*" (*Fairy Tales*, 24), a word with pejorative connotations of idleness and laziness (Perrault has only "s'amusant à cueillir," *Contes*, 144), which is in fact closer to the Grimms' moralistic *Märchen* than to Perrault's *conte*. Carter thus shifts the meaning of Perrault's text, where the narrator does not judge the behavior of the girl and only intervenes to express sympathy for "la pauvre enfant" to suggest that it is the girl's ignorance that is responsible for her tragic fate, even adding that the girl replies to the wolf innocently. But she also implies that the girl is punished for posturing as a lady (the *chaperon* was a headdress that was a clear class marker), and the introduction of a "grim" detail about the wolf's devouring "young ladies" "elegant red riding hoods and all" (*Fairy Tales*, 28) reinforces this point in the moral. Carter's moral also implies that social class and class markers are no protection against "wolves," at the same time as it warns girls against the dangers of dressing up as grown women. It also points out that unlike the ignorant girl of Perrault's *conte*, modern-day "young ladies" should know better: Having been "well-brought up" (and being already familiar with the tale), they do not have the same excuse as their predecessor.

In *The Fairy Tales of Charles Perrault* Carter praises Perrault's morals for turning the tales into "little parables of experience"

> from which children can learn, without half the pain that Cinderella or Little Red Riding Hood endured, the way of the world and how to come to no harm in it. . . . The wolf consumes Red Riding Hood; what else can you expect if you talk to strange men, comments Perrault briskly. Let's not bother our heads with the mysteries of sadomasochistic attraction. *We must learn to cope with the world before we can interpret it.* (*Fairy Tales*, 17–18; italics mine)

Carter favors Perrault's "parables of experience" in her translation because she wishes to foreground their "scheme of good sense." She plays down the sexual comedy of the bed scene, the implications of which are decoded in Perrault's moral. The wolf's ambiguous "envie de la manger" (*Contes*, 143) shifts to the imperative of hunger in "[he] wanted to eat her" (*Fairy Tales*, 23). Similarly, the wolf wants to eat the grandmother because "he had not eaten for three days," which, placed before the scene itself, ascribes the "devouring" of the old woman to literal hunger. More important, Carter redefines the cautioning message in the moral so as to make the sexual dimension of the threat fully understandable to an adult reader only. She clarifies the double meaning of the tale by opposing "real wolves, with hairy pelts and enormous teeth" (an addition to Perrault's text) to the metaphorical wolves who, "charming, sweet-natured and obliging," chat up "young ladies" (*Fairy Tales*, 28) the better to assault them. She also glosses *doucereux* (*Contes*, 145) as "smooth-tongued, smooth-pelted" (*Fairy Tales*, 28), thereby connecting language and body, text and texture—the exact opposite of Perrault's "abrasive" treatment of the story.[36]

Because she is retranslating what is now a bedtime story for children, Carter also attenuates the horror of Perrault's cruel ending. Perrault's "et la dévora" (*Contes*, 144) and "et la mangea" (145) are conveyed by "and gobbled her up" (*Fairy Tales*, 26) and "gobbled her up, too" (28).[37] This choice of verb is another echo of the Grimms' *Märchen*, where the equivalent verb *verschlucken* anticipates the happy ending that so strikingly contrasts with Perrault's: In "Rotkäppchen" the girl and her grandmother are rescued from the wolf's belly, unharmed because they have been swallowed up whole. The pressure of the German version of the tale thus attenuates the bloodiness and horror of devouring because the point of the tale for Carter is to teach them a lesson, not scare them to death. In contrast, the rewritings play up the horror of the tale and its connections with ancient folklore and werewolf stories. Even more so, the radio play and film script exploit the emotional scare to the point of parody, as Carter herself noted in her introduction to *Come unto These Yellow Sands*, where she remarks that "*The Company of Wolves* [took] on more of the characteristics of the pure horror story" and "became almost an exercise in genre" (10).[38]

By couching the story in a familiar style, basic vocabulary, repetitions, simple syntax, and "blunt and succinct manner,"[39] Carter's translation reflects modern conceptions of the genre that owe a lot to the Grimms' idea of the folktale, but it also reflects Carter's understanding of the practical purport of Perrault's *conte* as distinct from it. The translator seeks to convey a *modern* moral that could be summarized as follows: Spoiled girls whose taste for pretty but inappropriate clothes is encouraged by mothers and grandmothers are at risk because they live in ignorance of the dangerous desires of cynical (i.e., etymologically, like dogs, and therefore wolflike) male predators. The wolf exploits this when he cunningly dresses up as a woman to lure the child into the bed, and, to the reader's surprise, the girl does not see the difference, so unaware is she of the existence of wolves.

The moral especially reflects the translator's understanding of the story and her social and literary project. Carter knew that Perrault's morals "put the tales into the worldly context of late XVIIth century France and the court of the Sun King" (quoted on the dust jacket). Perrault's French text reads as follows:

> On voit ici que de jeunes enfants,
> Surtout de jeunes filles
> Belles, bien faites, et gentilles,
> Font très mal d'écouter toute sorte de gens,
> Et que ce n'est pas chose étrange,
> S'il en est tant que le loup mange.
> Je dis le loup, car tous les loups
> Ne sont pas de la même sorte;
> Il en est d'une humeur accorte,
> Sans bruit, sans fiel et sans courroux,

> Qui privés, complaisants et doux,
> Suivent les jeunes Demoiselles
> Jusque dans les maisons, jusque dans les ruelles,
> Mais hélas! qui ne sait que ces Loups doucereux,
> De tous les Loups sont les plus dangereux.
>
> (*Contes*, 145)

Jack Zipes notes that Carter's morals are remade into "prosaic folksy proverbs that often contradict what Perrault endeavored to communicate."[40] And yet Carter also saw in them a worldly wisdom that she modernized and disambiguated for young readers as follows:

> *Moral*
> Children, especially pretty, nicely brought-up young ladies, ought never to talk to strangers; if they are foolish enough to do so, they should not be surprised if some greedy wolf consumes them, elegant red riding hoods and all.
>
> Now, there are real wolves, with hairy pelts and enormous teeth; but also wolves who seem perfectly charming, sweet-natured and obliging, who pursue young girls *in the street* and pay them the most flattering attentions. Unfortunately, these smooth-tongued, smooth-pelted wolves are the most dangerous beasts of all. (*Fairy Tales*, 28; italics mine)

As Zipes notes, Carter's style is deliberately prosaic, matter-of-fact, and clean-cut. Almost brutal in its directness, it even adds a comic touch to the grim ending typical of English humor.[41] Instead of turning Perrault's message upside down, however, Carter adapts it to her own times; her version of the moral is resolutely cautionary and even *moralizing* because her modern-day girls are "nicely brought-up," unlike Perrault's *jeunes filles*, whose education had been neglected by their aristocratic parents. By addressing "children" and especially "young ladies" qualified as "foolish," Carter transforms the meaning of the tale into a typical twentieth-century warning that reflects changing concerns and perceptions of the danger faced by children in the modern world. Carter's "Little Red Riding Hood" is also addressed to mothers and grandmothers who take pride in their (grand) daughters' beauty and dress them inappropriately. Carter's dry humor, then, is not unlike Roald Dahl's.

Carter's modern moral, vigorously expressed through a commonplace imperative, situates the action in an urban environment, a mistranslation of Perrault's *ruelles*, which designated the space between the bed and the wall in seventeenth-century France. Whereas for Perrault the danger lay in the bedchamber where high society women used to receive guests who could compromise their reputation by taking advantage of the situation, for Carter the danger shifted to the open space of the modern city where wandering children are at risk. In this sense Carter's translation anticipates Sarah Moon's powerful series of black-and-white photographs illustrating Perrault's "Le Petit Chaperon rouge" published by Grasset in 1986, where the "wolf" who hunts down the girl cruises the streets of a city in his luxurious black car.

From Martin Ware's Illustrations to Carter's Rewritings: The Better to See You With

Vision is the art of seeing things invisible.

—JONATHAN SWIFT, *THOUGHTS ON VARIOUS SUBJECTS*, 181

Finding one's way in a wood is a common metaphor for the reader's experience of a book. Although Carter favors the straight path to drive the point of the fairy tale home in her translation, her retellings explore more meandering routes, with no well-traced paths or clear destination.[42] The story becomes an occasion to explore the sexual subtext hidden in the translation for children, and it exhumes ancient beliefs and customs, and tales of the supernatural, of witchcraft, werewolves, and vampires, and of strange encounters, seduction, abandonment, revenge, and transformation.

In *Lector in Fabula* Umberto Eco takes "Little Red Riding Hood" as a paradigmatic text to study the involvement of the reader in fiction and the way texts operate on the level of narrative. The reader, who is like the little girl wandering in the forest of the text, is invited to "fill in a whole series of gaps"[43] and become an active participant in the story, and this invitation is definitely shared by Carter, for whom reading and translating naturally led to rewriting. "Woods," Eco continues, "are a metaphor for the narrative text, not only for the text of fairy tales but for any narrative text," and "the reader is forced to make choices all the time as Jorge Luis Borges himself suggested in 'The Garden of Forking Paths,' 'a wood is a garden of forking paths. Even when there are no well-trodden paths in a wood, everyone can trace his or her own path, deciding to go to the left or to the right of a certain tree and making a choice at every tree encountered.'"[44] Eco also contends (and Carter would have surely agreed) that "this experience of re-reading a text over the course of forty years has shown me how silly those people are who say that dissecting a text and engaging in meticulous close reading is the death of its magic."[45] Each rewriting therefore explores an alternative path (filling gaps, solving enigmas or contradictions, etc.) based on a narrative, thematic, formal, or linguistic possibility. Accordingly, Carter makes sure to relate form and sense as she retells the story in different periods and cultures.

In "The Better to Eat You With" Carter explains that what she admires most about Perrault's "Le Petit Chaperon rouge" is the narrative economy of the tale, which so effectively conveys its basic conflict by privileging action over narration and description and by relying on characters reduced to types or "functions," the plot "aris[ing] from the interaction of the wolf and his hunger, and the child and her ingenuity" (454). Carter is here concerned with the politics of style and narrative form. Her reading of the tale as a warning against deceptive speech and rhetorical manipulation, embodied by the wolf, is reflected in the straightforward language used in her translation of Perrault's text. And yet clear-cut binary oppositions and fixed roles are inevitably complicated, insofar as the plot revolves around deception, disguise, and substitutions.[46] This is what Martin Ware's full-page etching suggests (Figure 2.2); it depicts two brief moments of narration inserted between the famous dialogues.

> Le Loup ne fut pas longtemps à arriver à la maison de la Mère-grand; il heurte: Toc, toc. . . .
> Ensuite il ferma la porte, et s'alla coucher dans le lit de la Mère-grand, en attendant le petit chaperon rouge, qui quelques temps après vint heurter à la porte. Toc, toc. (*Contes*, 144)

> The wolf soon arrived at Grandmother's house. He knocked on the door, rat tat tat. . . .

Updating the Politics of Experience   93

Then he closed the door behind him and lay down in Grandmother's bed to wait for Little Red Riding Hood. At last she came knocking on the door, rat tat tat. (*Fairy Tales*, 24, 26)

Although the tale is plot driven, centering on dramatic action, dialogue, and sound effects (onomatopoeia), Ware chooses to focus on a formal or structural aspect, namely, repetition with variation.

Ware translates this visually on the page by juxtaposing images that represent those two transitional moments as variations on the same situation. In the top frame (Figure 2.2) the spectator is inside the grandmother's bedroom, looking out. The old lady, seen almost in profile, is wearing a nightcap and nightgown. She sits straight in bed (as if waiting for someone to arrive), staring stonily ahead, while the head of the wolf, framed by

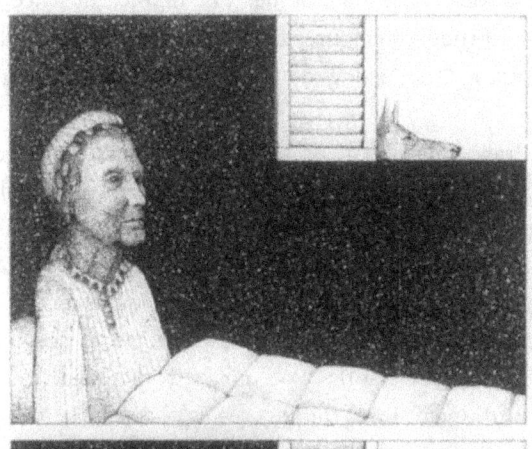

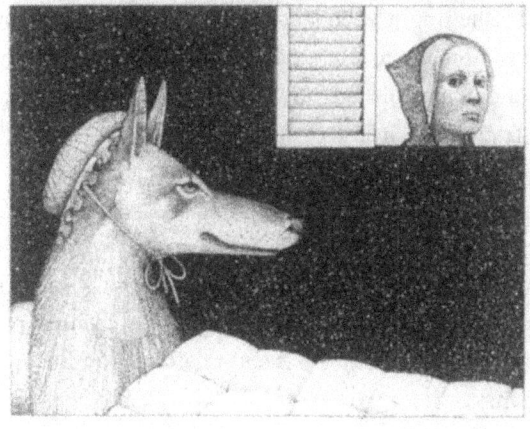

Figure 2.2. Illustration for "Little Red Riding Hood" in the 1977 edition of The Fairy Tales of Charles Perrault. *Courtesy of Martin Ware.*

the open window, is visible from the spectator's point of view but not his future victim.[47] In the bottom frame the setting and perspective are identical, except for the characters swapping places. The wolf has now replaced the grandmother, and he is wearing her nightcap (but no nightgown) to signal his usurpation of her identity, while the head of the heroine (light-haired, age uncertain, wearing her hood) is visible through the window. She is looking in, seemingly at the reader, who can only stare back helplessly. *We* know that wolves are dangerous, but *she* does not and we cannot warn her of the impending danger. Thus, whereas Carter seeks to emulate the masterfully constructed plot and effective style of Perrault's tale in her translation, Ware interprets the story visually as being about the old woman's and the little girl's inability to *see* the wolf and the danger that he represents. Ware's characters are impassive, still, and expressionless, to the point of undermining the dramatic action and its impact on the reader that supposedly drives the cautionary message home. The marked absence of visible emotions (in face, attitude, or gesture) in the pictures thus shifts the focus from action to narrative form, story to discourse, affect to reflection and critical distance.

Ware's illustrations draw attention to important differences between the visual and textual regimes, but they also complicate them, because the juxtaposition of two almost identical scenes conveys an idea of elementary sequence and development that is characteristic of narrative, as opposed to the descriptive nature of illustration. The brutality and violence of the devouring of the grandmother and the girl that follows upon each scene of waiting is elided, although the fact that the wolf moves from outside to inside the house, from background to foreground, creates a sense of suspense and threat, suggesting that he might even step out of the frame to devour the reader. Ware also pays homage to his predecessors. The night bonnet worn by the grandmother and appropriated by the wolf alludes to Gustave Doré's well-known illustration of Little Red Riding Hood in bed with the wolf (Figure 2.3).

Significantly, the bonnet passes from grandmother to wolf in the tale, just as the motif passes from Doré to Ware in the iconographic tradition. In other words, Ware has assimilated his predecessor just as the wolf has eaten the grandmother. Illustrators are therefore also rewriters, and the interplay between text and image characteristic of the fairy-tale tradition becomes central in Carter's rewritings.

Figure 2.3. Le Petit Chaperon rouge in Les contes de Perrault, *illustration by Gustave Doré, 1867.*

"Little Red Riding Hood" in "The Company of Wolves," "The Werewolf," and "Wolf-Alice," or Fleshing Out the Bare Bones of the Tale

Wolves are less brave than they seem.

—ANGELA CARTER, "THE WEREWOLF"

The wolf may be more than he seems.

—ANGELA CARTER, "THE COMPANY OF WOLVES"

She saw how pale this wolf, not-wolf who played with her was.

—ANGELA CARTER, "WOLF-ALICE"

The Bloody Chamber proposes several variations on the story of "Little Red

Riding Hood" that explore the disquieting confusion between the grandmother and the wolf, the girl and the wolf, the hunter and the wolf, and so on. Before appearing together in the volume, "The Company of Wolves" was published separately in the periodical *Bananas* (April 1977), "The Werewolf" in *South-West Arts Review* (October 1977), and "Wolf-Alice" in the literary magazine *Stand* (winter 1978). In her preparatory notes (undated) for "The Company of Wolves," Carter writes:

> In Perrault [crossed out several times]
> There is a conflict between the pleasure principle and the reality principle—dawdling along, picking the pretty flowers just as you please; or doing what mother tells out [sic], taking the presents to granny.
>
> I suppose, analysing own reworkings of the story. I've felt a compulsion to make Red Riding Hood less passive ["less passive" crossed out] than her folk-tale avatar; some internal rather self-reliant censor has also made her, in one story, rather older. The story called "the Werewolf" is still in the process of completion, but there's enough of it to show where it's going.[48]

As I have suggested, Carter's translation of Perrault foregrounds Freud's reality principle at the expense of the pleasure principle that is explored in "The Company of Wolves." We also note that the author's understanding of the tale is colored by memories of the Grimms' "Rotkäppchen," which invites a Freudian interpretation whereby pleasure is "censored" in favor of obedience to the mother, much more so than "Le Petit Chaperon rouge," where there are no warnings or prohibitions. The fact that Perrault's name is crossed out several times in her working notes even intimates that Carter changed her mind as to the significance of the story. More surprisingly, she eliminates "less passive" to describe the characterization of the girl in her own retellings of the story perhaps because she is now referring to the folktale. Carter's heroines are notoriously bold, determined, courageous, sensual, or simply forewarned Red Riding Hood figures.

Carter's remark on the variable age of the girl is also intriguing, as if in response to the moral of Perrault's *conte* addressed to *jeunes filles*. Her own portrayal of the girl as a child in "The Werewolf" and then as a pubescent girl in "The Company of Wolves" and "Wolf-Alice" turns the tale into a coming-of-age story.[49] Likewise, the radio play insists on the metamorphoses undergone during adolescence as a transitional, metamorphic, and magical age. When Granny calls her a little girl, Red Riding Hood observes: "Twelve. Going on thirteen, thirteen, going on fourteen . . . not such a little girl, for all that you baby me, Granny. Thirteen going on fourteen, the hinge of your life, when you are neither one thing nor the other, nor child, nor woman, some magic, in-between thing" (Carter, *Curious Room*, 64–65).

In her perceptive analysis of Carter's variations on "Little Red Riding Hood," Cristina Bacchilega proposes that Carter writes against the two most popular literary versions of the story, where "the wolf is either a 'smooth-tongued' seducer . . . or the natural instrument of punishment."[50] Whereas Perrault's *conte* is a coded fable meant to warn aristocratic girls against the danger of compromising their reputation, the Grimms' *Märchen* serves to educate little girls in keeping to the straight path of virtue, obedience, and good behavior. By contrast, "Angela Carter's postmodern rewritings are acts of fairy-tale archaeology that release this story's many other voices. . . . Carter tells tales that reactivate lost traditions, trace violently contradictory genealogies, and flesh out the complex and vital workings of desire and narrative."[51]

The phrase "fairy-tale archaeology" is particularly apt, as it captures Carter's taking the tale in different directions, making it travel in time and in space. Accordingly, "The Werewolf" imagines an archaic source for "Little Red Riding Hood" set in Northern Europe ("It is a northern country," *Bloody Chamber*, 108) during the early modern period. The presence of the Germanic term *Walpurgisnacht* (108) suggests that it might have served as a basis for the Grimms' moralized and Christianized "Rotkäppchen." In this "quasi-ethnographic sketch"[52] ancient pagan beliefs are shown to compete but also to mix with Christian ones, leading to witch hunting and brutal violence against women. Imitating the dry, paratactic, matter-of-fact style that Carter associated with the ancient storytelling tradition, the narrator tells of a girl's fearful encounter with a female werewolf, unless the mythical beast merely serves to disguise the ruthless appropriation of an old woman's belongings by her granddaughter. The tale is set in an economic and cultural context that reveals the ambivalent social function of folk beliefs that empower the girl but lead to the scapegoating of the grandmother. A werewolf in disguise, she is neutralized by her bold and armed granddaughter; alternately (depending on how we read the tale), the granddaughter can be seen as plotting against her elder, accusing her of being a witch to get rid of her and take her house. The moral of the tale remains ambiguously open, as Bacchilega notes.

> Though her lamb-like purity is rewarded, this girl only wears "a scabby coat of sheepskin." Is she too in disguise? Economics after all can turn sheep into wolf—the grandmother into a witch, the girl into a killer. And economics, which the narrator juxtaposes from the beginning against the moral dichotomies of popular sentencing, are also at issue when the girl "prospers" after taking over her grandmother's house.[53]

Far from seeing folk culture as an occasion to celebrate female solidarity against hardship, then, Carter uncovers the brutality of pre-Enlightenment scapegoating rituals and intergenerational rivalry.[54] The stylized and barren setting thus matches the brisk retelling, which highlights the violence, mutilation, and shedding of blood that Perrault's text memorably suggests but does not represent.

Likewise, "Rotkäppchen" contains no scene of bloodshed despite the two devouring scenes, as the wolf's "gobbling up" leaves the girl and her grandmother unharmed. The girl's revenge, however, is quite troubling, although never commented on; her cruel idea to fill the wolf's belly with stones provokes his pathetic and grotesque death, which reappears in a different configuration in the stoning to death of the grandmother/werewolf in Carter's retelling. The villagers "pelted her with stones until she fell down dead" (*Bloody Chamber*, 110) echoes the Grimms' text, where Rotkäppchen fetches stones so heavy that when the wolf wakes up he tries to jump but collapses and falls dead. Carter's retelling even subtly shifts the reader's sympathy from the girl to the wolf when she wounds him with a knife. When she is attacked in the forest, the girl slashes off the (were)wolf's paw and the beast limps away, "leaving a trail of blood behind it" (*Bloody Chamber*, 109); the beast even briefly becomes the focalizer when he "let[s] out a gulp, almost a sob" when he is harmed, and leaves "disconsolately" on three legs (109). With its focus on bloody deeds, Carter's retelling emphasizes the moral complexity of the tale and explores violent confrontations—and crossovers—between the human world and the animal world. Further on, the vivid images of the wolf's paw turning into a human hand, and the "bloody stump . . . festering already" (109), suggest the physical horror of the story that is carefully contained (bottled up?) in the classic versions. Here, however, the blood spills over in the mutilation of the beast and the stoning of the old woman, just as Gothic horror paled before the killing fields of World War I at the end of Carter's "Lady of the House of Love."

"The Company of Wolves" contrasts with "The Werewolf" in almost every way, except for the basic plot and triangle formed by the girl, the wolf, and the grandmother. In contrast to her translation of Perrault's tale, in which "foolish" girls are blamed for chatting with strangers in the moral, Carter explores female desire and restores agency to the adolescent heroine, insisting on her knowingness in the seduction game. The girl's bold confrontation with the manly beast and her ultimate embrace of the otherness that he represents—in terms of gender, class, and even species—explore the dangerous attraction of the "sweet-talking wolves" of Perrault's moral but this time stripped of moral condemnation.[55] The dark and handsome gentleman is both wolf and man (he is, after all, a werewolf), but he is also a mix of predator and helper, because he is dressed like the huntsman in "Rotkäppchen." Moreover, when the girl strays from the main path, she knows that she disobeys her mother and is likely to get into trouble. And yet, older and bolder than her predecessors, she admits to being attracted to the seductive hunter and deliberately plays his game, as "she *wanted* to dawdle on her way" (*Bloody Chamber*, 114; italics mine) to make sure that he would kiss her. The elaborate style of the retelling also references a literary tradition reminiscent of nineteenth-century fairy-tale books, illustrated editions, and even opera.

The possibilities opened up by conflations, role switching, substitutions, and shifting perspectives are spectacularly exemplified in "The Company of Wolves." The story is retold several times in different modes, styles, genres, and contexts, as if to condense in a single story the many possible refractions or diffractions of the tale when it is transposed in a different time, place, context, and medium.[56] It foregrounds the musical aspect of the text through a highly alliterative style ("Fear and flee the wolf," *Bloody Chamber*, 111) and references to wolf song as musical accompaniment, including the "aria of fear" (110) sung by the wolves, their "canticles" (112), "carols" (117), and "threnody" (117), even the "high soprano" (115) and false "falsetto" (116) of the wolf imitating the grandmother, followed by the "prothalamion" of the climax (*Bloody Chamber*, 118).

The visual dimension of the tale captured by Martin Ware is also fully present in the prose retelling. In keeping with the association of the wolf's smooth tongue with the dangerous seductions of speech and the discrepancy between seeming and being, the following passage combines literary and visual effects to ambiguous ends. It is written in an excessive and self-consciously visual style that evokes a scene full of eyes and (literal and metatextual) reflections.

> At night, the eyes of wolves shine like candle flames, yellowish, reddish, but that is because the pupils of their eyes fatten on darkness and catch the light from your lantern to flash it back to *you*—red for danger; if a wolf's eyes reflect only moonlight, then they gleam a cold and unnatural green, a mineral, a piercing colour. If the benighted traveller spies those luminous, terrible sequins stitched suddenly on the black thickets, then he knows he must run, if fear has not struck him stock-still. ("The Company of Wolves," *Bloody Chamber*, 110–111; italics mine)

The narrator interpellates the implied reader as "you" and thus casts "him" in the role of Little Red Riding Hood, as prey and future victim, even referring to "your smell of meat" (*Bloody Chamber*, 110). But the central trope of the reflecting eyes governing the passage suggests that there is something wolflike about the reader too. If, as Hans Belting suggests, "images send us back our gaze," then some texts have the same effect too. Who, then, is the narrator/storyteller in this retelling? Although Carter's intent seems to be to warn the reader, the elaborate, ornate, alliterative style dazzles and confuses all the better to trap "him" in the yellow, red, and green lights reflected in the wolves' eyes that glow in the dark.

The narrator's role becomes even more ambiguous when she invites the "benighted traveller" to run, only to stop "him" "stock-still" at the end of the sentence, and the paragraph. This strategy is also reminiscent of "The Bloody Chamber," which seemingly condemns the perverse (and deathly) seductions of art represented by the murderous Marquis and yet couches the story in a densely allusive and baroque, artful, and artificial language that ambiguously enacts what it cautions the reader against. Unlike the straightforward cautionary message conveyed by the translation, then, Carter's rewritings appeal to readers who can cope with "overheated poetic diction" (454) and they teach a lesson in the ambiguity, complexity, and shifting nature of meaning and address.

"The Company of Wolves" also clearly references Delarue's reconstructed folktale, albeit in a more sensual and literary fashion. The passage

> "Undress, my child," said the bzou, "and come and sleep beside me."
> "Where should I put my apron?"
> "Throw it in the fire, my child; you don't need it any more,"[57]

is echoed in Carter's text as

> Since her fear did her no good, she ceased to be afraid.
> What shall I do with my shawl?
> Throw it on the fire, dear one. You won't need it again. ("The Company of Wolves," 138)

Carter's Red Riding Hood takes her shawl off and throws it in the fire, continuing the ritual striptease until she appears naked, so that "by acting out her desires—sexual, not just for life—the girl offers herself as flesh, not meat."[58]

Moreover, "By eating the flesh and drinking the blood, the young girl incorporates the grandmother's knowledge and takes her place."[59] This testifies to Carter's fascination for archaic beliefs and rituals combined with sophisticated narrative skills and acute self-consciousness, as the idea of incorporation also functions as an apt metaphor for storytelling itself. The rewritings thus play with the various meanings of consumption (i.e., the act of consuming and, conversely, the state of being consumed) and consummation (sexual intercourse and climax).

"The Company of Wolves" fleshes out the bare bones of "Little Red Riding Hood" (and its first retelling in "The Werewolf") as it picks on Carter's addition of "smooth-pelted" to the dangerous "smooth-tongued" wolves in the moral of the translated tale. The motif of blood still runs through the multiple retellings that compose the story, revolving as it does on the transformation of flesh into meat in the course of an encounter with the wolf as "carnivore incarnate" ("The Company of Wolves," 118). The story starts with the "smell of meat" of the traveller/reader "as you go through the wood unwisely late" (110) in the frame narrative and moves to the killing of the werewolf and the transformation of his mutilated body into a man described or performed ("the bloody trunk of a man, headless, footless, dying, dead," 111) in the first anecdote. It carries on with the return of a groom who had vanished on the wedding night and comes back home after several years and is furious to find out that the young woman has remarried; he turns into a wolf "and tore off the eldest boy's left foot before he was chopped off with the hatchet" and "lay bleeding and gasping" (112) as he changes back into a man. And finally, in the fourth and most elaborate retelling, the little girl becomes a "strong-minded child" (113) who wears her red shawl, which "has the ominous if brilliant look of blood on snow" (113). She is menstruating for the first time, so that "the clock inside her . . . will strike, henceforward, once a month" (113).

This female blood, which symbolizes both sexuality and the possibility of procreation, transforms the potentially deathly encounter with the attractive werewolf into a potentially regenerative union. While he decides to cut through the woods to the grandmother's house with the help of a compass (another instance of "technology meets folklore"), the girl chooses "the winding path" (115) because "she wanted to dawdle on her way to make sure the handsome gentleman would win his wager" (115), that is, a kiss. Still a virgin but no longer ignorant or naive, the girl "knew the worst wolves are hairy on the inside and she shivered, in spite of the scarlet shawl . . . although it was as red as the blood she must spill" (117), when she realizes that the werewolf has devoured her grandmother.[60] And yet she "took off her scarlet shawl, the colour of poppies, the colour of sacrifices, the colour of her menses, and, since her fear did her no good, she ceased to be afraid" (117). She undresses, kisses the werewolf, and laughs when he pronounces the final repartee of the prescribed script, "All the better to eat you with": "The girl burst out laughing; she knew she was nobody's meat" (118), and the tale departs from the familiar plot to suggest the possibility of a happy ending that reconciles the young woman and the beast as she sleeps "between the paws of the tender wolf" (118). The semantic possibilities of the word *tender* invite further complications of the prey-predator divide. Carter's "Company of Wolves" would become emblematic of *The Bloody Chamber* volume, and anticipated numerous revisions of the tale for adults in the last decades of the twentieth century, from sensual or erotic retellings to versions of the story told from the wolf's point of view or presenting the wolf as a victim.

As we know, Carter's fascination for "Little Red Riding Hood" also took another turn when she rewrote the story as a radio play that served as the basis for the film script, both reproduced in *The Curious Room*.[61] This detour through a nonvisual medium is one of the many ways in which Carter activates the potentiality of the tale as a generating matrix for new stories. Carter significantly begins her preface to *Come unto These Yellow Sands* by expressing her interest in writing for radio in visual terms as "a kind of three-dimensional story-telling" (7). She explains that although storytelling unfolds in a more or less linear fashion, radio allows for a more simultaneous experience "so that a great number of things can happen at the same time" (7). Providing an aural equivalent of the perspective created in the toy book, then, the radio play juxtaposes elements that stimulate the imagination of the listener: "It is this necessary open-endedness of the medium," she says, "that gives radio story-telling its real third dimension, which is the space that, above all, interests and enchants me" (7). Carter goes on to elaborate on her efforts "to create complex, many-layered narratives that play tricks with time. And also to explore ideas . . . since, for me, a narrative is an argument stated in fictional terms" (7). Further on, she states that "The Company of Wolves" began as a short story, which the medium of radio turned into a "pure horror story" (10), "almost an exercise in genre" (10).

The third retelling of "Little Red Riding Hood" is yet another, even more self-conscious "exercise in genre." "Wolf-Alice" explores the unlikely encounter of a wild child raised by wolves and a necrophagous Duke borrowed from *The Duchess of Malfi*. The girl fully belongs to neither species, and the monstrous Duke is also a hybrid being and social outcast. This unlikely coupling reopens the issue of predation, unholy appetites, and the incorporation of the other within the self, although it also verges on (self-) parody. Carter comically recycles all the "juicy bits" of the familiar story in this baroque text that mixes (self-)transformation, Grand Guignol horror, mutilation, dismemberment, and menstrual bleeding. The Duke's room itself is a "bloody chamber" of sorts filled with "shrouds, nightdresses and burial clothes that had wrapped items on the Duke's menus" ("Wolf-Alice," *Bloody Chamber*, 123). Carter even exploits the unsavory image of necrophagy as French cuisine, with a pinch of salt: "He is white as leprosy, with scrabbling fingernails, and nothing deters him. If you stuff a corpse with garlic, why, he only slavers at the treat: cadavre provençale" (121). In the story that concludes *The Bloody Chamber* volume, or so Carter's parodic retelling suggests, the familiar tale has now been chewed over and squeezed dry.

Through the figure of the wolf-girl, Carter explores an altogether different strand of the story, namely, the real-life cases of wild children who raise the fraught issue (and ever-changing definition) of the division between humanity and animality (as distinct from beastliness, represented by the Count). Wolf-Alice indeed lives in an intermediary state between humanity and animality, and the story explores the gradual emergence of her sense of identity through contemplation in the mirror in a kind of mock Lacanian fable.[62] She flees the cruel world of the humans and the brutal educational methods of the nuns. This gives Carter an occasion to explore the paradoxical "humanity" of the wolves and their maternal instinct, solidarity, and unselfconscious beauty. Carter's abundant notes on wolves also testify to her fascination for the wild animal and attempt to rehabilitate it.[63] They document the wolf's ecology and behavior as an endangered species that Carter sees as a "test of human wisdom & good intentions." She adds a note about "the beast in man" in brackets, probably because she meant to explore this theme in one of her retellings—and so she did. Carter references not only books about wolves but also literary predecessors who, like her, were attracted to the mysterious beauty and "wisdom" of beasts, especially felines. In the 1977 journal, Carter mentions Blake's "The Tyger" and Baudelaire's cat poems, even quoting (in French) his homage to "la belle Féline" in the "Petits poèmes en prose." The narrator of "Wolf-Alice" clearly expresses her preference for wolves over human beings (though without romanticizing or sentimentalizing them) to the point of presenting the union of the wolf-girl and the man-wolf as a possible utopia. In this sense Carter's essay "Little Lamb, Get Lost" published in *New Society* in 1978, can be seen as the companion piece to "Wolf-Alice."

"Little Lamb, Get Lost" begins by challenging Blake's mythology of wild beasts and goes on to discuss the prey-predator divide. Carter wittily expresses her preference for the predator category in her usual epigrammatic style: "Carnivores, flesh eaters, predators, are dumb beasts, and beastly. Herbivores are just dumb" (306). She observes that "it is one of the more insinuatingly baleful effects of Judeo-Christianity that we can't treat the beasts as, in a sense, equals, but persist in projecting on them either our own beastliness or our fantasies of innocence" (306–7). Further on, Carter argues that wolves are "fine mothers," as ancient mythology suggests, but have more recently come to represent the "id," even though, she remarks sarcastically, "They are certainly less sexually voracious than the rabbit, but if Red Riding Hood had found a bunny in granny's bed, all it would have meant that it was Easter. Yet the wolf is virtually synonymous with 'id,' and with a particularly bestial type of ravening lust" (307–8). This is what Carter mocked in the reference to the "huge" genitals of the wolf attacking the grandmother in "The Company of Wolves." The more animal relation that the wolf-girl establishes with the beastly Duke in "Wolf-Alice" represents an alternative to the projection of various mythologies onto the "other."

Whereas "The Company of Wolves" draws on the sonorous qualities of the wolf "song" as natural music, "Wolf-Alice" dramatizes other modalities of the "fugue," as Carter's preparatory notes signal.

> Title: Red Riding Hood/ 3 Wolf Alice [crossed out: The Duke at Midnight]
> *Wolfsong*
> Female werewolf
> The moon and menstruation?
> Le [*sic*] tour tenebreuse
> Fugue: a polyphonic composition constructed on one or more short subjects or themes which are harmonised according to the laws of counterpoint, and introduced from time to time with various contrapuntal devices.[64]

The sequence of rewritings itself enacts the idea of the fugue, as embodied by the wild child: The wolf-girl runs away from the convent in which nuns train her into becoming a fully socialized human being, and she embraces freedom with another marginal character who is humanized thanks to her ministrations at the end. The idea of the counterpoint and the importance of sounds would become central in the radio play.

Storyteller and Fairy-Tale Author: Carter's Double Act from Grandmother to Godmother

As we have seen, Carter liked role playing and often endorsed the role of the storyteller as experienced grandmother or its literary variation as the pragmatic, wry, and worldly-wise fairy godmother inspired by Perrault. In her Foreword to *The Fairy Tales of Charles Perrault* she shrewdly observes that Perrault's fairies are powerful, experienced women ready to "help along a little sister" (19). The posture of the fairy godmother (with a touch of the anticonformist sorceress) was one that Carter herself liked to adopt on occasion, with her long, white, flowing hair and unconventional wisdom. In "Notes from the Front Line," Carter famously presents her work as a critique of myth, which she saw, after Roland Barthes, as a form of discourse encoding conservative values and patriarchal interests: "I believe that all myths are products of the human mind and reflect only aspects of material human practice. I'm in the demythologising business. I'm interested in myths—though I'm much more interested in folklore—just because they *are* extraordinary lies designed to make people unfree" (38). After Perrault, Carter opposed dominant myths, or rather mythologies in Barthes's sense of the term, a vision of art seen as a vehicle for practical wisdom, primarily if not exclusively addressed to women. Carter thus borrowed from Perrault the idea of the tale as a carrier of a useful moral adapted to her own time, public, and concerns.

Some feminist critics have objected to Carter's use of the fairy tale in *The Bloody Chamber*, arguing that they merely reproduce the narrative structures and patriarchal models that they see as inherent in classic tales. In the 1980s Patricia Duncker accused Carter of falling into "the infernal trap inherent in the fairy tale" that Carter rewrites "within the strait-jacket of their original structures."[65] Kay Stone also rejected fairy tales as inherently sexist on the (questionable) grounds that they offer "narrow and damaging role-models for young readers."[66] But this is to ignore the sexual politics of the classic texts and their reworking in Carter's many-faceted project; this does not so much retrieve the female victims trapped in the belly of a masculine fairy tradition as bear witness to the semantic richness, topicality and relevance, and emancipatory potential of the old tales, which have been forgotten in the course of time and neglected by the dominant cultural and critical reception.

Carter's lifelong interest in the fairy tale partly stemmed from a recognition of the extraordinary potential of the genre to carry out poetic and artistic experiments, and it also reflected an awareness of its crucial social role in shaping a sense of self and understanding of the world from an early age. But Carter was not so much breaking away from Perrault as following his plea for a modern literature as she transposed his worldly tales in the late twentieth century. They both shared a concern to protect girls from harm and initiate a reflection on the dangers of ignorance. Carter's translation, then, is best viewed as the pursuit of Perrault's effort to inject some new blood in an age-old tradition in order to make it meaningful to present-day readers.

3

Looking Through the Keyhole of Culture, or the Moral Function of Curiosity

FROM "LA BARBE BLEUE" TO "BLUEBEARD"
AND "THE BLOODY CHAMBER"

The Moral Function of Curiosity,
or Bluebeard Revisited (with a Vengeance)

Rereading is the magic key to rewriting.

—CRISTINA BACCHILEGA, *POSTMODERN FAIRY TALES*, 50

In the course of her research Angela Carter became aware of the manifold cultural inflections and shifting significance of the Bluebeard story. More visibly grounded in a history of violence against women than most fairy tales, every retelling positions itself implicitly toward the protagonists, either by siding with the bloodthirsty husband or with the disobedient wife. Through her translation and rewriting, Carter reflects these shifts of focus when she engages with the sexual politics of the tale in contrapuntal fashion. Her translation cautions children against marriage, and her rewriting self-consciously revisits a long history of physical, psychological, and symbolic violence against women. In both cases Carter draws attention to the progressive potential of the tale, which is often obscured by the conservative myths with which it is often confused. The creative role that Carter gave to active reading indeed enabled her to interpret Perrault's "La Barbe bleue" against the grain of its dominant reception in order to revalue female curiosity. Carter said in an interview with John Haffenden: "If morals are to do with the way people behave, then I do think the novel has a moral function. But the moral function should not be hortatory in any way—telling people how to behave. I would see it as a moral compunction to explicate and to find out about things. I suppose I would regard curiosity as a moral function."[1]

In keeping with Carter's double project as a translator of Perrault's classic tales and as an author revisiting a lesser known folktale tradition, "The Bloody Chamber" echoes two of the Grimms' variations on the Bluebeard story collected in *Kinder- und Hausmärchen*, starting with "Fitchers Vogel" (Fitcher's Bird). Both the German tale and its English equivalent, "Mr. Fox," refer to a bloody chamber and can even be seen as the key to Carter's collection as originating in childhood reading revisited from an adult perspective. In "Fitcher's Bird" a pretty girl snatched away by a wizard discovers the mutilated bodies of her sisters in a *Blutkammer* (*Kinder- und Hausmärchen*, 1: 237), pieces their limbs together and brings the young women back to life. The word also appears in "Mr. Fox," an Anglicized version of the German tale collected by Joseph Jacobs, who saw himself as an English Grimm: "Mr. Fox looked about a bit . . . went on dragging the young lady up the stairs into the Bloody Chamber" (*English Fairy Tales*, 150).[2] Carter's own "Bloody Chamber," however, is literally set in another version of the story collected by the Grimms, "The Castle of Murder" ("Das Mordschloss"), as Jean-Yves, the blind piano tuner, tells the horrified bride.[3] Jean-Yves reproaches himself for dismissing the sinister stories attached to the place as mere "old wives' tales, chattering of fools, spooks to scare bad children into good behaviour!" (*Bloody Chamber*, 33). In contrast to the local legend that exposes, condemns, and even punishes male violence toward women, "The Bloody Chamber" recapitulates a time-honored and culturally valorized tradition of misogynist representations of women through which the Bluebeard tale is commonly understood. Pitting high culture against the homey truths of popular tales, Carter creates a reading experience that rehabilitates curiosity through allusion and intertextual density. "The Bloody Chamber" thus encourages the reader to develop an inquiring, even inquisitive mind, instead of the classic caution against female curiosity found in Perrault's first moral.

But Carter's tale also suggests that Perrault's text cuts both ways and is more ambiguous than it seems. To quote Carter herself, the reader is encouraged to explicate the text, that is, to unfold, explain, elucidate, and analyze it closely and thereby become a better reader capable of deciphering the arcane text (or "grammar") of the world. This image, used in the second moral of Perrault's *conte*, which Carter left out of her translation, becomes a key principle in her rewriting, and it governs its reading protocol: "Pour peu qu'on ait l'esprit sensé, / Et que du Monde on sache le grimoire" (*Contes*, 154) (Provided we have some common sense and know the arcane book of the world; translation mine). Perrault's second moral is indeed explicitly addressed to an older, more experienced, sensible reader who knows how to decipher the implicit and elaborate codes of courtly society. We remember that in the same interview with Haffenden, Carter declares that she "put[s] everything in a novel to be *read* . . . on as many levels as you can comfortably cope with at the time."[4] Just like the heroine of the Bluebeard tale, then, the reader is encouraged to become a curious explorer of the bloody chamber of patriarchal culture; the palimpsest quality of the text has an important pedagogical function; it teaches the reader to decipher its hidden meanings and look into the dark corners of "the lumber room of the Western European imagination"[5] in order to better grasp the workings of "the cultural production of femininity."[6]

I showed in Chapter 2 that Carter's fiction derived a new energy from revisiting the cultural and literary past in the course of her rediscovery of Perrault's *contes* and her parallel research into the fairy-tale tradition. Because every reader is a potential author who can tease out new meanings in old texts, translation and rewriting are two forms of dialogic activity and creative and critical commentary on her sources. Carter famously draws on the new wine in old bottles analogy to describe this process, and she notes that the ferment of the new wine will in some cases liberate energies that will shatter the container itself. The bottle metaphor conveys the profoundly transformative impact of anticonventional readings of old texts that challenge expectations and certainties and undermine efforts to contain meaning. In connection with "Bluebeard" the image takes on new resonances. We cannot help noticing that in the Grimms' "Castle of Murder," the "bloody chamber" is in fact not a *cabinet* (storeroom) as in Perrault but a bloody cellar (*Keller*), which invites a rapprochement with Carter's famous bottles metaphor.

My contrapuntal analysis of Carter's translation of Perrault's *conte* and rewriting in *The Bloody Chamber* revolves around these two spaces. More specifically, it hinges on the striking image of the mirror of blood that Carter cut from her translation but that probably inspired the idea of the bloody chamber as a metaphor for the problematic representation of women in Western art and culture.

In Perrault's *conte* Bluebeard's house is filled with riches, splendid furniture, and precious objects, including mirrors framed with glass, silver, and gold "in which you might see yourself from head to foot" (*Histories*, 21).[7] In Carter's translation, the bride's friends and neighbors admire "the number and beauty of the tapestries, the beds, the sofas, the cabinets, the tables, and the long mirrors, some of which had frames of glass, others of silver and gilded vermilion—all more magnificent than anything they had ever seen" (*Fairy Tales*, 33) ("elles ne pouvaient assez admirer le nombre et la beauté des tapisseries, des lits, des sofas, des cabinets, des guéridons, des tables et des miroirs, où l'on se voyait depuis les pieds jusqu'à la tête, et dont les bordures, les unes de glace, les autres d'argent et de vermeil doré, étaient les plus belles et les plus magnifiques qu'on eût jamais vues" *Contes*, 150). Carter keeps the word cabinet, which Perrault uses repeatedly in this passage (here in the sense of cupboard), but she leaves out the idea of the women looking at themselves in the mirrors. The wonder that these extraordinarily crafted objects provokes in the visitors soon gives way to a different kind of wonder when the bride finds the murdered bodies mirrored in blood in another "cabinet," this time associated with fear and horror. In this early scene particular attention is paid to the mirrors, which are described in some detail and arrest attention, all the more so in a *conte* whose short form hardly allows for elaborate descriptions. Bluebeard, as it turns out, collects not only artistically crafted objects but also women, as foreshadowed in the little *cabinet* (here used in the sense of a small storage room) situated down the long gallery of the ground-floor apartment ("Pour cette petite clef-ci, c'est la clef du cabinet au bout de la grande galerie de l'appartement bas," *Contes*, 150). The location of the forbidden room in Perrault's text subtly establishes a connection between the paintings lining the gallery of the grand palaces of the wealthy and the bodies hidden away in the secret chamber; in other words, the *cabinet* is both art storeroom and ogre's larder.

In Perrault's time the *cabinet* was indeed a secluded room where the most valuable paintings were kept, and this is where Bluebeard hides the bodies of his murdered wives. The idea of women being killed into art—in both senses of killed for art and killed as an act of art—that Carter would elaborate on in the rewriting, is therefore already contained in the word *cabinet* which surely intrigued Carter and aroused her curiosity.[8] A particularly macabre detail also alerts us to a possible connection between Bluebeard's deeds of blood, his fascination with art, and the "perversions" of style. When the bride opens the forbidden door, what she sees is described in a disturbing image that aestheticizes the horrid spectacle of the murdered women.

> Après quelques moments elle commença à voir que le plancher était tout couvert de sang caillé, et que dans ce sang se miraient les corps de plusieurs femmes mortes et attachées le long des murs (c'était toutes les femmes que la Barbe bleue avait épousées et qu'il avait égorgées l'une après l'autre). (*Contes*, 151)

> After some moments she began to perceive that the floor was all covered over with clotted blood, on which lay the bodies of several dead women ranged against the walls; (these were all the wives whom Blue Beard had married and murdered one after the other). (*Histories*, 22)

In this chapter I trace the striking image of the female bodies mirrored in the pool of blood in Carter's translation for children, Martin Ware's illustration, and Carter's "Bloody Chamber" as a key moment reinterpreted for different audiences and purposes. Whereas the macabre image disappears in the fairy tale for children, it becomes a central metaphor in the rewriting to address the sexual politics of representation. Reading Carter's "Bluebeard" and "The Bloody Chamber" contrapuntally, then, shows how Carter toned down and cleaned up the disturbing elements of the tale for children but foregrounded them in her rewriting to reflect on the poetics and the politics of visuality. Not only does the tale provoke reactions of horror and terror that we associate more with Gothic literature than with the fairy tale, but its vivid visual images also invite reflection (an inner, intellectual, modality of vision) and reworking. Because the story of Bluebeard raises the age-old theme of female curiosity, it gave Carter an opportunity to open up the issue of the shaping of female identity through cultural and artistic representations. The happy ending of the French *conte*, however, contradicts the condemnation of female curiosity articulated in the moral; Carter did not so much break away from Perrault as exploit the contradiction between the tale and its alleged message in order to rehabilitate curiosity as a moral function.

Carter's Sources and Background Reading on "the Terrible Story of Bluebeard"

In *Perrault's Popular Tales* Andrew Lang says of "La Barbe bleue" that the story is "the most apt to move pity and terror. It has also least of the supernatural. Here are no talking beasts, no fairies, nor ogres" (lx), apart from the magical key. He observes that "in all else the story is a drama of daily and even contemporary life" set in Perrault's own milieu. In Lang's opinion the main interest of the story lies in its "moral motive," namely, the curiosity of the wife. He also mentions "the vision of the slain women" and the suspense that "make up the terrible story of *Blue Beard*" (lx).

Because of its realistic undertones, Bluebeard has been related to the historical figure of Gilles de Rais and to the legend of Comorre, who married and murdered a young woman canonized as Saint Tryphine. The tale also has resonances in myth: "The leading idea, of curiosity punished, of the box or door which may not be opened, and of the prohibition infringed with evil results, is of world-wide distribution."[9] In "The Bloody Chamber" Carter explores the idea of the possible historical basis of the tale (down to its Breton location) and its real-life implications in the portrayal of perverse marital relations. But she also spells out its resonances in the myth of Pandora and the Fall in order to show how these grand narratives neutralize the social critique of the folktale to legitimize misogynistic attitudes toward women instead.

In *Perrault's Popular Tales* Lang mentions a number of parallel stories, including the Grimms' "Robber Bridegroom," although "except for the 'larder' of the Robber, and of Mr. Fox in the English variant, these stories do not resemble Blue Beard." He finds a closer resemblance with "Fitcher's Bird" but jokingly remarks that "it would have been highly inconvenient for Blue Beard's surviving bride if the dead ladies had been resuscitated" (lxiii). Lang also notes that "the Story of the Third Calender in the *Arabian Nights* (Night 66) has nothing in common with Blue Beard but the prohibition to open a door" (lxiii) and the association of Bluebeard with the Devil in the Italian tradition. Lang concludes that Perrault's tale is more artful than its "popular rivals": "It is at once more sober and more terrible, and . . . possesses an epical unity of idea and action" (lxiv). And yet, he asserts, "Perrault's tale is clearly of popular origin, as the existence of variants in the folk lore of other countries demonstrates" (lxiv).

In their *Classic Fairy Tales* Iona and Peter Opie also remark on the near-absence of supernatural elements "except for the magic key" (103). Like Lang, they claim that Perrault adapted popular tales, and they note that the Bluebeard story reads like "a legend imperfectly recollected" on the grounds of a narrative "gap" between the bride's discovery of Bluebeard's secret and the husband's unexpected return, and his willingness to wait a "quarter of an hour" before killing his wife, which they deem improbable. Although they acknowledge that "no earlier telling of the tale has been discovered," they contend that "it may be taken for granted that one existed" (103). The Opies also relate female curiosity in the tale to a number of analogues in Western culture, from Lot's wife to Pandora's box, and Psyche's overpowering desire to see the face of her lover in Apuleius's *Metamorphoses*. Forbidden chambers, they remark, "are not unknown in pre-Perrault literature" (103), from Basile's *Pentamerone* to *The Arabian Nights* and the Grimms' "Fitcher's Bird."[10]

Among other parallel tales in Europe, the Opies signal an oral version recorded in the Vendée region (western France) by Eugène Bossard, where the wife's excuse for not coming downstairs is that she must put on her wedding dress. They mention the English "Mr. Fox," alluded to in Spenser's *Faerie Queene*, and Shakespeare's *Much Ado About Nothing*. Carter would later anthologize "Mr. Fox" in *The Virago Book of Fairy Tales* (1990), which presents a particularly macabre version of the story that nevertheless stresses female agency and the role of storytelling in denouncing the murderer. The Opies also signal the historical figure of Gilles de Rais, whose horrible deeds "had a lasting influence on Breton folklore" (*Classic Fairy Tales*, 105). The "ruinous extravagance" (104) of the character and his perverse enjoyment of murdering little children are perhaps echoed in Carter's decadent Marquis, who also eroticizes death and the act (as well as the spectacle) of murder. The story of Comorre the Cursed, Count of Vannes, is also briefly recounted, including the circumstances of his bride's death by decapitation.[11] Interestingly, the canonization of Tryphine may have impelled Carter to reactivate the idea of the bride's saintliness as a decadent fantasy of her perverse husband. The fact that Carter's Marquis is an aristocrat referencing both Sade (on whom Carter was writing at the time) and Comorre gives further evidence that "The Bloody Chamber" borrows from the multilayered tradition of the Bluebeard tale and other affiliated stories of murder and perversity.[12]

"The Bloody Chamber" also combines two images drawn from Carter's sources that function as keys to her own bloody chamber. Both Lang's "larder" and the Opies' "mortuary collection" (*Classic Fairy Tales*, 103) anticipate Carter's preoccupation with the treatment of "flesh" as "meat" throughout the collection and, more specifically, the characterization of the Marquis as a perverse collector of artistically displayed female corpses in "The Bloody Chamber." Carter thus shifts the focus from the wife's disobedience to her discovery of the true motive of the husband's crimes as originating in his deeply ingrained misogyny, which is itself nurtured by high art and culture. The writer thus picks up on two "inconsistencies" that the Opies had faulted Perrault's version with: Her own rewriting fills the gap between the macabre discovery and the husband's return and accounts for the protracted beheading scene as a macabre mise-en-scène staged by the sadistic Marquis. For Carter, then, the sexual subtext of the story has nothing to do with the bride's unfaithfulness that Bruno Bettelheim read into the story but rather with the husband's perverse enjoyment of the spectacle of his wife's "martyrdom." He can relate to women only through stereotypes as saints and whores. Carter's rewriting also follows Lang's and the Opies' remarks on the realistic nature of Perrault's Bluebeard tale by situating the story in a specific geographic (Breton castle), historical (early-twentieth-century France), and cultural (decadent and symbolist) context.[13]

The Opies' choice of illustrations indicates that the iconographic tradition played a crucial role in shaping the perception of the tale and its cultural significance, and it in turn constitutes an important source of inspiration for Carter in "The Bloody Chamber." Not only does the rewriting focus on visual culture, but it is also set in the same period as several of the illustrations in *The Classic Fairy Tales*. Both the Art Deco frontispiece by John Austen (1922) and Harry Clarke's decadent Bluebeard (1922) anticipate Carter's location of the story in early-twentieth-century culture (which can be dated through the Poiret dress worn by the bride).[14] Clarke's Bluebeard points toward himself with his eyes closed, suggesting vanity and self-absorption; his sophisticated costume, cane, goat legs, and long pointed beard portray him as a demonic, Orientalized dandy (Figure 3.1).

In the course of her reading, then, Carter was made aware of the potential of Perrault's *conte* for retelling and of the textual richness and visual variety of the fairy-tale tradition. She also realized that "depending on the treatment of the story, Bluebeard can be used to confirm traditional stereotypes of women as daughters of Eve and serve patriarchal interests, or on

Figure 3.1. Bluebeard portrayed by Harry Clarke, 1922, in The Classic Fairy Tales *by Iona and Peter Opie.*

the contrary (sometimes simultaneously) to criticize them."[15] The wealth of adaptations reaffirms the topicality of the tale against Perrault's moral that safely locates it in the past. Against the reassuring moral, the possibility that Bluebeard might be revived from the dead is implied by the text itself: "Ils lui passèrent leur épée au travers du corps, et le laissèrent mort" (*Contes*, 153), rendered in the early translation as "They ran their swords through his body, and left him dead" (*Histories*, 26). Carter, however, opts for "They thrust their swords through him and left him *for* dead" (*Fairy Tales*, 37; italics mine), hinting at Bluebeard's possible survival and return to life, in keeping with the rich literary and cultural afterlife of the tale, down to Carter's rewriting in "The Bloody Chamber."

From "La Barbe bleue" to "Bluebeard": Containing Visual Horror

A contrapuntal analysis of Carter's translation and rewriting shows how a children's classic informed by the normative force of its reception shifts to a complex, multilayered, and densely intertextual story of mystery, perversion, and crime in "The Bloody Chamber." In her foreword to *The Fairy Tales of Charles Perrault*, Carter presents Perrault's *contes* as "nursery tales" (9) that children can learn from. This establishes a somewhat strained connection between Perrault's public and Carter's own in the translation, as it takes Perrault's intentions at face value and anachronistically conflates the early reception of the tales with what they subsequently became. Although "The Bloody Chamber" would offer a corrective to this idea, Carter's translation can be seen as a means to intervene in the field of children's literature by going against the dominant trend promoting imagination and escapism.

To meet the expectations and needs of her young audience, Carter creates a homogeneous narrative voice, erases the ironic comments and explanatory parentheses, fuses the narrative voice and the fictional universe, reestablishes the chronological order of the narrated facts, and neutralizes the horrific visual details of Perrault's text. The self-same elements are foregrounded in her retelling of the story for adults. Probably in agreement with the publisher, Carter multiplies the paragraph divisions of the original text to facilitate reading, in keeping with the modern conventions of children's books, so that the continuous text of Claude Barbin's original

1697 French edition is broken into twenty-odd paragraphs, discounting the dialogue.

Carter also translates the text in a modern idiom. She subtly updates the language and world of the text ("soap and sandstone," *Fairy Tales*, 34) for *sablon* (fine sand) and *grais* (sandstone) (*Contes*, 151) and uses a familiar vocabulary: "a very fine fellow" (*Fairy Tales*, 32) for "un fort honnête homme" (*Contes*, 149) (a most honest man, a gentleman).

Perrault's complex sentences become much shorter and the somewhat convoluted syntax of the French text is replaced by a paratactic style. In the scene of the keys, for example, the husband utters one long sentence separated by two colons in Barbin's edition, whereas Bluebeard's speech contains one exclamation mark, five semicolons, and three full stops in the translation. The use of emphatic punctuation increases the dramatic impact of the scene: "'You don't know!' said Bluebeard. 'But *I* know, very well!'" (*Fairy Tales*, 36) ("Vous n'en savez rien, reprit la Barbe bleue, je le sais bien, moi," *Contes*, 152; that is, "You don't know anything about it, resumed Bluebeard, I know it well myself"). Similarly, "Ne manquez pas . . . de me la donner tantôt" (*Contes*, 152) ("'Fail not,' said Blue Beard, 'to bring it me presently,'" *Histories*, 23) is conveyed by the imperative "'Give it to me'" (*Fairy Tales*, 36) in Carter's translation, which creates a sense of immediacy and enhances the emotional involvement of the young reader or audience.

The narrator also clarifies meaning with the help of strong contrastive conjunctions ("But this little key"; "but she took no pleasure"; etc.) and reinforces the cohesion of the text for the benefit of a young reader. Thus, when Bluebeard comes back home earlier than announced, he does so "unexpectedly" (*Fairy Tales*, 34) in the translation in order to convey the bride's surprise. Similarly, when the bride has to give the stained key to her husband, the statement of bare fact ("Il fallut apporter la clef," *Contes*, 152; the key had to be brought) is reinforced by an introductory phrase that encapsulates the bride's hopeless situation in a commonplace image: "But there was no way out; she must go and fetch the key" (*Fairy Tales*, 36). Or when Anne spots a cloud of dust ("Sont-ce mes frères?—Hélas! non, ma soeur, c'est un Troupeau de Moutons," *Contes*, 153; "'Are they my brothers?' 'Alas! no, my dear sister, I see a flock of sheep,'" *Histories*, 25), Carter elaborates as follows: "'Is it the dust my brothers make as they ride towards me?' / 'Oh, no—it is the dust raised by a flock of sheep!'" (*Fairy Tales*, 37), which adds to the dramatic impact of the anticlimax.

By couching the story in a familiar style and chatty tone ("Bluebeard threw a lavish house-party," *Fairy Tales*, 32) and by using short, simple words and repetitions, basic syntax, and a "blunt and succinct manner,"[16] in her translation Carter reflects modern conceptions of the genre that owe a lot to the Grimms' idea of the folktale as "simple," "direct," "naive," and "sincere." Whereas the paragraph divisions facilitate the reading of the tale by a child, the use of emphatic punctuation anticipates its oral delivery in performance and, more important, encourages identification with the heroine.

The original title of Perrault's tale is "La Barbe bleue." Although the article is kept in Robert Samber's early translation ("The Blue Beard"), it disappears in the "G. M." edition ("Blue Beard"), and the villain's characteristic feature was crystallized into a proper name well before Carter retranslated the tale. "La Barbe bleue," which is the only tale not designated as a *conte* in Perrault's 1697 edition, opens with the "Il était une fois" (*Contes*, 149) (Once upon a time) formula and is told in the third person by a matter-of-fact narrator who occasionally makes subtly ironic comments on the story. Whereas Samber has "There was once upon a time a man" (*Classic Fairy Tales*, 106), G. M. simply has "There was a man" (*Histories*, 18). Like G. M., Carter chooses *not* to repeat the traditional formula and has only "There once lived a man" (*Fairy Tales*, 31), possibly to convey the idea that the tale is not, strictly speaking, a wonder tale (as Lang and the Opies had already noted).

Carter shifts the focus of the tale from class and gender relations to a critique of loveless marriage. In contrast to "Cendrillon ou la petite pantoufle de verre," which begins with "Il était une fois un *Gentilhomme*" (*Contes*, 171, italics mine), "La Barbe bleue" opens with "Il était une fois un *homme*" (149, italics mine), which immediately draws attention to his status as an immensely wealthy but common (literally ignoble) man. The entire *conte*, in fact, revolves around the idea of *honnêteté* as class marker and moral attitude, especially toward women. The young woman's perception of the man's physical abnormality and his social identity changes when she lets herself be seduced by his wealth and entertaining parties ("la Cadette commença à trouver que le Maître du logis n'avait plus la barbe si bleue, et que c'était *un fort honnête homme*," 149 [italics mine]). It is significant that the phrase recurs at the end of the tale with reference to the bride's *second* husband, but by this time she knows better and marries a "*fort honnête* homme" (154; italics mine), a real gentleman who is true to his name.

Likewise, Perrault's allusion to the aristocratic origin of the mother's bride disappears when "Dame de qualité" (*Contes*, 149) (Lady) is translated as "the mother of two beautiful daughters" (*Fairy Tales*, 31). Carter thus eliminates the underlying social critique of impoverished aristocrats marrying off their daughters to wealthy parvenus of dubious reputation in Perrault's *conte*.[17] She focuses instead on the superficiality and naïveté of young "girls" who marry for the wrong reasons but learn from their terrible experience to grow into wiser women able to choose a suitable husband for themselves.

Carter accordingly opposes "girls" to "women." The blue beard is so ugly and frightening that *both* women and girls run away from Bluebeard in the French text ("Il n'était ni femme ni fille qui ne s'enfuit de devant lui," *Contes*, 149), but *only* "women flee ... at the sight of him" (*Fairy Tales*, 31) in Carter's translation. Unlike the *women* who know better, then, the younger girl is soon seduced by his wealth. Carter also emphasizes her young age in the language of the text. Even after her marriage, she is treated like a child by her husband. When he announces his departure, he tells her that "he must leave her to her own devices" (*Fairy Tales*, 32) ("Il était obligé de faire un voyage," *Contes*, 150; "He was obliged to take a country journey," *Histories*, 19–20). In keeping with her representation of the bride as a young and foolish girl taken by appearances, Carter eliminates the ambiguity of the young woman's apparent repentance in Perrault's text: "She was *truly* sorry she had been disobedient" (*Fairy Tales*, 36; italics mine) ("avec toutes les marques d'un vrai repentir," *Contes*, 152; "with all the signs of true repentance," *Histories*, 24). When the young wife is confounded by her husband, the translator insists on the girl's childlike fear of punishment, as in "She wondered if he would punish her" (*Fairy Tales*, 34), to convey the bride's weighing the risk of disobeying her husband ("considérant qu'il pourroit lui arriver malheur d'avoir été désobéissante," *Contes*, 151; "considering what unhappiness might attend her if she was discovered," *Histories*, 22).

Because she is addressing a child reader, Carter also eliminates the *galanterie* (sexual allusions) of Perrault's knowing and playful prose. The gender of the guests invited to the lavish eight-day party organized by

Bluebeard is unknown in Carter's translation ("three or four of their closest friends and several neighbours," *Fairy Tales*, 32), but Perrault is more specific, distinguishing between three or four among their best female friends and a few young men living nearby ("trois ou quatre de leurs meilleures amies, et quelques jeunes gens du voisinage," *Contes*, 149; "three or four ladies of their acquaintance, with other young people from the neighbourhood," *Histories*, 19). Likewise, the fun and games, especially the nightly entertainment, are more innocuous ("The guests . . . spent the night playing practical jokes," *Fairy Tales*, 32) than in Perrault's more ambiguous version ("On passait toute la nuit à se faire des malices les uns aux autres," *Contes*, 149; "All passed the night in rallying and joking with each other," *Histories*, 19). In this way Carter self-consciously reads Perrault against Bettelheim's psychoanalytical interpretation of the tale as a story about sexual betrayal: "It is left to our imagination what went on between the woman and her guests with Bluebeard away."[18]

Carter's purpose as a translator for children is indeed quite different. In "The Better to Eat You With," Carter celebrates Perrault's matter-of-fact treatment of the tale against "the mysteries of sado-masochistic attraction": "We must learn to cope with the world before we can interpret it. The primitive terror a young girl feels when she sees Bluebeard is soon soothed when he takes her out and shows her a good time, parties, trips to the country and so on. But marriage itself is no party. Better learn that right away" (453). Carter adds that Perrault "blithely dismisses all the Freudian elements in the tale that galvanise the twentieth century. The troubling and intransigent images are incorporated into a well-mannered scheme of good sense" (453). Because she wishes to foreground "good sense" rather than the ghastly horror of the Bluebeard story, especially "the dismembered wives lying in their own blood in the secret chamber" (453), Carter also eliminates several details that hint at the macabre spectacle being staged by the murderous husband and to some extent aestheticized by the narrator: "Le plancher était tout couvert de sang caillé, et . . . dans ce sang se miraient les corps de plusieurs femmes mortes et attachées le long des murs (c'était toutes les femmes que la Barbe bleue avait épousées et qu'il avait égorgées l'une après l'autre)" (*Contes*, 151). Both Samber and G. M. simplify the text and eliminate the disturbing image of the blood mirroring the bodies of the dead women: "The floor was all covered over with clotted blood, on which lay the bodies of several dead women ranged against the walls; (these were all the wives whom Blue Beard had married and murdered then cut their throat one after another)" (*Histories*, 22). Carter compresses the passage further: "In the blood lay the corpses of all the women Bluebeard had married and then murdered, one after the other" (*Fairy Tales*, 34).

Carter's confinement of the horror and cruelty of the tale probably stems from her own dread at reading scary "bed-time stories" as a child (see "The Better to Eat You With") and her desire to stress the new moral instead (reinforced by the alliteration of "married" and "murdered"). Whereas the "adult" elements of Perrault's *conte* disappear from the translation, the dense intertextuality, complex irony and ambiguity, and disturbingly macabre images are all taken up and refracted in "The Bloody Chamber," in the manner of the multiplied images of the bride in the mirrors decorating the marital bedroom as antechamber to the bloody chamber.

Carter's translation nevertheless anticipates a central motif in her rewriting—namely, the association of the Bluebeard figure with God, which frames the reception of Perrault's text in the literary and iconographic tradition (as in Walter Crane's famous illustration).[19] Whereas in Perrault the blue beard is the result of misfortune (*par malheur*), Carter attributes the protagonist's features to God, including his blue beard ("but, alas, God had also given him a blue beard," *Fairy Tales*, 31). This is echoed later, when Bluebeard warns his wife: "nothing will spare you from my wrath" (33). Although this may reflect the pressure of a Christian reading of the story, the socialist Carter may also deliberately be linking the accumulation of material possessions with monstrosity. This would tie in with the shift of focus to the appeal of social status and material wealth as the source of the bride's shame in "The Bloody Chamber" (her forehead bears a heart-shaped mark, like the stained key). Carter's Bluebeard behaves like an angry and vengeful Old Testament God in the translation, and he becomes an elderly art collector and decadent pervert in "The Bloody Chamber."

Carter also eliminates the satirical jibes that the narrator of Perrault's *conte* directs at the bride's female friends when he suggests that they are hypocritical ("Elles ne cessaient d'exagérer et d'envier le bonheur de leur amie," *Contes*, 150; "They ceased not to extol and envy the happiness of their friend," *Histories*, 21). Reflecting a feminist sensibility, the translator has a more straightforward and neutral "They never stopped congratulating their friend on her good luck" (*Fairy Tales*, 33). Likewise, Carter eliminates the gendered address to women ("n'en déplaise au sexe," *Contes*, 154;

may the gentler sex not be offended) in the first moral, presumably to avoid repeating the old sexist topos harping on female curiosity.

Carter also broaches the theme of vision in her translation. Thus added emphasis is put on Bluebeard's paradoxical invitation to look at the moment he articulates the prohibition to see: "'Look!' he said to her. 'Here are the keys, . . .'" (*Fairy Tales*, 32) conveys "'Voilà, lui dit-il, les clefs . . .'" (*Contes*, 150) ("'Here,' said he, 'Are the keys,'" *Histories*, 20).

Relatedly, the idea of physical repulsion, disgust, and revulsion, which Carter explicitly relates to sexuality and the obscure nature of desire in "The Bloody Chamber," is already present in her translation. Whereas women flee at the sight of Bluebeard because his blue beard "le rendait si laid et si terrible" (*Contes*, 149) ("which made him so frightfully ugly," *Histories*, 18), the word "ghastly" (*Fairy Tales*, 32) used by Carter connotes fear but also loathing. Even more than the blue beard, women flee this man because he has already married several times but nobody knows what happened to his previous wives: "Ce qui les *dégoûtait* encore, c'est qu'il avait déjà épousé plusieurs femmes" (*Contes*, 149; italics mine). Both Samber and G. M. convey *dégoûtait* by "disgust and aversion" (*Histories*, 19) and Carter by "profound distaste" (*Fairy Tales*, 31). In seventeenth-century French *dégoûter* combined the meanings of physical aversion (provoked by ugliness or old age, as in Molière's plays about forced marriages) and spiritual or moral displeasure. This enables Carter to emphasize the repulsive effect provoked by Bluebeard's strange feature. When the bride's friends come to visit her in Bluebeard's absence, "à cause de sa Barbe bleue qui leur faisait peur" (*Contes*, 150) ("which frightened them," *Histories*, 21), Carter again insists on the unpleasant sensation provoked by the blue beard that "was so offensive" (*Fairy Tales*, 33). In the rewriting she explores the complex nature of desire as the bride acknowledges a mix of attraction and repulsion toward her husband after her first sexual experience.

Because it inevitably involves some degree of cultural transposition, translation affects the tale's intertextual dimension. Carter's choice of the word *attic* to convey Perrault's *garde-meubles* ("wardrobes" in the early translations) is a good case in point: Both "Here are the keys to my two large attics" (*Fairy Tales*, 32) and "They climbed into the attics" (33) present an interesting case of double address as it resonates in the ears of the cultured feminist reader. Indeed, *attic* evokes Charlotte Brontë's *Jane Eyre* (where Jane explicitly refers to Thornfield as Bluebeard's castle), which would take on new resonances after the publication of Sandra Gilbert and

Susan Gubar's groundbreaking feminist study, *The Madwoman in the Attic: The Woman Writer and the Nineteenth-Century Literary Imagination*, published the same year as *The Bloody Chamber*.

The most telltale part of the translation, however, is undoubtedly the morals, where Carter articulates her own interpretation of the relevance of the moral for a modern reader.

> La curiosité malgré tous ses attraits,
>   Coûte souvent bien des regrets;
> On en voit tous les jours mille exemples paraître.
> C'est, n'en déplaise au sexe, un plaisir bien léger;
>   Dès qu'on le prend il cesse d'être,
>   Et toujours il coûte trop cher.
>   (*Contes*, 154)

Carter translates the first moral as follows:

> Curiosity is a charming passion but may only be satisfied at the price of a thousand regrets; one sees around one a thousand examples of this sad truth every day. Curiosity is the most fleeting of pleasures; the moment it is satisfied, it ceases to exist and it always proves very, very expensive. (*Fairy Tales*, 41)

Emphasizing what she saw as the matter-of-factness of Perrault's message, Carter shifts from verse to prose. She eliminates the gendered address ("N'en déplaise au sexe," which the early translators convey as "O may it not displease the fair," *Histories*, 27), which is commonly interpreted as the expression of Perrault's conservative views on women. By cutting off the problematic line, Carter simply erases the suspicion of Perrault's alleged sexism. If read in the light of its hidden intertexts (especially Boileau's misogynist "Satire X"), however, Perrault's first moral can be understood as an ironic quotation of his adversary's fierce attack on educated women who want to know more about the world and its secrets. In this perspective "La Barbe bleue" does not condemn but on the contrary encourages women eager for knowledge. It is thanks to her curiosity that the young woman reveals her criminal husband's secrets and inherits his fortune, which enables her to marry both herself and her sister to partners of their own choice, this time regardless of their fortune. In his "Apologie des Femmes," published shortly before he wrote the manuscript version of "La Barbe bleue," Perrault explicitly criticized not only Boileau's misogynist view of women but also the current marital politics of parents imposing marriage for financial reasons on their daughters. Perrault claimed the right for young aristocratic women to be considered individuals who should be allowed to choose their own partners, contrary to current practice, as his version of "Bluebeard" shows. By omitting Perrault's pique and transforming the first moral into a more general consideration that can apply to all readers (and especially young readers tempted by this "charming passion"), Carter skillfully avoids the possibility of misreading the story as endorsing a patriarchal stereotype. She also considerably modifies Perrault's second moral by infusing it with new meaning.

> AUTRE MORALITE
> Pour peu qu'on ait l'esprit sensé,
> Et que du Monde on sache le grimoire,
> On voit bien tôt que cette histoire
> Est un conte du temps passé;
> Il n'est plus d'époux si terrible,
> Ni qui demande l'impossible,
> Fût-il malcontent et jaloux.
> Près de sa femme on le voit filer doux;
> Et de quelque couleur que sa barbe puisse être,
> On a peine à juger qui des deux est le maître.
> (*Contes*, 154)

Carter translates:

> *Another moral*
> It is easy to see that the *events* described in this story took place many years ago. No modern husband would dare to be half so terrible, nor to demand of his wife such an impossible thing as to stifle her curiosity. Be he never so quarrelsome or jealous, he'll toe the line as soon as she tells him to. And whatever colour his beard might be, it's easy to see which of the two is the master. (*Fairy Tales*, 41; italics mine)

Instead of the complex image of the world (high society) as a book of spells that can be deciphered with a modicum of good sense, Carter opts for "It is easy to see," which equates vision with the ability to understand and therefore to know. She eliminates the irony of the royal court as a place where social interactions are ruled in such an arcane fashion that it seems like a difficult grammar book. Whereas Perrault's reader needs to be able to decipher obscure and complex codes to realize that the Bluebeard story is a tale of ancient times, it is much easier for Carter's modern reader to realize that "the events took place many years ago."

The reason for this significant difference becomes clear in the second half of the moral: "No modern husband would dare to be half so terrible, nor to demand of his wife such an impossible thing as to stifle her curiosity." This sentence says much more than Perrault's "Il n'y a plus d'Epoux si terrible, Ni qui demande l'impossible," because it confirms that times have thoroughly changed in the twentieth century: It has become evident that no husband would even dare to behave like Bluebeard in the aftermath of the feminist movement. Carter's translation thus moves the focus of the old story away from female curiosity, transgression, and punishment to an investigation of changing masculine behavior. Bluebeard's perverse and provocative demand is "bluntly dismissed" as having become so unacceptable for modern women that no man would even *dare* to behave like this. Carter's stressing of the fact that this understanding of the story is so *easy* to grasp makes the second moral even more reassuring for young readers. It leaves no doubt that times have changed since the Bluebeard "event" happened and that even if curiosity can be an expensive pleasure according to the first moral, it is now disconnected from Bluebeard's threat of punishment, as his threatening itself is disqualified as unacceptable and unlikely to happen. Carter's translation of Perrault's morals thus conveys an optimistic message and promise of relief for her young readers.

Perrault's double morals require more effort from their adult readers. "Pour peu qu'on ait l'esprit sensé" is an oblique reference to the "lettre-dédicace" to "Mademoiselle" opening the *Histoires ou contes du temps passé*, in which Perrault declares that his tales contain (or enclose) a sensible moral that readers can discover according to their degree of perception or intelligence. The "morale très sensée" reveals itself only to the more perceptive or insightful readers and depends on their interpretative skills. The insight that there is no such terrible husband anymore also needs the reader's skill of deciphering Perrault's tale and the capacity to elucidate the obscure grammar of the world—that is, young ladies must learn to read the signs that spell out the true personality of individuals like Bluebeard (his beard as a sign of his barbarity) in order to avoid being married off to perverse monsters.

In "The Bloody Chamber" Carter explores precisely the sociopolitical subtext (i.e., the hidden violence and misogyny of high society) and complex textual strategies of her source. By doing so, she thematizes and enacts the dangers of literal reading, inviting the reader—after Perrault—to interpret the world (and especially suitors' real personalities underneath their social masks) as a matter of survival. Carter's move from a young readership to a knowing adult audience in "The Bloody Chamber," as we will see, is anticipated in Martin Ware's realistic portrayal of a black-cloaked Bluebeard wearing a monocle and elegantly dressed in a top hat and waistcoat, evoking Carter's monocled Marquis. As in Perrault's *conte*, curiosity is finally rewarded in "The Bloody Chamber": The bride gains useful knowledge from opening the door of the bloody chamber, and this knowledge becomes the means through which Bluebeard's awful secret is revealed, triggering a chain of events that ends his career as a serial killer and enables his wealth to be redistributed more equitably. Instead of seeing the Bluebeard story as a misogynist condemnation of female curiosity, then, Carter reads it as an invitation to look through the keyhole of culture. This sometimes implies disobedience and transgression but more often requires good interpretative skills (as Perrault himself pointed out) and leads to knowledge and emancipation from socially prescribed behavior and superficial values.

This revaluation of female curiosity undermines conventional interpretations of Bluebeard as an illustration of women's guilt and untrustworthiness. The bride's self-conscious identifications with Eve and Pandora in "The Bloody Chamber" signal her awareness of the pressure of biblical and Greek myths on conservative interpretations of Bluebeard. Carter shows that the same story may serve to keep women in the dark or, on the contrary, to enlighten and liberate them from oppressive patriarchal structures.

From Vision to Revision: Martin Ware's Etchings

Ce que nous voyons ne vaut—ne vit—à nos yeux que par ce qui nous regarde.

—G. DIDI-HUBERMAN, *CE QUE NOUS VOYONS, CE QUI NOUS REGARDE*, 9

The Bluebeard tale is centrally concerned with vision, as it notoriously centers on the female transgression of a male visual prohibition. As such, it provides a paradigmatic plot to explore the interactions between the verbal and the visual and to investigate the sexual politics of representation. As the title "The Bloody Chamber" indicates, attention is displaced from the male villain to the bride-narrator's discovery of his monstrous secret in the forbidden chamber. It focuses on the conditioning of the bride to be seduced by his material wealth but also to submit to her husband's voyeuristic gaze and visual power. The bride's first-person narrative stresses the ability of language to undo (or at least resist) masculine tyranny through delaying strategies when she tries to escape his murderous wrath and, later, when she retells the story from her own perspective and reflects on the implications of the rapprochement with the Bluebeard story. As she reflects on her experience of marriage to a wealthy and perverse aesthete, the surviving bride amply comments on the effects of her visual training into subjection. The Marquis exerts absolute control over her image and identity, and he shapes and reshapes it at will. The young woman is made to enact his increasingly cruel erotic fantasies, all of which are derived from visual images, and she becomes complicit in her own victimization to the point of almost accepting her death as the price of her disobedience, her status changing from *tableau vivant* to still life.[20]

In Perrault's "La Barbe bleue" the climactic moment of the opening of the door and gradual discovery of the corpses of Bluebeard's former wives is characterized by description, the visual mode par excellence.

> D'abord elle ne vit rien, parce que les fenêtres étaient fermées; après quelques moments elle commença à voir que le plancher était tout couvert de sang caillé, et que dans ce sang gisaient les corps de plusieurs femmes mortes et attachées le long des murs (c'était toutes les femmes que la Barbe Bleue avait épousées et qu'il avait égorgées l'une après l'autre). (*Contes*, 151)

> The windows were shuttered and at first she could see nothing; but after a few moments, her eyes grew accustomed to the gloom and she saw that the floor was covered with clotted blood. In the blood lay the corpses of all the women whom Bluebeard had married and then murdered, one after the other. (*Fairy Tales*, 34)

In turn, Ware represents the key moment of transgression in a strongly contrasted full-page illustration that represents the arrested movement of the wife's hand on the doorknob; the door opens up onto the black space of the forbidden room (Figure 3.2). The hand of the young woman holds the (typically English) knob of a banal white door, which opens onto a dark room where three realistically depicted skeletons (one torso and two skulls) are visible in the lower portion of the page. We recall that in Perrault's *conte* Bluebeard's victims are very present in their flesh and blood physicality: Their bodies are hanging from the wall, and the floor is covered in their blood. Shed of their flesh and blood materiality, however, only the women's bones remain in Ware's image, as though to confirm that Bluebeard's murders took place in a faraway past.

The almost abstract composition of the picture also raises the issue of the limits (and ethics) of visual representation. Half-hidden and half-revealed (or only gradually revealed if the image is read from top to bottom), the horror of the macabre discovery is to some extent neutralized by the black and white technique that contrasts with the gore, mutilated corpses, and violent murders of Perrault's lurid pose already attenuated in Carter's translation. Ware's illustration further contributes to rendering the disturbing passage more abstract by referencing the tradition of seventeenth-century vanitas paintings: three white skulls whose shape is not unlike the door knob (one vertical, one horizontal, both "grinning" at the viewer) and a human skeleton torso are seen in profile.[21] Bluebeard's murders belong to a distant past and thus become an occasion to meditate on human cruelty rather than an opportunity to exploit the sensational horror provoked by the spectacle of bloodshed.

As in Ware's illustrations for "Little Red Riding Hood," the climactic scene of the discovery of Bluebeard's murders is represented in a chilling but distant manner that is not unlike the matter-of-fact commentary of the narrator bracketed in Perrault's text. Ware deliberately eschews sensationalism and the voyeuristic mix of horror, disgust, and fascination provoked by the description of the scene in Perrault's text. The visual medium shapes Ware's interpretation of the passage, as distinct from the text, while also drawing attention to devices and effects that are lost in translation. Ware's illustration thus draws attention to the constant interplay of word and im-

Looking Through the Keyhole of Culture   131

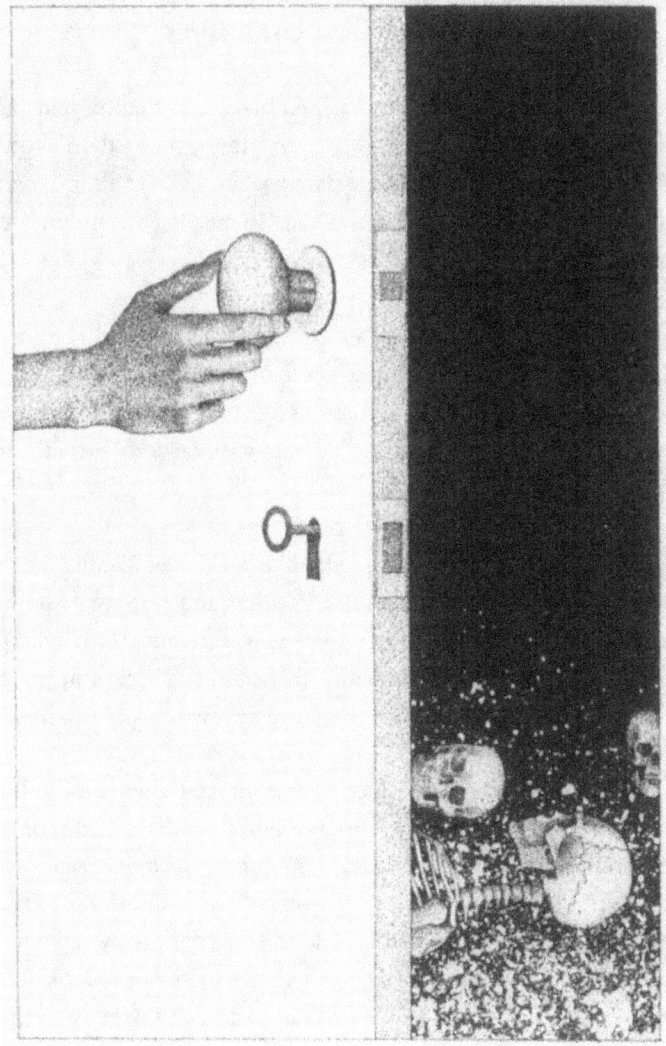

Figure 3.2. Illustration for "Bluebeard" in the 1977 edition of The Fairy Tales of Charles Perrault. *Courtesy of Martin Ware.*

age, as it transposes visually Perrault's verbal strategy (the brackets) as well as the popular idiom "to have skeletons in the closet."

Another climactic moment in the tale is the scene of the attempted beheading of the bride, preceded by a scene of repentance. When the young woman asks for forgiveness in Perrault's "La Barbe bleue," it is said that Bluebeard is unmoved because his heart is "harder than stone."

> Elle se jeta aux pieds de son mari, en pleurant et en lui demandant pardon, avec toutes les marques d'un vrai repentir de n'avoir pas été obéissante. Elle aurait attendri un rocher, belle et affligée comme elle était; mais la Barbe Bleue avait le Coeur plus dur qu'un rocher. (*Contes*, 123)

> She threw herself at her husband's feet, weeping and begging his forgiveness; she was truly sorry she had been disobedient. She was so beautiful and so distressed that the sight of her would have melted a heart of stone, but Bluebeard's heart was harder than any stone. (*Fairy Tales*, 36)

Ware represents Bluebeard as a tall, black-cloaked gentleman wearing a monocle and elegantly dressed in a top hat and waistcoat; he faces the reader and fixes him (or her) in the eye, indifferent to his young wife's pleading (Figure 3.3). The choice of this moment is significant, because illustrators traditionally focus on the more dramatic and visually arresting scene of near decapitation.[22]

By contrast, Ware pictures Bluebeard as impassive and motionless in the scene that precedes this suspenseful and emotionally loaded moment and, as such, prefigures Carter's Bluebeard epigone as a coldhearted aesthete in "The Bloody Chamber." The young woman kneels in front of her formally dressed husband, hiding her face in shame or despair. No weapon is visible, and the violence of the scene is suggested only by the *stony* look and visible hand of the man, as though he were about to grab his wife by the hair. The visual detail of the monocle, which comes to symbolize the Marquis's perverse eroticization of the spectacle of sexual violence and murder in "The Bloody Chamber," draws attention to the connection between visual power and sexual perversity (sadism and scopophilia). This is already hinted at in Gustave Doré's engraving of the handing down of the keys, where the idea of Bluebeard's visual obsession, which motivates his attempted entrapment of his wife, is represented by his eyes literally popping out as he stares at her while she looks at the keys with fascination (Figure 3.4).

As I will develop later, Carter's "Bloody Chamber" is replete with refer-

Figure 3.3. Illustration for "Bluebeard" in the 1977 edition of The Fairy Tales of Charles Perrault. *Courtesy of Martin Ware.*

ences to symbolist art (Moreau, Redon, Rops, Ensor, etc.) and ekphrastic passages. Moreover, the discovery of the Marquis's murders is followed by a lengthy description of the bloody chamber and its display of "exquisite corpses" as a "little museum of his perversity" (*Bloody Chamber*, 31). The

Figure 3.4. "La Barbe bleue" in Les contes de Perrault, *illustrated by Gustave Doré, 1867.*

bride senses that this macabre mise-en-scène was deliberately designed for her to discover, so that her husband could enjoy the spectacle of her horror, fear, and punishment. In "The Bloody Chamber" the intriguing visual detail of the Marquis's "carnal avarice" being "strangely magnified by the monocle lodged in his left eye" (11) is a telltale sign of his visual obsession.

Upon discovering that his wife has disobeyed him, his masklike face loses its gravity and stillness, and when he announces that she will be decapitated, she observes that "the monocle had fallen from his face.... I saw how he had lost his impassivity and was now filled with suppressed excitement" (35).

Ware and Carter also pick up on Perrault's image of the heart of stone. The visual artist translates the metaphor of Bluebeard's stony or pitiless look into the stone wall that stands behind the characters while the kneeling bride hides her face with her hand. The masculine character's massive black-cloaked body, rectangular face, and top hat, whose shape evokes the crenellations of the castle wall, suggest that Bluebeard embodies the fortified structure in which the heroine is confined. Once again, the scene is frozen, as in a snapshot. The climactic scene of the attempted beheading is described as follows in Perrault's text:

> La pauvre femme descendit, et alla se jeter à ses pieds toute éplorée et toute échevelée.
> —Cela ne sert de rien, dit la Barbe bleue, il faut mourir.
> Puis la prenant d'une main par les cheveux, et de l'autre levant le coutelas dans l'air, il allait lui abattre la tête. (*Contes*, 153)

> Bluebeard now shouted so loudly that all the house trembled. His unfortunate wife went down to him and threw herself in tears at his feet, her dishevelled hair tumbling all around her.
> "Nothing you can do will save you," said Bluebeard. "You must die." With one hand, he seized her disordered hair and, with the other, raised his cutlass in the air; he meant to chop off her head with it. (*Fairy Tales*, 38)

In "The Bloody Chamber" Carter introduces a new character at the climactic moment, because it is the bride's mother who comes to rescue her child (and not her brothers, as in Perrault). The Marquis's reaction is described as follows: "The Marquis stood transfixed, utterly dazed, at a loss. ... And my husband stood stock-still, as if she had been Medusa, the sword still raised over his head as in the clockwork tableaux of Bluebeard that you see in glass cases at fairs" (*Bloody Chamber*, 42). The mother's murderous look, compared to Medusa's, so surprises Bluebeard (unless of course it is the unexpected twist in the plot) that he stops and, standing "stock still," is killed by the heroic mother. Carter reinterprets the famous scene from a feminist perspective, and the reference to Medusa itself signals the reappropriation of the Greek myth by women critics and artists of the period, most notably Hélène Cixous in "Le rirede la Méduse" (1975; "The Laugh of the Medusa," 1976). In Carter's rewriting a further irony is of course that it is Bluebeard who is now killed into art. By invoking Medusa, the female narrator symbolically recuperates visual power for women, and it is to be noted that the mythological figure retains her agency even after being beheaded by Perseus, in an ironic nod to the Marquis's (very fin de siècle) obsession with decapitation.

The interplay of text and image in *The Fairy Tales of Charles Perrault* thus renews the significance of Perrault's *conte* and the power it exerts over our imagination. The tale comes to exemplify the intricate relations of visual and literary culture and becomes an occasion to reinterpret the conservative cultural myths with which it is often confused.

From "Bluebeard" to "The Bloody Chamber": Murdered Bodies in Mirrors, or the Perversions of Vision

Mais il en a toujours été ainsi; les queues de siècle se ressemblent. Toutes vacillent et sont troubles.

—JORIS-KARL HUYSMANS, *LÀ-BAS*, 363–64

It looks like the *fin* is coming a little early this *siècle*.

—ANGELA CARTER, "FIN DE SIÈCLE"[23]

In *The Bloody Chamber* Carter ransacks the storeroom of European culture as she questions the various myths of femininity that shape women's lives and identities. The title story is characterized by its complex dialogue with the long history of pictorial and literary representations of women in Western art and culture. It bears witness to the power of stereotypes that reduce women to innocent virgins or dangerous whores, passive victims or wicked Eves, and shows how these images operate in the service of patriarchy. "The Bloody Chamber" is a programmatic story insofar as it uses the tale of Bluebeard to articulate the interactions between the literary and the folk tradition, high and popular culture, and text and image, and to investigate the politics of representation from a woman's perspective. As the title of Carter's story indicates, attention is displaced from the male villain to the bride-narrator's discovery of his monstrous secret in the forbidden chamber. Although the tale has often been read, after Perrault, as cautioning against the dangers of female curiosity, "The Bloody Chamber" focuses instead on the conditioning of the bride to submit to her husband's visual power. This power consists of the absolute control he exerts over her image (and self-image) as he shapes and reshapes it at will. In this sense Carter goes against a long tradition that diverts attention away from Bluebeard's horrific murders to blame the curiosity of his wives. Maria Tatar notes that "nearly every nineteenth-century printed version of 'Bluebeard' singles out the heroine's curiosity as an especially undesirable trait."[24] This dominant reading based on Perrault's first moral was reinforced by illustrators, commentators, and adapters alike.

As the bride is made to enact the Marquis's increasingly cruel erotic fantasies, all of which are derived from visual images, she becomes complicit in her own victimization to the point of almost accepting death as the price of her disobedience. Carter thus pursues and radicalizes the argument made by John Berger in *Ways of Seeing* (1972), his popular study of the representation of women in European painting. Berger shows how "according to usage and conventions which are at last being questioned but have by no means been overcome . . . *men act* and *women appear*. Men look at women. Women watch themselves being looked at. This determined not only most relations between men and women but also the relation of women to themselves."[25] Establishing a connection between the economic dependency of women over men and pictorial conventions, Berger argues that in European art from the Renaissance onward, women have been depicted as being "aware of being seen by a [male] spectator,"[26] adding that paintings of female nudes reflect the woman's submission to "the owner of both woman and painting"[27] so that "almost all post-Renaissance European imagery is frontal . . . because the sexual protagonist is the spectator-owner looking at it."[28] This argument anticipates the work of feminist critics who would protest against the predominance of visual modes that reify the feminine. Although "The Bloody Chamber" associates vision with the Bluebeard figure and thus with masculine domination and oppression, it also suggests that the structure of representation analyzed by Berger becomes more complex when we move from visual to verbal art.[29]

Written during the heated debate on pornography that polarized Anglo-American feminists in the late 1970s, Carter's activation of the latent sexual content of the Bluebeard tale allows her to investigate the dominant representational modes at work in European culture. Challenging the conventional distinction between high art and mass culture, Carter defines "eroticism" as "the pornography of the elite" (*Sadeian Woman*, 17).[30] By playing with the conventions of pornographic address, in "The Bloody Chamber" Carter uncovers the structure of representation underlying male erotic iconography of women and explores its effects on female subjectivity. The connection established between sexual imagery and masculine violence serves to demonstrate the cultural foundation for the sadomasochistic scenario that the perverse Marquis imposes on his young bride. In this sense the revelation of Bluebeard's secret dramatizes the impact of visual culture on gender relations by following its implications to their logical and deathly extremes.

The main changes introduced by Carter as part of her adaptation—namely, the choice of a heroine-narrator who documents the masculine bias of visual art and the presence of two helper figures, the blind piano tuner Jean-Yves and the avenging mother—confirm the need to move attention away from the alienating effects of visual conventions, shaped as they are by the male gaze, as part of a strategy of female empowerment. On a first reading the story even seems to set up an opposition between visual and literary representation, insofar as the Marquis's despotic rule of vision is exposed by the female narrator and overthrown by her heroic mother. But the narrative process in fact complicates this opposition by dramatizing the interdependency of text and image. In a typically postmodern fashion "The Bloody Chamber" denaturalizes the borders between text and image by mixing, parodying, and subverting their conventions, codes, and modes of address.[31] It provides ample evidence of patriarchal visual traditions but also shows that the male gaze can be mirrored back in a different medium and mode to undo the Marquis's despotic rule over women.

"The Bloody Chamber" and Decadent Art: Rops and the Voyeuristic Scenario

Sensuality is touch;

eroticism is look.

Skin versus regard.

—ANGELA CARTER'S JOURNAL FOR 1977

In "The Bloody Chamber" Bluebeard becomes a wealthy French aristocrat and compulsive art collector driven to murder by his fascination for decadence.[32] Set in a Breton castle, the story is transposed to a fin de siècle environment and frame of reference. Carter's refined, perverse, and world-weary Marquis highlights the link between the aesthetic sensibility characteristic of the decadent movement and the violence done to women. By situating her story at the turn of the twentieth century, Carter also indirectly comments on her own cultural context at the moment of writing. In "Fin de Siècle," an article written shortly after her return from Japan, Carter registers her sense of shock and dismay at the changes that had taken place during her absence. She describes London in the early 1970s as a "monstrous harlot" (154) bathed in a decadent atmosphere reminiscent of the fin de siècle: "It looks like the *fin* has come a little early this *siècle*" (153). Carter identifies the signs of a conservative backlash that marks the end of the utopian spirit of the preceding decade in the nostalgic return to the musical styles of the 1950s and repressive dress codes for women, part Victorian, part fetishistic. More important, she is struck by the atmosphere of anger and conflict that manifests itself in a "class war" as well as a "sex war" (155). In "The Bloody Chamber" Carter thus suggests parallels between three fins de siècle that shared concerns about class and gender: the early decadence that Carter diagnoses in the 1970s, the fin de siècle atmosphere in which her story is set, and Perrault's "La Barbe bleue" (1697), itself marked by the decline of Louis XIV's reign. But she also revisits the past with a vengeance, using satire, parody, and pastiche as her main weapons, and she contradicts Perrault's reassuring moral about male violence being a thing of the past.

Carter's anchoring of "The Bloody Chamber" in a specific social, cultural, and historical setting suggests that the fantasy world of the Bluebeard tale is not as divorced from reality as we may think. Far from being safely located in an imaginary past, Bluebeard's sordid murders serve to illuminate the darkest and more disturbing aspects of symbolist and decadent art. As she transposes Bluebeard in fin de siècle culture, Carter articulates an incisive—if double-edged—critique of its misogynist bias. In the course of the story she traces the cultural bases and major aesthetic principles of this movement and reflects on its implications for women by critically engaging with some of its visual productions.

Carter's examination of the sexual politics of Decadentism anticipates feminist critiques like Elaine Showalter's, who observes in *Daughters of Decadence* that the figures associated with the fin de siècle are mostly men, although their subject matter was often women.[33] Because Carter shares Showalter's concern with the suppression of women in literary history, she imaginatively recovers the female side of the story in "The Bloody Chamber" by having the story narrated by the young bride, who survived to tell the tale. The adoption of first-person narrator shifts the focus from the Bluebeard figure to the psychological, moral, and intellectual development of the female protagonist as she explores "the unguessable country of marriage" (*Bloody Chamber*, 7). The story thus offers a woman's point of view on the related issues of gender, power, sexuality, vision, and decadent aesthetics.

Showalter notes that "decadent artists like Huysmans and Baudelaire were notoriously contemptuous of women," and she quotes the French critic Jean Pierrot, according to whom antifeminism was "widespread in artistic and literary circles during the decadent era." Specifically, "women are seen as bound to Nature and the material world because they are more physical than men, more body than spirit. They appear as objects of value only when they are aestheticized as corpses or phallicised as *femmes fatales*."[34] In "The Bloody Chamber" Carter also thematizes the transformation of Bluebeard's wives into masculine fantasies, sex objects, and ultimately into "exquisite corpse[s]" (*Bloody Chamber*, 39). Her feminist standpoint is perceptible in the treatment of decadent painting, the misogynist implications of which are both spelled out and neutralized in the shift from image to writing. The bride is confronted with the sexual politics of Decadentism through her husband's morbid reduction of sex and life to an imitation of pictorial art. For the Marquis desire is inseparable from visual representation, and a key to his obsession lies in his collection of erotic art and illustrated pornographic books. He even exhibits the portraits of his previous wives by fin de siècle artists in his portrait gallery. Symbolist and decadent painting is seen as a form of symbolic killing of women into art, which foreshadows their murder and gruesome display in the bloody chamber. By linking the Marquis's murders with the imaginative portrayal of women in the realm of the aesthetic, Carter's story establishes connections between modes of representation and social forms of power and domination. When the bride realizes that her husband has framed her (in more senses than one), she calls her mother to the rescue. The mother saves her life, but not without the help of a blind piano tuner, who sets up a music school with the surviving bride at the end. Even though the unexpected intervention of the mother gives a feminist twist to the Bluebeard plot, the blind piano tuner symbolizes to an almost parodic degree the need to move away from the tyranny of the male gaze.

In a more complex and subtle way the act of narrating her own story enables the bride to explore the relation between word and image and to reflect critically on her apprenticeship to the male point of view. In Carter's version the bride not only survives her monstrous husband but also goes on to tell her version of the story, so that her role shifts from passive object of the Marquis's sadistic fantasies to active, (self-)critical, and creative subject of her own tale. Whereas the Marquis systematically seeks to repress female individuality by reducing his wives to stereotypical images, the young woman reaffirms the power of naming (when she identifies him as Bluebeard) and writing as an assertion of self. The bride's confession shows that she has learned from her experience and that she is able to identify the dangers of the aesthetic sensibility as a negation of female realities. But she also realizes that gender relations, and even the most apparently "natural" aspects of human experience such as sexuality, are culturally determined. Decadent conceptions of nature as artifice, self as performance, and sexuality as mise-en-scène contribute to this new understanding.

The bride appropriates narrative and visual power not only by retelling the story from her own point of view but also by reflecting on her visual education and on the role of vision as an instrument of female oppression in the sadomasochistic relations imposed by the Marquis. She describes how she became gradually aware of the alienating effects of female objectification in the visual arts. She achieves this by subjecting several icons of decadent visual culture to critical scrutiny. There are four key moments when the central characters are associated with visual art. The bride first willingly embodies the child prostitute of a Félicien Rops etching, and her subsequent deflowering is inspired by pornographic illustrations. However, the Marquis's plan to make her enact the martyrdom of Saint Cecilia, foreshadowed in a painting he offers her as his wedding gift, is eventually foiled. Significantly, the climactic scene of the Marquis's demise, which marks a turning point in the development of the plot by reversing the traditional roles of female victim and male victimizer, is set up by the Marquis in visual terms as well. Thanks to her mother's intervention, the bride ceases to be the passive object of male eroticized violence. Her liberation from her husband's influence is reflected not only in the plot development but also in the narrative shift from an uncritical adoption of his set of cultural references to a re-presentation of the scene that freezes the dramatic action as a "clockwork tableau of Bluebeard" (*Bloody Chamber*, 40).

The plotting of the Bluebeard tale as a version of decadent misogyny raises the possibility of female emancipation from decadent images of evil temptresses, perverse nymphomaniacs, doomed prostitutes, and eroticized female martyrs. Carter's treatment of traditional material can be seen as dramatizing the idea of literary creation as a dynamic and transformative process that challenges traditional gender roles as they are encoded in fixed images and thus allows for positive and emancipatory change instead of mere (deadening) repetition.

During the courtship the girl is seduced by the Marquis's immense wealth, aristocratic rank and social status, worldliness and sexual experience, and refined tastes and sophistication, but she is also fascinated by the enigmatic power of his eye. She observes that in his still, masklike face, the eyes "always disturbed me by their absolute absence of light" (*Bloody Chamber*, 9). When he takes her to the opera, she "[sees] him watching [her] in the gilded mirrors with the assessing eye of a connoisseur inspecting horseflesh" (11). For the first time she acknowledges the action of his "carnal avarice," "strangely magnified by the monocle lodged in his left eye" (11). She adds: "When I saw him look at me with lust, I dropped my eyes but, in glancing away from him, I caught sight of myself in the mirror. And I saw myself as he saw me. . . . And, for the first time in my innocent and confined life, I sensed in myself a potentiality for corruption that took my breath away" (*Bloody Chamber*, 11). This first complex interaction of looks, mediated by the mirror, establishes the basis for their relationship.

The Marquis's gaze carries with it the power of action and possession as it sexualizes and objectifies his fiancée. Although the girl recognizes the dehumanizing effects of her suitor's look (which reduces her to "horseflesh"), she responds to it by identifying herself with his fantasy and internalizing his point of view.

After the wedding the Marquis and his young wife leave Paris for his Breton castle. When they arrive, the Marquis takes his bride on a tour of the castle and first brings her to the nuptial bedroom. It is furnished, the bride later writes, with a "grand, hereditary matrimonial bed" surrounded by mirrors "on all the walls, in stately frames of contorted gold, that reflected more white lilies than I'd ever seen in my life before" (*Bloody Chamber*, 14), lilies that suggest a comparison with "an embalming parlour" (18). Like the decadent figures he strives to imitate, the Marquis is bent on exploring extreme forms of sexual pleasure heightened by theatrical settings and sophisticated, morbid mises-en-scène.

The motif of the mirrors, in particular, links the gilded mirrors of Perrault's literary tale with the opening scene of Joris-Karl Huysmans's *A rebours* (1891).[35] The emphasis placed on the undressing of the bride exploits the sexual subtext of the Bluebeard story but more specifically connects it with decadent pornographic art. The husband "slowly, methodically, teasingly" undresses his docile and passive 17-year-old bride, in "a formal disrobing," which she associates with "a ritual from the brothel" (*Bloody Chamber*, 15).

> He stripped me, gourmand that he was, as if he were stripping the leaves off an artichoke—but do not imagine much finesse about it. . . . He approached his familiar treat with a weary appetite. And when nothing but my scarlet, palpitating core remained, I saw, in the mirror, the living image of an etching by Rops from the collection he had shown me when our engagement permitted us to be alone together . . . the child with her sticklike limbs, naked but for her button boots, her gloves, shielding her face with her hand as though her face were the last repository of her modesty; and the old, monocled lecher who examined her, limb by limb. He in his London tailoring; she, bare as a lamb chop. Most pornographic of all confrontations. And so my purchaser unwrapped his bargain. And, as at the opera, when I had first seen my flesh in his eyes, I was aghast to feel myself stirring.

At once he closed my legs like a book and I saw again the rare movement of his lips that meant he smiled. (*Bloody Chamber*, 15)

Explicitly associated by the narrator with the scene at the opera, the undressing illustrates the next stage in the Marquis's gradual transformation of his young bride into an object to be consumed sexually and commodified but also ultimately devoured and destroyed. This is confirmed by the presence of similar visual motifs (the "mirror," the "monocled lecher"), food imagery ("artichoke," "lamb chop," "unwrapp[ing]") and the financial transaction that marriage becomes without love ("bargain"). As the use of dehumanizing similes suggests, the erotic encounter between the experienced and predatory Marquis, for whom flesh is only meat, and his virgin wife foreshadows the death that is planned for her. Dandyism affirms the primacy of aesthetic values over the social, human, and moral order. Carter's Marquis is a coldhearted, manipulative, blasé, and cynical aesthete.

Identifying women with nature (and as such "abominable," to quote Baudelaire) and nature as abhorrent, the Marquis considers his latest wife in terms of the Goncourt brothers' claim that "everything that is not transformed by art is, for us, like raw meat."[36] But Carter's own reflections on flesh as meat are quite different, because for her the transformation results from existing power relations, as she argues in *The Sadeian Woman*; it is the system of "social dominance" that gives the consumer of pornography "the opportunity to purchase the flesh of other people as if it were meat" (14).

When she sees herself in the mirror, the bride realizes that her undressing is staged as a *tableau vivant*, although she is still ignorant of the fact that her husband's real intentions are to turn her into a *nature morte*. For the Marquis the scene derives its erotic force from being modeled on a pornographic etching from his collection, which the gap in the text (the suspension points) invites the reader to fill. The scene that the bride is made to enact as its "living image" is in fact based on an etching titled *Ma fille, Monsieur Cabanel!* by the decadent artist Félicien Rops, whose work Huysmans enthusiastically described in *Certains* (1889) (Figure 3.5).[37] The description of the girl's thin and naked body, her helpless gesture of shame, down to the details of the button boots and the gloves, evokes Rops's picture and suggests that the bride is being transformed into art.

Significantly, however, the grotesque and sinister figure of the mother/madam presenting her barely nubile daughter to the amateur of young flesh

Figure 3.5. "*Ma fille, Monsieur Cabanel!*" an etching by Félicien Rops, c. 1905.

in the etching (see Figure 3.5) is absent from the scene or, more exactly, replaced by the "old, monocled lecher . . . in his London tailoring" (*Bloody Chamber*, 15). Rops's nude constructs the spectator as a male voyeur cast in the role of the client of the child prostitute. By contrast, the reader of Carter's story identifies with the bride, who depicts the alienating effects of the male gaze on her sense of self. The voyeuristic scenario is even destabilized further by the absence of the complicit mother at this point.

The old woman of Rops's etching has, as it were, stepped outside the frame of the picture as the scene is reenacted, only to reappear in a radically different role at the end of the story. Instead of being the immoral accomplice of male abuse, ready to procure her own child for the pedophile client, the mother comes to her daughter's help in "The Bloody Chamber." Standing in for the brothers of the bride in Perrault's tale, the loving and courageous mother of Carter's tale heroically rescues her daughter as she is about to be beheaded, saving her life in the nick of time and shooting the Marquis. This unexpected (and humorously treated) twist in the patriarchal scenario so baffles the Marquis that he "stood transfixed, utterly dazed, at a loss. . . . The puppet master, open-mouthed, wide-eyed, impotent at last, saw his dolls break free of their strings, abandon the rituals he had ordained for them since time began and start to live for themselves" (*Bloody Chamber*, 39).

By surrounding himself with works of art that adopt a transgressive, sadomasochistic aesthetic amply illustrated by Rops, the Marquis is in fact conditioning the bride to accept the terms of a relationship based on the classic scenario of domination, violence, and death that he compulsively enacts with his successive wives. Without denying the complex nature of female desire (the bride recognizes the erotic appeal of such role playing), Carter draws attention to the cultural dimension of sex and highlights the problematic exploitation of the female body characteristic of much fin de siècle visual art. More important, the change that she introduces in the reenacted brothel scene, in the form of a reversal of gender roles, subverts the "iconography of sexual oppression" ("Fin de Siècle," 156) from within to suggest the possibility of positive change for women. Likewise, the unexpected intervention of the mother at the end dramatizes the idea of literary creation as a dynamic process that challenges prescribed gender roles and relations as they are encoded in fixed images and cultural scripts.

Uncovering the Pornography of the Elite, or High Art's Education into Submission

(eroticism, the pornography of the elite)

—ANGELA CARTER, *THE SADEIAN WOMAN*, 17

The bride's sexual initiation is deferred until after her visit to the Marquis's library. This symbolically significant space, where images and texts collaborate to define gender roles, prepares her for becoming the Marquis's sexual possession. In the library she is made to play another role that he has devised for her, also based on pornographic illustrations. There the bride admires the Marquis's collection of rare and richly bound volumes. As she observes, these books "seemed the source of his habitual odour of Russian leather" (*Bloody Chamber*, 16). The masterpiece of the collection, a luxury edition of Huysmans's *Là-bas*, is displayed center stage: "Row upon row of calf-bound volumes, brown and olive, with gilt lettering on their spines, the octavo in brilliant scarlet morocco.... A lectern, carved like a spread eagle, that held open upon it an edition of Huysmans's *Là-bas*, from some over-exquisite private press; it had been bound like a missal, in brass, with gems of coloured glass" (*Bloody Chamber*, 16). The bride's detailed description of the books focuses on the rich colors of their leather covers and elaborate bindings. She admires their formal beauty as artifacts, and even the sensual appeal of the smell of leather is reminiscent of the Marquis, but she does not seem to be aware that the open volume on the lectern provides a central clue to her husband's true identity, which is inseparable from the books he reads. The shape of the lectern, "carved like a spread eagle," displays an open copy of Huysmans's novel, an image that both parallels and contrasts with the open legs of the aroused bride in the previous scene, a scene in which the Marquis had nevertheless closed the legs "like a book," marking his preference for art over life and his negation of female sexual desire. Although less famous as a decadent manifesto than *A rebours* (1884), *Là-bas* explicitly links Bluebeard to Decadentism, as it relates to Durtal's research on Gilles de Rais, a historical figure associated with Bluebeard in the French tradition.[38]

Impatiently waiting for the wedding night now that her sexual curiosity has been aroused, the bride does not stop to read from Huysmans's novel. She glances at a few titles from "a glass-fronted case" but soon gets bored: "I squinted at a title or two: *The Initiation*, *The Key of Mysteries*, *The Secret of Pandora's Box*, and yawned. Nothing, here, to detain a seventeen-year-old girl waiting for her first embrace" (*Bloody Chamber*, 16). The uncurious bride literally overlooks books that all point to the Bluebeard subtext and testify to a revival of interest in occultism and mysticism at the fin de siècle, including Eliphas Levi's works on occultism, alchemy, and magic, such as the modern-day *grimoire* titled *La clef des grands mystères* (1861). The reference to *The Secret of Pandora's Box* also draws attention to the cultural myth of the femme fatale as a projection of male fears and desires. More important, the bride leaves *Là-bas* unread; only a "slim volume with no title at all on the spine" retains her attention. This turns out to be an eighteenth-century libertine book titled *The Adventures of Eulalie at the Harem of the Grand Turk*, complete with pornographic illustrations.[39] As she leafs through the volume, the young bride is shocked by a picture that depicts a flagellation scene and links sex and murder.

> When he showed me the Rops, newly bought, dearly prized, had he not hinted that he was a connoisseur of such things? Yet I had not bargained for this, the girl with tears hanging on her cheeks like stuck pearls, her cunt a split fig below the great globes of her buttocks on which the knotted tails of the cat were about to descend, while a man in a black mask fingered with his free hand his prick, that curved upwards like the scimitar he held. (*Bloody Chamber*, 16–17)

The pornographic picture, which the bride associates with the Rops etching, marks a new development in the representation of sexual domination, as it provides explicit, graphic evidence of the link between visual art and eroticized masculine violence. The description of the picture, introduced by a reference to Rops that deliberately blurs the conventional distinction between erotic art and pornography, is also framed by textual echoes ("connoisseur," "bargained") of the opera scene and the episode of the disrobing. The flagellation scene itself presents obvious similarities with the sadomasochistic relationship that the Marquis seeks to establish with his wife. While the figlike sex of the naked girl is reminiscent of the core of the artichoke image used by the bride in the previous scene, the masked man with the whip parallels the Sadeian Marquis whose masklike face so troubles the bride.

The picture's caption, "Reproof of curiosity," makes the connection with the Bluebeard tale and shifts the focus from male violence to female guilt. The Marquis surprises his wife as she is looking at another illustration, "Immolation of the wives of the Sultan," which repeats the scenario on a larger scale. He is delighted to see a young virgin take an interest in what he ironically calls his "prayerbooks" (*Bloody Chamber*, 17) and is aroused by the erotic potential of the scene. Catching his bride in the act of looking at transgressive material that foreshadows her own fate (decapitation) as the price of her curiosity, the Marquis seizes this opportunity to "punish" her and brutally "impale[s]" her in broad daylight: "All the better to see [her]," he says (17).

By acting out his sadistic sexual fantasies, the voyeuristic Marquis reaches a further stage in the subjugation of his wife to sexual violence. His desire is once again stimulated by the act of seeing, but it is interesting to note that he uses fairy-tale language and Baudelaire's poetry to make his bride submit to male abuse. At the moment of deflowering, the Marquis quotes a few lines from "Les Bijoux" (one of the *pièces condamnées* from Baudelaire's famous collection *Les fleurs du mal*, published in 1857): "Rapt, he intoned: "Of her apparel she retains / Only her sonorous jewellery" (*Bloody Chamber*, 17). The bride is made to embody the woman described in this erotic poem, her nakedness set off by the jewels of the title; however, the intertextual reference to "Little Red Riding Hood" that immediately precedes it shifts attention from the erotic and aesthetic dimension of the scene to its brutal and sexist aspects by framing it as an encounter between a wolflike predator and his young and helpless victim.[40] The quotation from Baudelaire, who was heralded as a forerunner of Decadentism by Bourget and Huysmans among others, serves to introduce the intersemiotic network (Rops, Moreau, Redon, Puvis de Chavannes, and the Flemish Primitives) created as the story unfolds and further contributes to situating Carter's narrative within the decadent or symbolist movement as a primary source of ideas, motifs, and references.

The bride's exploration of the Marquis's castle as a mirror of his fantasy world then takes her to his portrait gallery. Her sexual initiation has in fact fanned her curiosity and her desire to learn more about her husband. Before the Marquis's immediate and unexpected departure for New York, allegedly for business matters, he gives her the famous bunch of keys and encourages her to use them freely (except of course the one that gives access to the bloody chamber). The Marquis singles out "the key to the picture gallery, a treasure house filled by five centuries of avid collectors—ah! he *foresaw* I would spend hours there" (*Bloody Chamber*, 20; italics mine). The paintings displayed in the picture gallery provide further clues to the enigmatic personality of the Marquis. His passion for collecting decadent art is a key to a fuller understanding of his scopophilia and misogyny. As Showalter notes, "Fin-de-siècle misogyny was most dramatically and vividly apparent in painting. There images of female narcissism, of the femme fatale and the sphinx, of women kissing their mirror images, gazing at themselves in circular baths, or engaging in autoerotic play mutate by the end of the century into savagely 'gynecidal' visions of female sexuality."[41] For the Marquis, women have a decorative function, and their attraction lies in their ability to embody decadent perceptions of woman's alleged nature. The portrait of the Marquis's first wife is by Gustave Moreau, and his second wife was a fashionable model for Odilon Redon and Puvis de Chavannes, described as follows:

> Her face is common property: everyone painted her but the Redon engraving I liked best, *The Evening Star Walking on the Rim of Night*. To see her skeletal, enigmatic grace, you would never think she had been a barmaid in a café in Montmartre until Puvis de Chavannes saw her and had her expose her flat breasts and elongated thighs to his brush. And yet it was the absinthe doomed her, or so they said. (*Bloody Chamber*, 10)[42]

The description shows the process of sublimation and symbolization at work in decadent painting, which evacuates the actual conditions of the female models; their sufferings are aestheticized to represent the morbid decadent ideal of femininity—skeletal, enigmatic, and frail and marked by decay, disease, and death.

In fin de siècle painting women are objects of both attraction and repulsion, at once sublime in the idealization of the work of art and abject in their physical reality. In Carter's story the Marquis first murders his wives symbolically as he exhibits their portraits in the art gallery. But he completes the transformation process and pushes it to its logical if shocking extreme by literally putting them to death in a macabre mise-en-scène in the bloody chamber. The Marquis tells the bride "with a glint of greed" that he has "amply indulged his taste for the Symbolists" (*Bloody Chamber*, 20), including Moreau's great portrait of his [the Marquis's] first wife, the famous *Sacrificial Victim* with the imprint of the lacelike chains on her pellucid skin: "Did I know the story of the painting of that picture? How, when she took off her clothes for him the first time, she fresh from her bar in Montmartre, she had robed herself involuntarily in a blush that reddened her breasts, her shoulders, her arms, her whole body? He had thought of that story, of that dear girl, when first he had undressed me" (*Bloody Chamber*, 20).[43]

These paintings contribute to the visual education of the bride narrator. She first internalizes the tendency to reify women as mere art objects, but she will eventually escape the last role that the Marquis has prepared for her. Ever since the beginning of the story, the Marquis has sought to condition her to identify with a painting. As she recounts the courtship, the young bride prides herself on having caught the Marquis's attention, but she cannot quite understand what attracts him to her. At once flattered and anxious, she notes, "Married three times within my own brief lifetime to three different graces, now, as if to demonstrate the eclecticism of his taste, he had invited me to join this gallery of beautiful women" (*Bloody Chamber*, 10). The bride's choice of vocabulary ("demonstrate," "eclecticism of his taste," "gallery of beautiful women") immediately draws attention to the Marquis's collector spirit by associating his previous wives with art objects. Only later will she realize the dangers and implications of such assimilation.

During the courtship the Marquis showers his bride with gifts, which, as the material girl readily admits, "conspired to seduce [her] utterly" (*Bloody Chamber*, 12). One of them is "an early Flemish primitive of Saint Cecilia" (14), the patron saint of musicians, seemingly in homage to the bride's musical gifts.[44] When the bride is brought to the Marquis's castle, she discovers her wedding present in the "turret suite," which has been prepared for her. She readily identifies with Saint Cecilia but ironically misinterprets the gift of the painting as a sign of her husband's "loving sensitivity" (14). Only after the visit to the bloody chamber, however, does she realize that the gift foreshadows her own martyrdom: "My music room seemed the safest place, although I looked at the picture of Saint Cecilia with a faint dread; what had been the nature of her martyrdom?" (30). This assimilation is echoed by the Marquis, who, impatiently waiting for the bride to come down for the beheading, calls, "Shall I come up to heaven to fetch you down, Saint Cecilia?" (38). The Marquis thus reduces his wives to cultural icons, but the surviving bride is able to reflect on the destructive power that these icons may have as they are transmitted in the continuum of patriarchal myths which condition gender roles and relations.

The decadents highly valued painting and primitive art in particular. Huysmans's *Là-bas* begins with a detailed description of the altarpiece of Issenheim by Grünewald, which concludes with a celebration of primitive art as the realization of decadent ideals. In *A rebours* des Esseintes describes at length Moreau's *Salomé* as a monstrous deity. There follows a description of *L'apparition* by the same painter, where Salomé carries the severed head of John the Baptist. Carter is therefore like many decadent authors in including references to and descriptions of paintings and etchings in her story. Whereas the late-nineteenth-century authors celebrated an intense collaboration between the visual arts and the verbal arts, Carter suggests, however, that the visual regime is often used in the exercise of gendered power relations. Unlike the decadents, she questions the priority traditionally given to sight and criticizes the tyrannical power of images. Carter's reworking of the Bluebeard tale through the prism of Decadentism thus enables her to examine critically the pictorial and literary treatment of women in decadent art and suggests that literature can become a tool for emancipation. "The Bloody Chamber" challenges the patriarchal myths incarnated by the Marquis, whose death opens up new hopes for change.

Out of the Bloody Chamber: The Demythologizing Business of Fiction

Fine art, that exists for itself alone, is art in a final state of impotence.

—ANGELA CARTER, *THE SADEIAN WOMAN*, 13

The bride's visual education is completed when she acts out the role of the curious and disobedient wife and opens the door of the forbidden room. She is at first an eager apprentice and willing participant in the Marquis's power games and erotic fantasies, and the circumstances of her deflowering have been staged by the Marquis as a rehearsal for the role that she is supposed to play in the final scene. Her visit to the bloody chamber, however, gives her the final key to interpret her situation and understand the consequences of such role playing. There she realizes the full implications of her husband's invitation to join his "gallery of beautiful women" (*Bloody Chamber*, 10). The Marquis not only exhibits the portraits of his wives in the gallery of his castle but also keeps their bodies on display in a ghastly mise-en-scène. As she visits this "little museum of his perversity" (18), the bride comes to a full understanding of her husband's morbid taste for "exquisite corpse[s]" (39) turned into aesthetic objects: "Each time I struck a match to light the candles round her bed [where the embalmed corpse of a strangled wife lies], it seemed a garment of that innocence of mine for which he had lusted fell away from me" (28). For the perverse husband his bride's innocence is indeed the main source of her appeal; it enables him to shape her education and have her accept the power relations on which it is premised unquestioningly. Even though the bride admits her involvement in the sadomasochistic script laid out for her, she at long last distances herself from the appeal of the aesthetics of cruelty and the doctrine of art for art's sake dissociated from human concerns.

The revelation of the Marquis's murders provides a bitter commentary on the moral implications and sexual politics of decadent visual culture. Ironically, however, the Marquis's obsession with turning life into art will also be the cause of his undoing. From the Marquis the bride learns to interpret her experience as a version of the Bluebeard story, which enables her to demystify his power over her. On the level of the plot, as we have seen, the heroine's liberation from the perverse domination of her husband is made possible by the joint intervention of the blind piano tuner and her own mother. But as she narrates the scene of the Marquis's demise, the bride self-consciously uses the prewritten script of Bluebeard for her own ends, just as her mother appropriates the power of the gaze to suspend movement and arrest life by literally paralyzing the Marquis. Identified as a Bluebeard figure, the criminal husband is reduced to a stilled visual image and thus inevitably to death: "And my husband stood stock-still, as if she [the bride's mother] had been Medusa, the sword still raised over his head as in those clockwork tableaux of Bluebeard that you see in glass cases at fairs" (*Bloody Chamber*, 40).[45] The Marquis becomes a work of visual art in his turn, and it is this that kills him. As she describes the effects of her mother's intervention, the bride also reclaims the motif of the murderous look (Medusa) present in decadent culture to stress its liberating power when it is appropriated by women.[46] But the shift from classical mythology to the fairy-tale world and fairs suggests a move away from the misogynist exploitation of the classics in high bourgeois art (as Carter herself called it) to the emancipatory potential of popular culture.

Although the Marquis's serial crimes reveal the dangers of mere imitation and repetition (captured in the image of the mechanical Bluebeard), the bride subverts them from within as she introduces difference and ironic distance to prevent the perpetuation of patriarchal myths. The story of Bluebeard, then, serves different purposes depending on the perspective from which it is re-presented. For the Marquis it serves to confirm negative views of female curiosity and to justify its punishment. From the point of view of the surviving bride, however, the denouement of the tale is the main focus of interest, insofar as it puts an end to Bluebeard's deathly domination over women. This suggests that traditional tales cease to be carriers of a patriarchal ideology when they are reinterpreted against the grain of dominant readings. The act of rewriting thus reveals the emancipatory potential of old stories and images, which can be used to perpetuate conservative myths and values but which also provide the practical and intellectual means to subvert and escape them.

Carter's treatment of the structure of representation theorized by such feminist critics as Laura Mulvey is, however, fundamentally ambiguous. Although the story of "The Bloody Chamber" lends itself to a feminist reading as an allegory of the murderous effects of the male gaze and a critique of the misogynist implications of visual culture and decadent art, its generic affiliations, narrative mode, and writing style complicate its significance. The framing of the story as a version of the Bluebeard tale parodies the classic scenario of female victimization, with its strongly polarized representation of gender roles and thematic oppositions (male/female, dominant/submissive, active/passive, culture/nature), complete with a politically correct denouement where good triumphs over evil.

The choice of a female point of view and narrative voice, while supporting the idea of a feminist revisionist perspective on traditional material, nevertheless problematizes the model proposed by Berger and Mulvey insofar as the bride's narrative, far from adopting a fixed viewing position, shifts and multiplies them. Not only is the bride both subject and object of her own story, but as she demonstrates in the various scenes analyzed, she can be a critical and ironic spectator of herself, see herself through the Marquis's eyes, but also sympathetically identify with the girl in the Rops etching or the crying victim in the flagellation scene. The narrator's deliberate use of a sensual, rich, ornate, baroque, self-conscious, and intensely visual style, the move away from the constraints of realism, the experimental combination of genres, the elaborate descriptions of art works and paintings, the dense intertextuality, arcane references, and hidden allusions, and the open exploration of transgressive sexuality—all testify to the influence of decadent motifs and strategies on "The Bloody Chamber."

Carter's story can thus be read as engaging in a critical dialogue with fin de siècle art, which the bride reappropriates and transforms to underline its problematic aspects and its creative potential. The rewriting process reflects Carter's deconstruction of the patriarchal myths and sexist biases prevalent in turn-of-the-century culture and her questioning of the doctrine of art for art's sake. The aesthetic sensibility gives way to a reflection on the power of images as a means for social and cultural conditioning. "The Bloody Chamber," however, is no place for easy certainties; it calls into question the primacy of vision and stresses the potentially destructive effects of visual culture on women while refusing to align itself with feminist pieties and rigid theories berating the so-called pornography of representation.

In "Notes from the Front Line" Carter presents her work as a critique of "mythologies" that carry conservative values and legitimize patriarchal interests and to which she implicitly opposes folklore. "The Bloody Chamber" challenges the patriarchal myths incarnated in the Bluebeard figure and in turn projected onto Perrault's text. But Carter also recuperates the emancipatory aspects of the tale and even its utopian ending, because Bluebeard's death opens up hopes for greater justice and equality. Carter thus borrows from Perrault the idea of the tale as a carrier of a useful moral that is not simply given but must be discovered in the text by the curious reader (with the help of textual clues). Unsurprisingly, the key is to be found in the shifting meanings of the word *cabinet* itself. Readers must enter the tale, which contains useful knowledge provided that they read it closely enough. In *The Sadeian Woman* Carter defends the idea of art "as a means of *knowing* the world" or else "art is relegated to a kind of rumpus room of the mind" (13). Even though both Perrault and Carter deploy textual strategies that resist critical containment, their cabinets and bloody chambers are no rumpus room.

4

Doing the Somersault of Love

FROM "LE CHAT BOTTÉ" TO "PUSS IN BOOTS"
AND "PUSS-IN-BOOTS"

The Comic Interlude of "Puss in Boots": Capering Along with the Figaro of the Nursery, or the Smiling Cat as Authorial Double

What a joy it is to dance and sing!

—ANGELA CARTER, *WISE CHILDREN*, 232

"Puss in Boots," Angela Carter's translation of Charles Perrault's "Le Maître Chat, ou le Chat botté," is the third tale in *The Fairy Tales of Charles Perrault*, and it brings comic relief after the human drama of "Little Red Riding Hood" and the shuddering suspense of "Bluebeard." The fact that Carter translated and rewrote the tale for *The Bloody Chamber* and for radio shows how much she liked a story that lends itself particularly well to experiments in genre, medium, and style. Flexibility in fact characterizes the tale as much as its feisty animal hero, as a contrapuntal analysis of the translation, short story, and radio play confirms. Taken together, all three versions draw attention to the multicultural make of the tale, as Puss's adventurous travels follow the story's rich history of cultural adaptations. Based as it is on Perrault's text, Carter's translation for children bows to the French fairy-tale tradition, but her radio play rather winks in the direction of "Dick Whittington and His Cat," an English folktale recounting the feats of the cat who makes his master's fortune overseas: "One fine day, curled up in an empty barrel, overcome with fumes, nodded off, next thing I knew, woke up in Genoa—took service as a ship's cat, learned to roll my r's in Marseilles, to caterwaul in Spain" (*Yellow Sands*, 122–23).[1] The radio play exploits the tale's comedic and musical potential, and it pays homage both to the riotous spirit of the commedia dell'arte and the popular English pantomime tradition.

As we move from translation to rewriting, Carter's multilingual Puss takes us not only from France to England but also further back to Italy, where he salutes his predecessors in Straparola's "Costantino Fortunato" in *Piacevole Notti* (1553) and "Cagliuso" in Giambattista Basile's *Lo Cunto de li Cunti*, also known as the *Pentamerone* (1634–1636). In this early version the trickster cat is female, which must have pleased the feminist Carter very much. Materializing the amorous (and productive) encounter between these various traditions, Carter's "Puss-in-Boots" features a male *and* a female cat (and, predictably, their litter of kittens at the end). In other words, the author stresses the promiscuous exchanges between the Italian, English, and French versions of the tale, and she explores its connections with popular theater and opéra bouffe and ultimately with the radical tradition of Enlightenment drama and rococo art. In this sense the worldly-wise and well-traveled cat who makes his master's fortune comes to embody the circulation and adaptation of the tale in its manifold guises throughout Europe and its ramifications with art forms that all toy with extravagance and excess. In his antics Puss himself incarnates the spirit of comic subversion as he turns the world upside down for our amusement and delight.

Carter explains in the preface to *Come unto These Yellow Sands* that the scripts of "The Company of Wolves" and "Puss in Boots" both "started off as short stories" but that "these aren't adaptations as much as reformulations" (10). Her preference for the term *reformulation* calls attention to the aspect of formal experiment in the creative process. Despite Carter's manifest interest in the tale's potential for re-creation in different media, it has attracted surprisingly little critical attention to date.[2] Nonetheless, examining the translation in counterpoint with its prose and dramatic retellings sheds light on Carter's understanding of the tale and on the translation-rewriting dynamic.

These related if distinct projects inflect the story in three main directions. The translation rereads Perrault through folklore as a trickster tale; the short story activates its sexual subtext and subversive edge and enhances its stylistic and visual exuberance; finally, the radio play explores its comic, musical, and even farcical side in the mood of "All the better to kiss me with" (*Yellow Sands*, 146). Based on intrigue, mistaken identities, and fast-paced action and dialogue but also containing an element of romance introduced by Perrault, the tale ends happily with a royal wedding, and the cat is rewarded by becoming a "great lord" who "gave up hunting mice, except for pleasure" (*Fairy Tales*, 53). In Carter's hands "Puss in Boots" is made to celebrate the force of desire, delight in the body, and pleasure in language against social rules, hierarchies, and constraints, encapsulated in the smile of the affabulating cat.[3]

Carter's association of the tale with popular culture and street theater (commedia dell'arte and Harlequin plays), which inspired the English pantomime tradition of which Carter was particularly fond, colors her translation and her retellings.[4] Although her translation of Perrault adapts the text for a young audience and introduces a moral that complies with the didactic and moralizing impulse of children's literature, the rewritings release the subversive energy of its sources: the exuberant spirit, irreverent humor, social satire, and sexual candor that the author read between the lines of Perrault's *conte*.

In marked contrast to her translation, Carter's variations on "Puss in Boots" even push the immorality of the tale by staging the murder of an old, miserly, and impotent husband; the reader's sympathy goes to the young wife and her lover and to the feline couple that mastermind the plot and thus become a double of the mischievous author herself. The bawdy tale of revenge on an old, impotent, and avaricious dotard who keeps his pretty wife under lock and key, although immoral in a conventional sense, becomes an occasion for fun, horseplay, sexual comedy, and social comment about forced marriages.[5] Carter's Puss and his female companion Tabs challenge social hierarchies (including the hierarchy of the species, because the cats as plot makers are a lot smarter than their human masters) in this subversive tale where class conflict ends happily with the triumph of an underclass of poor but lusty young men and women and their feline friends. The tale allows Carter to denounce the oppression of women under patriarchy through a comic reworking of the figure of the "princess in a tower" (*Bloody Chamber*, 70), and she makes sure to introduce a female companion for her male cat, Tabs, who plays an active role in the development of the plot. Furthermore, Carter's self-consciously baroque style becomes an occasion to explore a poetics that radically differs from the simple style that she praises in Perrault and emulates in her translation. The tame translation thus gives way to excess in action and language in wild, over-the-top retellings that mimic the tricks, turns, and acrobatics for which Puss, Harlequin, and Figaro are best remembered.

From Radio Play to Prose Reformulation: Commedia dell'Arte and the Somersaults of Love

Perhaps the phrase that best captures the spirit of Carter's variations on "Puss in Boots" is *somersault*, an acrobatic movement that conveys the literal meaning of the *tours de souplesse* in Perrault's text, whereby the Cat hangs upside down, hides in the flour, and plays dead to catch rats and mice: "Il lui avait vu faire tant de tours de souplesse, pour prendre des Rats et des Souris, comme quand il se pendait par les pieds, ou qu'il se cachait dans la farine pour faire le mort" (*Contes*, 157) ("He had however often seen him play a great many cunning tricks to catch rats and mice, as when he used to hang by the heels, or hide himself in the meal, and make as if he were dead," *Histories*, 49).[6] The trick materializes the carnivalesque, "head over heels" world of the tale, but in French *tour de souplesse* also has a figurative meaning as a verbal ploy or manipulation. It is also etymologically related to the word *trope* (turn), which hints at linguistic creativity and rhetorical power that the Cat also resorts to in order to persuade, frighten, manipulate, seduce, and charm his victims. The physical, intellectual, and linguistic qualities incarnated by the Cat are conveyed in the baroque and ornate style of the short story and in the twists and turns of the plot and fast-paced action of the radio play.

The fact that Carter translates Perrault's *tours de souplesse* as "cunning tricks" (*Fairy Tales*, 46) in "Puss in Boots" even echoes her introduction to *Come unto These Yellow Sands*, where she explains that adapting the tale for radio was for her an occasion to "explore all kinds of rhetorical devices and linguistic tricks" (8). This captures her interest in the interplay of sound and sense as well as visual comedy. Radio is paradoxically the most visual of media because it relies on the listener's visual imagination: "Radio always leaves that magical and enigmatic margin, that space of the invisible, which must be filled in by the imagination of the listener" (*Yellow Sands*, 7).

Puss is indeed the master trickster in that he is both quick-witted and physically agile (which, of course, is quite appropriate for a tale about social mobility); not only does he convince all the human characters he meets on the way to do as he pleases, but he also moves quickly, racing in front of the coach to secure possessions for his master. He even climbs on the roof of the castle in a jiffy when its owner, an ogre, turns into a frightening lion. As Perrault humorously notes, this is no mean feat for a booted cat: "Le Chat fut si effrayé de voir un Lion devant lui, qu'il gagna aussitôt les gouttières, non sans peine et sans péril, à cause de ses bottes qui ne valaient rien pour marcher sur les tuiles" (*Contes*, 160) ("Puss was so sadly terrified at the sight of a lion so near him, that he immediately got into the gutter, not without abundance of trouble and danger, because of his boots, which were of no use at all to him in walking upon the tiles," *Histories*, 54–55). This comic vignette is taken up by Carter, who makes a lot of the Cat's boots as well as his up-and-down movements. When Puss climbs up the wall of the miser's house to join his beloved Tabs in the young lady's bedroom, he is discovered by the old duenna who keeps an eye on her. But he escapes by jumping out the window and performs a triple somersault as he falls three stories down to the ground. The admiring Tabs exclaims as she watches the athletic feat, "He's DONE IT! THE TRIPLE SOMERSAULT!" (*Yellow Sands*, 141). Likewise, the penniless young man and unhappily married young woman *fall* in love, like the cats, but with grace and in style, when they perform "the triple somersault of love" (152), to use the euphemism for their enthusiastic up-and-down lovemaking. By contrast, the demise (or downfall) of the old and stiff-jointed husband is brought about when he slips on Tabs and falls down the stairs ("Our good man's taken a sorry tumble!" 153). Lacking the graceful agility of the young lovers and their cats, he conveniently breaks his neck, ushering in the happy ending.

In Carter's reformulations Puss retains his animal form as a ginger tomcat ("Felis domesticus by genus," as he introduces himself grandiosely in Latin on page 119 of the radio play), because, as Carter observes, his animal disguise is essential for the role. "Perrault's great hero," as she calls him, comes to embody the comic side of the irreverent and anarchic spirit that she admired, but in style. In "The Better to Eat You With," Carter nevertheless observes that

> Puss in Boots . . . embarks on a career of guilt, blackmail and low cunning that advances his master to the highest station in the land, with a lot of gravy left over for Cat as well. . . . Were the Cat not a small, furry animal but a Figaroesque valet—a servant so much the

master already that he doesn't need the outward apparatus of the role because then he'd become powerless—then *Puss in Boots* would be in no way suitable for children. (454)

When Carter wonders whether Perrault's *conte* is suitable for children, she probably has in mind *The Infernal Desire Machines of Doctor Hoffman* (1972), where the sadistic Count accompanied by his long-suffering valet Lafleur disapproves of one thing only, namely, "the death-defying double somersault of love" (124), because it threatens his absolute domination over others and over himself. "Puss in Boots" is an occasion to return to the idea of the disruptive power of love and explore its comic and subversive possibilities. But the question of the suitability of the tale remains; it even echoes the reactions of many editors and translators since the eighteenth century, for this merrily immoral story resists assimilation to the pedagogical and moral imperatives of children's literature.

Carter's translation accordingly turns the Cat into "a small, furry animal" ("The Better to Eat You With," 454) and stresses his role as a faithful helper in a paradigmatic "rags to riches" plot that reestablishes a form of social justice for the miller's son and even introduces a note of moral disapproval for the Cat's actions at the end. In her reformulations for a broader audience, however, Carter self-consciously references the commedia dell'arte tradition and Beaumarchais's social comedy to explore the connection between the Cat and Figaro: Puss becomes a version of the scheming valet who makes his master's fortune by turning established norms and conventions, the rigid class structure and social hierarchies, and even the patriarchal system on their heads—and to their mutual advantage.

Carter's rapprochement between Puss and Figaro probably comes from Andrew Lang's *Perrault's Popular Tales*. Lang indeed begins the section on "Puss in Boots" as follows: "Everybody knows Puss in Boots. He is, as Nodier says, the Figaro of the nursery, as Hop o' My Thumb is the Ulysses, and Blue Beard the Othello; and thus he is of interest to all children, and to all men who remember their childhood" (lxiv–lxv). The association of Perrault's resourceful Cat with Figaro is explored more fully in Carter's short story, which emphasizes the subversive, even revolutionary implications of the story. Carter references Beaumarchais's *Le Mariage de Figaro*, one of the most famous examples of Enlightenment satirical comedy; this allows her to celebrate various forms of emancipation, from the social constraints of arranged marriages to the repression of the body, the hypocrisy of religion, and various oppressive social structures that conspire against love, pleasure, and delight. This also allows for a challenge of literary conventions and proprieties that translates into scenes of explicit sex, scatological humor, and a jokey "moral" that mocks conventional morality. In a different way from drama, then, prose offers a linguistic equivalent for the Figaroesque cat's antics in a self-consciously rococo style. The word *rococo* itself is of French origin, and it is apparently a playful alteration of *roc* or *rocaille* (shell work, pebble work); so it is a humorous troping of the word *roc* that produces a linguistic triple somersault of sorts. Stylistically, rococo was used to designate lavishly decorated furniture or architecture of the time of Louis XIV and Louis XV, specifically the excessive use of shell designs.[7]

The radio play also focuses on Figaro, but this time in order to foreground its musical connections. It pays homage to Mozart's operatic adaptation of Beaumarchais, as it begins and ends with Figaro's aria from *The Barber of Seville*. But it also imitates Rossini's cat duet to convey sexual rapture (*Yellow Sands*, 124, 133, and 156), and even quotes or samples Tchaikovsky's *1812 Overture* with its climactic volley of cannon fire, ringing chimes, and brass fanfare finale to accompany the hero and heroine's lovemaking (applauded by the spectators or audience, on page 157). There is also a great deal of meowing, caterwauling, serenading, purring, shouting, and screaming, as well as "Hearts and Flowers music" (127), church bells, electric birdsong, harp, and organ music.[8] Characteristically, Carter explores the proprieties of the medium in which she writes and happily mixes classical music, popular song, and human voice to celebrate desire and pleasure in life. In this sense *Puss in Boots* can be seen as Carter's transposition of the musical fugue as radio drama.

Of course, Mozart's *Barber of Seville* is itself an operatic transposition of French comic drama as opéra bouffe in the Italian style (if you follow me). This cross-cultural, intermedial dynamic surely appealed to Carter, who also drew on the comic energy, irreverence, and orchestrated cacophony of Rossini's equally famous *duetto buffo di due gatti*, which consists of the word *meow* treated melodically by the singers; like a true artist, everything is music to Carter's ears, from the sounds of foreign languages to the most common noises of life. Because the radio play is paradoxically a visual medium, music is married to movement as in a comic ballet to convey the racy rhythm, twists, and turns of the plot and the emphatic (histrionic) gestures, even gesticulations, of its feline hero, who memorably bows, jumps, runs, and falls to secure a bright future for his master and himself.[9]

In her preface to *Come unto These Yellow Sands* Carter notes that the radio play allowed her to activate the dramatic form underlying the short story version, so that

> *Puss in Boots* reverted very nearly to the exact form of the *commedia dell'arte* on which I'd modelled the original story in the first place. Puss was Harlequin all the time, and Tabs was Columbine, while the young lovers, the old miser and the crone were all originally stock types from the early Italian comedy, from which the British popular form of the pantomime is derived. That is why the whole thing is set in Bergamo, the town in Northern Italy where the *commedia dell'arte* was especially cherished. (11)

Carter adds that "Recording *Puss in Boots* was the most fun I'd ever had in a radio drama studio and the actors, somewhat breathlessly, concurred, although the production staff, faced with co-ordinating bedsprings, heavy panting and Tchaikovsky's 1812 overture (with cannon) could not, at the time, see the funny side" (11).

Stressing the possibilities of each medium, Carter argues that radio provides an imaginative space for the representation of Perrault's tale in the spirit of the age-old tradition of sexual comedy or farce.

> If *Puss in Boots* is an Old Comedy for radio, it is one that could only have been done in radio, not just because of the copulations, both feline and human, with which the script abounds, but because of the army of rats; and the acrobatics; and . . .
> And the presence of the margin of the listener's imagination. . . . well, I'd envisaged, shall we say, a balletic effect, hadn't I. A ballet in words. A ballet for radio?
> Well, why not? (*Yellow Sands*, 11)

Written in the casual, dialogic, and seemingly improvised or spontaneous style of the commedia dell'arte, this passage captures Carter's relish in the orchestration of her radio play as a means to explore the technical possibilities of each medium and to conduct experiments in the creation of new and hybrid genres, in this case the "ballet for radio."[10] But the author's creative freedom was inevitably more constrained when she translated the tale for children in 1976, although this translation served as a springboard for her creative imagination.

Angela Carter's Sources, or the Twist in the Cat's Tale: The Problem of the Moral

In *Perrault's Popular Tales* Lang notes the relative neglect of folklorists when it comes to documenting the history of "Puss in Boots." He suggests that Perrault's *conte* may be related to a number of folktales featuring animal trickster figures throughout the world, noting that "the Zulus, the Germans, the French, and the Hindoos have all a nursery tale in which someone, by a series of lucky incidents and exchanges, goes on making good bargains, and rising from poverty to wealth" (lxvi). The tentative sketch of the development and spread of the story reflects Lang's efforts to find a source that contains an identifiable moral, in keeping with the genre (as he saw it) and conventional morality. But he admits that no conclusive evidence can be drawn from his research. Even the ancient Indian tale contrasting an animal helper with an ungrateful man only remotely evokes Perrault's version of the tale.

Evidently troubled by the absence of a moral, Lang tries to find a suitable explanation for it. He speculates that

> Monsieur Perrault was at a loss for a moral to his narrative. In fact, as he tells it, there is *no* moral to the Master-Cat. Puss is a perfectly unscrupulous adventurer who, for no reason but the fun of the thing, dubs the miller's son marquis, makes a royal marriage for him, by a series of amusing frauds, and finally enriches him with the spoils of a murdered ogre. In the absence of any moral Perrault has to invent one—which does not apply. (*Perrault's Popular Tales*, lxv)

The discrepancy between the tale and its moral is attributed to the fact that Perrault was at a loss for a suitable moral, because Lang sees him as a collector of folklore and not as an author who may have deliberately intended to make fun of the convention of moralizing morals. The resistance of the tale to easy moralizing may explain the unease of Victorian scholars, and even perhaps the surprising disregard of Carter's critics for her retellings of the tale. Lang notes that George Cruikshank even "felt *compelled* to rewrite it" on the grounds that it was unfit for children, which provoked Charles Dickens's famous attack in "Frauds on the Fairies" (1853).

Although Victorian uneasiness about the amorality of the tale may not come as a surprise, it is interesting to see that Iona and Peter Opie also try to rationalize away the absence of a suitable moral in their *Classic Fairy Tales*, this time on the grounds of a change of mentalities.[11] They argue that Perrault's "Le Chat botté" is "the most renowned tale in all folklore of the animal as helper," but they add that "the tale is unusual in that the hero little deserves his good fortune, that is if his poverty, his being a third child, and his unquestioning acceptance of the cat's sinful instructions, are not nowadays looked upon as virtues" (110). For the Opies the situation of the young "hero" justifies his "good fortune" from an anthropological or folkloric perspective, even though the means by which he secures it are questionable. The Cat's "sinful instructions" make him a doubtful guide, mentor, and "teacher" figure. This idea also informs Carter's understanding of the tale as elicited from her notes on "Puss in Boots." Here is what she writes on a loose sheet:[12]

1. The flaw—a flaw in the fabric of society, and the procedure for mending it:
    Beginning of "Puss in Boots"
2. Characters chiefly referred to by their social roles . . .
3. Plain narrative recounts real facts, or at least, facts typical of reality—fable depicts those same facts together with others that are fused or disjointed in ways which exist only in the imagination
    The talking cat
    The "fairy godmother"
    Preoccupation with extraordinary and marvellous things, in which problems are solved according to the logic of the extraordinary and the marvellous

Like the Opies, Carter sees "Puss in Boots" as a tale about the restoration of social justice ("a flaw in the fabric of society"), although she does not read it through the Judeo-Christian lens in which they couch their moral reservations ("sinful"). She is more interested in the social types that she associates with the folktale tradition and the presence of a "talking cat" that plays the role of a fairy godmother. She also sees in the fable a mixed type of narrative that offers magical solutions for real-life problems.

Another document titled "Fairy Tales," which probably gathers notes taken in preparation for a course on the fairy tale, sheds light on Carter's understanding of the moral.

> When I say "values" . . . I don't mean "moral" values—the fairy tale has often been the entertainment of people who are too poor to appreciate the refinements of conventional morality—I mean something else, often sometimes more primitive and atavistic—and the great hero of story-cycles . . . is the trickster—. . . in modern Europe, the trickster is amply represented—Puss in Boots is . . . a shape-shifter (which may, in fact, be why Puss wears boots—to indicate his half and halfy nature) . . . There's a degree of cynical realism common to most folk-tales.

Carter thus echoes the Opies, who admit that "certainly the Master Cat can be acclaimed the prince of 'con' men, few swindlers having been so successful before or since" (*Classic Fairy Tales*, 110–11).

In his turn Martin Ware translates the idea visually in his portrayal of the self-styled Marquis in *The Fairy Tales of Charles Perrault* (Figure 4.1). In the illustration the title character is a booted ginger cat standing on his hind legs in the background. The fake aristocrat is represented as a sleek-haired and mustachioed dandy (*Fairy Tales*, 49). Ware's interpretation of the Marquis of Carabas as "a kind of spiv" (personal communication, January 26, 2010), is visualized in the dahlia that the character wears on the lapel of his white tuxedo; the fact that it attracts flies draws attention to his fishiness or untrustworthiness, as opposed to the butterflies that flit around the positive characters. Likewise, the artificial roses printed on his waistcoat symbolize his ability to use language to manipulate and rob his victims, in keeping with the flower symbolism adopted in the illustrations for *The Fairy Tales of Charles Perrault*.

The Opies trace the Italian origins of the tale to Giambattista Basile's *Pentamerone* and Giovanni Francesco Straparola's *Piacevoli Notti*, which Perrault probably knew.[13] In turn, Carter interprets the significance of Per-

168 CHAPTER 4

Figure 4.1. Illustration of "Puss in Boots" in the 1977 edition of The Fairy Tales of Charles Perrault. *Courtesy of Martin Ware.*

rault's literary tale through its folkloric sources, and she pays homage to pre-Perrault versions of the tale. The colorful folding frontispiece to Orlando Hodgson's 1832 edition of "Puss in Boots" for children, reproduced in the Opies' book, already references the popular genre of the commedia dell'arte and its adaptation in pantomime (Figure 4.2). It presents key episodes elaborately framed as though presented on a stage, complete with red curtains and yellow tapestries, lavish ornamentation (green fronds, garlands, and potted flowers, complete with a radiating fairy), and flights of stairs that seem to connect the five tableaux or acts representing the main episodes of the tale (note the histrionic postures of the cat). This illustration may have inspired Carter's radio play and the self-consciously baroque style of her prose "Puss-in-Boots."

From "Le Maître Chat, ou le Chat botté" to "Puss in Boots": The Cat as Con Man and Class Rebel

The title of Perrault's *conte* is "Le Maître Chat ou le Chat botté." Unlike Samber's and G. M.'s early translations, which convey the full title as "The Master Cat, or Puss in Boots," most modern translations shorten the title on the model of other popular fairy tales simply known by the name of the hero or heroine, such as "Cinderella" or "Sleeping Beauty." In the present case only the second part of the original title is retained, which leaves out the idea of the cat as "master" that reinforces the comic incongruity of the situation developed in Perrault's *conte*, where a cat becomes the master of his own master, intimidates peasants, deceives a king and even tricks (and eats!) an ogre. The overturning of the traditional class structure and social order that makes this tale both comic and subversive is thus considerably attenuated in modern translations, including Carter's.

In characteristic fashion Carter's translation follows Perrault's text closely while also adapting the tale for a young audience. The language is modernized, the syntax is simplified, and the tale adopts a familiar tone and oralized style (e.g., "Even *our* cat was so scared," *Fairy Tales*, 52; italics mine). The text is disambiguated, and explanations are occasionally provided. The parenthetical asides are eliminated, and the text is divided into short paragraphs to facilitate reading and comprehension.[14] The meaning of the tale is also subtly reoriented to comply with the conventions of children's literature while also reflecting Carter's intentions as a translator.

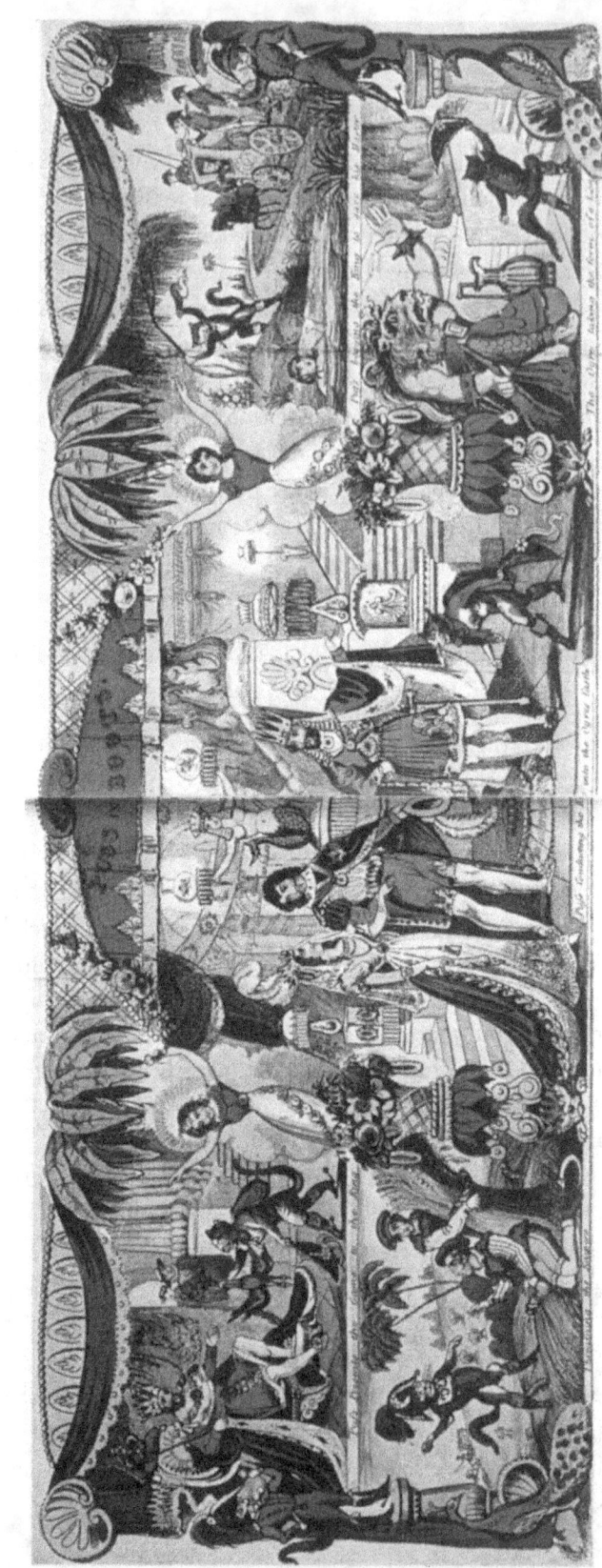

Figure 4.2. Folding frontispiece to Orlando Hodgson's edition of Puss in Boots, 1832, in The Classic Fairy Tales by Iona and Peter Opie.

In Perrault's text the clever and ingenious *Maître Chat* is contrasted with the witless and whining *Maître du Chat*. The latter complains about his situation and can only think of killing and eating his cat at the beginning of the tale ("Pour moi, lorsque j'aurai mangé mon chat, et que je me serai fait un manchon de sa peau, il faudra que je meure de faim," *Contes*, 157; "But for my part, when I have eaten up my cat, and made a muff of his skin, I must die with hunger," *Histories*, 49). But this is no ordinary cat; it's a Cat, with a capital "C" in Perrault (a fairy in disguise in Straparola's version), who manages to persuade his human master to do as he tells him. The man lacks initiative, and furthermore he enters his Cat's scheme without knowing what will come of it: "Quoique le Maître du chat ne fît pas grand fond là-dessus" (*Contes*, 157) ("Though the Cat's master did not build very much upon what he said," *Histories*, 49; "Although the cat's master could not really believe his cat would support him," *Fairy Tales*, 46). Subsequently, the Cat even takes the liberty to rename his master on a whim, inventing an aristocratic name and title for him and with it a new identity. The narrator observes in a parenthetical aside that *Marquis de Carabas* was the name "qu'il lui prit en gré de donner à son Maître" (*Contes*, 158); the obsolete phrase *prendre en gré* means to intend to do something ("volonté de faire quelque chose") but also to enjoy doing it ("prendre plaisir à faire quelque chose") according to the *Dictionnaire de l'Académie française* (1694). The element of pleasure, flippancy, and fun associated with renaming, remaking, and making up is emphasized in Carter's retellings but downplayed in her translation. Unlike the early translator who opts for "the title which Puss was *pleased* to give his master" (*Histories*, 50; italics mine), the tone of the modern translation is more disapproving: "without his master's knowledge or consent" (*Fairy Tales*, 46). Similarly, when the Cat stages the fake drowning scene, "Le Marquis de Carabas fit ce que son Chat lui conseillait, sans savoir à quoi cela serait bon" (*Contes*, 158) ("The Marquis of Carabas did what the Cat advised him, without knowing why or wherefore," *Histories*, 51). Carter has: "The Marquis of Carabas obediently went off to swim," *Fairy Tales*, 47). The master's blind trust in his Cat is mocked at first, but he will eventually be rewarded for it.

The English equivalent of Perrault's anthropomorphic Cat is Puss, which in its modern usage carries positive connotations through its association with pets and baby talk. This further softens the cunning character of Perrault's *conte* when the story is adapted for the nursery. Perrault's *Maître*

Chat is a comic but fierce and ruthless figure derived from the fabulistic tradition revived by La Fontaine, to which Perrault's *conte* self-consciously alludes; the Cat's tricks to catch mice come from Aesop and Phaedrus, by way of La Fontaine's "Le Chat et un vieux Rat" (*Fables*, 3: 18).[15] The translation, however, domesticates the text, as it includes intertextual references recognizable by modern-day English children: no longer fables from Antiquity but modern stories featuring anthropomorphized animals, such as Beatrix Potter's *Tale of Peter Rabbit* (1901; 1902).[16] In Perrault's *conte* the Cat's first catch is a young and naive rabbit, which is trapped in a bag filled with wild lettuce and bran.

> Il mit du son et des lasserons dans son sac, et s'étendant comme s'il eût été mort, il attendit que quelque jeune lapin, *peu instruit encore des ruses de ce monde,* vînt se fourrer dans son sac pour manger ce qu'il y avait mis. A peine fut-il couché, qu'il eut contentement; un *jeune étourdi* de lapin entra dans son sac. (*Contes,* 157–58; italics mine)

Unlike the early translator, who spells out the meaning of "peu instruit des ruses de ce monde" as "not yet acquainted with the deceits of the world" (*Histories*, 50), Carter evokes another animal story known to her young readers.

> He put some bran and a selection of juicy weeds at the bottom of the bag and then stretched out quite still, like a corpse, and waited for some *ingenuous* young rabbit to come and investigate the bag and its appetising contents.
>
>   No sooner had he lain down than a *silly bunny* jumped into the bag. (*Fairy Tales,* 46; italics mine)

Beatrix Potter's disobedient Peter Rabbit, himself remotely inspired by Perrault and Aesop, in turn colors or inflects Carter's translation in the choice of the word *ingenuous* to qualify the young rabbit. The phrase "silly bunny" echoes *The Tale of Peter Rabbit* (1901), one of the most successful children's books of all times, and its sequel, *The Tale of Benjamin Bunny* (1904), which features an encounter with a cat. In the first book Peter lives with his three sisters and their mother, Mrs. Rabbit, represented as cute animals dressed in human clothing and who, like Perrault's booted Cat, generally walk upright on their hind legs, although they live in a rabbit hole under a fir tree. The mother has forbidden her children to enter the garden of Mr. McGregor, where their father was killed. However, while Mrs. Rabbit is away and Peter's sisters are busy collecting berries, the adventurous "naughty" rabbit sneaks into the garden, feeds on vegetables until he gets sick, and is chased about by its owner, but he manages to escape and return home. Potter's rabbit story also centers on the dangers of greed, though it ends more happily for her young hero than his literary predecessor in Perrault's Cat-centered tale.

The English title "Puss in Boots" not only turns the composite title into a proper name (even more so in the hyphenated title of Carter's prose version), but it also suggests the singsong rhythms of nursery rhymes through its alliterative monosyllables and near-rhymes ("Puss"–"Boots") that reinforce the childlike, musical quality of the tale. This is in line with the reception of the French literary *contes* in England, which were often published together with songs, poems, and nursery rhymes.[17] According to the *Oxford English Dictionary*, the meaning of "puss" includes "a conventional proper or pet name for a cat" and "a person (frequently a girl or woman) who exhibits characteristics associated with a cat, as slyness, playfulness, attractiveness, etc. Now especially: a gentle, amiable, or submissive person." The feminization of the term in English may have played a part in Carter's decision to include a female counterpart, companion, and accomplice for her male Puss figure in her own reformulations of the story, apart from the pressure of her pre-Perrault sources. Moreover, the vulgar association of "puss" and "pussy" is clearly activated by the bawdy spirit and atmosphere of Carter's retellings.

When Carter translates the tale for a young audience, however, it is the childlike idea of the cat that prevails, as in the passage describing the boots as "une paire de Bottes pour aller dans les brousailles" (*Contes*, 85), conveyed as "a pair of boots *to protect my little feet* from the thorny undergrowth" (*Fairy Tales*, 11; italics mine) ("so that I may scamper through the dirt and brambles," *Histories*, 49). Here again, the cat is presented as a small, vulnerable pet, in contrast to Perrault's resourceful, scheming, cunning, manipulative, and sneaky Cat. In the French *conte* the *Chat botté* is indeed a human type representing the clever and scheming courtier or valet in animal form. Although the phrase "to protect my little feet" is added for explanatory purposes (why indeed would a cat choose to wear boots?), it contributes to making Perrault's *Maître Chat* into a more harmless and childlike Puss. In keeping with the opinion of folklore scholars, Carter sees Perrault's Cat as an animal helper and trickster figure, down to verbal echoes in "his cat might think up some *helpful* scheme" (*Fairy Tales*, 46; italics mine; for "il ne désespéra pas d'en être secouru," *Contes*, 157) and in "cunning *tricks*" (*Fairy Tales*, 46; italics mine). The qualities associated with the animal cat, namely, physical flexibility, gracefulness, and swiftness combined with the trickster's mental agility and social mobility, all contained in the French phrase *tours de souplesse*, become central in Carter's retellings.[18]

The choice of the familiar "Puss" also fosters an emotional identification with the title character. This marks a shift in cultural attitudes toward cats, as reflected in imaginative literature, but it also reflects the translator's special fondness for this animal.[19] As Susannah Clapp notes in *A Card from Angela Carter*, Carter was a lifelong cat lover: "Her first book, written at the age of six, was called 'Tom Cat Goes to Market'" (79). Carter also wrote the text for a children's book titled *Martin Leman's Comic and Curious Cats* (1979), a poetic alphabet of cats that lists feline characteristics.[20] The playful, alliterative text that accompanies Leman's naive illustrations begins with "I love my cat" and adds a list of characteristics beginning with three letters of the alphabet. Under the letters RST, the text associates the cat with personality traits dear to Carter: The cat is a lovable animal because he is "Rational, Sensitive and Tractable / Regal, Serene and Tolerant / Robust, Sincere and Thoughtful." The benevolent cat sports a funny name, he eats fruits and sweets ("Raspberries, Strawberries / And Toad-in-the-hole") and "He Rarely seems Troubled." Carter shared this love of cats with Baudelaire, and like him she devoted two poems to the animal. Clapp mentions a "Life-Affirming Poem about Small Pregnant White Cat" (*Card*, 79), and she even reproduces an untitled poem about a white cat likened to "a snow queen" (80), which evokes both d'Aulnoy's "La Chatte blanche" and Andersen's "Snow Queen." Carter also wrote a children's book titled *The Sea Cat* later in her life.

Obviously, a young reader is more likely to prefer a story about a familiar pet rather than a sly and cynical *Chat botté* who advances his master's interests through flattery, threats, lies, and deception. "Puss in Boots" features a likeable animal helper figure who makes his master's fortune and secures the happy ending. Carter's rendering of the opening paragraph already inflects Perrault's text in subtle but telling ways. Once again, the traditional "once upon a time" formula that is found in some English translations of Perrault's *conte* is absent from the translation.

> Un Meunier ne laissa pour tous biens à trois enfants qu'il avait, que son Moulin, son Ane et son Chat. Les partages furent bientôt faits, ni le Notaire, ni le Procureur n'y furent point appelés. Ils auraient eu bientôt mangé tout le pauvre patrimoine. (*Contes*, 157)

> A certain *poor* miller had only his mill, his ass and his cat to bequeath to his three sons when he died. The children shared out their patrimony and did not bother to call in the lawyers; if they had done so, they would have been quite stripped bare *of course*. (*Fairy Tales*, 45; italics mine)

The translation tends to naturalize the world of the tale, in contrast to the allegorical dimension suggested by the capitals and the intertextual echoes to the fabulistic tradition found in Perrault's *conte*.[21] Characteristically, Carter provides explanations and clarifications to facilitate reading and understanding by a child: The miller is immediately qualified as "poor" (probably echoing "le pauvre patrimoine" in the next sentence of Perrault's text), and his patrimony is distributed among his three "sons" instead of the more ambiguous "enfants" (in part because the English language has fewer gender markers), and only "after his death." This helps to clarify the opening situation and establish a logical sequence in the events. It also reflects the pressure of the folktale tradition, which favors prototypical plot patterns, recurrent motifs, and stock characters, as in "The King of England and His Three Sons" or "Whittington and His Cat," anthologized in Joseph Jacobs's *English Fairy Tales* (1890).

We remember that Carter owned a copy of *English Fairy Tales* in a popular 1895 edition illustrated by John D. Batten. Dick Whittington, of "Whittington and His Cat," is a destitute, hungry child, desperate for a job, who wanders the streets of London before being hired as a scullery boy, although he is so sorely beaten by the cook that he escapes. The boy's only possession is "Miss Puss" (Jacobs, *English Fairy Tales*, 172), a female cat who makes his fortune when she is sent abroad on a ship and gets rid of all the cats and mice that plague a king's palace and is handsomely rewarded. When the cat returns, Dick becomes rich and marries his sweetheart, Miss

Alice, his master's daughter: "History tells us that Mr. Whittington and his lady liven [*sic*] in great splendour, and were very happy. They had several children" (177).²² Here also we find a reference to a resourceful female cat who may have inspired Carter's Tabs in the radio play and prose retelling of the tale.

In Carter's translation the qualification of the miller as poor situates the man socially, but it also elicits compassion for the impoverished family, especially for the third son, who cannot live by honest means, like the young Dick Whittington: "My brothers can earn an *honest* living with their inheritance" (*Fairy Tales*, 45; italics mine). The French text, however, is more ambiguous: "Mes frères, disait-il, pourront gagner leur vie *honnêtement* en se mettant ensemble" (*Contes*, 157; italics mine). The old meaning of *honnêtement* could be "suffisamment, passablement,"²³ hence devoid of moral considerations. The young man complains that he will not be able to make a decent living, let alone an honest one. This is how the early translators understand it, G. M. opting for "handsomely enough" (*Histories*, 49) and Samber for "very handsomely" (*Classic Fairy Tales*, 113). By contrast, Carter emphasizes social injustice as an implicit justification for the cat's dishonest dealings to make his master's fortune (and his own). This complies with the idea of moral justice as characteristic of the fairy tale.

In the next sentence the ironic reference to the greedy "Notaire" (solicitor or notary) and "Procureur" (in the old sense of a law officer acting on behalf of someone else), which is often left out in translations for children, is kept by Carter in a more compact and simplified form ("the children ... did not bother to call in the lawyers"; the early translators have "neither scrivener nor attorney," *Histories*, 48). Carter even underlines the irony by adding "of course," an intensifier that drives home the social critique implicit in Perrault's text. The translation also triggers a different set of literary echoes, notably to the wealthy and sinister lawyer Tulkinghorn in Charles Dickens's *Bleak House*, itself a crossover novel long available in simplified editions for children.²⁴ Carter's decision to keep (and even emphasize) the satirical jibe or barb against men of law and the system that sustains them puts the cat's own predatoriness in perspective, as it suggests that the social structure itself condones the usurpation of other people's possessions (whether clothes, goods, houses, lands, titles, or even beautiful daughters).

Carter therefore stresses two types of injustice that need to be somehow counterbalanced if the story is to reflect the restoration of social justice typical of folktales: the unequal distribution of property among siblings, which, far from being corrected by law, is in fact made worse by its predatory representatives. Carter even isolates the next sentence, "He felt himself very ill used" (*Fairy Tales*, 45; for "Ce dernier ne pouvait se consoler d'avoir un si pauvre lot," *Contes*, 157), so that the narrator's mocking of the young man's self-pity and ineffectual behavior is replaced by the idea of injustice suffered by the youngest son.

Carter also suppresses another ironic feature of Perrault's *conte* that signals a change of audience and concerns. Despite the fact that the Cat's master is repeatedly (and emphatically) referred to as Marquis de Carabas throughout, Perrault oddly changes it to Comte de Carabas (*Contes*, 159) when he is presented to the princess, dressed in her father's own clothes (the possibility arises that she saw him naked when he was "rescued" from the river). This apparent error was probably meant to remind Perrault's aristocratic readers that the young man is emphatically *not* a marquis, thereby underlining the irony produced by this usurped title as a fiction that gradually becomes real. Obviously, Carter's modern-day readers are unlikely to know the difference between these titles (or for that matter that a count is hierarchically lower than a marquis), let alone care about it. They may not even notice this inconsistency in the designation of the young man's rank, especially when the tale is read out loud to them. But the point of Perrault's joke, which was *not* lost on his adult and courtly audience, is that the title is a fiction and subject to constant change, as the fake Marquis de Carabas evolves from dire poverty to princely status in the course of the story with the help of his smart and resourceful helper, who knows that social status has a lot to do with appearances and pretense.

The second moral itself echoes the worldly-wise Cat when the narrator observes that clothes, a pleasant face, and youth make a person likeable: "C'est que l'habit, la mine et la jeunesse / Pour inspirer de la tendresse, / N'en sont pas des moyens toujours indifférents" (*Contes*, 161) ("It must be remarked of fine clothes, how they move / And that youth, a good face, a good air, with good mien, / Are not always indiff'rent mediums to win / The love of the fair," *Histoires*, 57). The moral of the tale can be seen as a comic inversion of the French proverb "L'habit ne fait pas le moine" (you can't judge a book by its cover); here, dress, (fake) titles, and (deceptive) appearances create their own positive reality.[25] The tale thus becomes a celebration of the agency of words and the power of fiction making over reality.[26]

Carter, in her modern translation, also subtly reorients the gender politics of the tale in the passage about the king's daughter, who falls in love with the young man just rescued from the river and dressed in her father's clothes. Perrault's parenthetical explanation passes an appreciative judgment on the young man's physical appearance as the main reason for the princess's sudden attraction.

> Comme les beaux habits qu'on venait de lui donner relevaient sa bonne mine (car il était beau, et bien fait de sa personne), la fille du Roi le trouva fort à son gré, et le Comte de Carabas ne lui eut pas jeté deux ou trois regards fort respectueux, et un peu tendres, qu'elle en devint amoureuse à la folie. (*Contes*, 159)

> And as the fine clothes he had given him extremely set off his good mien (for he was well made and very handsome in his person), the King's daughter took a secret inclination to him . . . but she fell in love with him to distraction. (*Histories*, 52)

Carter prefers to give the princess's appreciative comment directly: "When the young man put them on, he looked very handsome and the king's daughter thought: 'What an attractive young man!'" (*Fairy Tales*, 48). The insertion of direct speech enables the readers to hear the princess's private thoughts or inner voice through her unmediated assessment of the young man's physical charm and its effect upon her. Consequently, Carter's feminine figure is given an opportunity to voice her feelings and even her desire for the young man directly, in conformity with the writer's feminist standpoint.

The scene in which the young man attracts the princess's amorous attention ("The Marquis of Carabas treated her with respect mingled with tenderness and she fell madly in love," *Fairy Tales*, 48) even forms a self-contained paragraph in Carter's translation, which lends more weight to the romantic element. The idea of being "head over heels in love" would of course reappear in the retellings, where the love interest and the princess's desire for the handsome young man (mirrored in the animal world) drive the plot. The prose "Puss-in-Boots," told from the cat's point of view, even proposes that "women, I think, are, of the two sexes, the more keenly tuned to the sweet music of their bodies" (*Bloody Chamber*, 78).

In Perrault's *conte* the king is seduced by the Marquis's great wealth, and after one glass too many (or so the text suggests), he offers his daughter in marriage without her consent. Carter's translation introduces a few slight changes that modernize the text: "The king was delighted with the good qualities of the Marquis of Carabas and his daughter was beside herself about them. There was also the young man's immense wealth to be taken into account. After his fifth or sixth glass of wine, the king said . . ." (*Fairy Tales*, 53). Carter attenuates the ironic and slightly derogatory "sa fille qui en était folle" (*Contes*, 161) when she opts for an idiom that conveys the king's daughter's attraction to the handsome young man in a more positive way; because she replaces the idea of being crazy in love with the image of "falling head over heels," she even anticipates the somersaults exploited in the rewritings and their associations with youth, agility, and practical intelligence. She also attenuates the passivity of the princess by changing the sequence of events in the sentence; the king's daughter seems to have discussed the advantages of the marriage with her father before the proposal, and her decision is apparently based on the good looks of the young man as well as on his great wealth. The princess, then, is not just governed by irrational feelings. She is in love but also quite matter-of-fact when it comes to choosing a suitable husband. In other words, she is no longer a mere pawn in the Cat's scheme, as in Perrault's *conte*, where the young man seduces and eventually marries the king's daughter as the final step in his social ascension; she actively contributes to and benefits from the fake Marquis's triumph.

Carter thus subtly shifts the focus and significance of the tale in her translation. This anticipates her own riotous and bawdy retellings for an adult audience, where she stresses the farcical elements and sexual comedy implicit in Perrault's *conte* and brings out the Cat's role as playwright; indeed, he directs the action and even dictates the speech of the minor characters that he brings into the plot when he tells his master what to do or threatens the peasants to "make mincemeat" of them (*Fairy Tales*, 48) ("vous serez tous hachés menus comme chair à pâté," *Contes*, 159) if they don't speak on cue. The cat thus orchestrates reality as though it were the stage on which the burlesque comedy of his master's advancement is being performed.

The fast pace of the action is even reinforced in the time scheme of the translation ("Une autre fois" [*Contes*, 158], conveyed by "the next day" [*Fairy Tales*, 47]). Tellingly, the phrase "répondit le Marquis" ("Vous voyez, Sire, répondit le Marquis, c'est un pré qui ne manque point de rapporter abondamment toutes les années," *Contes*, 159) is translated as "'The fields crops abundantly every year,' *improvised* the marquis" (*Fairy Tales*, 48; italics mine), which suggests the commedia dell'arte mode in the ability of actors to improvise on a given theme or plot.[27]

The translation of the moral also sheds light on the translator's interpretation of the tale. Here are Carter's comments on "Puss in Boots" in "The Better to Eat You With," which echo her notes quoted earlier:

> Of course, Perrault's great hero—hero of an age and a class—is Puss in Boots. . . . I'd forgotten what a masterpiece of cynicism this story is. "Keep quiet and leave everything to me," the cat requests the miller's son, and forthwith Perrault adds a moral as a sop to the emergent bourgeoisie—hard work and ingenuity will take you further than inherited capital. The Cat has certainly plenty of ingenuity, but his idea of a hard day's work is one spent collecting protection money; and the only task the miller's son himself performs is to pretend to drown. It's almost the frame work for a Stendhalian parable. (454)

Carter notes the cynicism of Perrault's *conte* hiding under the guise of the respectable moral and even associates the Cat's dealings with the Mafia. When she addresses a young reader, however, she foregrounds the fictional status of the text and of the talking cat, probably to disengage from his dishonest actions. This is particularly obvious in the translation of Perrault's ironic morals, in which Carter even introduces an element of moral condemnation. Instead of emphasizing, like Perrault, the role of dress, an amiable face, and youth as *efficient* means to win a princess's heart ("n'en sont pas des moyens toujours indifférents," *Contes*, 161), Carter translates "the means to achieve them are not always entirely *commendable*" (*Fairy Tales*, 53; italics mine).

Carter approvingly translates Perrault's first moral giving preference to "hard work" over inherited wealth, although she may not be aware of (or not willing to activate) the negative connotations of "savoir-faire" as "intrigue"[28] rather than "ingenuity."

> Quelque grand que soit l'avantage,
> De jouir d'un riche héritage
> Venant à nous de père en fils,
> Aux jeunes gens pour l'ordinaire,
> L'industrie et le savoir-faire,
> Valent mieux que des biens acquis.
>   (*Contes*, 161)

A great inheritance may be a fine thing; but hard work and ingenuity will take a young man further than his father's money. (*Fairy Tales*, 53)

We cannot help but notice that the praise of *ingenuity* (i.e., inventive skill or imagination; cleverness; imaginative and clever design or construction: a narrative plot of great ingenuity) both echoes and contrasts with the description of the *ingenuous* rabbit trapped and mercilessly killed by the ingenious cat. This anticipates Carter's prose retelling when Puss congratulates himself on his own ingenuity ("See how my ingenuity rises to this challenge," *Bloody Chamber*, 73) and later congratulates his partner-in-crime Tabs on hers ("I congratulate her ingenuity," 76) in plotting the cuckolding, and ultimately the death, of the old husband.

In sum, Carter's translation attenuates the immorality of Perrault's *conte* by emphasizing the injustice of which the youngest son is a victim at the beginning of the tale and by making the *Maître Chat* into a more harmless and sympathetic pussycat. This reflects Carter's understanding of Perrault's *contes* as "fables of the politics of experience" that contain an element of "moral instruction" ("The Better to Eat You With," 452) that is here interpreted as a lighthearted allegory of the class struggle for children in the guise of a funny fairy tale.

From "Puss in Boots" to "Puss-in-Boots": The French Connection, or Puss à la Beaumarchais

Already in 1976, Carter saw in Perrault's *contes* "the succinct brutality of the folktale modified by the first stirrings of the Age of Reason" ("The Better to Eat You With," 453). She was to pursue this idea in her own reformulations of the story through the twin influences of the Italian commedia dell'arte and French Enlightenment comedy.[29] In the radio play Carter picks up on the theatrical potential of "Puss in Boots" as commedia dell'arte. This popular form of theater, composed of improvisations based on traditional situations and characters, like Arlequin, Pantalon, and Colombine, was inspired by traditional comic characters such as the servant, the loving couple, the aged man, the lawyer, and the doctor (*Oxford English Dictionary*).[30] The genre is associated with the age-old tradition of street theater, characterized by free variations on a standard plot outline and the use of stock characters often dressed in traditional masks and costumes. All these types are present in Carter's radio play, most of them designated by their function: Pantaleone, Hero, Heroine, Hag, Puss, Tabs.[31] The doctor himself is played by the lover, who disguises himself to get into the house, cuckold the old husband, and eventually get rid of him with the help of the cats.

The influence of the commedia dell'arte is confirmed by Angela Carter's journal for 1977, which associates "Puss in Boots" with Harlequin, "his suit of lights, his patchwork coat, his wonderfully tessellated marmalade markings, lozenges, his fine, musical voice; his bird-entrancing eye; his whiskers." Under "Harlequin's acrobatics," she mentions "somersault," observing that "Harlequin is amoral but not vicious; never at a loss; sense of fun" and adding that "his character is a mixture of ignorance, simplicity, wit, awkwardness and grace ... The true mode of his performance is the suppleness, agility, grace of a kitten ... his role is that of a patient servant, loyal, credulous, greedy, always amorous, always getting his master or himself into a scrape." By contrast, Signor Pantaleone is "the bald-headed fool": "a Venetian; the old father, the greedy merchant, the doting husband, the silly guardian, the aged counsellor, ... a rich & almost always miserly old merchant, always decrepit and stumbling."

Through her retelling, then, Carter establishes a connection between her French source and an Italian cultural context associated with a popular theatrical tradition that celebrates creative freedom and the exuberant spirit of comedy and farce. The acrobatics ("suppleness, agility, grace") that Carter praises in real cats contrasts with the base flattery of Perrault's Cat-courtier who bows and grovels, the better to trick the king and the ogre:

"On le fit monter à l'Appartement de sa Majesté, où étant entré il fit une *grande révérence* au Roi" (*Contes*, 158; italics mine); "Le Chat ... demanda à lui parler, disant qu'il n'avait pas voulu passer si près de son Château, sans avoir l'honneur de lui faire la *révérence*" (160; italics mine) ("He made the king a tremendous bow," *Histories*, 46; "without paying his respects," *Fairy Tales*, 50).

Carter's prose "Puss-in-Boots" pursues the French connection by means of the Enlightenment tradition, in keeping with the rationalist strain that Carter identified in Perrault's *contes*. The short story features a ginger tomcat named Figaro; he tells the story ("as you shall hear," *Bloody Chamber*, 68) of his master's social elevation through dishonest if ingenious means along with their discovery of true love. The cat becomes the accomplice of a rakish young man modeled on the Venetian Casanova after receiving his boots as a "present" for his intempestive "singing" in the street. They live a carefree and hand-to-mouth life: The cat helps the young man seduce all kinds of girls and women, and they scrape a living by cheating at cards or even performing in the street, until the young man actually falls in love (to the cat's surprise and disapproval) with a young woman locked in a tower by a rich, old, impotent, and miserly husband. The cat helps the young man into the bed of his beloved by using various disguises to trick and fool the old husband and the young wife's keeper, an old chaperone who is allergic to cats. Figaro himself finds love with the young woman's pussycat, Tabs, and the two cats arrange the fortunes of both themselves and the young couple by having the old man trip and fall down the stairs to his death, so that in true fairy-tale fashion the young couple inherit his fortune and live happily ever after with their offspring (and the cat family). Whereas Carter's radio play seeks to recover the archaic energy and irreverence of "Old Comedy," the prose version of the story explicitly references Beaumarchais's *Mariage de Figaro* and more indirectly Casanova through the lecherous cavalry officer and his cat but also through the "sensible girl" (*Bloody Chamber*, 74) attracted to the handsome young man. Both intertexts contribute to reinterpreting the story as a celebration of true love and of the emancipating force of the Enlightenment. It is not so surprising as it may seem, since Carter associated cats with reason.

Carter's original plan for *The Bloody Chamber* collection explicitly connects the tale with Beaumarchais: "Puss-in-Boots, à la Beaumarchais; the feline factotum. Figaro, here! Figaro, there!"[32] In conformity with her political leanings and interest in French transgressive literature, Carter pays homage to *La Folle Journée, ou le Mariage de Figaro* (1778), a comedy in five acts first produced in 1784 after being banned for several years by Louis XVI on account of its subversive treatment of social hierarchies and aristocratic privileges. Carter's concerns with sexual domination and social inequality are echoed in the play, which shows how the valet Figaro rebels against the scheming Count Almaviva, who wants to use his "droit du Seigneur" (which he has apparently abolished himself as supreme judge of Andalusia!) and abuse Suzanne, a servant whom Figaro loves and is about to marry. Two years after its first performance, Mozart adapted the play for the opera (with a libretto by Lorenzo da Ponte), and it was produced as *Le nozze di Figaro* (*Les Noces de Figaro*). "Puss-in-Boots" pursues Beaumarchais's satire of the brutal, cynical, and corrupt Count Almaviva in a lighter mood as Carter reformulates the story in a different language, culture, period, and medium; her own retelling centers on the underclass of cats, an unhappily married woman, and a poor but handsome young man teaming up to outmaneuver and get rid of a rich, jealous, and tyrannical patriarchal figure in the name of true love.

Loosely based on Perrault's *conte* but filtered through many other traditions, Carter's "Puss-in-Boots" turns the tale into a "scatological fairy-tale about the omnipotence of desire"[33] with a political edge. The story follows more or less the same plot as Beaumarchais's play, with the cat's "tours de souplesses" turning into a "death-defying triple somersault" reminiscent of the page Chérubin's frantic action, and the dangerous jump through the window to escape the vindictive count. Both helper figures embody the resourceful and free nature of love as they eventually succeed in securing a partner and a sum of money for themselves. Some form of social justice is restored as the low-class characters have their way, whereas the characters belonging to the privileged class (i.e., the Count and Signor Pantaleone) end up losing their privileges and even, in the case of Pantaleone, his life.

Disguise, cross-dressing, and mistaken identities are of paramount importance in the play as well as in the tale. Apart from the booted cat, the cat's master is an impoverished but dandified soldier ("a man who keeps up appearances," *Bloody Chamber*, 69) who dresses as a rat catcher and finally as a doctor in Carter' short story. Finally the two texts present formal similarities as well, because both present Figaro as a character who shares the knowledge of what is going to happen later in the story. Carter's cat-storyteller even keeps his audience captive with teasers such as "which happened once, as you shall hear" (*Bloody Chamber*, 68), or "as you will hear" (70).

Another feature of Carter's reformulation is the sexual explicitness that characterizes *The Bloody Chamber* collection as a whole. The device of the double (or parallel) plot—that is, the human love story mirroring the animal one—is not only a staple feature of comedy but also a dramatization of the rewriting process itself. The theme of reproduction (biological but also structural and literary) further confirms this idea: Carter's rewriting indeed reproduces the tale, just as the cats give birth to three kittens at the end of the story (and the young couple are expecting a baby). This serves to celebrate desire as the creative impulse that drives both storytelling and lovemaking.

> Poor, lonely lady, married so young to an old dodderer with his bald pate and his goggle eyes and his limp, his avarice, his gore belly, his rheumaticks, and his flag hangs all the time at half-mast indeed; and jealous as he is impotent, tabby declares—he'd put a stop to all the rutting in the world, if he had his way, just to certify his young wife don't get from another what she can't get from him. (*Bloody Chamber*, 73)

Because the cat masters the art of telling stories that serve his master's interests, he deftly manipulates the reader's sympathy, so that we cannot but side with the young wife and her lover. Likewise, the scenes of lovemaking celebrate the pleasures of a sensual life in crude but comic fashion: "Then their strange dance breaks: that sentimental hovering done, I never saw two fall to it with such appetite. As if the whirlwind got into their fingers, they strip each other bare in a twinkling and she falls back on the bed, shows him the target, he displays the dart, scores in instant bullseye. Bravo!" (*Bloody Chamber*, 78). Even the undertakers cheer appreciatively at the spectacle when in the next encounter the lovers "conclude their amorous interlude amidst roars of approbation and torrents of applause" (83). The scene of lovemaking as comic interlude therefore comes to represent the role of the Puss in Boots tale within the *Bloody Chamber* collection.

Carter's short story ends with a mock moral. The narrator addresses the readers matter-of-factly (and humorously), wishing them "rich and pretty" wives or "young and virile" husbands, while subtly calling the institution of marriage into question in the concessive clause ("if you need them"; "if you want them").³⁴ The final reference to cats creates a circular movement (back to the title and beginning of the story) that emphasizes the dynamics of storytelling as caught up in repetition while also mimicking the looplike somersault that runs through the history of the tale.

> So may all your wives, if you need them, be rich and pretty; and all your husbands, if you want them, be young and virile; and all your cats as wily, perspicacious and resourceful as:
> PUSS-IN-BOOTS
> (*Bloody Chamber*, 84)

The circular movement of Carter's short story is related to the idea of repetition inherent in the storytelling tradition, but it also echoes Matei Calinescu's reflections on rereading, where "the linear (curious, end-oriented) movement of reading" is contrasted with and yet also intricately related to "the to-and-fro, back-and-forth, broadly circular (reflective and interpretive) movement of re-reading."³⁵ The ending not only echoes the title but even graphically reproduces its idiosyncratic typography and thereby draws attention to the fact that Carter's version of the tale *is* a rereading, a repetition with a difference, that reinterprets a familiar story that itself mimics the to-and-fro movements of lovemaking: "Up and down, up and down his arse, in and out, in and out her legs. Then she heaves him up and throws him on his back, her turn at the grind, and you'd think she'll never stop" (*Bloody Chamber*, 82). Love and literary creation as stories of holes, loops, and filling up loopholes thus become one—and for everybody's enjoyment.

In contrast to the radio play, which foregrounds the magic of "voices in the dark" (*Yellow Sands*, 13), Carter's prose "Puss-in-Boots" is also couched in a style that self-conspicuously alludes to and mimics visual decorative art and rococo architecture (architexture?), a style marked by elaborate ornamentation, a profusion of scrolls, foliage, and animal forms, and by extension an ornate style of speech or writing (*Oxford English Dictionary*). This further reinforces the association of the story with a movement in the visual arts contemporaneous with Casanova's and Beaumarchais's works. These elements are present in Carter's rewriting through references to architectural ornaments on the facade of the young master's house.

> I swing succinctly up the façade, forepaws on a curly cherub's pate, hindpaws on a stucco wreath, bring them to meet your forepaws while, first paw forward, hup! On the stone nymph's tit; left paw down a bit, the satyr's bum should do the trick. Nothing to it, once you know how, rococo's not a problem. Acrobatics? Born to them; Puss can perform a back somersault whilst holding aloft a glass of vino in his right paw and *never spill a drop*. (*Bloody Chamber*, 69)

The elaborate prose of the cat aptly mimics the acrobatics that he prides himself on (as a comic double of the author herself), but the old husband's more sober Palladian house is no "piece of cake." Because the agile cat manages to climb its facade at great risk, he is given an opportunity to perform the triple somersault that will win Tabs's heart: "If rococo's a piece of cake, that chaste, tasteful, early Palladian house stumped many a better cat than I in its time. Agility's not it, when it comes to Palladian; daring along can carry the day" (*Bloody Chamber*, 74–75). The influence of these two styles on Carter's rewriting can only be fully appreciated (or even understood) by an adult reader capable of enjoying a rich, profuse, even proliferating vocabulary, convoluted syntax and grammar, mix of language registers and even languages, alliterations, allusions, and inventive turns of phrase.

The story is written in an extravagant, almost self-engendering prose reminiscent of Basile's baroque prose, in contrast to the minimal vocabulary of Perrault's text:[36] "Aha! This hag turns out to be the biggest snag; an iron-plated, copper-bottomed, sworn man-hater of some sixty bitter winters who—as ill luck would have it—shatters, clatters, erupts into paroxysms of the *sneeze* at the very glimpse of a cat's whisker" (*Bloody Chamber*, 73). This obvious relish in rhythmic, alliterative, sensuous language echoes the sensuality of the characters and provides a linguistic equivalent for the cat's acrobatics. The rewriting thematizes the issue of cultural translation and the mix of multiple languages (French, Italian, English) through the well-traveled and worldly-wise cat, a cosmopolitan figure who even performs "a little Spanish dance" (70) on occasion. Puss is not only a speaking cat, as in Perrault's *conte*, but a polyglot, mastering several languages, including his master's native Bergamasque as well as French, "since it is the only language in which you can purr. / 'Merrrrrrrrrci!'" (68).

Perrault's *conte*, therefore, is only one intertext among many others that mingle and jostle in Carter's rewriting. Even specific echoes, such as the cat's famous boots that "click like castanets when Puss takes his promenade upon the tiles" (*Bloody Chamber*, 68), are given a Spanish musical twist. The boots are again mentioned when Puss mates with Tabs, who even asks him to remove them in a bawdy variation on the comical scene of Perrault's Cat climbing on the roof of the castle when the ogre changes into a lion. As in Perrault's tale, the cat's master does what his animal tells him without asking why: "Do as I say and never mind the reason!" (*Bloody Chamber*, 92). Both protagonists use dishonest means to get what they want, and both use a rat or a mouse to achieve their aims, and yet they are rewarded with a great fortune and a happy ending. Finally, both texts are generically hybrid: Whereas Perrault subtitles his tale "Conte" but self-consciously draws on the fable tradition, Carter revisits hers through the Italian commedia dell'arte tradition, French Enlightenment comedy, and rococo style.

Angela Carter's intentions in her translation and in her rewriting of "Puss in Boots" clearly differ, and they are best understood as contrapuntal responses to the tale, although every version underlies the next in palimpsest fashion. Unlike the domesticated and slightly moralizing translation, Carter's rewritings, while bearing the same name (only hyphenated) reference a wealth of other genres, traditions, and influences, and they are clearly aimed at an adult audience educated enough to identify the numerous allusions and enjoy the bawdy irreverence of the plot and the witty, baroque, and self-consciously over-the-top style of the writing.

5

Revamping Sleeping Beauty

FROM "LA BELLE AU BOIS DORMANT" TO
"THE SLEEPING BEAUTY IN THE WOOD"
AND "THE LADY OF THE HOUSE OF LOVE"

Except, I assure you, I did *not* await the kiss of a magic prince, sir! With my two eyes, I nightly saw how such a kiss would seal me up in my *appearance* for ever!

—FEVVERS, IN ANGELA CARTER'S *NIGHTS AT THE CIRCUS*, 42–43

From Magical Kiss to Lethal Bite: "Sleeping Beauty" Revamped, or New Blood in Old Bodies

When we think of "Sleeping Beauty," what immediately comes to mind is the magical kiss given by Prince Charming to the eponymous heroine, often filtered through Walt Disney's animated movie of 1959. A central icon of the Disney fairy-tale industry, the pink, gold, and light blue Sleeping Beauty castle used to feature a Barbie doll reproduction of the scene as the highlight of Disneyland's walk-through attraction before it was replaced by the original Eyvind Earle artwork. The emblematic scene was also represented in prominent Disney advertising campaigns on the occasion of the fiftieth anniversary of the film. In 2009 the kiss was reenacted by Hollywood movie stars Zac Efron and Vanessa Hudgens (themselves Disney Channel products), photographed in a glamorous mise-en-scène by Annie Leibowitz.[1] Newly-wed model Mariya Yamada and husband-actor Toru Kusano also posed in front of the original poster to promote the release of

Disney's *Sleeping Beauty* on Blu-ray and DVD. Both pictures testify to the ongoing appeal and global dimension of one of the most powerful myths exploiting the confusion between life and fiction, dream and waking life.[2]

No wonder that Charles Perrault's literary version of "La Belle au bois dormant" has been rejected by second-wave feminist critics on the grounds of its alleged reinforcement of patriarchal structures and values. In 1973 Marcia K. Lieberman condemned fairy tales for serving "to acculturate women to traditional social roles"[3] by shaping their behavior and aspirations. Taking Cinderella and Sleeping Beauty as paradigmatic examples, she remarked that Andrew Lang's *"Blue Fairy Book* is filled with weddings, but it shows little of married life,"[4] as most of the tales "literally end with the wedding."[5] A few years later, Karen Rowe pursued the same argument as she indicted fairy tales for romanticizing marriage, to the point of undermining the sociocultural changes promoted by the feminist movement.[6]

And yet, surprising though it may be, *there is no kiss* between the prince and the princess in Perrault's *conte*; nor is there one in the English translation published in Lang's *Blue Fairy Book*. Upon the arrival of the prince in the bedchamber, it is simply said that the princess wakes up now that the hundred years have elapsed: "Alors comme la fin de l'enchantement était venue, la Princesse s'éveilla" (*Contes*, 136) ("And now, as the enchantment was at an end, the Princess awaked," *Blue Fairy Book*, 59). What is more, far from concluding the tale, the marriage takes place roughly midway through the narrative, and rather than marital bliss, it leads to the horrific persecution of the bride and her two children by an ogrish mother-in-law while the new king is away battling his neighbor, the (funny-named) emperor Cantalabutte.

This crucial difference between Perrault's "La Belle au bois dormant" and the Grimms' "Dornröschen" struck Angela Carter when she translated Perrault's *Histoires ou contes du temps passé* into English. In the foreword to *The Fairy Tales of Charles Perrault* she notes that in contrast to Basile's version of the tale in *Pentamerone* (Day 5, Tale 5), in which a married king rapes the young woman during her sleep, "Perrault's prince is far too much of a gentleman to take such gross advantage of her. Indeed, he does not even presume to kiss her" (16–17). The apparent disparity between popular perceptions of "Sleeping Beauty" and the reality of Perrault's text alerted Carter to the fact that the fairy tale is a more complex document than most contemporary critics of the story were suggesting. For many feminists the story was representative of a genre that was inherently inimical to women. The lack of a romantic kiss in the source text, however, and the fact that the eventual marriage of Sleeping Beauty to the prince is not without its trials suggested to Carter that this narrative was no simple endorsement of saccharine patriarchal romance.

Another indication that the translation is closer to the textual tradition preferred by the Opies than to some generalizing idea about the tale type is Carter's decision to reproduce the full title in English: "The Sleeping Beauty in the Wood."[7] She even uses "wood" in the singular, after both "G. M." and Robert Samber's early English translations. The Opies, it is to be noted, praise Perrault's literary version over "the retellings which folklorists have subsequently found in oral tradition," which they deem "flat or foolish in comparison" (*The Classic Fairy Tales*, 81). They contend that the story of "Dornröschen" "is undoubtedly derived from Perrault's text, however reluctant the Grimms were to recognize it" (81), and they propose that Perrault's version does not give us "the whole story." In the Italian tale Talia's persecution by the wife of the unfaithful king is more strongly motivated than Perrault's episode with the ogrish mother-in-law, which the Opies dismiss as an "unnecessary appendage" (81). The Opies also note that Perrault's *conte* circulated in England in book form, although it mainly became popular through chapbooks and pantomime. They conclude by drawing attention to the absence of a kiss in Perrault, which is humorously seen as the dividing line between the literary and the popular traditions: "Pantomime producers have always known what apparently Perrault did not know, that the way to wake Sleeping Beauty was with a kiss" (83).

In counterpoint to the translation of Perrault's literary *conte*, Carter's radio play *Vampirella* and its prose retelling, "The Lady of the House of Love," unearth a headier tradition of vampire lore and ancient legends. Andrew Lang observes that the central motif of the Sleeping Beauty is "as old as the sleep of Endymion" (*Perrault's Popular Tales*, lii) and that the Fata, Moirai, or Hathors represented in birth scenes evoke several myths about "the impossibility of evading destiny" (lii). Lang also mentions the Grimms' "Dornröschen" ("Little Briar Rose") and "Schneewitchen" ("Snow White"), the medieval romance of *Perceforest*, and the story of Talia in Basile's *Pentamerone* (liv), before concluding that Perrault's "La Belle au bois dormant," "like all *contes*, is a patchwork of incidents, which recur elsewhere in different combinations" (liv).[8]

In Carter's own laboratory of creation, however, the combination of elements, types, and genres is even more fluid, unstable, and explosive. *Vampirella* and "The Lady of the House of Love" mix the fairy-tale and vampire stories to surprising effect when the iconic vampirical bite is neutralized by the fairy-tale prince's gentle kiss; instead of awakening the sleeping woman from her death-in-life slumber, as in Grimm, the childlike kiss kills the lady who has fallen in love with her potential victim. The idea of the vampire story as the fairy tale's dark double is further suggested by the fusion of the fairy-tale motifs of Sleeping Beauty pricking her finger on the distaff and the romantic kiss found in "Dornröschen." Revisited in the Gothic mode, the vampirical Beauty inflicts deathly wounds that masquerade as love bites, although in Carter's parodic retellings fairy-tale innocence returns with a vengeance through the unimaginative young man who unwittingly puts an end to the lady's curse.

The five illustrations of Sleeping Beauty reproduced in the Opies' *Classic Fairy Tales* already suggest a conflation of these key episodes and more generally hint at the merging of the French and German versions of the tale. The full-page image illustrating Samber's English translation of Perrault's *conte* represents the revengeful fairy as an old witch with a beaked nose and pointed chin, dressed in a flowing red cape, who darts her needlelike wand toward the face of the baby in her cot, as though she were about to stab her throat.[9] The color of the dress and threatening gesture of the malevolent fairy anticipate the young princess wounding herself on the distaff and shedding blood when she turns 15. On the next page we find a picture of the spinning woman in the tower while the princess is on the threshold of the room (c. 1925); this illustration links the two scenes of the malediction at birth and the realization of the curse. Finally, the three images reproduced on pages 89 and 91, taken from J. R. Planché's *Four and Twenty Fairy Tales* (1858), a nine-penny children's book (1777), and D. M. Craik's *Fairy Book* (1863), all focus on the scene of the "kiss" when the prince bends over the sleeping girl. The three scenes thereby reinforce the connection between curse, wound, and kiss that Carter would condense in her own retellings of the story as a vampire tale with a twist.

Robert Samber's early English translation already stresses the horrific and yet thrilling aspects of the tale in its gloss of the word "Ogre" (and "Ogress"), which had newly entered the English language by way of *The Arabian Nights*. When the peasants tell the young prince about the legends surrounding the mysterious castle, the translator adds in a footnote: "Now an *Ogre* is a giant that has long teeth and claws, with a raw head and bloody bones, that runs away with naughty little boys and girls, and eats them up" (*Classic Fairy Tales*, 87).[10] Likewise, the ogrish queen orders the cook to prepare the princess "with Sauce Robert," another borrowing from the French glossed in a footnote that lists the ingredients. Although the persecution of the bride in the second part of the French *conte* disappears from the Grimms' *Märchen* in favor of the romance element, the episode returns in Disney's 1959 *Sleeping Beauty* movie, with the important difference that the wicked queen is here filtered through the Gothic tradition. With her pale face, blood-red lips, satanic horns, and black and purple garments reminiscent of Dracula's flowing cape, Maleficent indeed strongly evokes vampire imagery, and this might have inspired Carter to explore the subterranean links between the genres.[11]

In "The Better to Eat You With" Carter says how scared she was by fairy tales as a child. Reworking "Sleeping Beauty" as a vampire story thus enabled her to explore the dark and disturbing aspects of Perrault's *conte* and the Grimms' *Märchen* that constitute the sinister underside of fairy-tale romance. Fusing the fairy tale and vampire fiction was probably also inspired by the sense of threat and transgression of boundaries that we find in Perrault's "La Belle au bois dormant," which features a doomed marriage, temporal distortions, and transgressive fantasies as well as the macabre image of the dead king's sons trapped in the thorns surrounding the castle in the Grimms' "Dornröschen." The translation-rewriting dynamic thus gave Carter an opportunity to reflect on the potential of the Sleeping Beauty tale to revive the highly coded (sub)genres of the fairy tale and the vampire story through fusion or, rather, transfusion.

The Interplay of Text and Image: From the Wonder of Love to Visual Disenchantment

Martin Ware's artwork for "The Sleeping Beauty in the Wood" harks back to the pantomime tradition, which dominates the reception of the tale in England. The black-and-white, drably realistic etchings foreground the dramatic dimension of the tale, against Disney's colorful and spectacular fairy-tale film. Ware depicts ordinary people cast in the roles of fairy-tale characters and placed on a stylized stage. The first full-page illustration represents the spinner in the tower as an old crone whose head and shoulders emerge from a cardboardlike tower. She sports tacky gauze wings to signify her supernatural nature, so she is also probably the bad fairy who puts a curse on the baby princess. The second image presents the emblematic scene of the encounter between the princess and the prince in an equally unconventional way.

Feminist critics of the male gaze have often indicted "Sleeping Beauty" as a sexist tale, but this ignores significant differences in the treatment of the story, from Basile to Perrault and Grimm. "The Sleeping Beauty in the Wood," as the title suggests, presents a variation on the topos of the *belle endormie*, which raises issues of visual power, sexual desire, and gender relations. In his critical edition of Perrault's *Contes*, Jean-Pierre Collinet lists dozens of references to the theme of beauty surprised in her sleep, from Boccaccio to La Fontaine, Colonna, and Melle de Scudéry (*Contes*, 319). The motif of the "songe amoureux" (though more often masculine than feminine), as Collinet observes, was a commonplace of *galant* poetry in Perrault's time. In Perrault's *conte*, however, the representation of the sleeping woman suggests both male visual desire and female erotic imagination. The erotic implications of the famous scene of discovery remain chastely "veiled" in Perrault's literary rendering and are only suggested by the curtains, which dramatize the conditions of visibility of the spectacle of the sleeping woman. This associates vision with intimacy, sensual pleasure, and desire, although the erotic charge of the scene is only subtly hinted at.[12] In fact, the main focus is on the erotic dreams of the sleeping woman and the sleepless wedding night that follows her awakening.[13] Whereas the voyeuristic implications of the discovery of Sleeping Beauty are muted, the sexual nature of Beauty's dreams is strongly suggested: When the young woman wakes up, she looks at the prince "avec des yeux plus tendres qu'une première vue ne semblait le permettre" (*Contes*, 136) ("looking on him with eyes more tender than the first view might seem to admit of" (*Histories*, 38–39).[14] She seems to have already seen him in her dreams, probably because, as the narrator speculates in a humorous aside, "la bonne Fée, pendant un si long sommeil, lui avait procuré le plaisir des songes agréables" (*Contes*, 136); ("for it is very probable . . . that the good Fairy, during so long a sleep, had given her very agreeable dreams," *Histories*, 39). The hurried wedding ceremony and sleepless night that follows further confirm the irresistible—and mutual—desire of the young couple.

Perrault's text makes gentle fun of the prince, who is literally dazzled at the spectacle of the sleeping princess, conveyed in a hyperbolic and humorous fashion: Enshrined in a golden room, her face radiates a "divine" light (*Contes*, 136) that captures the young man's rapture as an aesthetic, amorous, and mystical experience. When she translates the passage for children, Carter turns this overdetermined "marvellous" moment into a more ordinary "boy meets girl" episode ("She was so lovely that she seemed, almost, to shine," *Fairy Tales*, 64). The insertion of the qualifying adverb "almost" attenuates the magic of the scene and tones down the complex humor of Perrault's hyperbolic description of the prince's enchantment.

The encounter between the sleeping princess and the enamored prince represents a moment where vision is overdetermined in Perrault's text. Visual details abound: from the golden room and drawn curtains, to the supernatural light emanating from the girl, to the repetition of "seeing" and "admiring," which convey the surprise, wonder, and pleasure provoked by the spectacle of the sleeping beauty. We cannot help noticing, however, that the moment of the young prince's enchantment coincides with the princess's *dis*enchantment.

> Il entre dans une chambre toute dorée, et il vit sur un lit, dont les rideaux étaient ouverts de tous côtés, le plus beau spectacle qu'il eût jamais vu: une Princesse qui paraissait avoir quinze ou seize ans, et dont l'éclat resplendissant avait quelque chose de lumineux et de divin. Il s'approcha en tremblant et en admirant, et se mit à genoux auprès d'elle. Alors *comme la fin de l'enchantement était venue*, la Princesse s'éveilla. (*Contes*, 135–36; italics mine)

> At last he arrived in a room that was entirely covered in gilding and, there on a bed with the curtains drawn back so that he could see her clearly, lay a princess about fifteen or sixteen years old and she was so lovely that she seemed, almost, to shine. The prince approached her trembling, and fell on his knees before her.
>
> *The enchantment was over*; the princess woke. (*Fairy Tales*, 64; italics mine)

Carter's paragraph break underlines the shift from the prince to the princess, enchanted sleep to reality, though it is of course for the best since love wields its own magic. Martin Ware's visual rendering of the scene, by contrast, darkens the supremely romantic moment in order to emphasize its theatricality, perhaps even its tackiness, in pantomime (Figure 5.1). Ware's drab, somber, and almost sinister depiction of the scene in fact evokes *Hamlet* (another prince . . .). Framed by drawn curtains, the white horizontal rectangle on which the pale heroine (Ophelia?) is laid out is opposed to the vertical black backdrop. The young suitor, looking grim, surprised, or frightened, faces the viewer. The reclining girl is thin; she looks stiff and marmoreal in her plain dark dress, and her hair is neatly arranged in a bun. The prince's face is brightly lit from below, and the young woman's seemingly from above, as though by a spotlight, instead of radiating light as in Perrault's text. The visual treatment of the scene thus foregrounds the theatrical aspect of Perrault's text and its artificiality (or conventionality) but deprived of its wonder and splendor—in short, of its enchantment.

Ware's visual treatment of the famous bed scene self-consciously plays with the idea of disenchantment. Instead of referring to the end of the curse, it designates the neutral, detached, and disenchanted gaze of the viewer, which is set in ironic contrast with the young prince's subjective (enchanted or enamored) perception of the sleeping princess. In retrospect, Perrault's text already invites this unorthodox reading in the word *paraissait* (seemed), which suggests that the youthful beauty of the girl may be no more than an illusion and therefore hints at a discrepancy between the naive and enthralled prince and the ironic narrator.

The disenchantment of the fairy tale also characterizes Carter's rewriting of the story as a Gothic tale in "The Lady of the House of Love," when the female vampire (who is both Beauty and the Beast, Sleeping Beauty and her cannibal mother-in-law) lures a young man into her castle but falls in love with him, lets herself be kissed, and dies. The following morning, when the young man wakes up to find the room empty, the sinister decor of the Gothic castle is no more than a paltry illusion, and the morning light lays bare the device: "The shutters, the curtains, even the long-sealed windows of the horrid bedroom were all opened up and light and air streamed in; now you could see how tawdry it all was, how thin and cheap the satin, the catafalque not ebony at all but black-painted paper stretched on struts of wood, as in the theatre" (*Bloody Chamber*, 106). The glamorous lady was only a walking corpse, and the trappings of Gothic fiction are no more than

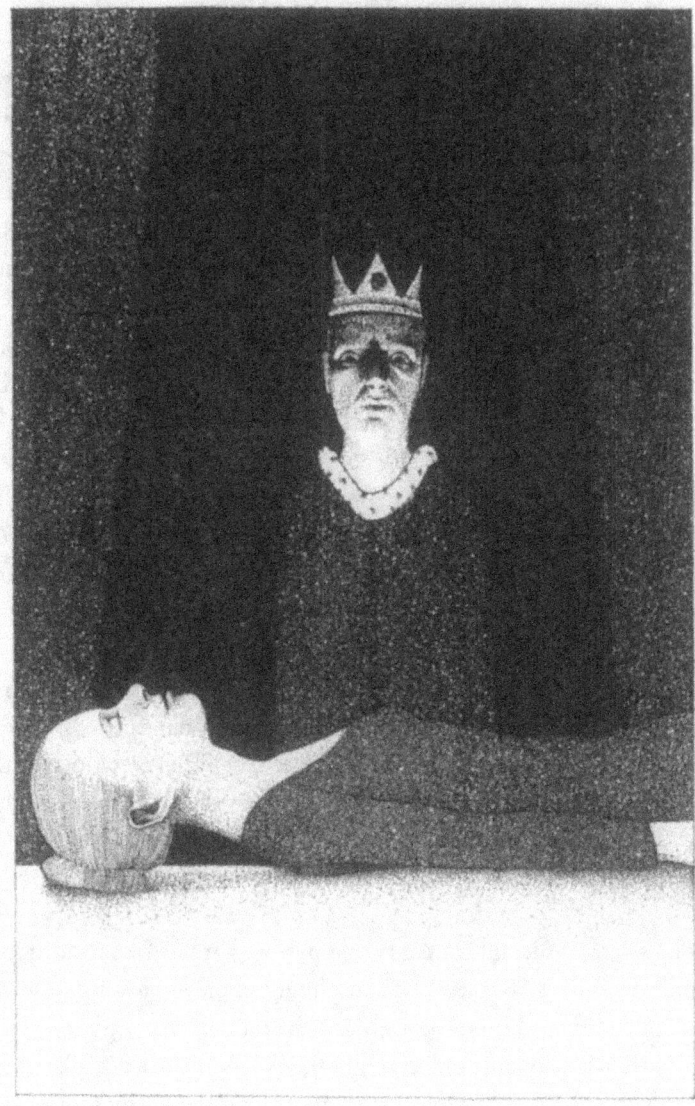

Figure 5.1. Illustration for "The Sleeping Beauty in the Wood" in the 1977 edition of The Fairy Tales of Charles Perrault. *Courtesy of Martin Ware.*

a cheap trick of the light—like the illusions of romance and fairy-tale magic in Ware's illustrations for *The Fairy Tales of Charles Perrault*.

From "La Belle au bois dormant" to "The Sleeping Beauty in the Wood": But Marriage Itself Is No Party

"The Sleeping Beauty in the Wood" is the fourth tale in *The Fairy Tales of Charles Perrault*. Carter adapts the story to accommodate a feminist agenda, but rather than contradicting Perrault's text, she uncovers its emancipatory potential against modern-day exploitation of Sleeping Beauty as a conservative myth. Indeed, Carter seeks to communicate a cautionary message about marriage already contained in Perrault's *conte*, although it of course resonates differently when the tale is retold in the present.

Because she wishes to foreground Perrault's "scheme of good sense" in her translation, Carter plays down the ambiguities, ironies, adult humor, and gruesome aspects of the French text. Instead, she uses the tale to caution her young readers (implicitly constructed as female in the text and explicitly so in the moral) against the seductions of the "Sleeping Beauty" myth. As it turns out, "La Belle au bois dormant" easily lends itself to a feminist reading that criticizes the influence of sentimental romance that fools girls into marrying young.

In "The Better to Eat You With" Carter praises the directness of Perrault's tales, which she strives to emulate in her translation by adopting a familiar tone, simple syntax, and vocabulary. In the same essay she explicitly reads Perrault against the grain of psychosexual interpretations of the tale prevalent in the late 1970s (first and foremost Bruno Bettelheim's influential study *The Uses of Enchantment* but also Anne Sexton's utilization of Sleeping Beauty to confront the taboo of incest in *Transformations*).

> The story of Sleeping Beauty is a perfect parable of sexual trauma and awakening. But Perrault resolutely eschews making any such connections; and quite right, too. Never a hint that a girl's first encounter with a phallic object might shock her into a death-like trance. She's the victim of a power struggle among the heavy female fairy mafia. We're dealing with the real world, not the phantasia of the unconscious. Children get quite enough of that in the privacy of their own homes. ("The Better to Eat You With," 453–54)

To emphasize the worldliness of the story, Carter resorts to familiar expressions, such as "put right any harm" (*Fairy Tales*, 58) to convey "réparer le mal" (*Contes*, 132). She also opts for active verbs and dynamic movement ("on vit entrer une vieille Fée" [*Contes*, 131] becomes "an uninvited guest came storming into the palace" [*Fairy Tales*, 58]) and eliminates what she considers superfluous details and redundancies. Thus the description of the enchanted castle—"on ne voyait plus que le haut des Tours du Château, encore n'était-ce que de bien loin" (*Contes*, 134; italics mine)—becomes "you could see only the topmost turrets of the castle" (*Fairy Tales*, 62). The juxtaposed subordinate clause becomes a consecutive clause that clarifies logic and sequence.

The translation also transforms the fairy tale into a bedtime story by constructing a child reader (addressed as "you" instead of the indefinite pronoun *on* in the French text) and a narrator as storyteller represented in the tale by the good fairy in charge of the princess's sleep. Thus the translator stresses the fairy's efforts to make "a *safe, magic place* where the princess could sleep her sleep out free from prying eyes" (*Fairy Tales*, 63; italics mine). Even the rhythmic language and sound patterns evoke lullabies. This contrasts with Perrault's text, which comically presents the fairy's supernatural intervention as a craft or "mechanical art" (*art mécanique*), to borrow the definition given in the *Dictionnaire de l'Académie française* (1694), and makes a veiled allusion to the erotic topos of the *belle endormie*: "On ne douta point que la Fée n'eût encore fait là un tour de son métier, afin que la Princesse, pendant qu'elle dormirait, n'eût rien à craindre des Curieux" (*Contes*, 134).[15] In both cases, however, the magical wood is conjured up to *protect* the sleeping girl—whether the eroticized young woman of Perrault's text or the little girl sleeping tight projected into Carter's modern translation.

Another change pertains to the narrative voice, so that the intrusive and *enjoué* narrator of Perrault's *conte* who plays with the codes of the *merveilleux* gives way to a more naive narrator who takes the fairy-tale world for granted. Thus the explanatory parenthetical comments and asides that disrupt the narrative flow are integrated as mere descriptive details (if they are retained at all). The painstaking efforts of Perrault's narrator to provide additional information produce incongruous *effets de réel* (to borrow Roland Barthes's term) in a story explicitly designated as a *conte* in the subtitle. For example, when the fairies are introduced, the narrator explains that "on donna pour Marraines à la petite Princesse toutes les Fées qu'on pût trouver dans le Pays (il s'en trouva sept), afin que chacune d'elles lui faisant un don, comme c'était la coutume des Fées en ce temps-là, la Princesse eût par ce moyen toutes les perfections imaginables" (*Contes*, 131). The translation, by contrast, normalizes Perrault's writing style and integrates the parenthetical information in a separate sentence placed at the end of the first paragraph: "After a long search, they managed to trace seven suitable fairies" (*Fairy Tales*, 57). Apart from giving more weight to the number of fairies, the adjective "suitable" implies that the fairies were selected among others, which situates the story even more firmly in the realm of fantasy. It also suggests that the curse is the consequence of the royal couple's snobbery, which leads to the revenge of the old fairy, who was deliberately excluded from the invitation. In Perrault's text, her anger is rather motivated by a breach of etiquette, in keeping with the author's barely disguised satire of his own times and milieu, the strict social hierarchies and sophisticated codes of court society, and the prickly egos of aging (but still powerful) aristocratic ladies. Although the tension between fairy-tale fantasy and the world of Versailles is a constant source of comedy in Perrault, Carter irons out the ironic asides and parenthetical comments and thus contributes to a naturalization of magic typical of the modern fairy tale.[16]

The presence of the narrator in Perrault's "La Belle au bois dormant" is also felt in his humorous allusions to people's naive beliefs in fairy-tale magic, in contradiction to the suspension of disbelief required by the genre, as in the passage quoted earlier ("*On ne douta point que* la Fée n'eût fait là un tour de son métier," *Contes*, 134; italics mine). Carter's translation, however, shifts attention from the collective perception of the magical power of the fairy to her efficient (and, to a young reader, reassuring) measures to protect the princess's long sleep in the absence of her parents: She has made "a safe, magic place" (*Fairy Tales*, 63) for the sleeping princess. Similarly, the rather convoluted (and risqué) passage about the princess's dreams ("*car il y a apparence (l'Histoire n'en dit pourtant rien)* que la bonne Fée, pendant un si long sommeil, lui avait procuré le plaisir des songes agréables," *Contes*, 136; italics mine) is simplified and disambiguated as follows: "Her good fairy had made sure she had *sweet dreams* during her long sleep" (*Fairy Tales*, 66; italics mine).[17] Instead of the erotic undertones of Perrault's text (even more explicit in the 1696 version published in *Le Mercure Galant*), the locution "sweet dreams" echoes the familiar formula used by parents after they have read a bedtime story to their children and kissed them goodnight.

The modern translation even draws the reader's attention to the only kiss found in Perrault's *conte*. In the scene where the king and queen kiss their sleeping child goodbye before leaving the castle forever, Perrault writes, "Alors le Roi et la Reine, après avoir baisé leur chère enfant sans qu'elle s'éveillât, sortirent du château" (*Contes*, 134) ("And now the King and Queen, having kissed their dear child without waking her, went out of the palace," *Histories*, 35). Carter's translation of this passage is consistent with her reorientation of the tale for a young audience. It stresses the pathos of the tender and moving gesture of the royal couple toward their beloved child, from whom they part "forever" (*Fairy Tales*, 62), and implicitly relates it to the circumstances of the telling of the tale: "The king and queen kissed their darling child but she did not stir" (*Fairy Tales*, 62). In this way Carter's "Sleeping Beauty in the Wood" marks a significant shift in the audience, reception, and transmission of the fairy tale in the late twentieth century, which identifies the young readers as the new "beauties" who are told a bedtime story before gently falling asleep.[18]

Carter's translation unsurprisingly modernizes the world projected by Perrault's "La Belle au bois dormant." To bridge the historical gap between the source text and its new audience and also perhaps to imitate her predecessor's playful anachronisms, the cures against infertility change from curative waters ("Ils allèrent à toutes les eaux du monde," *Contes*, 131) to "clinics" and "specialists" ("They visited all the clinics, all the specialists," *Fairy Tales*, 57).[19] Furthermore, to avoid overt cultural and historical references that have become opaque to a modern reader, the "étui d'or massif" (*Contes*, 131) (a medieval "hanap") becomes a "great dish of gold" (*Fairy Tales*, 58), and the "eau de la Reine de Hongrie" (*Contes*, 133) ("Hungary water," *Histories*, 33, glossed in Samber's translation but not in G. M.'s) is replaced by the more familiar "eau-de-cologne" (*Fairy Tales*, 61) invented by Jean Marie Farina at the beginning of the eighteenth century and adopted by Louis XV, becoming increasingly popular in the 1730s.

What "Sleeping Beauty" is best remembered for—quite apart from the romantic kiss introduced by the Grimms—is the magical possibility of suspended time. In addition to the 100-year-long sleep, references to age, duration, and timing abound in Perrault's "La Belle au bois dormant." The narrator even takes pains to give precise chronological indications about the unfolding of events in the otherwise timeless world of the *conte*: "Mais quand le Roi fut mort, *ce qui arriva au bout de deux ans*" (*Contes*, 137; italics mine). Carter's translation is less precise and focuses on the logical sequence of events: "But when the king died and the prince himself became king" (*Fairy Tales*, 67). Similarly, the old queen "commande *dès le lendemain au matin, avec une voix épouvantable qui faisait trembler tout le monde*, qu'on apportât au milieu de la cour une grande cuve" (*Contes*, 139; italics mine) is conveyed more directly and without further delay by "She ordered a huge vat to be brought into the middle of the courtyard" (*Fairy Tales*, 70). Perrault's humorous watch keeping therefore disappears in favor of a treatment of the story that is more consistent with the idea of the timelessness of fairy tales.

As we know, fairies like to play with time, whether to shorten human life or to put an entire castle to sleep in a moment. But as Perrault's narrator humorously points out, this creates comical paradoxes. Thus the princess's real age contrasts with her youthful appearance: "La jeune Reine avait vingt ans passés, sans compter les cent ans qu'elle avait dormi: sa peau était un peu dure, quoique belle et blanche" (*Contes*, 138) ("The queen was twenty, now, if you did not count the hundred years she had been asleep; her skin was white and lovely but it was a little tough," *Fairy Tales*, 69). Carter's casual "now" creates an effect of orality and presence in a tale otherwise told in the past tense. In keeping with the genre of the *conte du temps passé*, "La Belle au bois dormant" emphasizes time past by resorting to the *passé simple*, *imparfait*, and *plus-que-parfait*.[20] And yet Perrault also dramatizes the idea of suspended time in the use of the present simple (*présent de narration*) at particularly suspenseful moments. For example, when the heroine pricks her finger and time literally stops for her, "La bonne vieille, bien embarrassée, crie au secours" (*Contes*, 133) ("The old lady cried for help," *Fairy Tales*, 61). Later, when the prince progresses toward the bedchamber, "Il marche vers le château" (*Contes*, 135), "passe une grande cour pavée . . . monte, . . . entre . . . traverse, . . . entre" (*Contes*, 135) ("He saw the castle . . . walked towards it . . . went through a marble courtyard; he climbed a staircase; he went into a guardroom . . . He found several rooms . . . At last he arrived," *Fairy Tales*, 64). Finally, in the climactic scene that follows the discovery of the princess and her children, the ogress orders a vat to be filled with toads and snakes, before the family is saved in the nick of time by the unexpected arrival of the young king. All these instances are in the simple past in the translation, partly because the present of narration does not exist as such in English, but also because the actuality of the tale is conveyed by other means. In their own way, then, both Perrault and Carter foreground the magic of storytelling that abolishes the distinction between past and present, fantasy and reality, whether through reading or storytelling.[21]

Carter's translation also reflects modern conceptions of the fairy tale as distinct from the late-seventeenth-century *conte* and accordingly includes the traditional ingredients of "a castle in the country" (*Fairy Tales*, 60) ("une de leurs Maisons de plaisance," *Contes*, 132), a "tower" (*Fairy Tales*, 60) ("un donjon," *Contes*, 132), a "quest" ("Il ne laissa pas de continuer son chemin," *Contes*, 135), and common knowledge about fairies: "fairies *are* fast workers" (*Fairy Tales*, 62) instead of the more specific "*les* Fées *n'étaient* pas longues à leur besogne" (*Contes*, 134; italics mine). The presence of the word *happy* in the last line of Carter's translation in particular reflects the pressure of the conventional "happily ever after" formula associated with weddings and fairy tales. Perrault's text, in this instance, reads only "Mais il s'en consola bientôt avec sa belle femme et ses enfants" (*Contes*, 140), but in Carter's hands this becomes, "But his beautiful wife and children soon made him *happy* again" (*Fairy Tales*, 71; italics mine). The insistence on the happy ending, it can be argued, also contributes to neutralizing the sinister and frightening aspects of the text for young readers.

Another difference between Carter's translation and Perrault's text that prepares the reader for the point made in the moral is perceptible in the humorous description of the official ceremonies and grand celebrations that bring serious trouble, starting with the doomed baptism of the baby girl, followed 120 years later by her marriage to a not-so-charming prince. When at the beginning of the tale the young princess is born at last, Perrault simply states that "on fit un beau Baptême" (*Contes*, 131). In Carter's translation, however, the parents "were both *wild with joy*" (*Fairy Tales*, 57; italics mine) at the birth of the baby, and in a separate sentence the occasion is elaborated on as follows: "Obviously, this baby's *christening* must be the grandest of all possible *christenings*" (*Fairy Tales*, 57; italics mine). Carter thus presents the ceremony and ensuing dinner in emphatic, almost hyperbolic terms. Whereas the religious connotations of the event explain the presence of fairy *godmothers*, Carter's choice of the word *party* (*Fairy Tales*, 58) to convey Perrault's *grand festin* (great feast) reinforces its familiar and festive aspect: "Après les cérémonies du Baptême toute la compagnie revint au Palais du Roi, où il y avait un grand festin pour les Fées" (*Contes*, 131) becomes "After the ceremony at the church, the guests went back to the royal palace for a *party* in honour of the fairy godmothers" (*Fairy Tales*, 58; italics mine).

The party tellingly echoes Carter's translation of Perrault's "La Barbe bleue" as well as her interpretation of the tale in "The Better to Eat You With": "The primitive terror a young girl feels when she sees Bluebeard is soon soothed when he takes her out and shows her a good time, *parties*, trips to the country and so on. *But marriage itself is no party. Better learn that right away*" (453; italics mine). The textual and thematic connections that are thus established between "Sleeping Beauty" and "Bluebeard" draw attention to the dubious motivations women may have in getting married, which include cheap dreams of romance and hopes of social elevation or material advantage, as Carter's own variation on "Bluebeard," "The Bloody Chamber," would confirm. Tellingly, "The Sleeping Beauty in the Wood" conveys almost systematically the magical "don" of the fairies by the more material "present" ("magic present," "presents," "very unpleasant present," "time for present giving"), which prefigures the modern moral cautioning against early marriages motivated by the glamour of a grand church wedding and the prospect of receiving material presents. Carter's translation of this passage thus subtly expresses her critique of marriage, on which empty or naive dreams of fame, glory, prosperity, happiness, and babies are projected.[22]

In reflecting modern conceptions of the genre associated with fantasy and children, Carter's translation also expresses a desire to recover the cautionary dimension of Perrault's worldly *conte* in the moral. The French source already raises the issue of marriage and makes a tongue-in-cheek comment on women's attitudes toward it.

MORALITÉ

Attendre quelque temps pour avoir un Epoux,
Riche, bien fait, gallant et doux,
La chose est assez naturelle,
Mais l'attendre cent ans, et toujours en dormant,
On ne trouve plus de femelle,
Qui dormît si tranquillement.
La Fable semble encore vouloir nous faire entendre,
Que souvent de l'Hymen les agréables noeuds,
Pour être différés, n'en sont pas moins heureux,
Et qu'on ne perd rien pour attendre;

> Mais le sexe avec tant d'ardeur,
> Aspire à la foi conjugale,
> Que je n'ai pas la force ni le coeur,
> De lui prêcher cette morale.
>
> (*Contes*, 140)

Carter translates and condenses Perrault's twofold *moralité* as follows:

> *Moral*
> A brave, rich, handsome husband is a prize well worth waiting for; but no *modern woman* would think it was worth waiting for a hundred years. The tale of the Sleeping Beauty shows how long engagements make for happy marriages, but *young girls* these days want so much to be married I do not have the heart to press the moral. (*Fairy Tales*, 28; italics mine)

Even though Carter follows her source closely, the shift from verse to prose and the terse style match her prosaic, unsentimental, and matter-of-fact message. Perrault's sensible moral addressed to young women about the not so rosy realities of marriage is transposed to the late twentieth century, where Carter contrasts the "modern woman" prepared to wait for a suitable husband to the foolish "young girls" impatient to marry and live out an empty dream. The authorial voice ironizes their quest for a "brave, rich, handsome" husband, himself commodified as a "prize," and cautions against the attitudes encouraged by the Sleeping Beauty myth (but certainly *not* by Perrault's "La Belle au bois dormant"), namely, the desire to marry young because of the appeal of a fairy-tale-like marriage. What is remarkable about Perrault's text is that it lends itself to a feminist appropriation, down to the benevolent (if mildly ironic) tone expressed by the authorial voice in the concluding lines.

To an adult reader alert to the *galanterie* of Perrault's *conte*, the amused observation that his female contemporaries no longer sleep quietly as they wait for a suitable husband resonates in the erotic undertones of Carter's "long engagements"—a potential euphemism for premarital relationships in the aftermath of the sexual revolution. In a more veiled fashion female desire is already hinted at in "La Belle au bois dormant" when the narrator speculates that the princess, upon awakening from her long sleep, looks at the prince tenderly and addresses him with a charming wit and flirtatious eloquence that contrasts with his own inarticulateness. Of course, she has had plenty of time to think of a suitable line thanks to the thoughtful and foresighted fairy, as we remember. The subtle allusion to female desire and erotic fantasies is taken up again in Perrault's moral. Carter neutralizes these innuendoes when she addresses children (although adult readers can of course read an allusion to the benefits of the sexual revolution into the moral), unlike "The Lady of the House of Love," which uses the sexual subtext of the tale as an occasion to reflect on the conflict between predatory instinct and self-sacrificing love.

Aside from the moral, Perrault's *conte* itself already contains a critique of marriage. Indeed, what brings on the persecution of the bride is *not* the love story between the prince and the princess but the official announcement of their marriage when they move to the king's castle two years later. The happy couple are hurriedly married almost immediately after the princess's awakening, literally between supper and going to bed, and in the same sentence: "Sans perdre de temps, le grand Aumônier les maria dans la Chapelle du Château, et la Dame d'honneur leur tira le rideau" (*Contes*, 136) ("After supper, the chaplain married them in the castle chapel and the chief lady-in-waiting drew the curtains round their bed for them," *Fairy Tales*, 66). The wedding night is a sleepless one, the narrator humorously notes: "Ils dormirent peu, la Princesse n'en avait pas grand besoin" (*Contes*, 136) ("They did not sleep much, that night; the princess did not feel in the least drowsy," *Fairy Tales*, 66).

Unsurprisingly, two children are soon born of their union. It is only when the marriage is *officially* proclaimed and the new king brings his wife to the family castle in great pomp that trouble begins: "Il déclara *publiquement* son Mariage, et alla *en grande cérémonie* querir la Reine sa femme dans son Château. On lui fit une entrée magnifique dans la Ville Capitale, où elle entra au milieu de ses deux enfants" (*Contes*, 137; italics mine) ("He felt confident enough to *publicly* announce his marriage and install the new queen, his wife, in his royal palace with *a great deal of ceremony*," *Fairy Tales*, 67–68; italics mine). Marital happiness is therefore associated, both in Perrault's text and in Carter's translation, with the intimacy and privacy of the bedchamber, and it is threatened by officialdom (and ogress mother-in-laws). Moreover, the narrator points out in the same passage that the old king married an ogress out of interest, not love: "Le Roi ne l'avait épousée qu'à cause de ses grands biens" (*Contes*, 137) ("His father had married her only because she was very, very, rich," *Fairy Tales*, 67). This marriage is presented as unnatural, in opposition to the secret and happy union of the young lovers.

Carter's opinion on the subject of early marriages, already condemned in Perrault's moral, is expressed bluntly in "An I for Truth" (1977), an article for *New Society* published the same year as her translation. In the essay Carter stigmatizes the conservative ideology of the confession magazines targeted at women, observing, with characteristic sharpness, that "the ideology behind the romances and the confessions stinks" (456). Noting how these magazines, which "derive from Sunday School literature" (456), extol marriage and repress sexuality, Carter exclaims:

> They get married so young, these girls! Seventeen, eighteen, nineteen; and the babies come, to complete their happiness, except one girl miscarries and takes to the bottle, another miscarries and becomes frigid. . . . Yet the straightforward populist celebrations of marital love and family life are interspersed with downbeat narratives by people, often in their late thirties or older, coming to terms with divorce. . . . Yet marriage remains the principal obsession, even here. It is as if marriage functions as the sexuality of women. It occupies the imagination of these magazines to the same obsessive extent that sexuality itself does in the tit mags. (458)

Carter concludes with a thought-provoking redefinition of pornography directed against the Moral Majority and such antiporn feminists as Andrea Dworkin and Catharine MacKinnon: "They have the false universality of any other mythic places and the value system has the same false universality, too. And *what is really pornographic is the titillatory exploitation of the human heart, which is a lot worse than the titillatory exploitation of human flesh*" (459; italics mine).

Thus Perrault's *contes* can be bent to accommodate Carter's sex-positive feminism, which suggests that they contain a genuine potential for women's emancipation that the translator brings out. Echoing Perrault's plea for a modern literature that would speak to his contemporaries, Carter significantly uses the word *modern* in her moral, which of course resonates differently in the wake of the feminist movement, let alone Sexton's critique of the exploitation of fairy-tale patterns in the women's press and popular culture. For both Perrault and Carter, then, fairy tales serve to carry useful and empowering knowledge distinct from conventional morality, and as a modern genre par excellence, they can be (re)made to reflect ever-changing realities and concerns.

Carter, who in her translations sought to caution her young readers, saw herself as a worldly-wise, wry but sympathetic fairy godmother. In her foreword to *The Fairy Tales of Charles Perrault* she perceptively observes that Perrault's fairies are less reminiscent of ancient supernatural creatures than of "women of independent means" who "are prepared to help along a little sister who finds herself in difficulties" (19). As a modern-day equivalent of Perrault's *fées marraines*, Carter seeks to break the spell of the Sleeping Beauty myth and more generally of the mainstream culture that has co-opted fairy tales in the service of conservative values. Her translation of Perrault enables her to share her experience as a woman who married early, and not too happily either, before finding later in life a younger, kind, and loving partner. But the modern fairy knows that her own powers were limited, like Perrault's before her. To quote the Opies:

> In these deeply-penetrating tales, fairy godmothers do not suddenly materialize, waving wands that make everything come right. The power of the godmothers is limited. Sometimes all they are able to offer is *advice*. They are never able, it seems, to change a worldly situation, or alter a wicked heart. What they can do, on occasion, is assist in the breaking of a spell or in the alleviation of its ill effect. (*Classic Fairy Tales*, 14; italics mine)

The storyteller as fairy godmother therefore tries to break the Disney spell (to borrow Jack Zipes's phrase) and the wish-fulfillment fantasies encouraged by the Sleeping Beauty myth in favor of Perrault's worldly wisdom.

In her programmatic essay "Notes from the Front Line" (1983), Carter famously presents her work as a critique of the mythologies of her times. Seeing in the fairy tale a carrier of practical knowledge, she sought to transmit unofficial, empowering, and entertaining knowledge against the conservative manipulation and exploitation of the genre. Although it is no doubt tempting to argue that Carter's translations contest the cultural authority and alleged conservatism of her source, Perrault's "La Belle au bois dormant" is not to be confused with the Sleeping Beauty myth, which evacuates the moral and neutralizes its critique of marriage. Instead of kissing Sleeping Beauty goodbye (to borrow the title of a feminist manifesto), Carter's translation testifies to the capacity of the literary tale to accommodate an alternative feminist agenda. Carter, then, was not so much breaking away from Perrault as following his plea for a modern literature that cautions women against the falsity of cultural myths, romantic or otherwise.

From *Vampirella* to "The Lady of the House of Love": Vampirism as Metaphor

Once we have accepted the story we cannot escape the story's fate.

—P. L. TRAVERS, *ABOUT THE SLEEPING BEAUTY*, 65

mysterious solitude of ambiguous states

—ANGELA CARTER, NOTES FOR "THE LADY OF THE HOUSE OF LOVE"

(ANGELA CARTER PAPERS, BRITISH LIBRARY)

Angela Carter's radio play *Vampirella* (1976) opens with a chorus of birdsong, with doves cooing and a lark singing to the musical accompaniment of the title character's long and sharp nails against the bars of a birdcage. The melancholic vampire asks herself, "Can a bird sing only the song it knows or can it learn a new song" (*Yellow Sands*, 84), only to be interrupted by the screech of a bat. This is an apt prelude for Carter's own take on "Sleeping Beauty," from fairy-tale romance to creepy horror story. The idea of replay is everywhere at work in this allegory of creation in which the female vampire refuses to follow the predetermined script and takes her fate into her own hands. The "new song" line is not only repeated in the radio play but also echoed twice in slightly different circumstances (e.g., a series of tarot readings that always present the same configuration of cards) in the associated short story, "The Lady of the House of Love," included in *The Bloody Chamber*.[23]

An examination of the Angela Carter Papers shows that the two versions of the tale are part of a creative continuum. The file, titled "Thematic Variations: Vampirella/La Belle au Bois Dormante" (sic), contains various drafts of the story including a screenplay with the handwritten note: "This is actually NOT a screenplay, but a kind of intermediary version between screenplay and short story."[24] Carter's translation of Perrault "coincides with the transmission of her first radio play, *Vampirella*, in the summer of 1976. In turn, her initial work in radio informs her later fictional engagement with the genre."[25] In her preparatory notes for the "story version," Carter lists a number of changes, including narrative point of view ("1st person"), focus ("concentrate on erotic relation between Hero and Countess"), and guardian ("remove Mrs Beane—replace her by a deaf-mute"). Some isolated sentences also capture the spirit of the retelling: "mysterious solitude of ambiguous states" and "I give you as a souvenir the dark, fanged rose I have plucked from between my thighs, like a flower laid on a grave." Carter also quotes from Théophile Gauthier's "La morte amoureuse" (1836), a story much admired by Baudelaire about a beautiful female vampire who offers a young priest eternity in a kiss. Another probable influence is Charles Dickens's *Great Expectations* and the memorable scene of Pip's encounter with the old Miss Havisham in her yellowed bridal dress. The wealthy lady combines fairy-tale elements (she is designated by Pip as both a witch and a fairy godmother) and Gothic motifs, such as the decaying house, doomed love and a shameful secret, stopped clocks, and even a game of cards.

Carter's process of rewriting thus produces generic transformations that materialize the idea of "intermediary" states not unlike the vampire's own condition. It also hints at the double legacy of the tale through Gauthier's voluptuous French vampire and the Grimms' morbid roses in "Dornröschen." The name of the heroine indeed refers to the murderous hedge of thorns that surrounds the castle; the hedge's hand-shaped branches grab the young princes who try to get across it and die gruesome deaths: "Es war ihnen aber nicht möglich, den die Dornen, als hätten sie Hände, hielten fest zusammen, und die Jünglinge blieben darin hängen, konnten sich night wieder losmachen und straben eines jämmerlichen Todes" (Grimm, *Kinder-und Hausmärchen*, 1: 259). Ralph Manheim's translation conveys the haunting image of the personified and malevolent thorns as follows: "From time to time a prince tried to pass through the hedge into the castle. But none succeeded, for the brier bushes clung together as though they had hands, so the young men were caught and couldn't break loose and died a pitiful death" (*Grimm's Tales For Young and Old*, 176–77). When the prince eventually crosses the corpse-strewn hedge (*Dornenhecke*), he finds beautiful flowers that magically open up a path before him, but we cannot help associating the macabre human remains and the beautiful wild roses, as Carter herself did.

Another variation on the story of Sleeping Beauty serves as the basis for "The Snow Child." "The Snow Child" closely follows a variant of "Schneewitchen" found in the early manuscript version of the Grimms' *Kinder- und Hausmärchen*. This paragraph-long variant of the opening of "Schneeweisschen" or "Schneewitchen" is reproduced in the 1810 manuscript. The alternative opening begins as follows: "Es war einmal ein Graf u. eine Gräfin, die fuhren zusammen, u. fuhren an drei Haufen weissem Schnee vorbei, da sprach der Graf: ich wünsche mir ein Mägdlein, so weiss wie diesen Schnee. Sie fuhren weiter u. kamen an drei Gruben voll rothes Blutes, da wünschte der Graf u. sprach . . ." (*Kinder- und Hausmärchen*, 3: 79). Carter's rewriting of the story also features a count who wishes for a girl as white as snow, as red as blood, and with hair as black as a raven's, and a jealous countess. Although "The Snow Child" adds a new sexual component in its depiction of the rape of the snow girl, it replays the enigmatic opening with its winter scene and the vivid image of the hole full of blood. Characteristically, Carter fuses fairy-tale imagery, surrealist fantasies, and present-day cultural references. In her 1977 journal she makes a passing reference to Paloma Picasso as an inspiration for the rewriting.

> IMMORAL TALES: Paloma Picasso's black boots with red heels, a fetishistic image of erotic cruelty and high fashion. Note: use for "Sleeping Beauty"—the count & Countess rode out one snowy day, she wore a black cloak that rustled & black riding boots with scarlet heels.

Paloma Picasso played the bloody Countess Erzsébet Báthory in the *Contes immoraux*, an erotic movie directed by Walerian Borowczyk and released in 1974. Carter makes the connection between the actress's iconic use of red, black, and white in her self-fashioning and the Grimms' variations on "Snow White," when she proposes a "conclusion of Sleeping Beauty" (the count raping the snow child and the couple riding away) that would become "The Snow Child."

The Grimms' "Dornröschen" and "Schneewitchen," based as they are on the first and second parts of Perrault's *conte*, are therefore an important source of motifs in Carter's vampire stories. Her own retellings feature sinister roses feeding on dead suitors and replay the strange incipit where the queen pricks her finger and, as she gazes at the drops of blood on the snow, wishes for a baby girl white as snow, red as blood, and black as the ebony window frame, or its even more troubling variant that the Grimms relegated to the notes. In Carter's *Vampirella* the extraordinary pale skin, long dark hair, and "fleshy," "purplish crimson," "morbid" (*Yellow Sands*, 101) mouth of the Countess self-consciously draws (blood?) connections between the German *Märchen* and vampire fiction.

Carter's radio play also references "Snow White" in Vampirella's physical appearance as well as her death-in-life state. Like her fairy-tale predecessor encased in a glass coffin after being poisoned by her jealous stepmother, the vampire lies in her coffin during the day "as ruddy in the cheeks as if I had nodded off to sleep in my shroud" (*Yellow Sands*, 85). Ritually beheaded and bled ("Out gushes warm torrents of rich, red blood, like melted roses," 85), the vampire rises again, just like the fairy tales that are endlessly revived in multiple combinations, transpositions, and reinventions.

In the preface to *Come unto These Yellow Sands* (1978), Carter explains that she "took the script of 'Vampirella' as the raw material for a short story, 'The Lady of the House of Love.' It was interesting to see what would and would not work in terms of prose fiction" (10). Radio, she says, enables her "to create complex, many-layered narratives that play tricks with time. And, also, to explore ideas, although for me, a narrative is an argument stated in fictional terms" (7). She goes on to elaborate on the different possibilities opened by the two mediums.

> In radio, it is possible to sustain a knife-edge tension between black comedy and bizarre pathos. . . . This is because the rich textures of radio are capable of stating ambiguities with a dexterity over and above that of the printed word; the human voice itself imparts all manner of subtleties in its intonations. So "The Lady of the House of Love" is a Gothic tale about a reluctant vampire; the radio play, "Vampirella," is about vampirism as metaphor. The one is neither better nor worse than the other. Only, each is quite different. (10)

These comments on the impact of the medium on the message shed light on the dynamics of creation in Carter's work, whose remarkable inventiveness derived from the interplay of her various activities and her continual experiments in retelling stories—including her own—in different forms, styles, and media. Even though Carter's choice of the term "reformulations" (*Yellow Sands*, 10) to describe her own writing evokes the magic formulas associated with the fairy tale,[26] the ominous phrase "raw material" humorously tropes the creative process as a form of cannibalism or vampirism. It hints at the possibilities offered by unusual generic combinations (or transfusions) for transgressive retellings but also reveals the inherent hybridity of literary genres. Indeed, as I will show, Carter's reworking of "Sleeping Beauty" quickens to life that which remained dormant in Perrault's "La Belle au bois dormant" and gives it new bite.

Vampirella links Gothic horror and the fairy tale through the Countess, a self-loathing vampire who imagines that she is Sleeping Beauty, thereby fusing two powerful myths of femininity: the femme fatale and the *belle endormie*.[27] The leitmotif of the birdsong encapsulates her melancholic musings on the curse of being born a vampire condemned to repeat her ancestors' crimes, in a language that is itself marked by repetitions: "I am compelled to the repetition of their crimes; that is my life. I exist only as a compulsion, a compulsion" (*Yellow Sands*, 84). The "beautiful somnambulist" (105) passes the time in a dreamlike state, "an endless revery, a perpetual swooning" (90), wondering whether she will be able to escape a preordained fate. When she declares, "I am both the Sleeping Beauty and the enchanted castle; the princess drowses in the castle of her flesh" (90), the character signals her self-estrangement in the shift from the first to the third person and in her identification with the fairy-tale heroine and the castle in which she is confined, thereby playing on the ambiguous title of Perrault's "La Belle au bois dormant," where *dormant* (sleeping) qualifies the wood surrounding the castle as much as the princess herself.[28]

Carter's vampire stories suggest that the fairy tale and Gothic fiction have in fact a lot more in common than we might think. Not only do they explore the intermediary state of the vampire figure, but they also hint at the two genres' shared concern with liminal states and spaces, (self-)transformation, and the blurring of the boundaries between the human and the nonhuman. And because they are conventionalized genres, they also display a parodic self-consciousness.[29] Deliberately drawing on Gothic clichés, the Countess's self-dramatization as an embodied castle reactivates a staple feature of the genre while also evoking Sleeping Beauty's castle as a shrine for and extension of the sleeping woman. Her pleasant dreams, however, turn into the nightmare of the living dead condemned for all eternity to live in the castle of their flesh and feed on the blood of the living. As the Countess declares to the Hero in stilted language, periodic sentences, and pathetic accents: "I do not mean to hurt you, I do not want to cause you pain. But I am both beauty and the beast, locked up in the fleshly castle of exile and anguish, I cannot help but seek to assuage in you my melancholy" (*Yellow Sands*, 97).

The caged bird with which the female vampire identifies symbolizes the conflict of body and soul, fate and free will, compulsion to repeat and capacity to change, that is at the heart of Gothic literature.[30] It thus captures the Countess's quandary, trapped as she is in "the timeless Gothic eternity of the vampires" (*Bloody Chamber*, 97) and the age-old tradition of vampire stories associated with her father, Count Dracula. We remember that in Perrault's *conte* the fairies shower gifts onto the baby princess, including the ability to sing like a nightingale, a simile that becomes central in Carter's *Vampirella*, revolving as it does around the Countess's aspiration to "sing her own song." The vampire's pet bird, however, is not a nightingale but a "skylark" (*Bloody Chamber*, 98). Like Percy Bysshe Shelley's musical and literary bird, whose heart is said to pour "profuse strains of unpremeditated art" ("To a Skylark," l. 5), the Countess longs for free expression and self-determination.[31] In Shelley's poem the bird is in part a symbol for a spontaneous, natural form of poetry through song. Although, as a creature of light, joy, and freedom, the skylark is opposed in many ways to Carter's heroines, the romantic poet also likens it to a lonely maiden in a palace tower who soothes her lovelorn soul with music, not unlike Sleeping Beauty's creepy sisters, Vampirella and the Lady of the House of Love.

The leitmotif of the birdsong in these vampire stories thus plays a complex and manifold role as it comments on the situation of the main character: a poor "nightbird" (*Yellow Sands*, 102) trapped in the "castle of her flesh" (90) who aspires to the condition of the emblematic skylark. Enclosed in the "vast, ruined castle" (88) of her ancestors, she is condemned to the endless repetition of her crimes and, on another level, to the prison of literary referentiality and its inescapable echoes. By invoking romantic lyrical poetry through the musical bird, as a symbol of the redeeming power of love and song, the Countess seeks to liberate herself from her predetermined fate and from the constraints of the Gothic genre that keeps her captive.

Even the gloomy atmosphere of the Transylvanian castle in which she lives (whose battlements evoke "broken teeth," *Yellow Sands*, 89) is not unrelated to Perrault's *conte*. We recall that the prince's first impression on entering the sleeping castle is one of horror, as it confronts him with silent images of ruin and death ("C'était un silence affreux, l'image de la mort s'y présentait partout," *Contes*, 135; "An awful silence filled it and the look of death was on everything," *Fairy Tales*, 64). Likewise, the claustrophobic images of the body as a prison could be related to the heroine's subjective perception of her condition as a *belle endormie* condemned to passively submit to a preordained fate and to the male gaze.[32] The radio play, however, relying as it does on words and sound effects, shifts the visual economy associated with "Sleeping Beauty" to the aural stimulation of imagination, because for Carter "radio always leaves that magical and enigmatic margin, that space of the invisible, which must be filled in by the imagination of the listener" (*Yellow Sands*, 7).[33]

What is more, both *Vampirella* and "The Lady of the House of Love" reverse the traditional fairy-tale script insofar as the Sleeping Beauty figure becomes a predatory female who uses her charms to catch and kill the young men on whom she feeds, although this "feminist" twist in the plot does not represent a significant improvement in her condition but merely the move from one stereotype (the passive princess) to another (the bloodthirsty vamp). And yet Carter recasts the Countess as a victim as much as a predator; she becomes a persecuted romantic figure longing for true love and expressing herself in soulful (even melodramatic) tones.[34] Her inhuman beauty may be the sign of her monstrous condition, but in the cage of her body there is a trapped bird that wants to sing its own song; instead of a Wagnerian *Liebestod*, she thwarts all expectations when she simply asks the Hero for "a goodnight kiss" (*Yellow Sands*, 114).

In this sense the motif of the birdsong and the emphasis on voice fulfill an obvious metatextual function. The vampire who laments her predicament reflects on her status as a character caught in old, exhausted, and convention-ridden genres from which she can free herself only through an unexpected twist in the plot and a return to childlike innocence. This turns her into a double of the author herself, who with characteristic self-irony dramatizes her own struggle with a long and stifling legacy in order to ward off the curse of repetition and prewritten scripts. And so Carter manages to retell the familiar story without falling into the trap of the happy ending expected of fairy tales or the brutal killings of the vampirical others that we find in Bram Stoker's *Dracula*. Carter's Countess eventually conjures the twin curses of heredity and generic confinement, fate and plot, by singing her own song.

In mock Sleeping Beauty fashion the Countess awaits her Prince Charming and imagines that only a true lover's kiss can put an end to the curse that blights the line of vampires engendered by Count Dracula.

> COUNTESS. But love, true love, could free me from this treadmill, this dreadful wheel of destiny...
> COUNT. My daughter, the last of the line, through whom I now project a modest, posthumous existence, believes . . . that she may be made whole by human feeling. That one, fine day, a young virgin will ride up to the castle door and restore her to humanity with a kiss from his pure, pale lips. (*Yellow Sands*, 85–86)

The image of the wheel of destiny, which harks back to the age-old spinners of human fate, once again raises the question of the Countess's capacity to become a free agent of her own life. The existential musings of the heroine, couched as they are in direct speech, melodramatic tones, and pathetic accents, prefigure her ultimate choice to renounce the terrible gift ("terrible don," *Contes*, 132) of eternal life given to her at birth by her evil (god) father. She becomes human (and therefore mortal) when she lets herself be tenderly kissed by her potential victim, a young and naive traveler, in an ironic replay of the life-giving kiss found in the Grimms' version of the tale. This innocent kiss ("Softly, with my lips, I touched her forehead, as if I had been kissing a child goodnight," *Yellow Sands*, 114) is the exact opposite of her own deathly and erotically charged bites, and she dies in his arms. The Hero adds: "She felt quite limp in my arms. . . . Soon it will be morning; the . . . first light will dissolve this Gothic dream with the solvent of the natural" (*Yellow Sands*, 114). Dracula, enraged by this most unexpected turn in the Gothic tale of violence, murder, and terror, interrupted by the romantic cliché par excellence, "moans and gurgles: 'Is a millennium of beastliness to expire upon a *kiss*?'" (*Yellow Sands*, 114–15).[35] The following morning, Mrs. Beane, the governess, releases her protégée's pet lark: "Fly away, birdie, fly away!" (115). Like the bird, the Countess is free at last. She has overcome her predatory nature and compulsion to kill and has chosen her own destiny by recovering the childlike innocence of fairy-tale romance. The vampire with her "Strewelpeter's hands" (113) has vanished into the light, like Shelley's skylark, after singing her own sweet song of sadness.[36]

Modern Technology Meets Folklore, or the Magic of Voices in the Dark

In the preface to *Come unto These Yellow Sands* Carter explains that she was a child of the radio age and that *Vampirella* came to her as radio "in terms of words and sounds" (10). For her, "Writing for radio involves a kind of three-dimensional story-telling" (7) that relies on "the imagination of the listener" (7). Carter's decision to write *Vampirella* originated in the suggestiveness of the sound made by a pencil that she "ran idly along the top of a radiator. It made a metallic, almost musical rattle. It was just the noise that a long, pointed fingernail might make if it were run along the bars of a birdcage" (9). That is where the idea of the story originated, in that birdcage. The creation of the radio play, which brings together the pen and the radiator, writing and sound, is pursued in the alliterative logic that guided Carter's imagination in her description of the creative process.

> I alliterated her. . . . A lovely lady vampire; last of her line, perhaps, locked up in her hereditary Transylvanian castle, and the bird in the gilded cage might be, might it not, an image of the lady herself, caged as she was by her hereditary appetites that she found both compulsive and loathsome. . . . I invented for the lovely lady vampire . . . a hero out of the *Boy's Own* paper circa 1914, who would cure and kill her by the innocence of his kiss and then go off to die in a war that was more hideous by far than any of our fearful superstitious imaginings. . . . It *came* to me as radio, with all its images ready formed, in terms of words and sounds. (9–10)

Carter's radio play thus uses radiophonic technology as a new form of magic that revives the ancient, oral storytelling tradition, as it resorts to theme music, sound effects, lyrical speech, and dramatic intensity to create the peculiar mix of "black comedy and bizarre pathos" (*Yellow Sands*,

10) intended by the author. The Countess's anguished monologues and artificial diction together with the thematic emphasis on voice and song enacted in the sound effects reference melodrama as a hybrid artistic form enhanced by the sense of doom and theatrical setting of the Gothic castle. The combination of melody (from the Greek μελοιδια, or "song") and drama (δράμα, or "action") thus serves to dramatize the demise of Gothic fantasy in favor of historical fact; in *Vampirella* the extinction of the female vampire is followed by the return of morning birdsong, interrupted by the chuckle of the Fatal Count, whose shadow "rises over every bloody battlefield" (*Yellow Sands*, 116).

Gothic horror is similarly displaced and transformed at the end of "The Lady of the House of Love" by twentieth-century history and the real enough killing fields of World War I. Accompanied by birdsong, the Hero leaves the castle on his bicycle, "So I sped through the purged and rational splendours of the morning; but when I arrived at Bucharest, I learned of the assassination at Sarajevo and returned to England immediately, to rejoin my regiment" (*Yellow Sands*, 116). But it is the Count who has the last laugh, because the young man is off to a bloody war.

Carter's Countess arguably fuses various motifs from "Sleeping Beauty." Her sharp, pointed teeth evoke the lethal spindle of the traditional story, and her death-in-life state is not unlike the hundred years' sleep to which the princess is condemned by the old fairy's curse.[37] The self-loathing heroine is both Sleeping Beauty and her cannibal mother-in-law, thereby reviving the specters and scary monsters that haunt the fairy-tale tradition: "the flesh-eating ogre[s] and . . . death itself" that, as Marina Warner aptly observes, "are not always invoked in order to be dispelled."[38] As such, the vampire illustrates the dynamics of retelling at work in the fairy-tale tradition itself, endlessly reinvented through new combinations of characters, motifs, and images as well as cross-generic and intermedial transpositions.

Carter's radio play and short story therefore draw on a range of artistic forms, genres, and media that share a number of conventions, including stock characters, stylized language, and predictable plots. Whereas radio stresses the fairy tale's privileged connection with speech (which etymologically comes from *fari*, "to speak" in Latin), the short story explores its links with romantic literature and Gothic fiction. Historically, these genres are indeed interrelated, because the reception of French fairy tales in England influenced the development of Gothic fiction, out of which melodrama notoriously emerged.[39] Carter's vampires thus symbolize the author's awareness of the difficulties but also the potentialities of renewing and regenerating formulaic fiction by recovering hidden connections that lead to the recognition of the complex interpenetration of literary genres and the fact that vampire stories never die—at least as long as they prey and feed on other texts and artistic forms.

Reading "La Belle au bois dormant" Backward: Fairy-Tale Gothic

> A specific figure animates this essay: the figure is the vampire: the one who pollutes lineages on the wedding night; the one that effects category transformations by illegitimate passages of substance; the one who drinks and infuses blood in a paradigmatic act of infecting whatever poses as pure; . . . I think vampires can be vectors of category transformation in a racialized, historical, national unconscious.
>
> —DONNA HARAWAY, "UNIVERSAL DONORS IN A VAMPIRE CULTURE," 356

Carter's ingenious, self-conscious, and self-engendering retellings of the familiar tale of "Sleeping Beauty" enable us to discover anew the classic texts that she read so carefully and imaginatively. *Vampirella* and "The Lady of the House of Love" challenge the modern perception of "Sleeping Beauty" as a bland fairy-tale romance partly because it also revisits the folktale tradition exemplified by the Grimms. And yet Carter also brings to the fore the darker aspects of Perrault's "La Belle au bois dormant" and even picks up on a detail around which her translation for children arguably revolves: the tender farewell kiss given by the royal parents to their sleeping daughter, which has the power to dispel vampires, spooks, and other figures of nightmare.

Perrault's "La Belle au bois dormant" is much more complex and ambiguous than its subsequent reception has made it out to be. Although this is inevitably downplayed in the translation, Carter's blending or fusing of the fairy tale and the vampire story in her two retellings foregrounds the sinister aspects of the Sleeping Beauty story, such as family curses, doomed unions, and temporal distortions. It also draws attention to the threatening presence of the flesh-eating mother-in-law in the second half of Perrault's *conte*. This perversion is represented by the anthropophagous Beane family in *Vampirella*, and the familiar variation, vampirism, appears in both the radio play and the short story.

Carter's retellings of "Sleeping Beauty" not only play with the idea of the creative process as a deliberate vampirizing of the literary and cultural past but also explore the generic combinations, structural inversions, and semantic possibilities suggested by her main source. Reformulation (in the sense of finding a new chemical formula) thus becomes a key creative strategy that enables Carter to explore the potential for revival and renewal of formulaic (sub)genres.[40] Carter's vampire stories exploit the more disturbing aspects of Perrault's *conte* and the textual complexities that have been effaced or neutralized in simplified versions of the story.

As I argued earlier, *Vampirella* seeks to recover "the atavistic lure, the atavistic power, of voices in the dark" (*Yellow Sands*, 13). Carter accordingly draws attention to references to folklore in Perrault's "La Belle au bois dormant"; reported by the peasants to the prince, these stories spur him on to find the princess.[41] All kinds of scary legends surround the enchanted castle, which is said to be haunted by ghosts ("esprits") and wizards ("les sorciers de la contrée," *Contes*, 134). Most agree, however, that "un Ogre y demeurait, et que là il emportait tous les enfants qu'il pouvait attraper, pour pouvoir les manger à son aise, et sans qu'on pût le suivre, ayant seul le pouvoir de se faire un passage au travers du bois" (*Contes*, 134–35) ("But the most popular story was, that it was the home of an ogre who carried all the children he caught there, to eat them at his leisure, knowing nobody else could follow him through the wood," *Fairy Tales*, 63). A mere superstition, surely, except that the horrific stories and dark legends told by the peasants are closer to the truth than we might think, because the princess's mother-in-law turns out to be an ogress who will later try to devour her daughter-in-law and her two grandchildren.

Carter thus seems to elaborate on the orally transmitted tales embedded within Perrault's literary *conte* but left unexplored by the French writer. As it happens, the peasants tell these stories to the son of an ogress, who seems to have inherited from his mother the special gift of crossing the magical wood unharmed. The repetition of the word *passer* in this passage even seems to signal (and enact) the connection between the ogre of hearsay and the young prince crossing the forest unharmed: "A peine s'avança-t-il vers le bois, que tous ces grands arbres, ces ronces et ces épines, s'écartèrent d'elles-mêmes pour le laisser passer" (*Contes*, 135) ("No sooner had he stepped among the trees than the great trunks and branches, the thorns and brambles parted, to let him pass," *Fairy Tales*, 63). The next sentence reinforces this textual echo by insisting on the feat of the prince, for whom trees part and close after him ("Les arbres s'étaient rapprochés dès qu'il avait été passé," *Contes*, 135; "The trees sprang together again as soon as he had gone between them," *Fairy Tales*, 64).

Another scene in Perrault's text presents an equally intriguing confusion or crossing of antagonistic characters. The tale memorably opens with the grand dinner prepared for the fairies, which seals the young princess's fate.[42] After her disenchantment and marriage to the prince, the young princess is persecuted by the queen mother, who repeats over and over that she wants to eat, first "la petite Aurore," then "le Petit Jour," and finally "la jeune Reine" (*Contes*, 138). Combining her brutal atavistic drive with gourmet sophistication *à la française*, she declares that she wants to eat the little girl in an "ogrish" tone (note the importance of voice), one of the few descriptive elements given about her in Perrault's tale: "Je le veux, dit la Reine (et elle le dit d'un ton d'Ogresse qui a envie de manger de la chair fraîche), et je la veux manger à la Sauce-robert" (*Contes*, 138) ("The queen was twenty, now, if you did not count the hundred years she had been asleep; her skin was white and lovely but it was a little tough . . . ," *Fairy Tales*, 69). Perrault's cannibal humor here is particularly ferocious. Even the narrator temporarily adopts the perspective of the ogress by way of the cook to comment on the quality of the young queen's flesh, white and beautiful but probably a bit tough: "La jeune Reine avait vingt ans passés, sans compter les cent ans qu'elle avait dormi: sa peau était un peu dure, quoique belle et blanche" (*Contes*, 138) ("'She's just the very thing I fancy,' said the queen mother in the voice of an ogress famished for fresh meat. 'And I want you to serve her up with sauce Robert,'" *Fairy Tales*, 68).

Like Sleeping Beauty, Carter's vampirical Countess is at once young and ageless, uncannily beautiful and morbidly pale as befits her condition. Like the old queen, however, she hungers for young flesh and her nostrils quiver at the smell of the young man's blood. But the discovery of tenderness (*ten-*

dresse as opposed to *tendreté*, which in French distinguishes human softness of heart from the culinary quality of tender meat—an interlinguistic pun that seems to inform Carter's retellings) will humanize her when the Hero "touch[es] her forehead, as if [he] had been kissing a child goodnight" (*Yellow Sands*, 114).

The confusion between the fairy-tale heroine and her monstrous antagonist in Perrault's text is also subtly suggested when the queen mother and the young queen are both referred to as *Reine* and only distinguished by age. This ambiguity is reinforced by the old queen's urge to eat the younger one, a desire that is in a sense realized in Carter's vampire stories, where the two characters become one. When the cook kills a doe in place of the young queen and cooks it for the old one, the latter eats the dish heartily: "Il alla accommoder une biche, que *la Reine* mangea à son soupé, avec le même appétit que si c'eût été *la jeune Reine*. Elle était bien contente de sa cruauté, et elle se préparait à dire au Roi, à son retour, que les loups enragés avaient mangé *la Reine* sa femme et ses deux enfants" (*Contes*, 139; italics mine). The first sentence, however, is ambiguous, as "appetite" could equally well refer to the old or the young queen. This ironic effect disappears in Carter's translation, which distinguishes the two antagonists both grammatically and lexically: The butler "went to kill a young doe that the queen mother ate for supper with as much relish as if it had been her daughter-in-law" (*Fairy Tales*, 70). The confusion in the French text is further increased by the proximity of the phrase "la Reine-Mère" (the queen-mother) to designate the ogress and "la Reine sa mère" (the queen his mother) to refer to the young queen in the next paragraph.

Another kind of contamination arises when the old queen imagines a lie to disguise her crimes. She wants her son to believe that wolves ate his wife and children, a lie that is materialised in the very language of the text when the narrator describes her in animal terms immediately after.

> Un soir qu'elle *rôdait* à son ordinaire dans les cours et basses-cours du Château pour y *halener* quelque viande fraîche, elle entendit dans une salle basse le petit Jour qui pleurait, parce que la Reine sa mère le voulait faire fouetter. (*Contes*, 139; italics mine).[43]

> One night as she prowled about as usual, sniffing for the spoor of fresh meat, she heard a voice coming from the servants' quarters. It was little Day's voice; he was crying because he had been naughty

and his mother wanted to whip him. (*Fairy Tales*, 70)

The ogrish nature of the old queen is revealed by her tone of voice, and her connection with wolves is betrayed by the lie that she imagines to account for the disappearance of her daughter-in-law and her children. She thinks of accusing "les loups enragés" (*Contes*, 139) (ravenous or rabid wolves), but here again the (tall or telltale) tale within the tale is not so far removed from the truth, insofar as she behaves like a wolf.

Thus the performative function of language is not only thematized in "La Belle au bois dormant" in the opening scene of the cursing of the newly born baby but also enacted in the very text of the tale, to the point that the boundaries between prey and predator, story and discourse, are blurred. Carter's vampire stories thus encourage us to go back to Perrault's *conte* and reread it in the original language, as Carter herself did, and become aware of its textual complexities as a vein of inspiration.

"The Art of Horrorzines," or When Baudelaire Meets Vampirella

We have seen that Carter reworked the material of the familiar stories on which she preyed in characteristic postmodern fashion by experimenting with unexpected generic (trans)fusions and transpositions. These creative strategies also include a self-conscious exploitation of the transformative effects resulting from the crossing of linguistic, national, and cultural frontiers and the arbitrary boundary between "high" and popular culture. Carter's entire oeuvre indeed reflects the author's insatiable intellectual curiosity and her manifold activities as a cultural critic, translator, and editor. Always impatient at being seen as a British writer, Carter reveled in cross-cultural traffic, and this is comically dramatized in her vampire fiction, which stages a confrontation between "reason" (represented by the young British Hero who believes in science and bicycles) and the supernatural, transgressive forces epitomized by the Francophile heroine and the inhabitants of the Transylvanian castle.

Although *Vampirella* references Gothic literature as a European phenomenon, it also pays homage to the sexy comic book heroine created by the American Forrest J. Ackerman in 1969 and the subculture of comic books and Hammer films so popular in the 1970s (Figure 5.2). In "The Art of Horrorzines" (published in *New Society* in 1975), Carter celebrates this modern spin-off of Gothic fiction in popular culture, the fanzine.[44] And yet she also claims in the same article that "there's no denying, Vampirella's got a lot more class in French" (447). Her heroine is accordingly inspired by the sexy comic strip vamp filtered through the dark glamour of the Baudelairian vampire—decadent, artificial, macabre, moody, melodramatic, sensuous, sophisticated, and self-consciously theatrical.[45]

Carter observes that the vampire myth reflects culturally specific echoes and resonances and accounts for the reception of the American Gothic in France: "Baudelaire's version of Poe helps to distort, to etherealise, to surrealise the original image of the chubby Vampirella in all its native sexploitativeness and sensationalism" ("Art of Horrorzines," 448).[46] These obser-

Figure 5.2. Vampirella, *1977 special issue.* ® & © 2013 DFI. Courtesy of Dynamite Entertainment.

vations on the cultural inflections of the vampire myth are based on her reading of the French fan magazine *Vampirella*, which, she rejoices, "is the antithesis of that aspect of the British intellectual tradition typified by F. R. Leavis and those unable to see anything extraordinary in the juxtaposition of an umbrella and a sewing machine on a dissecting table" (448). Carter's enthusiasm for the magazine, as opposed to the Leavisite bourgeois ethos eager to maintain cultural hierarchies and impervious to the marvelous, stems from the shattering of arbitrary hierarchies between high and popular culture, good and bad taste, American pop culture and French Decadentism, which she sees at work in the "parody academe" characteristic of "sub-culture of the comic buff" (449). The metaphor popularized by the surrealists to celebrate the creative potential of incongruous juxtapositions that awaken all kinds of associations perfectly applies to her own creative method. Carter observes that the women's movement influenced the fanzine "in rather a complex way" (450).

Carter's Countess is not only inspired by the "sexually liberated" Marvel World heroine Angel O'Hara, who preys on her male victims, but also by Michael Morbius, with whom she shares a sense of her tragic condition, as "an existential kind of vampire" "consumed with self-loathing." Morbius himself, she remarks, is influenced by "those nineteenth-century French decadents with whose style the captions are heavily tinged" ("Art of Horrorzines," 450). Carter's own Vampirellas therefore draw on the "raw material" of a global culture that is itself marked by cross-cultural borrowings, adaptations, and reformulations, nourished as it is on the American comic strip as much as the French *poètes maudits* and thereby participating in the general circulation, blending, and transformation of texts, genres, and ideas.

Carter's reinvention of highly coded genres, such as Gothic fiction, the fairy tale, and the comic strip, thus illustrates the idea of literary creation as cultural traffic and the transfusion of new blood into old (textual and other) bodies, a variation on her well-known image of "new reading of old texts" as akin to "putting new wine in old bottles, especially if the pressure of the new wine makes the old bottles explode" ("Notes from the Front Line," 37). In this vampire context, of course, the wine is red.

6

Recovering a Female Tradition

FROM "LA BELLE ET LA BÊTE" TO "BEAUTY AND THE BEAST" AND "THE TIGER'S BRIDE"

Taming or Turning into the Beast? From "Sweetheart" and "Beauty and the Beast" to "The Courtship of Mr. Lyon" and "The Tiger's Bride"

Beast conquers Beauty & bestializes her.

—ANGELA CARTER, 1977 JOURNAL

Angela Carter also translated two *contes* by Jeanne-Marie Leprince de Beaumont: "Le Prince Chéri" and "La Belle et la Bête." The tales were published alongside her translations of Perrault in *Sleeping Beauty and Other Favourite Fairy Tales* (1982).[1] "Beauty and the Beast" inspired two stories included in *The Bloody Chamber* ("The Courtship of Mr. Lyon" and "The Tiger's Bride") that resolve the conflict between the female heroine and the male beast in radically different ways. Carter's rewritings revisit the literary and the rich visual tradition of the tale. Marina Warner notes in *From the Beast to the Blonde* that Jean Cocteau's film *La belle et la bête* (1945) had a profound impact on Angela Carter, "who specially remembered the way the Beast smouldered—literally—after a kill" (296). She also observes that Cocteau's film reflects a "masculine sympathy" that "divert[s] the story from the female subject to stress male erotic hunger for beauty as the stimulus for creativity" (296).[2] Although the surreal atmosphere of Cocteau's film and its preoccupation with instinct are perceptible in "The Tiger's Bride," Carter explores the female side of the story when she retells it from the perspective of Beauty.

Beaumont co-opted the fairy tale for her educational project, and she adapted it to serve the moral education of girls, who were encouraged to draw its lessons through her fictional alter ego, Melle Bonne. In the frame narrative the governess comments that an ugly face is soon forgotten when the person has a good heart and that duty is always rewarded. Carter admired Beaumont's "Beauty and the Beast" for its artfulness and melancholy, but she made sure to tone down its pious sentimentality and heavy-handed moralizing in her translation. In "About the Stories" (in *Sleeping Beauty and Other Favourite Fairy Tales*) she praises the French governess for accommodating the fairy tale as children's literature in England, and she goes on to subtly reorient the message of the translated tales for modern-day readers. In her own retellings, however, Carter enhances the literary refinement, sensuousness, and psychological depth of Beaumont's tales of enchantment for an adult audience. "The Courtship of Mr. Lyon" and "The Tiger's Bride" explore the potential of Beaumont's *contes* for alternative retellings by taking the story in two different directions. Carter thus draws our attention to Beaumont's own doubling of the story in *Le Magasin des enfants* and to ambiguities within the texts themselves; in her turn, she uses the tale to explore the relationship between self and other and the possibility of bridging social, cultural, gender, and even deeper ontological or epistemological divides.

As an emblematic beast-marriage story, "Beauty and the Beast" revolves around the conflict between nature and culture, humanity and beastliness. Carter sees the fairy tale as an occasion to reappraise and deconstruct these rigid oppositions with a feminist and ecological sensibility, based on elements that already make them problematic in the source text, starting with the contrast of inner self and external appearance that characterizes the Beast. As such, Carter's own Beauty and the Beast stories can be seen as part of a broader investigation of beings who are not what they seem. *The Bloody Chamber* is peopled with beastly men and manly beasts, starting with the perverse Marquis as a beast in disguise in "The Bloody Chamber," the manly werewolf in "The Company of Wolves," and even (in a different key) the lusty booted cat in "Puss-in-Boots."[3] In one way or another, all the stories explore women's complex relations with various forms of beastliness (from the recognition of inhumanity at the heart of human civilization to the tenderness of wild animals) that culminate in "Wolf-Alice," the hybrid wolf-girl who ministers to the monstrous Count when he is wounded by villagers.

In both her afterword to *Sleeping Beauty and Other Fairy Tales* and her interview with John Haffenden, Carter insists on the literariness of Beaumont's *conte*.

> It seems to me important that Beauty and the Beast does not come out of oral tradition: it's an art story, written for children—just as my stories are art stories—and it was intended as a perfectly tuned moral tale. Actually, it's an advertisement for moral blackmail: when the Beast says that he is dying because of Beauty, the only morally correct thing for her to have said at that point would be: "Die, then."[4]

Carter therefore aligns her own "art stories" with Beaumont's, while ironizing their moral import.

Although her translation remains close to the original, Carter rectifies Beaumont's moral somewhat to reflect her own values. In the retellings, however, she openly queries the social, moral, and epistemological underpinnings of the classic story.[5] Whereas "The Courtship of Mr. Lyon" subtly complicates the opposition between Beauty and the Beast while following the familiar plot, "The Tiger's Bride" boldly deviates from it when the heroine rejects convention and humanity itself to embrace a beastlike condition and thereby draws the reader's attention to the ending of the tale as an ideologically—and even philosophically—loaded moment. The "nursery story" thus serves to interrogate anthropocentric categories and destabilize manmade hierarchies.

Sleeping Beauty and Other Favourite Fairy Tales includes two of Beaumont's *contes* from *Le Magasin des enfants* (1756): "La Belle et la Bête" and the lesser-known "Le Prince Chéri," which is a sort of prequel to the classic story. "Le Prince Chéri" tells about a young prince transformed into a Beast as a punishment for his bad behavior. Carter's translation of "Sweetheart" thus contributes to the rediscovery of a lesser-known variation on "Beauty and the Beast" that influenced her own fairy-tale rewritings. In this way Carter paid tribute to a female author obscured by the male canon of Perrault, the Grimm brothers, and Hans Christian Andersen. Beaumont indeed played an important role as a cultural mediator of the literary fairy-tale tradition in England, which she helped legitimize as a genre suitable for children, although her stories have deeper resonances and implications that Carter would explore in "The Courtship of Mr. Lyon" and "The Tiger's Bride."

Recovering a Female Fairy-Tale Tradition: Beaumont's Beast Stories as Transitional Texts

In her foreword to *The Fairy Tales of Charles Perrault* (1977) Carter makes a passing reference to Marie-Catherine d'Aulnoy and Jeanne-Marie Leprince de Beaumont as two outstanding fairy-tale authors slighted by literary history. She mentions Beaumont's "Beauty and the Beast" and d'Aulnoy's "White Cat," "with its handsome prince, magic castle and princess suffering the most exquisite feline transformation" (14), as two fairy tales "often assumed incorrectly to be part of Perrault's legacy" (14–15).[6] To some extent *Sleeping Beauty and Other Favourite Fairy Tales* remedies this injustice and hints at the masculine bias of the modern fairy-tale canon. Carter's plan to write a second book of "New Mother Goose Tales" based on the work of d'Aulnoy and Beaumont and her subsequent edition of two volumes of fairy tales by women for Virago contributed to restoring forgotten female voices.

Aside from the larger question of the gendering of the fairy-tale genre, Carter was acutely aware of the grounding of individual tales in specific historical and cultural contexts.[7] In "About the Stories" she elaborates on Perrault's and Beaumont's different use of the fairy tale as a result of an epochal change in perceptions of childhood and the development of edifying literature for children. Unlike Perrault's pragmatic (and sometimes morally doubtful) tales, Beaumont's stories seek to educate children by promoting obedience, filial duty, and selflessness but also courage, kindness, sincerity, self-control, and firmness of purpose. In short, as Carter puts it, Beaumont "believes that children need only be *good* in order to deserve happy endings" (*Sleeping Beauty*, 125).

In classic folkloristic fashion Carter associates Beaumont's "Beauty and the Beast" with the tradition of beast-marriage stories throughout the world. Significantly, she does not retain the Opies' disquisition on the literary origins of the tale in *The Classic Fairy Tales*, asserting instead that "*Beauty and the Beast* still has its origins deep in the antique, international heritage of the folk-tale" (*Sleeping Beauty*, 125).[8] As we have seen, Carter's valuing of a popular, oral tradition was congenial to her socialist and feminist stance, but she nevertheless refused to regard the literary tradition as a debased form of folklore; her artistic sensibility made her recognize the literary qualities of Beaumont's rendering of the tale, which she praised as the most fully accomplished realization of the story: "The formal perfection, tenderness and wit with which Madame de Beaumont retold Beauty and the Beast remain impossible to improve upon" (*Sleeping Beauty*, 126).

Carter also underlines significant differences between Perrault and Beaumont that hint at changing perceptions of the genre and shifts in practice, purpose, style, and audience. Her brief presentation of Beaumont's life, times, and work in "About the Stories" thus challenges a number of received ideas about the fairy tale as an authorless, unchanging, and artless narrative form. It also sheds light on Carter's own project as a translator for children and as a writer for adults. The French governess, Carter approvingly notes, worked for a living and gained a degree of independence by becoming an accomplished author. Carter retains the idea of the pedagogical value of the fairy tale in the translation, which she adapts to her own times and values, and goes on to use it as a tool for critical inquiry and intellectual development.[9] Carter thus portrays Beaumont as a literary "foremother" of sorts: a gifted woman traveling between languages and cultures, independent and active, who earned a living by writing fairy tales that combine artistic, social, moral, and pedagogical concerns.[10]

Like Carter, Beaumont indeed believed in education as a means to foster autonomous thinking and advance the cause of women.[11] Although politically conservative (a royalist) and a devout Catholic, Beaumont was a proto-feminist of sorts who started her writing career with a pamphlet against l'Abbé Coyer's conservative views of women. In her witty response to Coyer, titled "Lettre en réponse à l'auteur de *l'Année merveilleuse*," Beaumont argues that far from being inferior to Adam, Eve was God's ultimate achievement. God, she explains, was not at all satisfied with his creation after fashioning Adam out of dirt.

> Ce composé, dit-elle, ne donnait qu'une faible idée de sa science . . . . C'est son chef-d'oeuvre auquel il destine les derniers coups de pinceau. Il forme la femme: tout est accompli. Il cesse alors de créer de nouvelles créatures.[12]

> This composite being, she said, only gave a feeble idea of his science. ... It is to his masterpiece that he devotes his last painter brushes. He gives woman her shape: all is accomplished. Then only does he cease to create new creatures. (translation mine)

More fundamentally perhaps, Carter shared Beaumont's progressive views on education. Probably influenced by John Locke's treatise *Some Thoughts Concerning Education* (1693), Beaumont formulates her dissatisfaction with the stultifying educational methods of her days, promoting dynamic exchange and open dialogue with the governess, who can act as a firm but benevolent tutor. She remarks that children—especially girls—are taught to speak, to listen, and to look but not to think for themselves. By contrast, she declares, "Je veux leur apprendre à penser, à penser juste pour parvenir à bien vivre. Si je n'avais pas l'espoir de parvenir à cette fin, je renoncerais dès ce moment à écrire et à enseigner" (quoted in Robain's *Beaumont*, 74) ("My aim is to teach them to think, and to think well in order to live well. If I did not have hope that I can reach this aim, I would immediately stop writing and teaching" [translation mine]). Beaumont's lifelong ambition was to instruct through conversation and discussion rather than through rote learning and constraint. This pedagogical principle is conveyed in the dialogical structure of the *Magasin des enfants*, in which a number of fairy tales are embedded, the morals of which are elicited by the children themselves with the help of their governess. Like Beaumont, then, Carter wanted children, adolescents, *and* adults to learn to think for themselves in order to "live well."[13]

Carter also draws attention to the difference between the original editorial context of Beaumont's *contes de fées* and modern-day publication practices. She gives the full title of the *Magasin des enfants* in French, points out that the book was first published in London, and summarizes the author's stated purpose. "The book intended to blend 'the useful' with 'the agreeable' in the form of a collection of moral tales, of which *Beauty and the Beast* is one. It was translated as *The Young Misses Magazine* in 1761" (*Sleeping Beauty*, 127). Carter signals that "Beauty and the Beast" was originally part of a much more capacious and heterogeneous "magazine" from which it was subsequently isolated. She mentions its early reception in English, with a new title that explicitly targets girls. She also points out that Beaumont's *conte* was itself a rewriting for children of a longer *conte de fée* by

Gabrielle Susanne Barbot de Gallon de Villeneuve, in *La jeune Américaine et les contes marins* (1740). In doing so, Carter situates her own endeavor as part of a long chain of translations, adaptations, and retellings of fairy tales for children, but she also hints at an older tradition of literary tales for adults exemplified by d'Aulnoy and Villeneuve.

Carter also praises Beaumont's introduction of subjectivity and psychological realism in the fairy tale, innovations that will come to characterize the Victorian novel. She approvingly sees in the character of Beauty a modern "fully-realised heroine" exhibiting the qualities of "stoicism, courage and kindness" (*Sleeping Beauty*, 128) that she will promote in her own work. Carter situates Beaumont's intervention as a major one in the fairy-tale tradition, which itself is inseparable from the development of nineteenth-century fiction; the presence of rounded characters and the complex portrayal of father-daughter relationships, evolving feelings, and psychological insights would feed into the novels of Jane Austen and the Brontës. Carter thus makes a connection between French fairy-tale authors and the heyday of the English novel, bringing to light previously unacknowledged cross-cultural connections and hidden filiations and recognizing the importance of the "minor" genre of the fairy tale in the development of English literature.[14]

Probably because she is a writer herself, Carter is also sensitive to the literary merits of Beaumont's "self-conscious, sensuous, evocative" prose, which seduces the reader into the magical world of the tale.

> With Beauty's father, we shiver in the cold wind in the wood, shudder to hear the Beast's frightful roar; the haunted solitude of the Beast's palace enchants us as it does Beauty. We live inside the story until we, too, like Beauty, are almost sad to find, when we have learned to love the dear, ugly, irreplaceable Beast, that, after all, he is no more than a common or garden enchanted prince. (*Sleeping Beauty*, 128)

The evocative and affective style of Beaumont's writing is the true locus of magic; the strange, haunted atmosphere of the isolated palace echoes Beauty's complex emotional response to the Beast, translating physical sensations into feelings ("shiver," "shudder," "enchants," "sad," "love") and fostering identification with the female character.[15] Carter even observes that there is a hint of regret in Beauty's reaction to the metamorphosis of the

Beast into a prince, and this draws attention to the psychological and textual complexity of Beaumont's tale that will serve as a starting point for Carter's own rewritings. Thus the Beast in "The Courtship of Mr. Lyon" ends up with only a vague, "distant . . . resemblance to the handsomest of all the beasts" (*Bloody Chamber*, 51). This comes as a slight disappointment to the reader; the tale ends on a melancholic note where the enchanted world of the fairy-tale world gives way to a clichéd picture of bourgeois comfort and domestic bliss.[16] In contrast, the Beast returns to his animal state in "The Tiger's Bride," and so does Beauty, who relinquishes the alienating trappings of humanity. Whereas the first rewriting complies with the structure of the classic tale, the second follows up the hint in Beaumont's text that the animality of the Beast is part of its appeal to its logical conclusion.

Carter, then, presents Beaumont's *Magasin des enfants* as a prime example of the cross-cultural and transgeneric dynamic at the heart of literary history. While she pursues (and also modifies) the moralizing strain that "would dominate nineteenth century stories for children" (*Sleeping Beauty*, 128) in her translation, she foregrounds the literariness of Beaumont's tales in her own sophisticated, self-conscious retellings of the Beauty and the Beast tale in *The Bloody Chamber*, whose spell-binding power resides in the "magical art" (128) of language.

From "Le Prince Chéri" to "Sweetheart": Transformation as Self-Reformation

> The notion of the fairy-tale as a vehicle for moral instruction is not a fashionable one.
>
> —ANGELA CARTER, "THE BETTER TO EAT YOU WITH," 452

Carter's decision to publish her translation of Beaumont's "Le Prince Chéri" in *Sleeping Beauty and Other Favourite Fairy Tales* may seem at first surprising, because the tale is sentimental and heavily moralistic. Like other fairy tales adapted for children by Beaumont, "Le Prince Chéri" also finds its source in the literary tradition of the marvelous tale for adults, namely, Marie-Catherine d'Aulnoy's much longer "La Princesse Belle Etoile et le Prince Chéri" from her *Contes nouveaux, ou Les fées à la mode*, anthologized in Charles-Joseph Mayer's *Nouveau cabinet des fées* (1785). Beaumont's version of the tale is found in a few nineteenth-century anthologies, including Andrew Lang's *Blue Fairy Book* (1889). Carter may have wanted to reintroduce the story into the fairy-tale canon in a modernized form; she reorients Beaumont's praise of Christian virtues to respect, consideration, and empathy for others, especially women and animals, in her translation for children.

"Le Prince Chéri" tells the story of a good king who spares a white rabbit's life when he is out hunting. The animal turns out to be a fairy in disguise who agrees to look after the king's beloved son, the eponymous Prince Chéri. The fairy warns the king that her powers are limited and that she can only give the prince good advice. The prince receives a golden ring that pricks him every time he misbehaves. When he inherits the throne after the king's death, however, things go from bad to worse. Left to his own devices, the young king kicks his dog and becomes more and more tyrannical with his subjects. Irritated by the ring, which reminds him of his duty, he gets rid of it. He falls in love with a shepherdess named Zélie and tries to force her into marrying him. When she refuses, he is infuriated and locks her up. His old tutor liberates the girl, and he is imprisoned in his turn. At this point the fairy Candida reappears, scolds the young king, and transforms him into a beast that embodies his various vices (anger, pride, cruelty, impatience, etc.). The old tutor becomes king, and the monster is locked up in the menagerie, where he slowly begins to reform himself. Despite the bad treatment he suffers there, he saves his guardian's life and is set free. He gradually recovers his humanity after every good deed, first changing into a dog and then a bird before recovering his human shape when he confesses his love to Zélie in the presence of an old hermit who turns out to be the fairy in disguise.

The modernity of the tale must have struck Carter, who like Beaumont believed in nurture over nature and the idea of the moral tale as an educational tool. Aside from the theme of the enlightened prince typical of early children's literature, Beaumont's "Prince Chéri" targets the "enfant roi" (king child) turned into a little monster by a doting father and overindulgent relatives. The child thinks that the entire world turns around him and must do as he wishes, and he throws tantrums when contradicted. "Le Prince Chéri" seeks to reform the prince by preaching kindness to animals and the qualities of stoicism, courage, and kindness manifest in Zélie, who resists his tyrannical rule. A "good heart" therefore contributes to social and gender equality, respect for others (including animals), peaceful living together, freedom of speech and action, and respect and tolerance for difference. The tale even posits that love must be premised on goodness ("virtue" in Beaumont's terms) in order to last.[17]

When she translates the tale as "Sweetheart," Carter characteristically adapts its language and message for modern-day readers. The English translation remains close to its source, although a few marginal characters disappear, as do minor digressions that could distract from the main plot. The translator also opts for a familiar tone (e.g., "You really do look very comic, in such a tizzy!" *Sleeping Beauty*, 118; for "Je me moque de ta faiblesse et de ta rage," *Beaumont*, 197), and the character's speeches are less contrived. Carter also tones down the sentimentalism, probably because it is seen as a period marker but also because it is alien to her own ethos.

In the title the name of the beloved prince (Chéri) is translated as "Sweetheart," a term of endearment that ironically contrasts with his bad character. He is taught a lesson and learns to be true to his name in typical fairy-tale fashion. The emphasis placed on the heart also captures Carter's valuing of a "good heart" rather than on mere virtuous behavior and conformity to the norm. The avoidance of the word *prince* in the title also attenuates the connection between education and social class and also distinguishes the tale from Oscar Wilde's "The Happy Prince" (from the eponymous collection published in 1888) and "The Young Prince" (from *The House of Pomegranates*, 1891). Likewise, Carter's rabbit is not white, probably to avoid activating the *Alice in Wonderland* intertext. Indeed, Carter's aim is not to emulate Wilde's fin de siècle fairy tales or even Lewis Carroll's surreal fantasies but to carry a few simple messages home. When the old king saves the rabbit and this good deed results in the granting of a wish, the fairy Candida voices the moral as follows, which Carter translates in a slightly modified—and telltale—fashion:

> J'ai voulu savoir si vous étiez bon comme tout le monde le dit. Pour cela j'ai pris la figure d'un petit lapin et je me suis sauvée dans vos bras; car je sais que ceux qui ont de la pitié pour les bêtes en ont encore plus pour les hommes. (*Beaumont*, 191)

> I decided I would find out if the good things they say about you are

true. So I changed into a rabbit and threw myself on your mercy, because I know that people who are kind to animals are kinder still to men *and women*. (*Sleeping Beauty*, 113; italics mine)

Respect for animals will resonate in Carter's manifest admiration for wild animals in the rewritings, and the subordinate condition of women (which the translator added in her translation of the passage) under patriarchy will be stressed in "The Tiger's Bride."

The translation adopts a fluid style, short words, and a simple vocabulary and avoids relative clauses and subordination in favor of rhythmic, musical language, as in the opening sentence: "Once a good king went out hunting" (*Sleeping Beauty*, 113) ("Il y avait une fois un roi qui était si honnête homme, que ses sujets l'appelaient le *roi Bon*," Beaumont, 191). Because it avoids subordination and eliminates wordiness and superfluous details, the translation is somewhat shorter than the source text (4,528 words against 3,398 words).

The concern of the old father for his young son is couched in less openly moralizing language, as Carter conveys *virtue* by *goodness* ("Il n'y a que la vertu qui puisse rendre content," Beaumont, 191; "Only the good are happy," *Sleeping Beauty*, 114). She nevertheless retains Beaumont's reflections on the role of stories in educating children.

What is also interesting about the portrayal of the fairy is Carter's ready admission of her limited powers, like the governess/storyteller herself. She cannot "turn your Sweetheart into a good man in spite of himself. He must work hard at good deeds" (*Sleeping Beauty*, 114). She can only "give him sound advice" and, if he does not take heed, "punish him" (114) ("Mais il n'est pas en mon pouvoir de rendre le prince Chéri *honnête* homme malgré lui. Il faut qu'il travaille lui-même à devenir *vertueux*. Tout ce que je puis vous promettre, c'est de lui donner de bons conseils, de le reprendre de ses fautes, et de le punir s'il ne veut pas se corriger et se punir lui-même," *Beaumont*, 191; italics mine).

To ensure coherence in characterization and avoid lachrimose sentimentality, Carter cuts the prince's effusion of tears at the death of his father. The deterioration of the prince's character starts with his bad temper when he kicks his dog. The argument that he puts forward to justify his behavior shows the corrupting effect of power leading to abuse: "What point is there in being a king, if I'm not allowed to kick my own dog?" (*Sleeping Beauty*,

115). Here the fairy intervenes to explain to him that it is "no excuse for bullying" and that his responsibilities as a king are "to do as well as you can" (*Sleeping Beauty*, 115).

The bad influence of the prince's entourage is emphasized, starting with the "old nurse" who had "thoroughly spoiled him" (*Sleeping Beauty*, 115) ("une sotte nourrice qui l'avait gâté quand il était petit," *Beaumont*, 192) and encouraged his tyrannical and "selfish ways" (*Sleeping Beauty*, 115) ("fier, orgueilleux, opiniâtre," *Beaumont*, 192). When he got older, "He tried and tried to be good, but bad habits are hard to break, although he was not naturally bad-hearted, only used to getting his own way in everything" (*Sleeping Beauty*, 115) ("Il avait pris la mauvaise habitude de tous ces défauts; et une mauvaise habitude est bien difficile à détruire. Ce n'est pas qu'il eût naturellement le coeur méchant," *Beaumont*, 192). This echoes Rousseau's theory of education, and the belief in stories as a means to promote individual reform and social change.

Note that two feminine characters, namely, the good fairy and Zélie, voice the moral of the story. In Carter's translation the shepherdess who refuses to marry the young prince even expresses the kind of popular wisdom that Carter associated with the fairy tale through the proverb "Handsome is as handsome does." Angry at the girl "for speaking her mind" (*Sleeping Beauty*, 116) ("Il fut occupé toute la journée du mépris que cette fille lui avait montré," *Beaumont*, 193), the prince locks her up in the castle. The fairy punishes the prince for oppressing an outspoken girl, who also belongs to a low social class. His tyrannical behavior is encouraged by a false friend (who happens to be the nurse's own son), although Carter takes care to eliminate the snide remark about the nurse's son's lowly birth being naturally correlated with his vile character ("cet homme, qui avait les inclinations aussi basses que sa naissance, flattait les passions de son maître et lui donnait de fort mauvais conseils," *Beaumont*, 194), blaming instead "the family tradition of flattering, pampering and spoiling the prince" (*Sleeping Beauty*, 115). The friend reminds him of his prerogatives as a king and advises him to threaten and even kill the shepherdess if she persists in refusing to obey him "to teach the rest a lesson" (*Sleeping Beauty*, 115) ("pour apprendre aux autres à céder à vos volontés," *Beaumont*, 194). This suggests that the tale contains a *good* and a *bad* lesson. When Sweetheart objects that she has done nothing wrong, the false friend replies, "She has disobeyed you" (*Sleeping Beauty*, 115).[18] This argument echoes Bluebeard's own justification for punishing his wife with death, although it merely reveals his tyranny. It is therefore up to the reader to elicit the true lesson of the tale.

Carter eliminates certain details of the plot (e.g., three young knights who encourage the prince's bad ways and his project to sell Zélie as a slave) to retain only the episode of the drinking and the discovery that Zélie has escaped, which makes him even more furious. The influence of Oriental tales on Beaumont's *conte* is also perceptible in the name of the prince's "old tutor," Suliman, who liberates the girl. The wise man, however, is not able to reason with the young despot, for he is arrested in his turn. The fairy intervenes at this point to accuse the prince of not having followed her advice. Upon these words, she makes his appearance match his true nature, so that he becomes "a perfect monster" (*Sleeping Beauty*, 117):

> Henceforward, you shall look like what you are—angry as a lion, brutal as a bull, greedy as a wolf, and treacherous as a snake.... Take on in your new shape something beastly from all these creatures. (*Sleeping Beauty*, 117)

> Je vous condamne à devenir semblable aux bêtes dont vous avez pris les inclinations. Vous vous êtes rendu semblable au lion par la colère; au loup, par la gourmandise; au serpent, en déchirant celui qui avait été votre second père; au taureau, par votre brutalité. Portez dans votre nouvelle figure le caractère de tous ces animaux. (*Beaumont*, 195)

Left in a forest, the prince sees a reflection of himself in a pool, with the "head of a lion," "a bull's horns on top; limbs of a wolf; and a long, snaky tail" (*Sleeping Beauty*, 117). The matching of inner self and outer appearance enables him to gradually reform himself, although he is first beside himself with rage. He is caught by hunters and locked in with other wild beasts. There he begins to repent, becoming "as gentle as a lamb" (*Sleeping Beauty*, 120) ("devint doux comme un mouton," *Beaumont*, 196), and he even saves his cruel keeper when the latter is attacked by a tiger. Having integrated the Christian moral of returning good for evil, he becomes a "peculiar-looking monster" (*Sleeping Beauty*, 120) who, once tamed, lies down at the feet of his keeper "purr[ing]" (*Sleeping Beauty*, 120) after overpowering the tiger. In fact, the translator does *not* have the tiger killed, as in Beaumont's version ("ce monstre bienfaisant se jeta sur le tigre, l'étrangla, et se coucha ensuite aux pieds de celui qu'il venait de sauver," *Beaumont*, 197), and this "rescuing" of the tiger in "Sweetheart" will become a full-fledged rehabilitation in "The Tiger's Bride."

Sweetheart is rewarded for this good deed by turning into a "pretty little dog" (*Sleeping Beauty*, 121), when he learns to control his hunger. On another occasion he sees men begging for food and starving to death (a grim detail eliminated in the translation), and although very hungry himself, he gives his crust to a beggar girl. When he sees Zélie being dragged toward the house, he also feels remorse, and the beggar girl warns him that "this magic house is called the Mansion of Greed" (*Sleeping Beauty*, 122) ("Cette maison est le palais de la volupté, tout ce qui en sort est empoisonné," *Beaumont*, 198). Carter's change of *volupté* (sensual pleasure) into "greed" transforms Beaumont's Christian allegory into something closer to the fairy-tale world of the Grimms' "Hänsel and Gretel." Sweetheart, who has resisted temptation, turns into a dove ("un charmant oiseau de paradis," *Beaumont*, 198). Once again the slight alteration probably reflects the pressure of the Grimms' "Singing, Springing Lark" ("Das singende, springende Löwenekerchen"), a version of "Beauty and the Beast" in which the Beast is an enchanted lion; as in the Psyche story, he turns into a white dove when light falls on him, and so the heroine embarks on a long quest to reclaim him. Carter's choice of "dove" also avoids turning the moral tale into an exotic tale of wonder.[19] After searching in vain for Zélie around the world, Sweetheart finds her sharing a meal with a holy man. When she promises to love the bird always, the prince is disenchanted at last (Carter making sure to eliminate the rather verbose speech). He confesses his love, and they fall into each other's arms. The old man is in fact the fairy in disguise, who spells out the moral and blesses the young couple: "Now you have learned your lesson and are a changed man. She can love you without reservations. Go home and live happily ever after" (*Sleeping Beauty*, 124) ("Le changement de votre Coeur lui donne la liberté de se livrer à toute sa tendresse. Vous allez vivre heureux, puisque votre union sera fondée sur la vertu," *Beaumont*, 199). The conventional fairy tale ending no longer celebrates *virtue* but *goodness* leading to *happiness*, engineered by the fairy Candida and Zélie. Although the fairy tale focuses on Sweetheart, Zélie is in fact the true heroine of the story; courageous, kind, beautiful, and loving, this peasant girl is no less independent, shy, or submissive for it. She speaks her mind and resists the tyrannical rule of the young king, refuses to marry him even though she is in love with him, and thus becomes a spokeswoman for Beaumont and, after her, for the translator herself.

The Beast Illustrated: Visual Metamorphoses from *The Classic Fairy Tales* to *Sleeping Beauty and Other Favourite Fairy Tales*

The preparatory notes for *The Bloody Chamber* indicate that Carter thoroughly researched the history of "Beauty and the Beast." She was familiar with its critical reception and the illustrated tradition, and she mentions Iona and Peter Opie's *Classic Fairy Tales* and Mary Eastman's *Index to Fairy Tales, Myths, and Legends*.[20] She notes that the "68 printed editions" of "Beauty and the Beast" listed in the *Index* are "entirely dependent upon literary influence," adding that "B&B, while undoubtedy [sic] influenced by oral tradition, became a literary tale that returned to oral tradition as a new variant." She lists the most frequent animal spouses (bear, dog, snake, pig, wolf, and lion).[21] She also signals that unlike the ancient tale of Cupid and Psyche, "the Discreet Governess Beaumont subdues the sexual element (thus making it more obviously about sex)"; Carter's parenthetical comment hints at an element that she will bring to the fore in "The Tiger's Bride." The appeal of the tale resides in the tension between natural instinct and respect for the other, which prolongs Carter's reflection on education; Carter observes that "the ancient power of the Beast's presence, controlled by a gentle nature and respect for another individual, makes Beauty and the Beast appealing to modern readers. Irrepressible instincts allied with good intentions are so palatable." This slightly ironic comment on the appeal of Beaumont's fairy tale also applies to Carter's "Courtship of Mr. Lyon."

The reception of "Beauty and the Beast" in England is also covered in some detail in Carter's notes, including its adaptations for the popular stage, illustrated books, and film. Carter lists Charles Lamb's Orientalized *Beauty and the Beast* (1811) in verse, with the dismissive comment: "rhyming versions; dumb beast, dumber beauty."[22] She also mentions J. R. Planché's 1841 pantomime where, she says, "levity rules." She notes also that Andrew Lang's version of the tale in *The Blue Fairy Book* (1889), loosely based on Madame de Villeneuve's literary tale in the *Cabinet des Fées*, was widely known in the late nineteenth century, and she adds parenthetically that this editorialized translation was accepted in England as the "authentic" form of the tale. Her own (re)translation therefore serves as a corrective of sorts.

Carter also lists "3 Gallant Plays: Fernand Nozière, lightweight pre-WWI version: when her kiss transforms the beast, she is furious—'Here I was smitten by an exceptional being, and all of a sudden, my fiancé becomes an ordinary distinguished young man.'" This picks up on an ambiguity in Beaumont's text that Carter would return to in her own retellings of the tale.

Carter's interest in the reception of the tale extends to the visual tradition. In her notes she mentions Edmund Dulac's turn-of-the-century "Moorish illustrations," which "marked a shift towards increased compartmentalization of the juvenile," and Jean Cocteau's *La Belle et la Bête* (1946), noting that Cocteau apparently complimented his cameraman for achieving "a supernatural quality within the limits of realism." Carter adds: "It is the reality of childhood. Fairyland without fairies."[23] She also exclaims "innumerable B&Bs MORE!" in the 1970s, including "1979 movie"[24] and Robin McKinley's *Beauty: A Retelling of the Story of Beauty and the Beast* (1978), glossed as "247 page novel 'about honour' back to Madame de Villeneuve." Carter ends this section with a brief summary of Betsey Hearne's interpretation of the tale as "also a moral tale," adding that "Beast shows traditionally female attributes of delicate respect for Beauty's feelings, nurturance, comfort, gentleness and patience, all of which he has learned through a humbling experience . . . Beauty must learn the same."[25]

In "The Courtship of Mr. Lyon," which long predates Hearne's study, the moral force of the tale is also seen to reside in the protagonists learning consideration for the other, which leads to their mutual humanization. "The Tiger's Bride," however, takes the story in another direction: from human, and especially gender, relations to a more profound and radical inquiry into psychology and moral philosophy. Warner notes that "Beauty has to learn to love the beast in him, in order to love the beast in herself."[26] Accordingly, the tale becomes an occasion to question the humanization of the Beast, let alone Disney's cute anthropomorphized animals. Its radical critique of anthropo- (phallogo-)centrism can even be said to anticipate contemporary debates about the status of animals.[27]

Carter's 1977 journal references Iona and Peter Opie's *Classic Fairy Tales* as an important source of information and inspiration. Apart from the texts themselves, the illustrations in the book probably stimulated Carter's imagination, including her representation of the Beast as a lion in both her translation and her rewriting of the tale. The first image of the Beast is a woodcut from *Popular Tales of the Olden Time* (c. 1840) "entreating Beauty to become his wife" (*Classic Fairy Tales*, 137). The Beast's appearance seems to be modeled on the description of the metamorphosed Prince Chéri; he looks like a lion, muscular and big-breasted and equipped with sharp teeth, curly mane, knitted brow, snub nose, claw-tipped fingers, and scaly tail. The hybrid (and soulful) monster is dressed in a kind of toga, and his posture, one hand over his heart, the other hand extended toward Beauty, looking mournfully in the other direction, evokes the melodramatic gesture of the pantomime actor.

As its etymology already suggests, the word *monster* triggers the writer's, reader's, and illustrator's visual imagination. Unlike Chéri, who turns into a composite monster whose various parts are borrowed from animals that symbolize capital sins, Beaumont's Bête is more mysterious, because he (it?) is described only through the reactions of fear that he provokes in his human visitors.[28] Thus Robinson's lion-headed Beast, complete with horns and big ears, plays with the adult resonances of the tale; the Beast becomes a perverse dandy, even a Sadeian figure, almost to the point of suggesting echoes between Beaumont's Beast and Perrault's Bluebeard (down to the alliterations of beast and beard) (Figure 6.1).[29]

Captioned "The Beast as visualized by W. Heath Robinson, 1921," the picture does not present the Beast as a scary monster but is more suggestive of a man wearing a mask; he is dressed in black leggings and a flowing striped shirt with frilled ruff and cuffs. The posture of the Beast is peculiar, standing on tiptoes, with bent knees and arms level with his head, one tapered-fingered, thin, and bony hand extended, the other one closed. The figure stands out in the open and is seen in three-quarter profile; the mouth is half-open and full of pointed teeth, as if he were about to pounce on and devour his victim. The Beast is not so much a supernatural being as a man in disguise, wearing a mask, and out to frighten a passer-by (as a highwayman in disguise) or even a flasher waiting for girls on a deserted road. This highly anthropomorphic Beast is faunlike and demonic (his strange posture suggests that he has cloven feet). The half-human, half-beastly nature of the figure evokes both Carter's Marquis, whose face is said to be like a mask, and his double and opposite, the Tiger, who hides his animal features behind a human mask.[30]

In her preparatory notes for her "New Mother Goose Tales—Beauty & the Beast sequence,"[31] Carter imagines a scene that could in fact have

Figure 6.1. The Beast as visualized by W. Heath Robinson, 1921, in The Classic Fairy Tales *by Iona and Peter Opie.*

been inspired by Robinson's image, which itself evokes Chéri's "head of a lion, with a bull's horns on top." The association of the Beast with a lion and with a faun through the proverbially lustful goat suggests that the beastliness of this particular Beast may have to do with the sexual instinct. In contrast to the lion defeating the tiger in "Sweetheart," which heralds the triumph of culture (and education) over nature and of humanity over animality, Carter chooses to walk on the wild side and go for the tiger in "The Tiger's Bride."[32] In her notes she associates the Beast figure with Sade and Byron, probably through their association with Venice. In a kind of rough sketch for a possible rewriting of the tale, the lion and the sexual danger represented by the glamorous Byronic hero (including his mysterious and slightly demonic club foot), all seem to coalesce in a story where "Beast conquers Beauty & bestializes her." Set in Venice, whose emblem is a winged lion, the Beast is associated with Byron; the Romantic poet famous for his glamour and sexual attractiveness (despite or perhaps because of his animalistic physical defect) notoriously visited Venice twice. After sketching out the opening situation, Carter describes the climax as "Beast takes off its mask; Beauty flinches." The story is set in "a fabulous 18th c. Venice, a Byronic beast with legs like a satyr; gondolas, black as agents of death—the Virgin with the Lion." Carter also observes that "it was not Byron's genius that excited public interest about him. It was his rank, his beauty, his fortune, and his mysterious reputation for strange adventures." Noting the erotic dimension of the tale, and perhaps fusing Byron's sex appeal and Sleeping Beauty's dreams, Carter jots down that Beauty "dreams she makes love with Beast."

Another well-known illustration reproduced in the Opies' book seems to have inspired Carter's "Tiger's Bride," even though there is nothing tigerlike about the Beast. This illustration represents Beauty bending over a manly Beast sporting a boarlike head with wolf's ears (Figure 6.2). Walter Crane's illustration (1874) reproduced in *The Classic Fairy Tales* (146) portrays two monkeys dressed like their master in red livery and white shirts and sporting gray hats. Looking anxiously at the dying Beast, they are pouring water or spirits into a goblet to revive it. The formally dressed Beast (in contrast to his threatening boarlike head), the posture of the two protagonists with Beauty anxiously leaning over him, and the accompanying animal servants evoke "The Tiger's Bride."

Despite their differences, Crane's image and Carter's text indeed have a few elements in common.[33] When she encounters the Beast, the rebellious bride traded off by her father remarks that she "never saw a man so big look so two-dimensional, in spite of the quaint elegance of The Beast, in the old-fashioned tail-coat" (*Bloody Chamber*, 53). The presence of his retinue denoting aristocratic status, sophistication, and human manners (the monkeys assume that their fanged master can drink out of a water goblet) also finds its parallel in Carter's version of the tale, where the tiger-man "could take a glass of ale in his hand like a good Christian" (56) and the valet-interpreter turns out to be a gibbering monkey (66). In this sense Carter's rewritings are composite "monsters" that draw on various texts and images and therefore are not unlike the Beast himself.

We have seen that the literary and iconographic tradition often represents the Beast as a lion or a tiger but also as a boar, a bear, a snake, and a wolf, because the precise nature of his beastly appearance is left to the read-

Figure 6.2. Color wood engraving by Edmund Evans, after a drawing by Walter Crane, 1874, in The Classic Fairy Tales *by Iona and Peter Opie.*

er's imagination. Michael Foreman's illustration of "Sweetheart" in *Sleeping Beauty and Other Favourite Fairy Tales* represents him as a lion-headed beast in a realistic style that contrasts with his otherwise dreamlike rendering of a fairy-tale atmosphere. Foreman's illustrations for "Beauty and the Beast," however, are realized in a quite different spirit and style inspired by Gothic imagery. One vignette represents Dracula's shadow behind a dripping candle-lit chandelier decorated with a skull (*Sleeping Beauty*, 45), and in one full-page scene Beauty and her father mournfully journey in a forest of tall, spiky trees toward an anthropomorphized castle (the door of the entrance is a gaping maw whose eyelike windows survey the surroundings in a literal depiction of a watchtower). The Beast is a loathsome creature: toady, pustulated, fanged, single-eyed, and of a mottled brownish-gray color (unlike Cocteau's shaggy Beast). Beauty, her father, and the Beast are first represented in profile sitting at the table, and in another image the monster looks the reader in the face so that we are made to share Beauty's fright and disgust when she first dines with him. The sophisticated green apparel of the Beast, with its heart-shaped neck and Elizabethan collar and white frills, evokes Jean Marais's lavish costume in Cocteau's film, but it is also reminiscent of the frog turning into a Prince Charming in the Grimms' "Frog King" ("Der Froschkönig oder der eiserne Heinrich"). The full-page illustration depicting Beauty kneeling beside the dying Beast, surrounded with frogs and lizards, further reinforces the connection with the German tale.

One of Michael Foreman's illustrations for "Sweetheart" represents the scene of the lion fighting with the tiger, which seems to have served as a starting point for Carter's twin retellings for *The Bloody Chamber*. Unlike the lion, however, the tiger will not be tamed. When their cruel keeper is asleep, the tiger attacks the man, but Sweetheart, after a moment of hesitation, comes to his rescue and kills the wild beast. When Sweetheart intervenes to save the keeper's life, he reneges on his kinship with the tiger and sides with a man, bad though he may be. He is rewarded for this "heroic" deed by turning into a tame animal—a pet dog. The episode of the tiger is made to illustrate the Christian moral of Beaumont's tale, formulated by Sweetheart himself as "I must return good for evil."

But Carter is not interested in Sunday school teaching, and she turns the tale of "Sweetheart" into a reflection on the mutually humanizing power of love in "The Courtship of Mr. Lyon." The rewriting exploits the biblical imagery of lamb versus lion and follows the strain of Beaumont's tale, inasmuch as Mr. Lyon is ultimately disenchanted by Beauty's kiss, the story ending in a bland image of domestic happiness. In "The Tiger's Bride," however, the bride chooses to explore the other possibility left open by Beaumont's story: She does not side with men who have reduced her to a pet, rejects the hierarchy of species that underlies Beaumont's tale, and embraces the tiger's condition instead.

From "La Belle et la Bête" to "Beauty and the Beast": Strange Attraction, or When an Adventurous Beauty Meets a Melancholic Beast

> Part of Angela Carter's boldness—which made her unpopular in some quarters of the feminist movement in the 1970s—was that she dared to look at women's waywardness, and especially at their attraction to the Beast in the very midst of repulsion.
>
> —MARINA WARNER, *FROM THE BEAST TO THE BLONDE*, 308

Carter's decision to keep the opening fairy-tale formula in her translation of "Beauty and the Beast" captures the essential difference that she saw between Perrault's brief and worldly "fables of experience" and Beaumont's artful literary tales. Moreover, "Once upon a time" ("Il y avait une fois") contrasts with the early English translation reproduced in the Opies' *Classic Fairy Tales* ("There was once," 139). Except for this departure from her usual translation style, Carter characteristically simplifies and reduces Beaumont's French text from 5,517 words to 5,122 words in English. The opening paragraph is a good case in point.

> Once upon a time, there lived a rich merchant who gave his three sons and his three daughters the best that money could buy. They had private tutors for everything. (*Sleeping Beauty*, 45)

> Il y avait une fois un marchand qui était extrêmement riche. Il avait six enfants, trois garçons et trois filles, et comme ce marchand était un homme d'esprit, il n'épargna rien pour l'éducation de ses enfants, et leur donna toutes sortes de maîtres. (*Beaumont*, 177)

Carter gets rid of redundant information to convey the passage in a familiar, easy, and reader-friendly style suitable for a young audience. As in her translation of Perrault, she opts for short sentences and simple syntax and avoids parenthetical clauses and emphatic turns of phrase.[34] She also modernizes the cultural references to education that are humorously referred to by Beaumont, who was herself in charge of providing children from a wealthy family with a good education. Carter also replaces Beaumont's stilted prose with "folksy" proverbs (to borrow Zipes's term), such as "Pride goes before a fall" (*Sleeping Beauty*, 46) ("Elles ne méritent pas qu'on les plaigne, nous sommes bien aises de voir leur orgueil abaissé," *Beaumont*, 177). Likewise, female schadenfreude gives way to a comic vision of poetic justice typical of the fairy tale. Unlike her sisters, Beauty similarly accepts her fate with a lively and rhythmic "I shall try to be happy without a penny" (*Sleeping Beauty*, 46).

Besides the nature of the relationship between Beauty and the Beast, the most significant changes introduced by Carter pertain to education, family relations, and the gender politics of the tale. The conflicted relationship between Beauty and her sisters is depicted in somewhat less negative terms than in Beaumont's text. It is less the beauty of the youngest girl that causes her sisters' jealousy, because they are all said to be "very pretty" ("très belles"), than her being singled out from birth and nicknamed "Little Beauty" (*Sleeping Beauty*, 45) ("la *Belle Enfant*," *Beaumont*, 177). Just as Sweetheart's father dotes on his son, Beauty's feckless father unwittingly causes his beloved daughter's misfortune, first by marking his preference for her and then by refusing to take responsibility for the rose incident, when he breaks off a rose from the Beast's garden and provokes the owner's fury. Contrary to Cinderella, whose sufferings are provoked by her father's weakness or indifference, Beauty's misery originates in her father's obvious preference for her, which causes her sisters' jealousy.

Beaumont insists on the importance of the nickname given to the heroine in a parenthetical aside, which suggests that this element is a clue to the message (or moral) of the tale directed to the adult readers. Characteristically, Carter eliminates the parenthetical comment that nods at Perrault's signature style: "Beauty, the youngest, thanked everyone politely for their proposals" (*Sleeping Beauty*, 45) for "la Belle (car je vous ai dit que c'était le nom de la plus jeune), la Belle, dis-je, remercia bien honnêtement ceux qui voulaient l'épouser" (*Beaumont*, 177). Beaumont even adds *dis-je*, which on one level creates an effect of orality, because it refers to the frame situation in which Melle Bonne tells the fairy tale to her pupils, and on another level suggests that the author is self-consciously writing back to Perrault. Intertextual echoes to Perrault's *contes* are indeed interspersed in "La Belle et la Bête"; the authorial narrator insists on the name of the heroine being inseparably linked to her destiny, just like "Cendrillon," or "La Belle au bois dormant," which her young readers were probably familiar with.[35]

The pairing of "Beauty and the Beast" and "Sweetheart" in the 1982 *Sleeping Beauty* collection foregrounds the issue of education, although Carter takes care to exonerate the nurse blamed by the governess Beaumont.[36] Far less openly than in "Sweetheart" where the effects of a bad education are blamed on doting adults and false friends, "Beauty and the Beast" nevertheless points to the responsibility of the father in Beauty's situation. Carter attenuates sibling jealousy and the sharp comedy of the girl's enemies rejoicing about the proud sisters' downfall. Instead, she turns female pettiness into a funny vignette of the girl's humbled situation, with chickens added for comic effect: "Don't waste your pity on those two! Pride goes before a fall. Let them see how long they can keep up their high-faluting ways among the sheep and chickens" (*Sleeping Beauty*, 46) ("Elles ne méritent pas qu'on les plaigne, nous sommes bien aises de voir leur orgueil abaissé; qu'elles aillent faire les dames en gardant les moutons," *Beaumont*, 177). The humor of the scene and familiar language even present female gossip as a source of fun and creativity.

The characterization of Beauty's personality also shifts from being virtuous (with its connotations of obedience to prescribed behavior and Christian morality) to being "nice" and "generous" (*Sleeping Beauty*, 45).[37] Further on, Beauty's father "loved her all the more, and respected her too" (*Sleeping Beauty*, 46) when she does not react to her sisters' taunts ("il admirait la vertu de cette jeune fille, surtout sa patience," *Beaumont*, 178). The modern values of love and respect replace the conventional praise of female virtue and patience.[38] Unlike Beauty, the elder sisters are arrogant snobs, and Carter's choice of the adjective *stuck-up* echoes her translation of Cinderella's stepmother, drawing attention to similarities between the two tales. The fact that Cinderella colors Carter's translation (and perhaps already Beaumont's original French text) is further confirmed by the reference to dress in the description of the girls walking in the park "wearing the most beautiful clothes" (*Sleeping Beauty*, 45) (a detail that is absent from the source text). This spells out the cultural implications of "aller à la promenade" (*Beaumont*, 177) (i.e., promenading to see and to be seen), but it also carries over a central theme of Perrault's *conte* into Beaumont's translated tale.

The characterization of Beauty is subtly but significantly altered in the translation to convey Carter's own concerns and values. When faced with a turn of fortune, Beauty faces up to it with courage, determination, and endurance, as in the source tale, but without pathos or appeals to duty and self-sacrifice: "But then she told herself to pull herself together" (*Sleeping Beauty*, 46) ("Mais elle s'était dit en elle-même: 'Quand je pleurerai, mes larmes ne me rendront pas mon bien; il faut tâcher d'être heureuse sans fortune,'" *Beaumont*, 178). In Carter's translation Beauty's steadfast attitude could even be seen as an indirect critique of female self-pity and self-victimization. Beauty is indeed a heroine after Carter's own heart; she prefers reading and playing music to any other entertainment, even though her sisters make fun of her for it. She also politely turns down suitors, arguing that she is too young (in keeping with the moral of "Sleeping Beauty") and wants "to stay with her father a little while longer" (*Sleeping Beauty*, 45), whereas her snobbish sisters only want to marry men of aristocratic rank ("a duke, or a count," *Sleeping Beauty*, 45).[39]

Beauty, then, is self-composed, generous, and kindhearted but no self-sacrificial "angel in the house." She bears her family's downfall with equanimity and does not mind hard work, reasoning with herself that shedding tears is useless. In her spare time she plays music, spins, or reads while her work-shy sisters mock her for doing a servant's job and liking it. Beauty is also reproached by her sisters for being coldhearted when she does not cry when her father tells his children of his misadventure with the Beast. But, she declares, "Crying won't help."

> Besides, why should I cry for my father's fate when that fate can be averted? If the beast will take a daughter instead of the father, then I shall gladly go instead.
> (*Sleeping Beauty*, 50)

> Cela serait fort inutile, reprit la Belle. Pourquoi pleurerais-je la mort de mon père? Il ne périra point. Puisque le monstre veut bien accepter une de ses filles, je veux me livrer à toute sa furie, et je me trouve fort heureuse, puisqu'en mourant j'aurai la joie de sauver mon père et de lui prouver ma tendresse. (*Beaumont*, 182)

Carter avoids the self-sacrificial accents of the dutiful daughter who is ready to die for her father and is even afflicted by a rather surprising death wish

("Je ne suis pas fort attachée à la vie," *Beaumont*, 182) altogether omitted in the translation.[40] The translator instead insists on Beauty's sense of responsibility toward her father ("remorse" conveying "mourir de chagrin") but also her strong will and determination.

> If the Beast will take a daughter instead of a father, then I shall gladly go instead. (*Sleeping Beauty*, 50)

> Puisque le monstre veut bien accepter une de ses filles, je veux me livrer à toute sa furie, et je me trouve fort heureuse, puisqu'en mourant j'aurai la joie de sauver mon père et de lui prouver ma tendresse. (*Beaumont*, 183)

The translation is much more sober and matter-of-fact, and the focus is on Beauty's determination: "You can't stop me following you," she says. She is "determined"; she "insisted" on accompanying her father to meet the Beast. Beauty's self-possession, courage, and adventurous spirit are consistent with the translator's values, and her attitude will indeed be rewarded at the end. Even when Beauty at last sees the Beast, though much frightened, "she put on a brave face" ("La Belle ne put s'empêcher de frémir en voyant cette horrible figure," *Beaumont*, 183).

Beauty's vocation for martyrdom is thus turned into a mix of daughterly love and curiosity for the Beast. As a matter of fact, the Beast is *never* designated by the term *monster* in the translation (e.g., "Quoique je sois jeune, je ne suis pas fort attachée à la vie, et j'aime mieux être dévorée par ce monstre que de mourir du chagrin que me donnerait votre perte," *Beaumont*, 183; "Young I may be, but how could I spend the rest of my life full of remorse because I caused my father's death?" *Sleeping Beauty*, 50). This introduces a significant change in the representation of the Beast, whose status shifts from horrible monster to incarnation of animality, which will be developed in Carter's rewritings. When Beauty is left alone in the Beast's castle, she is not so much afraid of being devoured alive as bracing herself to meet a wild animal. The animal normality of the Beast rather than his supernatural monstrosity is systematically stressed by the translator: "She guessed the Beast must take his meals in the evenings, *as animals do*, and she would pass the waiting hours in exploring the palace" (*Sleeping Beauty*, 53; italics mine), for "Elle croyait fermement que la Bête la mangerait le soir. Elle résolut de se promener en attendant, et de visiter ce beau château" (*Beaumont*, 184).⁴¹

Carter thus depicts the Beast as a feline, in stark contrast to the source text, which systematically designates him as a monster. This probably reflects the pressure of the lion-headed Prince Chéri, the lion husband in the Grimms' affiliated *Märchen*, and fairy-tale iconography, as I have argued. But more fundamentally, it hints at a change in the perception of beastliness in the twentieth century that echoes Marina Warner's reflections in *From the Beast to the Blonde* and captures Carter's fascination with animality. Interviewed for *Marxism Today* in 1985, Carter declared, "Well, we are animals, after all" (21), and she elaborated: "I'm a Darwinian. I like animals and I'm interested in animals. I'm also interested in human beings' projections upon animals of negative qualities, which very often the animals don't have. . . . I'm interested in the division that Judeo-Christianity has made between human nature and animal nature" (21).

Indeed, Beaumont does not describe the Beast, only insisting on his monstrosity and the effect of horror that he provokes in human beings.⁴² Carter's own Beast, by contrast, is described as a wild animal who "roars" and "growls" and even declares that he would rather "cut off his right *paw*" (*Sleeping Beauty*, 57; italics mine) than cause Beauty pain ("J'aime mieux mourir moi-même, dit le monstre, que de vous donner du chagrin," *Beaumont*, 186).

Further on, the talking Beast reproves Beauty's father, who addresses him as Monseigneur, for trying to soften him through flattery.

> "Nobody calls me 'sir,'" *growled* the Beast. "My name is Beast. I don't like compliments. I don't care what anybody thinks of me and flattery will get you nowhere." (*Sleeping Beauty*, 49; italics mine)

> Je ne m'appelle point Monseigneur, répondit le monstre, mais la Bête. Je n'aime pas les compliments, moi; je veux qu'on dise ce que l'on pense; ainsi ne croyez pas me toucher par vos flatteries. (*Beaumont*, 182)

The Beast, then, owns up to his name and is no dupe when the father humbles himself. Tellingly, Carter translates "Je veux qu'on dise ce que l'on pense" as "I don't care what anybody thinks of me," which turns the Beast's rejection of hypocrisy into a declaration of independence.⁴³ Tellingly, "the Beast growled" when he spoke ("répondit le monstre"). The only passage where the word *monster* is used in the translation is when the Beast designates *himself* as a monster, which is immediately contradicted by Beauty and by the narrator herself, who, unlike Beaumont, refuses to endorse the Beast's opinion of himself.

What is more, the enchanted realm of the Beast is both a prison of sorts (although Beauty is granted permission to go back home for a limited period of time) and a woman-friendly space. Beauty has a "room of her own," where she reigns supreme, filled with books and musical instruments. She is even granted permission to rule over the Beast's dwelling. When she says, "You are the master in your own house," the Beast courteously replies that this is not so and that she "must give the orders, here" (*Sleeping Beauty*, 54). At this point, Beauty acknowledges the Beast's "good heart" and registers its effect on her perception of him: "When I think how kind you are, you seem less ugly, somehow."⁴⁴ This reassures her, and she eats her supper heartily, until he asks her to marry him.⁴⁵ Although troubled by his repeated marriage proposals, which she keeps refusing, she begins to appreciate the Beast's "good, plain, common sense" ("bon sens"). The nature of their relationship is based on Beauty's rational appraisal of the Beast's many virtues in the source text rather than on emotional attachment in the translation: "Every day, Beauty found she *liked* more and more things about him. She soon grew used to his ugliness" (*Sleeping Beauty*, 56; italics mine) to the point of looking forward to having dinner with him. In the same spirit the final speech addressed by the fairy to Beauty's envious and cruel sisters explains that they will be turned into stone statues and yet will keep their "human feelings" ("votre raison," *Beaumont*, 189) until they are "cured of their enviousness" (*Sleeping Beauty*, 62) ("On se corrige de l'orgueil, de la colère, de la gourmandise et de la paresse, mais c'est une espèce de miracle que la conversion d'un coeur méchant et envieux," *Beaumont*, 189). Carter thus replaces the fairy's Christian moralizing about the seven deadly sins with the ability to develop a generous heart.⁴⁶

The translation praises true feelings, but it tones down Beaumont's emphatic language and pathos. Thus, when Beauty is allowed to go home for a little while, she is happy to see her father again, and they hug and kiss (rather than Beauty's father "nearly dying of joy"). Likewise, her sisters "felt quite ill" upon seeing her (instead of "nearly died of spite"). Even their jealousy is conveyed by an idiom centering on the heart (they "eat their hearts out with envy"), so that Beaumont's praise of the relatively abstract notion of goodness becomes a celebration of "good hearts" in the translation. Likewise, when Beauty ponders the many qualities that a woman should value in a husband, namely, "strength of character, goodness and kindness" (*Sleeping Beauty*, 60), she reflects that in return, she "mustn't break his heart" (instead of "make him unhappy").

At the end of the translated tale, when Beauty finds the dying Beast lying near a canal, she exclaims: "No, Beast! Don't die! Live and marry me! . . . I cannot live without you" (*Sleeping Beauty*, 69). In the source text a less passionate Belle soberly declares, "Non, ma chère Bête, vous ne mourrez point, lui dit la Belle; vous vivrez pour devenir mon époux. . . . Je ne pourrais vivre sans vous voir'" (*Beaumont*, 189). These words (and not a kiss!) provoke the metamorphosis of the Beast into a Prince Charming. The possibility arises, however, that Beauty is not altogether pleased with this change. This is hinted at in Beaumont's text and further emphasized in the translation.

> But Beauty scarcely spared these wonders a glance, she was so concerned for her dear Beast. Yet what a surprise! For her Beast was gone and, at her feet instead of him, lay a handsome young prince, thanking her profusely for freeing him from the spell he had been under.
>
> Although this prince was worth all her undivided attention, still she puzzled: "What has happened to *my* Beast?" (*Sleeping Beauty*, 62; italics mine)

> Mais toutes ces beautés n'arrêtèrent point sa vue; elle se retourna vers sa chère Bête, dont le danger la faisait frémir. Quelle fut sa surprise! La Bête avait disparu, et elle ne vit plus à ses pieds qu'un prince plus beau que l'Amour, qui la remerciait d'avoir fini son enchantement.[47]
>
> Quoique ce prince méritât toute son attention, elle ne put s'empêcher de lui demander où était la Bête. (*Beaumont*, 189)

Carter remarks on this ambiguity in her notes, which opens up a possibility for retelling that she explores in her radical transformation of the dénouement in "The Tiger's Bride," where not only does the Beast discard the false trappings of humanity but also Beauty herself reclaims her own beastliness. In the translation already the voice of Beauty can be heard in direct speech, when she expresses her surprise and disappointment (depending on how we read the passage) at the disappearance of the Beast. This focus on Beauty's affect and subjectivity is fully realized in Carter's second rewriting, which retells the story in the first person from the perspective of the reluctant bride who is furious to have been traded off by her father but who ends up being won over by the Beast and what he represents. Even the choice of the possessive "my" in "my Beast" already suggests not only that Beauty has made the Beast her own but also that beastliness itself has become part of her own being. The fascination for and attraction to the Beast as a desirable "other" and the idea of the beastliness within are developed in the rewriting, where the freedom of the animal realm contrasts with the social roles imposed on women by patriarchy.

The last sentence of the tale complies with the conventional ending and follows the moralizing message of Beaumont, except for the significant shift from virtue to goodness.

> The prince married Beauty and they lived happily ever after, in a contentment perfect because it was founded on goodness. (*Sleeping Beauty*, 62)

> Il épousa la Belle, qui vécut avec lui fort longtemps et dans un bonheur parfait, parce qu'il était fondé sur la vertu. (*Beaumont*, 189)

The translation reflects the pressure of fairy-tale conventions and formulaic language ("They lived happily ever after") but it also promotes true feelings coming from the heart rather than Beaumont's abstract moralizing and conformity to the norm. Carter's rendering of Beaumont's text thus subtly reorients the treatment of beastliness and gender relations and remakes the young heroine after the translator's own heart.

From the Blonde to the Beast:
Carter's "Courtship of Mr. Lyon" and "The Tiger's Bride"

> Lautréamont seeks to reduce human pride & thereby find peace through a fraternization with the animal world & finally through actual metamorphosis.
>
> —ANGELA CARTER, JOURNAL FOR 1977

Carter explores the shifting boundaries between the human and the non-human in "The Courtship of Mr. Lyon" and "The Tiger's Bride."[48] In *The Bloody Chamber* collection the "Beauty and the Beast" sequence follows Carter's take on "Bluebeard," which can be seen as an inverted retelling of Beaumont's tale. In each story a human bride is confronted with a beastly monster, and the story traces the evolution of their relationship; because a human appearance may conceal a perverse, manipulative, and predatory personality or, conversely, a monstrous appearance may hide great qualities, the opposition between man and beast is more complex than it may seem. In "Sweetheart" the badly named prince is changed into a beast that reflects his true nature, whereas in "Beauty and the Beast" Beauty eventually learns to love the kind and respectful Beast. In Beaumont's tales the power of metamorphosis is attributed to women, whether fairies or young women (Zélie and Belle), who redeem the beastly characters through love. "Sweetheart" grows into a selfish, cruel, domineering, and insensitive man and is eventually reformed after a series of trials in a Christian parable masquerading as a fairy tale. It is the Beast's attentions, respect, patience, and thoughtful attitude toward Beauty that distinguish him from most men, to the point of seducing the heroine in spite of his frightening appearance. Carter stresses the Beast's "humanity" in her translation, and she pushes the paradox further in her rewritings by linking the destabilization of the human-animal divide with the condition of women under patriarchy, reduced as they are to pets ("The Courtship of Mr. Lyon") or automatons ("The Tiger's Bride").

In fact, "The Tiger's Bride" goes so far as to reverse the manmade hierarchy of species when the Beauty figure does *not* humanize the Beast but chooses to embrace an animal state in which she discovers (or rather recovers) a mode of being where language and vision give way to touch and smell—a utopian move whose possibilities and limits are explored more fully in "Wolf-Alice." The bride thus embraces the animal nature of her beastly consort against an anthropocentric and phallocentric order sanctioned by religion that excludes, exploits, or negates the "otherness" that animals and women represent. The shift from monstrosity to wild nature is already initiated in the translation, as we have seen.

In the rewriting the young woman, who is perforce brought into contact with the Beast, overcomes her fear and comes to see the animal realm as a valid alternative to human society (just as the heroine is attracted to the werewolf and ends up sleeping with him in "The Company of Wolves"). In this sense the Beast is the exact opposite of the Marquis in "The Bloody Chamber," with his hatred of nature, misogyny, and murderous obsession with art.[49] In "The Tiger's Bride" the natural, animal state of the Beast is no longer seen as a threatening otherness that needs to be tamed, domesticated, and humanized; although profoundly unsettling, it becomes something desirable for the bride, who literally embraces it at the end.[50] For Carter, then, the story of "Beauty and the Beast" presents a profound ethical challenge based on an existential mystery: Who are we? Where do human beings stand in the greater scheme of things? What discourses (or "mythologies") have they invented to legitimize anthropocentric hierarchies, and what role does the fairy tale play in reinforcing or challenging them? How do human beings treat those who are excluded from the category of the human? And where do women stand on this scale of being? To what extent are women and animals reduced to the role of commodities or "meat"? What are the implications of reclaiming the in-between status (neither fully human nor fully animal) to which they have been relegated?

The manifold transformations that occur in Beaumont's *conte*, at once physical, emotional, social, and societal, invite further intellectual inquiry. By engaging affect (fear gradually giving way to trust, affection, and even attraction), social relations (hierarchy giving way to equality and reciprocity), and moral philosophy, the tale becomes an occasion to question man-made divisions, rethink our relations to various forms of otherness, and even consider the possibility of interspecies bonding beyond the nature-culture, prey-predator divide.

The evolving relationship between Beauty and the Beast thus provokes further complications and deeper transformations in the rewritings. "The Courtship of Mr. Lyon" explores the idea of the mutually humanizing power of love in a sentimental, sensual, and relatively consensual variation on the familiar plot, whereas "The Tiger's Bride" takes the tale in a completely different direction. The retelling is more speculative, exploratory, and experimental and features a rebellious bride who breaks away from the social order and human nature itself.[51]

"The Courtship of Mr. Lyon" develops the theme of education raised in "Sweetheart," which made a case for the shaping of character through upbringing. Because Carter addresses her rewriting to older readers, she makes a more subtle argument about sentimental education being able to counterbalance the corrupting power of money and privilege. She pursues the psychological insights that she admired in Beaumont's story in her depiction of the father-daughter relationship and even suggests that the metamorphosis of the Beast may be an effect of Beauty's subjectivity more than an actual transformation of the (already tame) lion into Mr. Lyon. Carter characteristically transposes the story into a modern context (complete with a car and telephone) while retaining elements of magic and fantasy associated with the landscape surrounding the Beast's house. Even the knocker is "in the shape of a lion's head, with a ring through the nose" (*Bloody Chamber*, 42); this detail hints at the master's domestication in a gentrified English setting. The Beast lives in an "atmosphere of suspended reality" and "a place of privilege" (42) that enchants Beauty, though she at first rejects the otherness of the Beast and his "bewildering difference," which she finds "almost intolerable" (45). And yet something about the Beast's sad eyes moves her: "A lion is a lion and a man is a man and, though lions are more beautiful by far than we are, yet they belong to a different order of beauty and, besides, they have no respect for us: why should they? Yet wild things have a far more rational fear of us than is ours of them, and some kind of sadness in his agate eyes, that looked almost blind, moved her heart" (*Bloody Chamber*, 45).

Beauty adopts the point of view of the Beast and is even touched by an emotion that she recognizes in the lion's eyes; her musings enact her changing opinion and perception of the Beast, from the tautological affirmation of radical distinction, separateness, and separation to an admission of difference that leads to a shift of perspective. As this passage shows, the tale thematizes and enacts how *affect* may question established boundaries between the species. In this case the Beast is not particularly threatening. His roaring is impressive, but he wears "a smoking jacket of dull red brocade" and is emblematic, looking like "the first great beast of the Apocalypse, the winged lion with his paw upon the Gospel, Saint Mark" (*Bloody Chamber*, 46) in Venice. Mr. Lyon even ends up "bur[ying] his head in her lap" (47) like a big cat. Beauty interprets his licking of her hands as a kiss, thereby showing her ability to "translate" from the animal to the human realms: "She felt his hot breath on her fingers, the stiff bristles of his muzzle grazing her skin, the rough lapping of his tongue and then, with a flood of compassion, understood: all he is doing is kissing my hands" (47). But when she leaves Mr. Lyon's house to return to London, "she could not bring herself to touch him of her own free will, he was so different from herself" (48).

"The Courtship of Mr. Lyon" therefore draws on Beaumont's valuing of sense and sensibility but subtly reorients it toward a reflection on the relationship of self and other. It is because Beauty's feelings for the Beast ("compassion") are stronger than her intellect but also because she eventually overcomes her self-centeredness that they end up living happily together. As in "Sweetheart," the father's doting on his daughter, and even more so the opulence in which they live once the Beast has rescued them from poverty, spoil her character. Back in London she becomes vain and superficial, and this alters her appearance: "She smiled at herself in mirrors a little too often, these days, and the face that smiled back was not quite the one she had seen contained in the Beast's agate eyes. Her face was acquiring, instead of beauty, a lacquer of the invincible prettiness that characterizes certain pampered, exquisite, expensive cats" (*Bloody Chamber*, 49). The idea of physical appearance reflecting inner self central to "Sweetheart" therefore reappears in Carter's first retelling of "Beauty and the Beast," which also establishes a connection between moral and physical beauty.

Through Beauty's reverse transformation into a cat (if only by means of an analogy), Carter also establishes a thematic connection with Marie-Catherine d'Aulnoy's "La Chatte blanche" (The White Cat), and the style of Carter's first retelling recalls the ornate manner characteristic of the heyday of the literary *conte de fées*.[52] During her stay in Mr. Lyon's "miniature, perfect, Palladian house" (*Bloody Chamber*, 42), Beauty even finds in a rosewood revolving bookcase "a collection of courtly and elegant French fairy tales about white cats who were transformed princesses and fairies who were birds" (46). The "lovely girl" (41), whose skin glows like snow, is her father's "beauty, his girl-child, his pet" (41). It is her encounter with the Beast, and her sudden guilt at having broken her promise, hence the development of her moral consciousness, that will humanize her. When she hurries back to the Beast's derelict house and finds the dying Beast, she notices "that his agate eyes were equipped with lids, like those of a man." Is it, she muses, "because she had only looked at her own face, reflected there?" (51). Her kiss and her tears bring about Mr. Lyon's "soft transformation" (51) into a man, "with an unkempt mane of hair and, how strange, a broken nose, such as the noses of retired boxers, that gave him a distant, heroic resemblance to the handsomest of all the beasts" (51). The story ends in bourgeois domesticity and marital bliss, the couple walking in a garden covered with drifting petals.

In "The Tiger's Bride," however, Carter's heroine refuses to comply with the prewritten script and chooses animality over humanity.[53] Unlike her predecessor, she does not refer to herself as Beauty and refuses to be reduced to her physical appearance. Furthermore, she rebels against the patriarchal system that treats her like a commodity. Refusing the role assigned to her by her irresponsible father, who trades her at cards, she leaves the human world behind and turns into a she-tiger once she has established a pact with her unlikely consort. She thereby achieves a form of equality with the wild beast once their shared alienation in the human world has been acknowledged and overcome.

Mocking the biblical utopia where "the lion lies down with the lamb" (*Bloody Chamber*, 51), which recalls the taming of Sweetheart, the young woman reassesses the true nature of her father's "love" with "furious cynicism," when she is given away to "La Bestia," with a reputation for ferocity and a knack at playing cards. This time the Beast is not a lion but a tiger (the defeated feline in "Sweetheart") who can barely master his wild nature. His efforts to mask his pungent smell and animal habits make him a much more threatening figure than Mr. Lyon: "He has an air of self-imposed restraint, as if fighting a battle with himself to remain upright when he would far rather drop down on all fours" (53). Unlike his predecessor, he needs the help of a valet (a monkey in disguise), who interprets for him and who reproaches Beauty's father for being careless. The Beast's palazzo is a strange, decaying place where animals reign supreme: The horses have been given the use of the dining room, swallows nest in the tall roof, and the doors and windows are open to the winds. "Nothing human lives here" (59), remarks the simian valet.

Although she has been told "old wives' tales, nursery fears" (*Bloody Chamber*, 56) to "tame [her] into submission" (56) as a child, Beauty refuses to give in to panic and starts reflecting upon the nature of "beastliness" (55), going so far as to share "Gulliver's opinion, that horses are better than we are" (55).[54] When the Beast wants to see her naked, however, she is angry and humiliated to be treated like a prostitute, and her reaction strikes him "to the heart" (59). During her stay in the Beast's run-down palazzo, she reflects on her condition and meditates on the rich ironies of gender discrimination in the name of reason.

> I knew they lived according to a different logic than I had done until my father abandoned me to the wild beasts by his human carelessness. This knowledge gave me a certain fearfulness still; but, I would say, not much. . . . I was a young girl, a virgin, and therefore men denied me rationality just as they denied it to all those who were not exactly like themselves, in all their unreason. (*Bloody Chamber*, 63)

She goes on to ponder the fact that women are denied a soul in "the best religions of the world" and engages in "metaphysical speculation" (*Bloody Chamber*, 63)—"I certainly meditated on the nature of my own state, how I had been bought and sold, passed from hand to hand" (63)—as they go riding in the wilderness, until the tiger shows himself stripped of his human trappings. Beauty realizes that the Beast proposes a "reciprocal pact" and feels her breast being "ripped apart as if I suffered a marvellous wound" (64). She undresses in her turn and, feeling free for the first time in her life, she decides not to go back to her father but to send her clockwork double instead. She then joins the Beast in his den "reek[ing] of fur and piss" (66) and overcomes the "earliest and most archaic of fears, fear of devourment" (67). The Beast begins to purr and licks her skin, revealing her own fur underneath: "My earrings turned back to water and trickled down my shoulders; I shrugged the drops off my beautiful fur" (67).

This profound rewriting of the classic tale, then, hints at a new humanism of alterity and vulnerability as it reconsiders various forms of otherness that have been dominated, exploited, or excluded. "The Tiger's Bride," inasmuch as it challenges anthropocentric categories and modes of thinking, reads like a fable of deep ecology.

7

Giving Up the Ghost

FROM "CENDRILLON OU LA PETITE PANTOUFLE DE VERRE" TO
"CINDERELLA: OR, THE LITTLE GLASS SLIPPER"
AND "ASHPUTTLE *OR* THE MOTHER'S GHOST"

The Bloody Chamber contains retellings of well-known tales such as "Bluebeard," "Beauty and the Beast," "Sleeping Beauty," "Puss in Boots," and "Little Red Riding Hood." "Cinderella" is surprisingly absent from the collection, especially when we consider that Angela Carter had translated "Cendrillon ou la petite pantoufle de verre" for *The Fairy Tales of Charles Perrault*. In her 1977 journal Carter even plans to write a "very primitive, very archaic" Cinderella story. And yet her "Ashputtle *or* The Mother's Ghost" would be published nearly ten years later. One part, "The Burned Child," first appeared in *Cosmopolitan* in July 1987 and in *Merveilles et Contes* later that year (1.2, December 1987). The complete threefold text, composed of "The Mutilated Girls," "The Burned Child," and "Travelling Clothes," was anthologized in *The Virago Book of Ghost Stories* (1987) and reprinted in *American Ghosts and Old World Wonders* (1993).[1] Whereas Carter's translation of Perrault, "Cinderella: or, The Little Glass Slipper," seeks to recover a preromantic tradition compatible with her pedagogical aims, the rewriting for adults harks back to a folk tradition associated with the Grimms in contrapuntal fashion. Upon reviewing the first English translation of the German legends for *The Guardian*, Carter declared that "no home was complete" without a copy of the *Kinder- und Hausmärchen*.[2] And it is to the Grimm brothers' version of Cinderella (or rather Ashputtle) that Carter returned in "Ashputtle *or* The Mother's Ghost."

Unlike Carter's translation for children, whose message is neatly encapsulated in the moral, "Ashputtle *or* The Mother's Ghost" celebrates the mutability of the tale and its openness to (re)interpretation.[3] The subtitle,

"Three Versions of One Story," already underlines this; there is no canonical version of the tale but rather a multiplicity of unique retellings. Unsurprisingly, Perrault's "Cinderella" and the Grimms' "Ashputtle" generated strikingly different responses from Carter. Her translation of the worldly and humorous French *conte* communicates a matter-of-fact message to young girls about how to get on in the world and marry happily. In contrast, her rewriting of the German *Märchen* captures the cruelty, dark poetry, and disturbing psychological insights of ancient folktales about mothers who magically return from the grave to help—but also to haunt—their mistreated daughters.

Carter's double take on Cinderella/Ashputtle highlights significant differences in the plot, language, motifs, tone, and atmosphere of Perrault's and the Grimms' texts. And yet both the translation and the rewriting amalgamate them in subtle ways, revealing the palimpsestic dimension of the fairy-tale tradition and showing how fusion can be used as a creative strategy.[4] Markedly different traditions of the tale indeed tend to become mixed in the process of translation, adaptation, and re-creation. Whereas Carter's Perrault-based translation is colored by memories of the Grimms' *Märchen*, her Grimm-based rewriting still contains traces of Perrault's text, starting with its title: "Cendrillon ou la petite pantoufle de verre" becomes "Ashputtle *or* The Mother's Ghost." Although the name of the heroine clearly affiliates the tale with the German *Märchen*, the title's syntax is modeled on the French *conte*.

The Grimmification of Perrault in English: The Two-Faced Cinderella, or Perrimm and Grimmault

> Ghost, fiend, and angel, fairy, witch, and sprite.
>
> —ELIZABETH BARRETT BROWNING, *AURORA LEIGH*

A reversible head of Cinderella and her Fairy Godmother illustrates Iona and Peter Opie's introduction to *The Classic Fairy Tales*. Drawn by Rex Whistler "to amuse a child" (10), this optical illusion suggests that the two emblematic fairy-tale characters can metamorphose into each other depending on how we look at the picture, in the manner of an Escher drawing (Figure 7.1). The illustration portrays the Fairy Godmother as a grotesque, wild-eyed, monkey-faced peasant woman and Cinderella as a waiflike, hollow-eyed girl who looks nothing like Perrault's dainty heroine. Her heavy eyes and down-turned mouth express the grief of the disconsolate Aschenputtel shedding tears over her mother's grave rather than the French Cendrillon who cries only when she cannot go to the ball and is immediately consoled by her resourceful godmother. This draws attention to a discrepancy between image and caption. The head is identified as "Cinderella" in one orientation and as "The Fairy Godmother" in the rotated orientation, hence referencing Perrault, although the portrait depicts a mournful girl in a headscarf and her aged double more reminiscent of "Frau Holle" (or "Frau Trude").[5] Perrault's *conte* and the Grimms' *Märchen* indeed present different versions of the tale in spite of superficial similarities, and Whistler's picture illustrates the fusion of the two distinct texts and traditions in the process of reception.

Another game for children reproduced in the Opies' *Classic Fairy Tales* is a cutout of Cinderella representing "Cinderella's coach, her changes of costume and transferable head, from a paper doll book, 1814" (118–119). Based on Perrault's version and centering on dress and fashion, the cutout plays on the mutable identity of the fairy-tale heroine and her magical transformations, hinting at retellings of "Cinderella" as so many *refashionings* of the tale.

Whereas the playful magic of dress, childlike delight in disguise, and changing appearance are central to modern perceptions of the tale, including Perrault-based translations and games for children, Carter's subsequent retelling of Ashputtle as a ghost story centering on the dead mother explores its dark underside—its harsh, brutal, and cruel aspects as well as its metafictional resonances. "Ashputtle *or* The Mother's Ghost" also hints at the worldwide distribution of the story, because it references parallel versions featuring animal helpers in Indian and Celtic folklore and the custom of foot binding in an early Chinese version of the tale. Whereas "Cinderella: or, The Little Glass Slipper" harks back to the literary tradition, "Ashputtle *or* The Mother's Ghost" imaginatively reconstructs ur-versions of the tale in the manner of folklorists.[6]

Carter's twofold response to Cinderella and Ashputtle reflects a nuanced position in the debate between folklorists and literary scholars in the twentieth century. Folklorists tend to value oral culture, whereas literary scholars and book historians give primacy to printed texts. A folklorist at heart,

Figure 7.1. Cinderella and the Fairy Godmother. Reversible head by Rex Whistler, c. 1935, in The Classic Fairy Tales *by Iona and Peter Opie.*

Carter was also influenced by Iona and Peter Opie's textual approach to the fairy-tale tradition.

> Folklorists today are so preoccupied with orally communicated texts

that literary research has become unpalatable. Certainly a great gulf has opened up since the days of Andrew Lang, between the collector of *Märchen* and the student of popular literature. The folklorist today commonly eschews texts that have come under literary influence, even when these texts are the sources of the most-loved stories of a nation. (Opie and Opie, *Classic Fairy Tales*, 5)

Carter negotiates the critical divide outlined by the Opies when she pays close attention to the linguistic, verbal, and textual details of Perrault's version in her translation while celebrating the "dark poetry" and creativity of a lesser known folk tradition in her rewritings. In fact, Carter's invention of hypothetical urtexts in "Ashputtle *or* The Mother's Ghost" posits folklore as a prime source of inspiration, but it also suggests that recovering lost origins is an illusion, except as fictional re-creation. In other words, Carter evokes the possibility of an archetypal version of the story only to stress the uniqueness of each retelling. "Ashputtle *or* The Mother's Ghost" thus blurs the distinction between creative and critical discourse as it engages with the reception of the tale in scholarly discourse.

The Opies stress the antiquity and ubiquity of the story of Cinderella throughout the world. They also note the strangeness and cruelty of folk versions where "the magical assistance the heroine receives [often] comes to her from the spirit of her dead mother" (*Classic Fairy Tales*, 13). By contrast, "Perrault's story, for all its wit and compassion, is a worldly and somewhat sentimentalized version of older and darker stories, which have many strange undertones" (13). Whereas the playful magic of dress, disguise, and changing appearance characterizes Perrault's (and Disney's) version, the persecuted heroine owes her triumph to her dead mother in "Aschenputtel." Carter's double focus on the figure of Ashputtle and her mother clearly aligns her retelling with the folklore tradition, down to its tripartite structure, which parallels the three sources found in Hesse on which the Grimms based their own *Märchen*.

The folklorist Andrew Lang, whose work Carter also knew well, similarly contrasts Perrault's urbane and "civilized" *conte* to what he calls the "wild justice" (*Perrault's Popular Tales*, cii) of the Grimms' "savage *Märchen*," where Ashputtle's stepsisters are mutilated by their own mother and blinded on the heroine's wedding day (xxxv).[7] Lang treats the German tale as an anthropological document recording ancient beliefs and customs, and he mentions the Chinese custom of foot binding as a probable source for Ashputtle's tiny feet.[8] He also notes that the tale has archaic parallels in the Egyptian story of "Two Brothers" and a Russian story in which the mother survives in different shapes. The mother also magically aids her daughter "from her tomb" (xviii) in the Scottish "Rashin Coatie," in which the persecuted heroine receives help from a cow, a red calf, and even the magical bones of the calf when the animal is killed by the stepmother. Focusing on the bare bones of the tale ("the bare necessity of fairy tale," to quote Carter in *American Ghosts*, 113) and the cruel acts found in the folk tradition, Carter's "Ashputtle *or* The Mother's Ghost" taps into the "wild" folklore of the "lower races" (*Perrault's Popular Tales*, xciv).[9] In this way the modern author unearths an obscured fairy-tale tradition in conformity with her interest in international folklore, which she rehabilitates as literature.

In her introduction to *The Virago Book of Fairy Tales* Carter observes that "although the content of the fairy tale may record the real lives of the anonymous poor with sometimes uncomfortable fidelity—the poverty, the hunger, the shaky family relationships, the all-pervasive cruelty . . .—the form of the fairy tale is not usually constructed so as to invite the audience to share a sense of lived experience" (xiii). Unlike "Cinderella: or, The Little Glass Slipper," which fosters identification with the heroine and purports to communicate a message about charm being more powerful than "a fancy hairdo," "Ashputtle *or* The Mother's Ghost" suggests a darker psychological truth about mother-daughter relations conveyed in a dry, distant, and unsentimental fashion. Carter uses the tale to explore the mysterious nature of maternal love. In the first retelling, upon finding her stepsister's cut-off toe in the fireplace, Ashputtle "feels both awe and fear at the phenomenon of mother love. Mother love, which winds about these daughters like a shroud" (*American Ghosts*, 115). When Carter shifts from translation to rewriting, Cinderella's beautiful dresses turn into the mother's shroudlike love.

From "Cendrillon ou la petite pantoufle de verre" to "Cinderella: or, The Little Glass Slipper": Perrault's Making of a Princess Refashioned Anew

"Cinderella" is usually seen as a fairy tale that vindicates a long-suffering, kind, and pretty girl who is rewarded with a princely marriage thanks to the help of her Fairy Godmother.[10] In Disney's fairy-tale film the stepsisters are even depicted as comically ugly to heighten the contrast with the fairy-tale heroine. When Carter translated Perrault's "Cendrillon ou la petite pantoufle de verre" into English, however, she discovered that her French source neither exploited nor endorsed the idea of a beauty contest. Perrault certainly mocks the bitter competition to win the Prince's heart, and he pokes fun at the courtier culture he knew so well, but in his version of the tale (unlike the Disney movie) Cinderella's stepsisters are said to be less pretty than the heroine and are essentially described in moral terms: They are haughty and proud like their mother, rude and mean to Cinderella, only concerned with dress and appearance, and mostly characterized by their bad character and manners. When the stepsisters ask the heroine for forgiveness at the end, she magnanimously grants it. Moreover, the first moral explicitly distances itself from the conventional praise of female beauty to focus on the benefits of education instead. This made it easy for Carter to turn Perrault's text into a critique of the beauty myth targeted by second-wave feminists and to praise the heroine's charm as the new locus of magic. The translation seeks to communicate a homey truth about seduction and marriage and thus uses Perrault's *conte* against the cultural stereotype of Cinderella.

"Cendrillon ou la petite pantoufle de verre" thinly disguises its satire of the extravagant court milieu at the time of Louis XIV and its obsession with fashion and appearances under the veneer of the marvelous. It mocks female obsession with dress in the fierce competition for a socially desirable partner but also targets male foolishness. The two morals even challenge received ideas about success, stressing the role of education over beauty and of experienced and well-connected women in the making of the princess, hence reinterpreting "magic" as power and influence in high society. In the first moral social training is seen as the key to social elevation; because she is prepared and raised ("dressée," i.e., disciplined) to attract the Prince's attention through her pleasant company and accomplishments, Cinderella gets a prince as her "prize."[11] In her translation Carter mistranslates *dresser* as "dressed," however, and so part of Perrault's point (including his mocking of fashion) is lost.

Because "Ashputtle *or* The Mother's Ghost" activates the negative connotations of the word *dresser* as the brutal training of an animal to obey (in modern French usage), the rewriting can be seen as a corrective to the translation.[12] The stepmother "is prepared to cripple her daughters" (*Amer-*

ican Ghosts, 115), and even the mother's reincarnation as a dove stays close to Ashputtle at the ball, "pecking her ears to make her dance vivaciously, so that the prince would see her, so that the prince would love her, so that he would follow her" (115). "Ashputtle *or* The Mother's Ghost," then, captures the darker sociopsychological implications of the tale as it raises the issue of intergenerational transmission from mother to daughter. The shift from translation to rewriting, then, arguably hinges on the word *dresser*, whose meaning slips from dress to tough love, with steely social-climbing matriarchs shaping generations of Cinderellas in the world. Their motivations are more complex than we might think; Carter suggests that they range from personal ambition and desire for revenge to concern with their daughter's economic security once they are gone. Whereas Carter's translation warns young girls that there is more to the seduction game than a "fancy hairdo," the rewriting set in an immemorial past focuses on what binds one generation of women to the next.

Carter's translation of Perrault took place at a time when the fairy tale was being debated and accused of perpetuating patriarchal norms and values. "Snow White," "Sleeping Beauty," and "Cinderella" in particular were seen as providing role models and perpetuating stereotypes of femininity that went against the progressive ideals promoted by the women's liberation movement.[13] The influential interpretation proposed by Bruno Bettelheim in *The Uses of Enchantment* (1976) further reinforced the belief that in these tales "the rescuers fall in love with these heroines because of their beauty, which symbolizes their perfection" (277). Bettelheim devotes a long chapter to "Cinderella," which he presents as a story about "sibling rivalry." He sums up several versions of the tale, including the ancient Chinese tale that associates sexual attractiveness with tiny feet in accordance with the custom of foot binding. He admits, however, that "neither in Basile's story nor in the much more ancient Chinese tale is there any mention of Cinderella being mistreated by her siblings" (246). This is probably why Carter, who was critical of the reductive nature and sexist bias of Bettelheim's psychosexual readings, chose to focus on mother-daughter relationships instead. Significantly, there are no stepsisters in "The Burned Child" or "Travelling Clothes."

In his reading of Grimm, Bettelheim also predictably associates the striking image of the bloody shoe with the bleeding vagina as a manifestation of castration anxiety. Like Anne Sexton before her, Carter reinterprets the motif not as a Freudian symbol but as the real enough bodily mutilation perpetrated by mothers on their own daughters to secure a princely marriage for them. She even makes bitter fun of Bettelheim's reading when she writes, "Brandishing the carving knife, the woman bears down on her child, who is as distraught as if she had not been a girl but a boy and the old woman was after a more essential portion than a toe" (*American Ghosts*, 115).[14] Although Carter reads into the bloody deeds described in the Grimms' *Märchen* the brutal consequences of a patriarchal order perpetuated by women themselves, her translation of Perrault's *conte* conveys a much more lighthearted message to young girls about how to achieve happiness.

Carter's "Cinderella: or, The Little Glass Slipper" characteristically modernizes the language and message of the tale while also paying homage to Robert Samber's or G. M.'s early translations of the French *conte* into English. The title is indeed modeled on Samber's "Cinderella: or, The Little Glass Slipper" or on G. M.'s similar translation, which is referenced here. Probably to highlight the difference between Perrault's text and the cultural stereotype of Cinderella, Carter reproduces the full title and distinctive punctuation of these early translations, thereby drawing attention to her own project as a *re*translation of the tale. The double title suggests a double thematic focus (the girl and the shoe) and a double meaning, if only because Perrault proposes two alternative morals. The first moral is consistent with fairy-tale logic, as it teaches that the true gift of fairies lies in a good education because "bonne grâce" is superior to beauty, although this is ironized in a metatextual aside ("Car ainsi sur ce conte on va moralisant," *Contes*, 177). The second moral, however, is more worldly and cynical: To be socially successful, one needs all the qualities listed earlier as well as powerful godmothers or godfathers.[15] The contemporary resonance of "godfathers" (Francis Ford Coppola's famous crime film *The Godfather* came out in 1972) probably explains Carter's reference to "the female fairy mafia" in "The Better to Eat You With" (453), against Disney's elderly, benign and rather silly fairy godmother.

Carter finds in Perrault's *contes* useful lessons that enable children to be spared "half the pain that Cinderella or Red Riding Hood endured" and "to come to no harm in [the world]" (*Fairy Tales*, 17). Specifically, they learn "the advantages of patronage from Cinderella" ("The Better to Eat You With," 454): "Cinderella's godmother and the guests at the Sleeping

Beauty's wedding," she notes, "have less the air of supernatural beings derived from pagan legend about them than of women of independent means who've done quite well for themselves" (454). In the same essay Carter even draws a parallel between Perrault's worldly fairy and Mae West in *She Done Him Wrong* (1933). She voices the moral to be elicited from the tale through this modern-day equivalent of Cinderella's Fairy Godmother, who consoles a seduced and abandoned girl by giving her "nice clothes and good advice" (454). Although the memory of the romantic comedy may have induced Carter to mistranslate *dresser* as "dressed," the worldly-wise Lady Lou (Mae West) also gives the girl hard-nosed advice: Instead of useless moralizing, she points out that "hard work and ingenuity, virtue and beauty are all very well. But somebody's got to run the racket" (454). Carter's translation, though obviously quite different from the French *conte*, thus carries a matter-of-fact message that is surprisingly close to the spirit of the source.[16]

Carter's modern translation for children also fosters and facilitates the young reader's identification with the fairy-tale heroine. The three young women competing for the Prince's attention in Perrault's text become significantly younger in the translation. The marriageable daughters of the *conte*, who laugh mockingly at Cinderella, become giggling children in Carter's text (*Fairy Tales*, 83, 94). The cultural references to fashion, hair, and beauty rituals in preparation for the ball are updated to a fresh haircut and makeup; the stepsisters' elaborate headdress ("cornettes à deux rangs," *Contes*, 172) and beauty patch ("mouches de la bonne Faiseuse," *Contes*, 172), fashionable at the time of Perrault, change into their modern-day equivalent: "a good hairdresser" and "the best cosmetics" (*Fairy Tales*, 86).[17] Despite these differences, the implicit critique of artifice remains, and Carter shares with Perrault a project of "worldly instruction" inflected by her own feminist concerns about the education of young girls on the topics of seduction, love, and marriage.

Steeped in a courtly culture and aristocratic milieu, Perrault's *conte* shows how dress is inseparable from social status, determining identity as well as desirability. When Cendrillon dresses like a princess, even her stepsisters do not recognize her. When she runs away at midnight, the guards see only a peasant girl leaving the castle ("On demanda aux Gardes de la porte du Palais s'ils n'avaient point vu sortir une Princesse; ils dirent qu'ils n'avaient vu sortir personne, qu'une jeune fille fort mal vêtue, et qui avait plus l'air d'une Paysanne que d'une Demoiselle," *Contes*, 176). The prince himself seems to be more enamored with the glass slipper than with the mysterious young woman wearing it at the ball. The twofold title of Perrault's *conte* itself suggests that the fairy-tale heroine is one with her marvelous shoe. In her turn, Carter stresses the comedy of fashion that she would explore further in her brilliant essays for *New Society*, which reveal her strong and perceptive insights into self-fashioning. The translation portrays Cinderella as lovely and kind, but also strong, smart, and determined, displaying a good dose of practical intelligence and humor (she knows that appearances are deceptive and fools her stepsisters twice with obvious delight), all contained in the quality of "charm" praised in the moral.[18] Far from being passive, Cinderella is not resigned to her fate, and she seizes an opportunity to reinvent herself with the help of her godmother.

The very name of the heroine reflects her mutable identity and opens up the possibility of self-transformation. Cendrillon is anglicized first as Cinderilla in both Samber's and G. M.'s translations before stabilizing as Cinderella.[19] The girl is given two derogatory nicknames by her clothes-conscious stepsisters, the more insulting of which, Cucendron (*Contes*, 171) (Ash-bottom), is attenuated in the early translations as Cinderbreech (*Histories*, 59).[20] Carter modernizes it as Cinderbritches (*Fairy Tales*, 86),[21] so that the girl is associated with a type of ungendered working outfit, further reinforced by the phrase "workaday overalls" (88) ("clothes" and even "nasty old clothes" in *Histories*, 67). Because "britches" is also found in the English idiom "to wear the britches," Cinderella's elusive identity becomes linked to girl power. In this sense Carter's fairy-tale character is recast as a working-class heroine who turns an insult into a strength and makes a name for herself by reclaiming her nickname.

Perrault disguises his critique of the aristocracy under the formulaic "once upon a time" opening. The capitalized word "Gentilhomme" ("gentleman") that designates the heroine's father clearly functions as a class marker: "Il était une fois un Gentilhomme qui épousa en secondes noces une femme, la plus hautaine et la plus fière qu'on eût jamais vue. Elle avait deux filles de son humeur, et qui lui ressemblaient en toutes choses. Le Mari avait de son côté une jeune fille, mais d'une douceur et d'une bonté sans exemple; elle tenait cela de sa Mère, qui était la meilleure personne du monde" (*Contes*, 171).

Unlike Samber, Carter does *not* opt for the traditional fairy-tale formula. The generic signal is considerably attenuated ("There *once* lived a man . . ."), perhaps to emulate "Aschenputtel," which begins in medias res ("Einem reichen Manne, dem wurde seine Frau krank," *Kinder- und Hausmärchen*, 1: 137). Carter's translation reflects the pressure of the folktale tradition in its adoption of a simple, paratactic style and symmetrical oppositions to convey the conflict that opposes two family lines of women competing for a man.

> There once lived a man who married twice, and his second wife was the haughtiest and most stuck-up woman in the world. She already had two daughters of her own and her children took after her in every way. Her new husband's first wife had given him a daughter of his own before she died, but she was a lovely and sweet-natured girl, very like her own natural mother, who had been a kind and gentle woman. (*Fairy Tales*, 83)

To clarify the oppositional logic at work in the tale, Carter resorts to elementary syntax and parallel structures, parataxis ("and," "and," "but"), basic vocabulary and short words, contrasted pairs ("once" versus "twice," "second wife" versus "first wife," "daughters of her own" versus "daughter of his own," "her children took after her in every way" versus "very like her own natural mother"), and repetitions ("new husband," "new wife," "new daughter"). Whereas Perrault resorts to the marvelous to mask his critique of the pettiness, intrigues, and vanities of the world of the court, Carter follows the conventions of the genre as (re)defined by the Grimms, namely, "the bare necessity of the fairy tale, with its characteristic copula formula, 'and then'" to quote the self-conscious narrator of "Ashputtle *or* The Mother's Ghost" (*American Ghosts*, 113).

Carter's translation of Perrault in fact reflects the pressure of the "Gattung Grimm" on language, syntax, and style but also on the story itself. This style had already been emulated by Ralph Manheim in his celebrated new rendering *Grimms' Tales for Young and Old*, which Carter mentions in her course notes.[22] Whereas much is made of the death of Ashputtle's mother in the German *Märchen*, the French text only implies that she has died through the husband's remarriage. Carter disambiguates Perrault's text by adding a subclause: "[The] first wife had given him a daughter of his own *before she died*" (*Fairy Tales*, 83; italics mine). The recomposed family is also seen as unnatural, unlike Cinderella, who is "like her own *natural* mother" (83). Carter's addition reflects a long tradition of cruel stepmothers on the translator's understanding of the tale, which probably owes something to the Grimms.

The narrator of "Ashputtle *or* The Mother's Ghost" even muses on this word ("natural") introduced in the translation when she speculates that the secondary meaning of "natural" as "being born outside marriage" could explain the stepmother's hostility toward Ashputtle if the girl were her husband's illegitimate daughter. She nevertheless rejects this interpretation as providing motivation, hence moving away from fairy-tale logic toward bourgeois realism.

In short, Carter's translation of Perrault is already haunted by the memory of the Grimms, and as such it anticipates the mother's comeback in the rewriting as a returning ghost, based on the promise made by the dying mother in "Aschenputtel": "Liebes Kind, bleib fromm und gut, . . . und ich will vom Himmel auf dich herabblicken und will um dich sein" (*Kinder- und Hausmärchen*, 1: 137), translated by Manheim as "Dear child, be good and say your prayers . . . and I shall look down on you from heaven and always be with you" (*Grimms' Tales*, 83).

Another perceptible shift in the translation pertains to class. Perrault's characters belong to an aristocratic milieu. The downgrading of Cinderella within the recomposed family results from the father's inability to hold his place in the household. He is a weak nobleman who lets himself be entirely ruled by his second wife ("qui se laissait gouverner entièrement," *Contes*, 171). Cinderella is made to serve "Madame" and "Mesdemoiselles ses filles" (171) and finds herself relegated to the role of servant in the family. This concern with rank is further reflected in the trying on of the slipper in decreasing order by princesses, then duchesses, the entire court, Cinderella's stepsisters, and so on ("On commença à l'essayer aux Princesses, ensuite aux Duchesses, et à toute la Cour, mais inutilement. On l'apporta chez les deux soeurs," *Contes*, 176). The German *Märchen*, however, takes place in a bourgeois household, where a first daughter is born to a rich man (*Kinder- und Hausmärchen*, 1: 137) before his wife dies and he remarries.

It is noteworthy that although in her translation Carter simply refers to the husband as "a man" (*Fairy Tales*, 83), her rewriting focuses on the economic stakes of marriage and remarriage. The first section, titled "The Mutilated Girls," begins with a commentary on the German text, based on a quotation from Manheim's translation, which sought to recapture the oral quality of the tales: "A rich man's wife fell sick, and, feeling that her end was near, she called her only daughter to her bedside" (*American Ghosts*, 110; *Grimms' Tales*, 83). The narrator draws attention to "the absence of the husband/father" (110) and accounts for female conflict as a result of women's economic dependence on men: "In the drama between two female families in opposition to one another because of the rivalry over men . . . , the men seem no more than passive victims of their fancy, yet their significance is absolute because it is ('a rich man,' 'a king's son') economic" (110–111).[23] Even though Carter's translation tends to erase class markers, her rewriting focuses on women's obsession with marriage as a consequence of their subservient social, legal, and economic status under patriarchy.

Perrault's critique of courtly society is conveyed through the portrayal of arrogant aristocrats contrasted with the first wife and her daughter, who display inborn qualities. Unlike Cinderella, who is "d'une douceur et d'une beauté sans exemple" and owes these qualities to her mother, who was "la meilleure personne du monde" ("of unparallelled goodness and sweetness of temper"; "the best creature in the world," *Histories*, 58–59), the second wife is unbearably proud and haughty ("la femme la plus hautaine et la plus fière qu'on eût jamais vue," *Contes*, 171; "the proudest and most haughty woman that was ever seen," *Histories*, 58). Carter follows the early translators when she uses the superlative form to describe Cinderella's stepmother as "the haughtiest and most stuck-up woman" (note the familiar word mocking pretentiousness), but she does not reduce the heroine and her mother to stereotypes. Cinderella is "a *lovely* and *sweet-natured* girl" and her natural mother is "a *kind* and *gentle* woman" (*Fairy Tales*, 83; italics mine). Because she omits "sans exemple" (unparalleled), her modern heroine is no longer a paragon of virtue but an ordinary "lovely" girl, just like the "lovely ladies" addressed in the moral, which strengthens the link between Cinderella and the modern-day readers. The translator therefore inflects the praise of beauty, sweetness, and goodness of the heroine to emphasize the lovable character and natural kindness of the girl ("sweet-natured").[24] Unsurprisingly, the translation reflects Carter's effort to avoid reducing Cinderella to a mere stereotype or "Angel in the House" type.[25]

Carter shifts the subtle critique of the aristocratic milieu depicted in Perrault's *conte* onto the conflict that opposes the heroine to her foster family. The violent power relations result from the father's inability to hold his place in the household and protect his daughter. Many readers, including the narrator of "Ashputtle *or* The Mother's Ghost," have wondered at the father's indifference to the persecution of his daughter. In "About the Stories" Carter even notes that "Cinderella's father is no more than a function of the plot" (*Sleeping Beauty*, 128), and she goes on to account for his absence in "Ashputtle *or* The Mother's Ghost" in similar terms. When she translates "Gentilhomme" as "man" and, at the end of the first paragraph, designates the first wife as a "gentle *woman*" (and not "lady"), the implicit critique of aristocrats' indifference toward their children reorients the tale and redefines its significance for a modern audience.

Carter's concern with women is already perceptible in the grammar of the translated text. "Cinderella: or, The Little Glass Slipper" begins with the husband, defined by what he "has," namely, a wife and a daughter. But he quickly moves from generic subject ("a man") to a mere pronoun and object of dispute. The conflict that opposes two women for the *possession* of a rich and noble husband (who is furthermore easy to influence and manipulate) is replayed in the next generation.[26] Cinderella avenges her mother and wins all, although her stepsisters also benefit from her triumph (in contrast to the German *Märchen*, in which they are cruelly punished). In the first sentence already, the insignificant husband is replaced by his domineering second wife, who becomes the grammatical subject of the next sentence ("She already had two daughters of her own"). She is in turn replaced, in the sentence that follows, by the first wife's own daughter, whose role will be to put an end to the usurpation. Even though the tale starts with "a man," then, the first paragraph of Carter's translation significantly ends on the word "woman" (note that Perrault's text was not divided into paragraphs). The incipit therefore introduces the main characters, their roles and relationships within the family, and the conflict that opposes them, but it also sums up the entire tale and its resolution. Because the attention quickly shifts from the weak husband and indifferent father to the world of women, it even anticipates the rewriting of the tale in "Ashputtle *or* The Mother's Ghost."

The conflict between the two families is underlined by parallel grammatical constructions with the possessive form. The second wife has "two daughters *of her own*," whereas the first wife "had given him a daughter *of his own*" (*Fairy Tales*, 83; italics mine). This suggests a biological link between the father and the heroine that makes his indifference toward her even more mysterious or unnatural. The idea of a female struggle for the possession of a husband in turn informs Carter's rewriting, where the narrator comments:

> Although the woman is defined by her relation to him ("a rich man's wife") the daughter is unambiguously hers, as if hers alone, and the entire drama concerns only women, takes place almost exclusively among women, is a fight between two groups of women—in the right-hand corner, Ashputtle and her mother; in the left-hand corner, the stepmother and *her* daughters. (*American Ghosts*, 110)

The harsh world of the tale sheds a crude light on naive notions of sisterhood and idealized motherhood invoked by second-wave feminists, which Carter saw as mere consolatory fictions. Rather, as a socialist and materialist feminist, she blamed women's economic dependency on men as the main source of conflict, brutality, and cruelty among women.[27]

Each version of the tale, then, proposes an interpretation shaped by the teller's own concerns and context. The moral in particular becomes a privileged site where the translator can voice her views on the upbringing of girls. A brief comparison of Perrault's and G. M.'s texts shows how Carter responds to both the source text and the intermediary translation. In Perrault's *conte* the first moral brings up the controversial subject of the pros and cons of educating girls, which Molière had raised in *Les femmes savantes* and Boileau bitterly mocked in his *Satire X*. Perrault, however, argues that female education should not be neglected because, as the story of Cinderella demonstrates, it is the key to a young woman's social elevation and royal marriage:

MORALITE
La beauté pour le sexe est un rare trésor,
De l'admirer jamais on ne se lasse;
Mais ce qu'on nomme bonne grâce
Est sans prix, et vaut mieux encor.
C'est ce qu'à Cendrillon fit avoir sa Marraine,
En la dressant, en l'instruisant,
Tant et si bien qu'elle en fit une Reine:
(Car ainsi sur ce Conte on va moralisant.)

> Belles, ce don vaut mieux que d'être bien coiffées,
> Pour engager un Coeur, pour en venir à bout,
> La bonne grâce est le vrai don des Fées;
> Sans elle on ne peut rien, avec elle, on peut tout.
>
> AUTRE MORALITE
> C'est sans doute un grand avantage,
> D'avoir de l'esprit, du courage,
> De la naissance, du bon sens,
> Et d'autres semblables talents,
> Qu'on reçoit du Ciel en partage;
> Mais vous aurez beau les avoir,
> Pour votre avancement ce seront choses vaines,
> Si vous n'avez, pour les faire valoir,
> Ou des parrains ou des marraines.
>
> (*Contes*, 177–78)

Perrault's twofold moral reads like an intervention in an ongoing argument about female values and virtues (the concessive "mais" in the first and "sans doute" in the second suggest possible objections). The first part, presumably addressed to young women, places the *bonne grâce*, which Antoine Furetière's *Dictionnaire universel* (1690) defines as "affabilité, amabilité, gentillesse" (i.e., affability [pleasant to speak to], amiability [or lovableness], and pleasantness [or gracefulness and even wit according to Littré]), *above* beauty, seemingly against public or dominant opinion. The obsolete meaning of *bonne grâce* is therefore surprisingly close to Carter's qualification of Cinderella as "lovely" in the main body of the tale, inasmuch as both Perrault and Carter seem to place a good education over good looks, although Carter puts more emphasis on the girl's innate qualities. The training and good advice is provided by the *fée marraine* (Fairy Godmother), to whom the girl owes her success and promotion. However, the parenthetical comment that concludes the second quatrain in Perrault's moral introduces an ironic distance that calls into question its truth value. It contradicts the conventional praise of talented young people to wryly assert that they will remain unnoticed and unrecognized unless powerful "parrains" and "marraines" intercede in their favor.

The early English translation attenuates the ironic discrepancy between the first and second moral as it eliminates the subtle humor (*ton enjoué*) of the parenthetical aside, reasserting the truth of the moral instead. Furthermore, the fairies who teach young women *bonne grâce*, guaranteeing success, disappear when the tale is Christianized. This acculturation characterizes the reception of French *contes de fées* in Puritan England, which was deeply suspicious of the "pagan" origin and influence of the *contes merveilleux* and of "frivolous" literature in general.[28] Whereas Perrault's moral asserts that "la bonne grâce est le vrai don des Fées," the connotations of "good grace" take a religious turn in Samber's and G. M.'s translations (*Histories*, 70), where "grace" evokes the godly favor that "in scriptural and theological language [designates] the free and unmerited favour of God" (*Oxford English Dictionary*). The new meaning of "grace" is confirmed by two additions: "fate" associated with "heaven" in the first moral and "rich graces from above" in the second moral. The English equivalent of "parrains et marraines" ("Godsires" and "Godmothers") reinforces the shift to divine grace and determination still further.

Perrault's worldly message is thus filtered through Protestant homily, thereby exemplifying the adaptation of Perrault's *conte* to the discursive practices and cultural references of early-eighteenth-century England. Carter, however, gives a modern twist on the moral, as follows:

Moral

Beauty is a fine thing in a woman; it will always be admired. But charm is beyond price and worth more, in the long run. When her godmother dressed Cinderella up and told her how to behave at the ball, she instructed her in charm. Lovely ladies, this gift is worth more than a fancy hairdo; to win a heart, to reach a happy ending, charm is the true gift of the fairies. Without it, one can achieve nothing; with it, everything.

Another moral

It is certainly a great advantage to be intelligent, brave, well-born, sensible and have other similar talents given only by heaven. But however great may be your god-given store, they will never help you to get on in the world unless you have either a godfather or a godmother to put them to work for you. (*Fairy Tales*, 95–96)

Carter characteristically opts for prose to convey a practical (but certainly not a preachy) message suited to her young public in the morals.[29] Perrault's first moral lends itself particularly well to Carter's feminist point of view because it recognizes the admiration provoked by beauty in a young woman but immediately demarcates itself from it. Carter mistranslates *dressant* as "dressed," as we have seen, and redefines *gentillesse* (which her source presents as the true nobility of the heart) as "charm." Placed above beauty, coquetry, and artifice, which the translator comically conveys as a "fancy hairdo," charm is the new magic that emanates from the modern-day heroine. Moreover, Carter's own version of the happy ending emphasizes love and romance rather than social success. In this sense the translated text is not unlike Cinderella herself, always dressed anew. Like a true fairy godmother, Carter thus put the fairy tale back in fashion in the twentieth century.

Martin Ware's illustrations represent yet another dressing of the tale as he translates elements from Carter's text into visual images. Ware characteristically figures the sun as a headpiece for the Cinderella story, either in homage to the art-loving Sun King and his fashion-conscious court or because the worldly wisdom of the morals heralds the Enlightenment period, as Carter herself points out. The first full-page illustration of the tale (*Fairy Tales*, 85) presents an elderly, bespectacled, stiff-upper-lip woman wearing a strict dress but an extravagant hat decorated with roses, feathers, and butterflies (Figure 7.2). Although her identity is ambiguous (the text on the left mentions the stepmother, not the godmother), she seems to represent the Fairy Godmother, whose magical powers are associated with speech, usually symbolized as roses by the illustrator.

The lady's lavishly decorated hat also evokes the amusing and droll custom of wearing fancy hats (typically featuring flowers, butterflies, and feathers) at Ascot, where society ladies gather not so much to watch the horse races but rather to see and to be seen, to attract the attention of a suitable party for themselves or their children, or to appear in the papers the next day. Ascot and similar events thus represent the modern-day British equivalent of the lavish balls and spectacles organized by Louis XIV at Versailles that Perrault subtly ridiculed in his *conte*. But the ambiguous identity of the woman portrayed by Ware also suggests new possibilities for retelling; the stern lady may be a benevolent godmother determined to

Figure 7.2. Illustration for "Cinderella" in the 1977 edition of The Fairy Tales of Charles Perrault. *Courtesy of Martin Ware.*

help a girl in distress or a cruel matriarch ready to do anything to promote her own daughter(s). This hints at the ambivalence of mother-daughter relationships that becomes central in "Ashputtle *or* The Mother's Ghost."

The second illustration for Cinderella is equally ambiguous. It shows the six lizards metamorphosed into footmen or the different stages in the transformation of one single lizard. The image captures a magical moment and decomposes what happens in an instant in the text. The metamorphic process stresses the hybrid identity of the animal as it changes into a human being. The next full-page illustration (*Fairy Tales*, 93) represents a scene favored by illustrators of "Cinderella." It portrays the heroine in a simple, low-cut dress as she leave the castle in a hurry. She seems to be caught in flight after running down the palace stairs, the movement of her hair suggesting that she has just turned her head, while her abandoned slipper is visible on the left. The next page presents a close-up of the slipper as a delicate, semi-transparent, high-heeled shoe, placed at the bottom of page, as though the stairs were represented by the paragraphs of the text (Figure 7.3). The shape of the glass shoe strangely evokes the body and muzzle of the lizard on the facing page (perhaps through an association of the metamorphosed footmen and the foot wearing the slipper?). It is also noteworthy that the shoe is inserted at the exact moment of Cinderella's triumph and final transformation, when her godmother touches her "overalls with her ring [*sic*] and at once the old clothes were transformed into garments more magnificent than all her ball-dresses" (*Fairy Tales*, 94–95).

Ware therefore focuses on the transformative process, from the flowers, butterflies, fruits (including a tiny pumpkin!), and leaping frog decorating the aristocratic lady's hat that come alive on page 85 (*Fairy Tales*) to the lizards turning into footmen on page 89.[30] All these images have to do with magic and transformation; the glass slipper even connects enchantment and reality as well as text and image, each representing a new metamorphosis of the tale. The shoe as ultimate marvelous accessory thus frames the story textually (in the title) and visually (in the illustration), functioning like a decorative element that contains the fairy tale and symbolizes it. In her rewriting, by contrast, Carter discards all unnecessary ornamentation to focus on the bare bones of the tale.

Figure 7.3. Illustrations for "Cinderella" in the 1977 edition of The Fairy Tales of Charles Perrault. *Courtesy of Martin Ware.*

From "Wolf-Alice" to "Ashputtle *or* The Mother's Ghost": Eating Mamma, or Puns and Pumpkins

A masterpiece always moves, by definition, in the manner of a ghost.

—JACQUES DERRIDA, *SPECTERS OF MARX*, 18

The Grimms' *Märchen* gave Carter an occasion to reflect on another kind of magic, this time associated with biological and literary motherhood.[31] Whereas the German tale praises the uncanny influence of Ashputtle's mother after her death (provided that the girl remains good and pious), the modern writer prefers to probe the enigma of "mother love" (*American Ghosts*, 115) that drives a woman to manipulate and even mutilate her own daughters, because "the girls, all three, are animated solely by the wills of their mothers" (111). When Carter decided to include "Ashputtle *or* The Mother's Ghost" in *American Ghosts and Old World Wonders*, however, it came to express an even more personal and intimate concern about the author's own legacy.

"Ashputtle *or* The Mother's Ghost" shifts the focus from the fairy-tale heroine to the figure of the mother: "It is really always the story of her mother even if, at the beginning of the story, the mother herself is just about to exit the narrative because she is at death's door" (*American Ghosts*, 110). The first section of the rewriting reads like a prologue that accounts for the new focus adopted by the reader/writer. It also suggests that Carter's understanding of the tale is inseparable from its critical reception. The authorial narrator's speculations on the tale's significance respond to Sandra Gilbert and Susan Gubar's *Madwoman in the Attic* (1979), Bruno Bettelheim's *Uses of Enchantment* (1976), and possibly even Nancy Friday's *My Mother, My Self* (1977), Friday's interest in intergenerational legacy and sex-positive feminism being close to Carter's.

"Ashputtle *or* The Mother's Ghost" also provides a skeptical counterpoint to Carter's celebration of a female fairy-tale tradition of "wise, clever, perceptive, occasionally lyrical, eccentric, sometimes downright crazy . . . great-grandmothers . . . and their great-grandmothers; and of the contributions to literature of Mother Goose and her goslings" (Carter, *Virago Book of Fairy Tales*, xxii). Although Carter's two edited volumes for Virago are consistent with the press's endeavor to recover female voices, her rewriting of "Ashputtle" is more suspicious of uncritical appeals to female genealogies and legacies. Sarah Gamble rightly observes that "Carter uncovers a deeper, more subversive history of the fairy tale, bringing to the surface not only what Warner terms its 'harshly realistic core' but also 'the suspect whiff of femininity' from which it has never been completely disassociated," although "her reclamation of the position of female storyteller does not lead to her exoneration of the female gender from complicity with—and even an active perpetuation of—the circumstances of its own oppression."[32] "Ashputtle *or* The Mother's Ghost" is a good case in point because it revolves around the figure of the mother, who comes back from the dead to take control of her daughter's fate. By fusing the "good" mother and her dark double (the stepmother), Carter intimates that the nature of mother-daughter relationships is fundamentally ambivalent, mixing love and negation of the daughter's individuality, self-denial and self-affirmation, identification and independence. The same applies to literary creation, which unfolds in the interplay of repetition and difference.[33]

In *The Bloody Chamber* the idea of the tale as a generative matrix is thematized in the last tale of the collection. In "Wolf-Alice" the wolf-child who "sleeps in the soft, warm ashes of the hearth" (121) remembers her foster mother killed by the peasants: "When [Wolf-Alice] curled up among the cinders, the colour, the texture and warmth of them brought her foster mother's belly out of the past and printed it on her flesh; her first conscious memory" (123–24). The sensory experience of early childhood, comfort, and reassurance associated with the wolf's belly makes the wolf-child into a wild Cinderella of sorts. "Wolf-Alice" is therefore a transitional text that borrows elements from "Little Red Riding Hood" but also fleetingly morphs into the ash girl. Carter's preparatory notes confirm that she used the material that she had collected for "Cinderella" in "Wolf-Alice," beside *Wolfsong* and *The Wild Boy: The Savage of the Aveyron*.

More specifically, how did "Ashputtle *or* The Mother's Ghost" come into being? As a cross-cultural, translatorial process, literary creation involves endless transformations. Accordingly, Carter mixed Perrault and Grimm as the starting point for her rewriting through a cross-linguistic pun when she connected the godmother's changing the pumpkin into a golden coach in Perrault with Ashputtle's orphan state in Grimm. In her notes for "Ashputtle *or* The Mother's Ghost" Carter indicates that the original version of her own story (its seed, as it were) was based on a pun. On a page titled "Eating Mamma" she picks the episode of the pumpkin transformed into a stage coach and even quotes the passage in French: "Va dans le jardin et apporte-moi une citrouille. Cendrillon alla aussitot [*sic*] cueillir la plus belle qu'elle peut [*sic*] trouver." In her commentary Carter astutely makes a connection between Cinderella's lack of family (or "kin") with the magic pumpkin. She muses over the word *pumpkin*, whose suggestive form becomes perceptible only through the detour of the French text, as Carter observes herself.

> The godmother asks the girl to fetch a pumpkin; poor orphan Cinderella, out she goes to fetch the only fruit that never wants for family because its "kin" go everywhere with it, as suffix, as indelible second syllable although this point is lost in French, of course.

Analogy between pumpkin and woman's belly ("full of seeds"), belly of the mother // pie; "there is always something going on in a woman's belly" // moon

The pumpkin-kin pun therefore becomes a key creative device, through associations of ideas that function like an umbilical cord linking Perrault's and the Grimms' texts, their crossing (cross-breeding?) generating the idea of pregnancy, mothering, and reproduction at the core of the rewriting. Carter thus locates magic in language, which becomes especially productive in translation because it has the power to reenchant language.[34]

One idea leading to another, Carter moves from the "pregnant" fruit to baking a pumpkin pie as equivalent to "eating a mother"; the pie becomes a cheerful "invocation of the mother," a homey "meal of motherhood," and even "a kind of transubstantiation" that harks back to ancient ceremonies where the participants consume the body of a venerated ancestor, as in the Eucharist. The kitchen itself becomes a "space of welcome, odorous and warm, place of time and metamorphosis, the womb, that mysterious, moist, magical vessel—the alembic of flesh."[35] The hearth, Cinderella's dwelling place, is no longer associated with the heroine's degradation and misery but with cooking as analogous to pregnancy: a magical, transformative process that allows a form of communion with the mother, set in the kitchen as a domestic and distinctively female laboratory of nourishing and nurturing creation and fiction making.

Cooking indeed strengthens the connection with storytelling as a metaphor for female production, in keeping with traditional fairy-tale imagery (the scene of storytelling by the hearth found in most frontispieces). When Perrault's pumpkin is transposed into an American context, however, it inevitably evokes Halloween, the festival of the dead, a connection that was further reinforced when "Ashputtle *or* The Mother's Ghost" was reprinted in *American Ghosts and Old World Wonders*. It took on new resonances and turned into a meditation on the author's own demise, as Carter knew that she was condemned by lung cancer; the tale served to speculate on Carter's disappearance and possible return in spectral form through the magic of writing. Carter's ultimate return to Ashputtle therefore became an occasion to reflect on her own legacy, the author staging herself as a maternal figure taking leave of her readers but also anticipating her continuing presence in ghostly fashion, because ghosts trouble the separation between the living and the dead.[36] Although the tale served as a matrix generating "daughter-texts," it later came to reflect Carter's own thoughts on her afterlife as a writer. Carter even played with the manifold meanings of *will* as mother's will to live (and accomplish herself) through her daughter, but also literary will (testament); she addresses her readers and invites them to use the gifts that she has bestowed on them but in their own way and in their own voice.[37]

A third set of notes for "Cinderella," subtitled "the seduction of the father," takes the tale in an altogether different direction. It sums up an alternative version of the story reminiscent of "Donkey-Skin," which found its way in the second retelling, "The Burned Child": "Cinderella, banished to the kitchen by the stepmother, plots and schemes her way back to her father's bed." She also adds "big, old house in the country—Hardup Hall," probably remembering a pantomime version alluded to in "In Pantoland."[38]

The story of Cinderella, then, takes new and unexpected turns in Carter's fiction depending on the tradition followed by the author. Characteristically, Carter explores the semantic possibilities and poetic associations of a word, image, or name defamiliarized through translation.[39] In his account of the significance of the tale, Bettelheim argues that Ashputtle acquires her distinct name and identity when she loses her mother and finds refuge in the kitchen hearth to mourn her. When Carter revisits Grimm (by way of Bettelheim), she explores the more sinister implications of ash as the mortal remains after combustion, so that the tale becomes a memento mori and meditation on the author's legacy after burning to death (she was, after all, a heavy smoker consumed by lung cancer).

"Ashputtle *or* The Mother's Ghost" brings back to life archaic "mother texts" buried by the dominant literary tradition and thus inevitably raises the issue of filiation. According to Lorna Sage, "The spectre that faced Angela Carter from the very beginning of her writing career [was] the thought that there was nothing new to do or be."[40] But the creative process testifies to the profoundly transformative nature of the fairy-tale tradition and the suggestive power of the ubiquitous tale that took the author from the pregnant belly of the pumpkin to the coffin that turns into a coach, from cooking and eating to breeding and dying, from Cinderella to Ashputtle, from dresses to ashes, dust to dust.

The Ambivalence of Mother-Ring: From Fairy to Fateful Mother

The cycle of her fate seems inexorable.

—SANDRA GILBERT AND SUSAN GUBAR, *THE MADWOMAN IN THE ATTIC*, 42

Escape the same fate!

—ANGELA CARTER'S HANDWRITTEN WORDS AT THE TOP OF A TYPEWRITTEN DRAFT OF THE STORY "ASHPUTTLE *OR* THE MOTHER'S GHOST"

"Ashputtle *or* The Mother's Ghost" summons up the German "Aschenputtel" in its anglicized form. Moving away from Perrault's witty and urbane *conte*, Carter picks up on the bloody and macabre details of the folk versions: Ashputtle's rivals are mutilated so they can slip their feet into the tiny shoe, and they are blinded by the mother's ghost (materialized as a bird) on the heroine's wedding day. Even the involvement of Ashputtle's mother in her daughter's fate is more ambiguous, or ambivalent, than we might think—or so Carter suggests.[41] This doubleness is implied in the italicized conjunction *or* in the title, which pairs Ashputtle with her mother's ghost, suggesting an uncanny splitting of identities as well as the generic doubling of the tale. Shifting from the *conte merveilleux* symbolized by the glass slipper to the Gothic tale and its maternal ghost, Carter reinvents the story of Cinderella "in a proliferation of intertextual possibilities" by "presenting versions that are to be read with and against each other" while also "engag[ing] in a productive dialogue with critics," to quote Cristina Bacchilega.[42]

"Ashputtle *or* The Mother's Ghost" indeed offers a threefold response to the creative and critical tradition of the tale. The first version, "The Mutilated Girls," takes the absence of the heroine's father in "Ashputtle" as its starting point, as though to prolong Gilbert and Gubar's reflections on "Snow White" in *The Madwoman in the Attic*. The second version, "The Burned Child," imagines a possible urtext for Ashputtle in the manner of folklorists, and the third version, "Travelling Clothes," briefly returns to the episode of the pumpkin changed into a coach to evoke the possibility of emancipation from the mother's influence in a kind of envoi.

"The Mutilated Girls" reads like preparatory notes, or even course notes on the tale, especially when we remember that Carter taught creative writing and folklore in England and in the United States. The narrator adopts the posture of a tutor who takes the reader/audience through a close textual analysis of the opening situation presented in "Ashputtle"; her commentary is interspersed with casual addresses to a vague "you" ("But although you could easily . . .," *American Ghosts*, 110) that soon turns into a collective "we" (111–112).[43] This prologue reflects on key questions raised by the tale and soon proposes new foci, from the heroine to the mutilated sisters, before settling on the figure of the mother. It identifies the basic components of the tale, thereby calling attention to its nature as a verbal construct that can be separated into its constitutive elements and remade into a different story.[44] The narrator acknowledges the enigmatic quality of the tale (from a Greek word meaning "to speak in riddles," itself derived from *ainos* [fable]), which triggers the interpretative and hence the retelling process. The father, the narrator observes, is "a mystery to me." He is "the unmoved mover, the unseen organising principle, like God, and, like God, up he pops in person, one fine day, to introduce the essential plot device" (110–112). This echoes Gilbert and Gubar's interpretation of "Snow White" as revolving around the absent father/husband, who symbolizes patriarchy as "the voice of the looking glass."[45] Instead of opposing mother and daughter around the male figure of authority, however, Carter draws attention to the ambivalent role played by the mother. Even though she leaves her own text ambiguously open rather than appeal to female solidarity, Carter nevertheless recuperates something of Gilbert and Gubar's portrayal of the Queen as "a plotter, a plot-maker, a schemer, a witch, an artist, an impersonator, a woman of almost infinite creative energy, witty, wily, and self-absorbed"[46] in her own portrayal of the mother's ghost as the main agent or dynamic principle behind Ashputtle's fate. After Sexton, Gilbert and Gubar also suggest that "the Queen and Snow White are in some sense one," so that even after her death, she "rises from her coffin" only to endlessly repeat the same story since "the cycle of her fate seems inexorable."[47] Carter's "Ashputtle *or* The Mother's Ghost" makes a similar point, and yet it is also possible to read in the third retelling a way out of the perpetuation of the logic of the same, generation after generation.

The first retelling comments on the conflict between two rival groups of women for the possession of a husband. The stepmother usurps the first wife's rightful place in the matrimonial bed while the dead mother lies in her tomb and Ashputtle sleeps in the hearth's ashes. To reverse the situation, the dead mother must come back and keep the promise she had made on her death bed: "I shall always look after you and always be with you" (*American Ghosts*, 111). The narrator departs from the Grimms when she speculates that the child is not altogether relieved at this return from the dead, because she understands that henceforth "she must do her mother's bidding" (111). The mother indeed wants to marry her off to the Prince, and she is ready to do what it takes to make it happen; she steals the stepdaughters' dresses and jewels, forces her daughter to exhibit herself at the ball (a "marriage market," as in Sexton's poem) and to dance like a marionette, "pecking her ears to make her dance vivaciously, so that the prince would see her, so that the prince would love her, so that he would follow her and find the clue of the fallen slipper" (115). The trial of the shoe leads the stepmother to mutilate her daughters, but the bird reveals the fraud and allows Ashputtle to try on the warm and bloody shoe, triumphantly exclaiming, "Her foot fits the shoe like the corpse fits the coffin!" (116).

The second retelling, "The Burned Child," is a short, terse tale about a burned child who mourns her dead mother and wins her father back with the help of friendly animals. The mother incarnates herself as a cow, a cat, and a bird to heal, groom, and dress her daughter in her own blood. Every gift is accompanied by a message of independence: "Give your own milk, next time ... you've milked me dry,"[48] "Comb your own hair," "Make your own dress" (*American Ghosts*, 118). The animals have sacrificed themselves to transform the mutilated child into a marriageable girl who succeeds in replacing her stepmother. The story ends with a muted happy ending: "She did all right." It imitates the features associated with the folktale: The distant, third-person narrator retells the story in the past tense; the deictic "now" (117 and 118) creates an effect of orality and presence; and the story adopts a threefold plot structure, lexical repetitions, and a simple and barren style characteristic of the Grimms' understanding of the *Volksmärchen*. Even the fairy-tale formula "Once upon a time" (117) comes up in the middle of the story. The matter-of-fact narrator does not comment on the tale being, at least implicitly, about incest.

The third story, "Travelling Clothes," more enigmatic still, revolves around a dialogue between mother and daughter. With a kiss the mother magically erases the scar made by the cruel stepmother, and she draws a precious gift from her own corpse: She turns a worm eating her eye into a ring. Unlike the animal helpers in the previous version, the mother urges her daughter to accept the objects that she inherited from her own mother (i.e., mortality as heirloom). The leitmotif "I had it from my mother when I was your age" (*American Ghosts*, 119) structurally enacts the idea of repetition and reproduction demanded by the mother. Intergenerational solidarity is inseparable from servitude, leading as it does to the endless repetition of female destiny. The story ends with Ashputtle stepping into her mother's coffin before it turns into a coach, in a macabre version of Perrault's pumpkin changed into a golden carriage by the Fairy Godmother. The mother's last call or last words are ambiguous: "Go and seek your fortune, darling." It remains uncertain whether the daughter will live her own life or simply reproduce the cycle of generations (or both). Although she dies at the beginning of the tale, the mother literally has the last word.

In the Grimms' Christianized tale the possibility of life after death is meant to comfort the daughter, and yet its implications of total control and constant surveillance are also sinister, as Carter suggests. The mother imposes her will in a domineering, tyrannical fashion because she condemns her daughter to replace her or, like Hamlet's ghost, to avenge her. Unlike Perrault's praise of the influence of powerful godmothers and godfathers or the Grimms' pious (if disturbingly cruel) celebration of motherly love beyond death, Carter explores the more obscure, complex, and disturbing implications of mother-daughter relations that echo modern psychology.

"The Mutilated Girls" focuses on the scene of the shoe, with a close-up on the vivid visual detail of the mother brandishing a knife over her terrorized child. The mutilation of the girl seems to be a prerequisite for marriage, if she wants to fit the mold and fulfill her prescribed destiny. The verb *to fit* is used in connection with the shoe, the coffin, and marriage, linking them together to suggest enclosure and imprisonment, even death. The narrator herself remarks that "it would be easy to think of it as a story about cutting bits off women, so that they will *fit in*, some sort of circumcision-like ritual chop" (*American Ghosts*, 110; italics mine). The spirit watching over Ashputtle sheds its Christian trappings when the mother reincarnates herself in various animals in the second rewriting, which desacralizes the religious imagery of the German *Märchen* (especially its representation of the mother as holy ghost and the horrific punishment of the stepsisters as righteous godly vengeance), as Carter submits the tale to cultural translation.[49]

The dead mother's intervention in her daughter's fate is marked by ambivalence, because she gives birth and therefore paradoxically dooms her child to death. The bloody shoe is described as an "open wound" and a "hideous receptacle" (*American Ghosts*, 116). Lucie Armitt notes that in "The Bloody Chamber" "chamber" designates simultaneously the secret room in which the Bluebeard figure hides his murdered wives, the bleeding female womb connoting sexuality, reproduction, and mortality, and the equally ambivalent space or site of literary creation.[50] Bettelheim also sees the glass shoe as a sexual symbol; according to him, however, Cinderella is the prototype of the "virginal bride."

> For the test to work, the shoe must be a slipper that does not stretch or it would fit some other girl, such as the stepsisters. Perrault's subtlety is shown in his saying the shoe was made of glass, a material that does not stretch, is extremely brittle and easily broken.
>
> A tiny receptacle into which some part of the body can slip and fit tightly can be seen as a symbol of the vagina.[51]

When Carter muses on the shoe, it is no longer a symbol of fetishized virginity but evidence of the physical, material reality of mutilation; Carter stresses the bloody, painful, and shocking aspect of the act and its unspoken consequences in the recognition scene.

> So now Ashputtle must put her foot into this hideous receptacle, this open wound, still slick and warm as it is, for nothing in any of the many texts of this tale suggests the prince washed the shoe out between the fittings.... Ashputtle's foot, the size of the bound foot of a Chinese woman, a stump. Almost an amputee already, she put her tiny foot in it. (*American Ghosts*, 116)[52]

Carter suggests that Ashputtle's small foot symbolizes her conformity to the patriarchal order. Against Bettelheim's assumptions, then, she reverses the traditional reading and transforms "Ashputtle *or* The Mother's Ghost" into a tale cautioning against conformity to the norm, whereas "Travelling Clothes" fuses the bloody shoe (in Grimm) and the magical coach (in Perrault) into a new motif: the coffin. This allows Carter to equate marriage (as female destiny involving child bearing) and death in a macabre analogy: "Her foot fits the shoe like the corpse fits the coffin!" (*American Ghosts*, 116).[53] The gradual disappearance of the authorial voice (in marked contrast to the first retelling) reads like an invitation to the reader: "Do your own reading next time."

"Ashputtle *or* The Mother's Ghost" in *American Ghosts and Old World Wonders*: From Halloween to Christmas, Carnival to Ash Wednesday

American Ghosts and Old World Wonders is a collection of miscellaneous texts published only a few months after Carter's death. Mercedes Gulin notes that "Ashputtle *or* The Mother's Ghost" takes on even deeper resonances when it is considered with the rest of the volume and the texts that frame it. Put together by Carter herself, the volume includes scenarios, legends, tales, sketches, and drafts that connect two continents: America and the Old World. In her introduction to *American Ghosts*, Susannah Clapp proposes to link these apparently disparate texts on the basis of their geographic location, shared metafictional concern, and carnivalesque spirit: "These stories, written late in Angela's life . . . divide between Europe and America and between old and new ways of story-telling: Angela enjoyed carnival in different forms" (xi).

Carter's writing has often been qualified as carnivalesque on the basis of its riotous, anarchic, and irreverent spirit, iconoclastic mixings, and subversive, parodic dimension.[54] The text that immediately precedes "Ashputtle *or* The Mother's Ghost" is "In Pantoland" (first published as an essay in *The Guardian* [1991] and later reprinted in Carter's collection *Shaking a Leg*). It stars Mother Goose as the prototypical storyteller that implies, as Benson observes, "a performative even a pantomimic notion of authorship."[55] Through the figure of the bawdy old gossip, Carter celebrates a submerged, popular, comic, and irreverent tradition of female storytellers that she identified with later in her writing life.[56] "In Pantoland" stages a carnival that almost reads like a self-parody. It pays homage to the popular art of pantomime inseparable from the reception of fairy tales in England.

In this festive world figure the heroes and villains of the most well-known fairy tales, presented in a series of tableaux. The Dame, a comic old woman usually played by a male actor, is introduced as an androgynous character: "double-sexed and self-sufficient," "the sacred transvestite of Pantoland" (*American Ghosts*, 100). Mother Goose also features among these hybrid figures.

> The Goose in Mother Goose is, or so they say, the Hamlet of animal roles, introspective and moody as only a costive bird straining over its egg might be. There is a full gamut of emotion in the Goose role—*loyalty and devotion to her mother; joy and delight at her own maternity*; heart-break at loss of egg; fear and trembling at the wide variety of gruesome possibilities which might occur if, in the infinite intercouplings of possible texts which occur all the time in the promiscuity of Pantoland, one story effortlessly segues into another story. . . . Note that the Goose, like the Dame, is a female role usually, though not always, played by a man. (*American Ghosts*, 103; italics mine)

The arch-storyteller is represented as both a maternal and a daughterly character (and also mocked for this reason). Like all the other motherly figures in the parade, she is a transvestite. Through her Carter makes fun of the overprotective mother hen, and its dark double, the threatening "phallic" mother, who foreshadows the tyrannical mother figure in "Ashputtle *or* The Mother's Ghost," although in a completely different mood and mode.

"Cinders," one of Cinderella's avatars in Pantoland, is a comic version of Ashputtle. Her father is in charge of finances, and her stepmother and sisters are similar to the Dame, in that they actively contribute to perpetuate the patriarchal system. In this mock phallic world the stick in the anus of the Dame is transformed into a magic wand. In "Travelling Clothes" and "Cinderella: or, The Little Glass Slipper," however, Carter replaces the magic wand with a ring, possibly because its shape evokes a more feminine symbol. The ring also opens up a reflection on circularity, repetition, and marriage as the perpetuation of the social order and the cycle of biological reproduction. The comedy of this upside-down world does not last, however, and the story ends on a sobering note, with the narrator quoting

Umberto Eco's remark that "an everlasting carnival does not work": "It is here today and gone tomorrow, a release of tension not a reconstitution of order, a refreshment . . . after which everything can go on again exactly as if nothing had happened" (*American Ghosts*, 109). Carter's fiction cannot and will not be reduced to a Bakhtinian carnival, and this cautionary note is an apt prologue for the dark retelling of the Cinderella story that follows.

After the carnival of Pantoland comes Ash Wednesday: an appropriate festival for Carter's take on Ashputtle, because the holiday derives its name from the practice of covering one's forehead with ashes as a sign of mourning and repentance. The radical shift of mood from "In Pantoland" to "Ashputtle *or* The Mother's Ghost" thus turns the familiar story of social triumph and sentimental romance into a memento mori contained or foreshadowed in the heroine's own name. Carter's retelling of "Ashputtle" can also be related to "Impressions: The Wrightsman Magdalene," which closes *American Ghosts*; the blood-red dress of "The Burned Child" and "Travelling Clothes" echoes Mary Magdalene's red dress in Georges de La Tour's painting. In this ekphrastic meditation Carter represents Mary Magdalene, the repentant prostitute meditating on candlelight, like a female Hamlet: "Something has already been born out of this intercourse with the candle flame. See. She carries it already. She carries where, if she were a Virgin mother not a sacred whore, she would rest her baby, not a living child but a *memento mori*, a skull" (*American Ghosts*, 146). Thus the figures of Mother Goose, Cinderella, and Mary Magdalene are strangely but productively linked. Likewise, the marvelous and the horrific, birth and death, life and art, are united in the vanitas.

Carter's Literary Testament, or the Power of Fiction: Magic, Haunting, (Dis)Enchantment

> Because I could not stop for Death—,
>
> He kindly stopped for me;
>
> The Carriage held but just Ourselves—
>
> And Immortality.
>
> —EMILY DICKINSON, "BECAUSE I COULD NOT STOP FOR DEATH"

Mary Magdalene represents the paradox of giving birth to death. This echoes Carter's retelling of "Ashputtle" as a reflection on motherhood and filiation, away from sentimental and idealizing stereotypes. Mercedes Gulin astutely observes that "Travelling Clothes" expresses this idea in a pun that Carter uses as a creative device and generating principle for several of her retellings: "mothering" becomes "mother-ring." The ring is both the circle that condemns to repetition or the equivalent of the magic wand that can transform a miserable life into a happy one (unless it merely means a reproduction of prescribed life patterns). In Carter's rewriting the ring is a worm eating the mother's eye, which evokes Edgar Allan Poe's "Conqueror Worm."[57]

The orphaned childhood of the famous author of Gothic tales even inspired Carter to write a short text, published in her *Black Venus*,[58] that presents another ghostly apparition: "Father! said Edgar; he thought their father must have reconstituted himself at this last extremity in order to transport them all to a better place but, when he looked more closely, by the light of a gibbous moon, he saw the sockets of the coachman's eyes were full of worms" (35). The return of the father's ghost is followed by the "Testament of Mrs Elizabeth Poe," including her legacy of "nourishment," "transformation" and "awareness of mortality" (36). This resonates with Ashputtle's duty, if she wants to accomplish her mother's (last) *will*. This means accepting her gifts of a red dress (life and femininity), the ring (magical object and marriage symbol), and the coach (travel and transformation but also marriage and death). The ring comes from "the eye," a homophone of "I," which suggests the transmission of the giver's identity or voice. Ashputtle, who remains voiceless in the text, must then embark on a quest to find her own after the farewell or envoi of her literary mother. The end of the text is the threshold of her own story, as yet unwritten. The coffin (as a symbol of the human condition) turns into a coach through which the daughter's quest can be accomplished. If we read the tale as a rite of passage, then, the coach carries the heroine through life to its final destination.

Carter knew that she was dying when she decided to include "Ashputtle *or* The Mother's Ghost" in *American Ghosts and Old World Wonders*.[59] The text thus reads like a poignant farewell to her readers/daughters, to whom the mother's ghost in "The Burned Child" addresses a last piece of advice: "Make your own dress, next time. . . . I'm through with that bloody business" (*American Ghosts*, 118). The mother is through with the messy bloodiness of life, including the possibility of bearing new life; but so is Carter herself with her "bloody (chamber) stories." Metaphorically, "dress" indeed captures the mutability of the fairy tale as a literary form that matches the heroine's changing identity. The (god)mother has striven to communicate a message of emancipation to her readers (another "business"—the demythologizing of Western culture, no less). More than a story of metamorphosis, then, Ashputtle becomes a story of transmission of life skills through a close reading that recognizes the value of individual interpretation and personal choice. The ghost returns to encourage the younger generation to complete the task that the author left unfinished as a result of her premature death.[60] As a unique and memorable retelling woven from the age-old history of the tale, "Ashputtle *or* The Mother's Ghost" represents both the possibility of change and the threat of repetition, which suggests that Carter's legacy has to be honored, celebrated, and itself turned into a new creation.

Conclusion

THE POETICS AND POLITICS OF TRANSLATION

Retraduire suppose sans doute plus fortement encore une théorie d'ensemble que traduire ce qui n'a jamais été traduit.

—HENRI MESCHONNIC, "TRADUIRE: ÉCRIRE OU DÉSÉCRIRE," 70

We should remember that it is the "inter"—the cutting edge of translation and renegotiation, the *in-between* space—that carries the burden of the meaning of culture.

—HOMI BHABHA, *THE LOCATION OF CULTURE*, 38

Angela Carter used the homey metaphors of wine making and potato soup to capture the experimental spirit, mix-and-match (mash?) approach, and nourishing (even nurturing) effect of her lifelong interest in and engagement with the fairy tale. She is best known today as the author of memorable novels and stories that escape easy categorizations and labels, precisely because they emerged from Carter's experiments across linguistic, generic, discursive, cultural, and artistic boundaries, as I have tried to show. Working *between* languages, traditions, and media, Carter wrote for the radio, the stage, and the screen; she was a trenchant journalist and astute cultural critic, a precise and thoughtful translator, a bold and polemical essayist, an enthusiastic editor for Virago, a maverick scholar, a funny and tender children's author, and even a poet and painter.[1] These various activities fed into each other, so that each individual project was somehow connected with the others and in turn became an occasion to try a new recipe, rethink an idea, reformulate a question, and explore another point of view for a different audience or occasion. Far from being conducted in isolation from her other activities, then, *The Bloody Chamber* was part of one continuous, lifelong endeavor that evolved over time, taking on various forms, just like the metamorphic genre of the fairy tale itself. In this sense, translation was for Carter not merely the laboratory of creation from which she evolved (or cooked up) her own fiction but the generating principle of her entire oeuvre, as she translated not just other people's works but also her own, continuously and self-consciously. Her fictional output has been valued over other projects and activities, including her translations of Perrault and Beaumont, although they were intricately connected. The reconstruction I have attempted here of the translation and rewriting process is a means to reaffirm this interconnectedness and to revalue the act of translation as a form of active, productive reading of foreign texts that re-enchanted language and stimulated imagination and creativity.

The time has come to recognize the significance, both personal and cultural, of Carter as a translator who, once again, was ahead of her time. Indeed, Susan Bassnett observes:

> Once upon a time, it was deemed to be unsafe and undesirable to occupy a space that was neither one thing nor the other, a no-man's land with no precise identity. Today, in the twenty-first century, political, geographical and cultural boundaries are perceived as more fluid and less constraining than at any time in recent history. . . . In such a world, the role of the translator takes on a greater significance.[2]

Translation, I have tried to argue, was Carter's favorite mode of critical and creative inquiry, and in this respect too she was an avant-garde artist and thinker. Her work owes part of its rich resonances, mysterious beauty, playful elusiveness, thought-provoking nature, and sharp edge to a translational poetics that I have documented and celebrated in this book. It stresses the heretofore neglected role of translation that turned out to be a crucial source of inspiration for Carter's fairy-tale-inspired fiction. Beyond translation *stricto sensu*, however, generic, cultural, and intermedial transposition informs Carter's entire oeuvre, nourishing, complicating, and taking it into new directions like a movable feast.

Translation determines a particular poetics that also has ethical implications and political ramifications. Margaret Atwood said of Angela Carter that she "was the opposite of parochial. Nothing, for her, was outside the pale: she wanted to know about everything and everyone, and every place and every word. She relished life and language hugely, and revelled in the diverse."[3] As the spatial metaphors suggest, Carter's translation practice was a means to challenge the stifling and arbitrary divisions, exclusions, and hierarchies that structure the social, national, cultural, and literary spheres. Well before translation was recognized as a major force of change and innovation in literary history, Carter's view of reading as inseparable from translating and (re)writing emphasized the generative and transformative role of translation both in her own work and for English culture as a whole.

In this sense, interpreting Carter's work through the prism of translation not only unsettles conventional boundaries but also captures how the movement of crossing itself sets creation in motion, from the author's deliberate self-estrangement in Japan to her cross-cultural intellectual ventures, her interest in speculative fiction, and her fascination with transgressive French art. Mirroring her life, Carter's work derived its energy from the translation, transposition, hybridization, and transformation of ideas, languages, texts, words and images as material for new creation and food for thought.

Angela Carter's impatience with received ideas and pieties and her constant positioning on the borderline of languages, cultures, countries, genres, movements, and media make her an important figure in an age of heightened global exchanges and problematic return to fixed and rigid notions of identity. A free, curious, restless, daring traveler, Carter used the interstitial space of translation and rewriting to test and explore new ideas, find new ways of expressing them, and encourage her readers to exercise their reading skills, intellectual curiosity, and ability to think on their own. She conceived of writing as a fundamentally dialogic mode of inquiry that in turn calls forth new responses. This was consistent with her choice of the fairy tale as an open, ever-changing tradition that became her favorite mode of expression. The dynamics of reading, translating, and (re)writing, then, is at the heart of an artistic, human, and intellectual endeavor in which we are all invited to participate by cooking—and serving—our own homemade soup or wine.

Notes

INTRODUCTION

1. Neil Forsyth, personal communication, summer 2011. Lorna Sage makes the rapprochement between Carter's (self-)estranging experience of Japan and Barthes's *Empire of Signs* in *Angela Carter* (26–28). Sarah Gamble also observes that "living in Japan, a country in which she was outlandishly foreign, also caused her to look back at her own European ancestry from the perspective of a foreigner. The experience of alienation was to shape her subsequent fiction" (*Fiction of Angela Carter*, 66).

2. Susan Rubin Suleiman reports that the novel was written "in three months, in a Japanese fishing village on an island where she seemed to be the only European" (Suleiman, in Sage, *Flesh and the Mirror*, 100). *The Infernal Desire Machines of Doctor Hoffman* can be seen as a fictional exploration of Gauthier's feminist critique of the surrealist movement. Born into a working-class family in 1942 (and therefore of the same generation as Carter), Xavière Gauthier (pen name of Mireille Boulaire) is an important figure of the feminist movement in France. Her groundbreaking study *Surréalisme et sexualité*, based on her doctoral thesis, was published by Gallimard in 1971. Like Carter, Gauthier was polyvalent; an academic, writer, journalist, and editor, she founded the literary and artistic journal *Sorcières* in 1975. Her work deals with women's sexuality and its representation and with the history of the feminist struggle for contraception and abortion rights. Gauthier contributed to the rediscovery of the proto-feminist activist and anarchist Louise Michel. No wonder Carter saw in Gauthier a kindred spirit. See Watz, "Angela Carter." Carter later translated into English a short story by the French surrealist artist and writer Leonora Carrington, "La Débutante" (from *La Débutante, Contes et Pièces*), for her edited anthology of stories *Wayward Girls and Wicked Women*.

3. Carter refers to the collection as *Contes du temps passé* in "The Better to Eat You With," but she uses the full title (in French) in the foreword to *The Fairy Tales of Charles Perrault*. Some of the stories that inspired Perrault for his collection were also known as *Contes de ma mère l'Oye* (Mother Goose Tales), as she also points out. Carter's translation seems to be based on Perrault's 1697 *Histoires ou contes du temps passé*, edited by Andrew Lang as *Perrault's Popular Tales* (1888). Because Lang's scholarly edition reproduces the seventeenth-century spelling and punctuation of Perrault's French text, I have decided to refer to the slightly modernized (but authoritative) critical edition

304 NOTES TO INTRODUCTION

of the *contes* by Jean-Pierre Collinet instead, to facilitate readers' comprehension of the text.

4. Carter's famous statement of intentions expressed in "Notes from the Front Line" (38) echoes almost verbatim her enthusiastic account of the gist of Perrault's *contes* as "*this world is all that is to the point*" in "The Better to Eat You With" (453).

5. Carter had already used the phrase "new wine in old bottles" in the conclusion of her BA thesis, "Some Speculations on Possible Relationships Between the Medieval Period and the 20th c. Folk Song Poetry": "These songs survived the centuries, being continually re-moulded to suit each new generation of country singers, but often retaining ancient features; and newly written or adapted songs were often, new wine in old bottles, cast in ancient forms" (98) (Angela Carter Papers, British Library, 1/116).

6. Zipes, "Remaking of Charles Perrault," ix.

7. Benjamin, "Task of the Translator."

8. Berman, *Experience of the Foreign*, 293–94.

9. Derrida, "What Is a 'Relevant' Translation?" 425. See also Derrida, "Les tours de Babel." Derrida's thoughts on texts as affiliated with but never simply belonging to one single genre is also relevant for Carter's generic experiments ("La loi du genre").

10. Venuti, *Translator's Invisibility*. In *Scandals of Translation* Venuti addresses the political implications of translation as he explains the translator's marginal status on account of her questioning the authority of dominant cultural values and institutions, especially national myths of autonomous development.

11. Jakobson, "Linguistic Aspects," 233.

12. "Le terme de *translation* est suffisamment plastique pour décrire ce qui advient lorsque l'on passe de l'image au texte et vice-versa en une sorte de système de dialogue ou de réponses, en une opération de traduction ou d'interprétation . . ., un transport . . . un *rapport* plutôt" (Louvel, *Texte/Image*, 148). "Le processus dynamique de la translation s'effectue en réponse à l'écart entre l'image et le texte. Le passage entre deux codes sémiotiques se lit entre-deux" (149). Louvel's model is based on an interlinguistic pun, because the word *translation* combines the French sense of spatial or geometric displacement and the English sense of linguistic transposition. The translations are my own. See also Louvel, *L'oeil du texte*.

13. Carter, *Yellow Sands*, 13.

14. See Crofts, *Anagrams of Desire*; and the recent 2012 BBC program *Writing in Three Dimensions: Angela Carter's Love Affair with Radio*, http://www.bbc.co.uk/iplayer/episode/b01by8n1/Writing_in_Three_Dimensions_Angela_Carters_Love_Affair_with_Radio/ (accessed July 23, 2012).

15. Likewise, Louvel suggests that mixing text and image materializes the dialogue between the arts and hence proceeds from an ethics of opening and a decompartmentalization of disciplines (*Texte/Image*, 259).

16. Lefevere and Bassnett, *Constructing Cultures*, vii. See also Bassnett, "Writing and Translating." Lefevere describes translation as "a rewriting of an original text" (*Translation*, xi). Inasmuch as different languages reflect different worldviews, mediating these differences in translation inevitably involves "attempts to naturalize the different culture to make it conform more to what the reader of the translation is used to" (Lefevere, *Translation*, 237). Bassnett further argues that translated texts need to be

considered as independent literary productions. Lefevere points out that of the different forms of adaptations that writers commonly engage in (i.e., translation, criticism, commentary, historiography, and anthologies), translation is the most influential in shaping the image of original writers and their works beyond the boundaries of their culture of origin (*Translation*, 9).

17. "By translation I first of all mean a process by which, in order to objectify cultural meaning, there always has to be a process of alienation and of secondariness *in relation to itself*. In that sense . . . [cultures] are always subject to intrinsic forms of translation. This theory of culture is close to a theory of language, as part of a process of translations—using that word . . . not in a strict linguistic sense of translation as in a 'book translated from French into English,' but as a motif or trope as Benjamin suggests for the activity of displacement within the linguistic sign" (Homi Bhabha, qtd. in Rutherford, "Third Space," 210).

18. This comic detail is reminiscent of Perrault's ogress in "La Belle au bois dormant," who declares to her cook that she wants her grandchild Aurora cooked "à la sauce Robert"; the ineffectual use of garlic to ward off vampires is also made fun of in Roman Polanski's *Fearless Vampire Killers* (1967).

19. Even Carter's English is sometimes colored by French syntax (convoluted or verbless sentences), grammar (present of narration), and lexis (recherché vocabulary, abstract language, French borrowings) and makes creative use of the phenomenon known as interlanguage (see Toury, "Interlanguage").

20. I treat the role of other key agents in the translation process, such as the Victor Gollancz publishing house and its editorial policies, the book market, and the terms of contract with the translator, only marginally in this book for lack of documentary evidence.

21. For Simon "the very meaning of the activity, the values which it engages, the changes it invokes, must be understood in relation to 'something else'—the ideas and projects with which it is allied" (Simon, *Gender in Translation*, 83).

22. Simpson, "Femme Fatale."

23. See Oittinen's pioneering study *Translating for Children*; O'Sullivan, *Comparative Children's Literature*; van Coillie and Verschueren, *Children's Literature in Translation*. See also Lathey's *The Translation of Children's Literature* and *Role of Translators in Children's Literature*. For the reception of Grimm's *Märchen* as international fairy tales, see Dollerup, *Tales and Translation*. Other critics have engaged with the specific problems posed by the mixed nature of children's illustrated books, including Nicolajeva and Scott in *How Picturebooks Work*.

24. See Haffenden, "Angela Carter," for example.

25. See Benson, *Cycles of Influence*; and Joosen, *Critical and Creative Perspectives*.

26. Jacques Barchilon's name was mentioned in Carter's black notebook of 1977 (Angela Carter Papers, British Library, MS 88899/1/96).

27. Jack Zipes's influential *Fairy Tales and the Art of Subversion*, which documents the socializing function of fairy tales in shaping children's behavior, attitudes, values, and expectations, has become a reference not only for critics but also for many writers and artists working on the fairy tale. Aside from Marina Warner, critics who have also greatly contributed to the field and recognized the importance of Carter's work are

Cristina Bacchilega (*Postmodern Fairy Tales*), Elizabeth Wanning Harries (*Twice Upon a Time*), Donald Haase (*Fairy Tales and Feminism*), and Stephen Benson (*Contemporary Fiction* and the special issue of *Marvels & Tales* guest-edited by Benson and Teverson). The rediscovery of the French *conteuses* of the ancien régime was initiated by Jacques Barchilon, and scholars working on this corpus today are too many to name. I can, however, mention Jean Mainil's landmark study *Madame d'Aulnoy* and the various contributors to *Féeries* in France as well as Lewis Seifert, Sue Bottigheimer, and the various contributors to *Marvels & Tales* in the United States. In Germany the important work conducted by Heinz Rölleke radically changed perceptions of the Grimms' *Kinder- und Hausmärchen*.

28. Benson, "Angela Carter," 31.
29. See, in particular, Sage, *Angela Carter*; Bristow and Broughton, *Infernal Desires*; Day, *Angela Carter*; Gamble, *Angela Carter: Writing from the Front Line and Angela Carter: A Literary Life*; Roemer and Bacchilega, *Angela Carter*; Lepaludier, *Métatextualité*; Munford, *Re-Visiting Angela Carter*; and Benson, *Contemporary Fiction*. To quote Benson: "Carter's extensive work on the traditions of the fairy tale—as author, editor, and critic—was preeminently influential in establishing a late-twentieth-century conception of the tales, the influence of which has continued into the new millennium.... Her work establishes in ... vibrant and polemic fashion what might be called the contemporaneity of the fairy tale" (2). He rightly observes that "the conception of the fairy tale we have today, in English speaking areas at least, is in no small part a product of the Carter generation" (5).
30. Zipes, "Crossing Boundaries"; Crofts, *Anagrams of Desire*; Murai, "Voicing Authenticities."
31. Barchilon, "Remembering Angela Carter," 28.
32. Heidmann and Adam, "Text Linguistics."
33. Hennard Dutheil de la Rochère, "Modelling for Bluebeard." See also Hennard Dutheil de la Rochère and Heidmann, "New Wine in Old Bottles"; Hennard Dutheil de la Rochère, "Updating the Politics," "Marriage Itself," and "Les métamorphoses de Cendrillon."
34. Zipes, "Remaking of Charles Perrault," 1.
35. Zipes, "Remaking of Charles Perrault," 1.
36. Barchilon, "Remembering Angela Carter," 26.
37. In the 1960 introduction to Samber's 1729 edition of Perrault's *contes* in English, titled *The Authentic Mother Goose Fairy Tales and Nursery Rhymes*, Barchilon and Pettit see the fairy tale in the time of Perrault as children's "apprenticeship to life" (27). In his introduction to the *Nouveau cabinet des Fées*, Barchilon asserts that the authors of the literary fairy tales anthologized in *Le cabinet des fées* deserve to be known by modern readers. He even adds: "Même les deux 'grands,' Perrault et Madame d'Aulnoy, sont relativement méconnus: ils ne circulent le plus souvent qu'à travers des éditions édulcorées pour un jeune public" (*Nouveau cabinet des fées*, xvii).
38. In *Art baroque* Jean Perrot convincingly demonstrates Perrault's affiliation with the baroque and its imitation of a childlike imagination.
39. See *Marvels & Tales*, 2 (2011), special issue in honor of Jacques Barchilon.
40. Said and Carter also believed in the profound worldliness of texts, whether critical or creative (or both). Carter pays homage to Said's foundational work in *Come unto*

These Yellow Sands, when the Shopkeeper embarks on a lecture on Orientalism (1983: 30–32). In her notes for "Wolf-Alice" Carter provides a definition of *fugue*, a term also beloved by Said, as follows: "a polyphonic composition constructed on one or more short subjects or themes which are harmonised according to the laws of counterpoint, and introduced from time to time with various contrapuntal devices."

41. Zipes, "Remaking of Charles Perrault," 1. Likewise, Sarah Gamble describes *The Bloody Chamber* as a "gleeful, subversive commentary" (*Angela Carter: A Literary Life*, 131) on Carter's translation of Perrault.

42. Carter, journal from March 1977, Angela Carter Papers, British Library, MS 88899/1/96.

43. Carter also jots down: "Venice again: swimming cat a handsome ginger tom with white feet." Although the ginger tom evokes Puss, her delightful children's story "Sea-Cat and Dragon King" (2000) features a swimming cat dressed in lovingly decorated clothes made by his own mother, who will succeed in placating a dragon.

44. On the last page of the 1977 journal, Carter lists five "Stories for fairy tale book 2."

45. Carter would pursue her "uncovering" of a marginalized female fairy-tale tradition in her subsequent edition of two volumes of "fairy tales" by women from around the world for Virago: *Wayward Girls and Wicked Women: An Anthology of Subversive Stories* (1986); and *The Virago Book of Fairy Tales* (1990) (aka *The Old Wives' Fairy Tale Book*). Carter also produced *The Second Virago Book of Fairy Tales* (1992) (aka *Strange Things Still Sometimes Happen: Fairy Tales From Around the World* [1993]) and *Angela Carter's Book of Fairy Tales* (2005) (which collects the two Virago books).

46. Escola, *Commentaires* (150–151). See also Heidmann and Adam, *Textualité*, for a revaluation of the gender politics of Perrault's *contes*.

47. For a useful reflection on Carter's connections between Sade and the fairy tale, see Sheets, "Pornography"; and Gamble, "Penetrating."

48. See Blom, "Life and Works of Samber."

49. Gamble, *Fiction of Angela Carter*, 8.

50. It is interesting to note that Perrault translated Gabriel Faërne's *Fables* into French (1699).

51. Perrault's purported aim in *Contes* is quite complex, because he wishes to instruct his dedicatee, a young aristocratic lady, into the life of the people, who themselves use the genre to instruct their own children: "Il est vrai que ces Contes donnent une image de ce qui se passe dans les moindres Familles, où la louable impatience d'instruire les enfants fait imaginer des Histoires dépourvues de raison, pour s'accommoder à ces mêmes enfants qui n'en ont pas encore" (*Contes*, 127). On the complications of the reading experience induced by the morals, see Escola, *Commentaires*.

52. An interesting variation on the new wine in old bottles metaphor is found in Carter's notes for *The Bloody Chamber* (Angela Carter Papers, British Library, undated, 1/33), where she states her intentions to explore narrative form and the archaic imagery that she associates with the folktale as follows: "What I want to talk about, and hopefully to demonstrate, is the way that the marvellous tale functions as narrative and its rather more curious function as a kind of gusher of crude imagery, like crude oil [the rest is crossed out]. As if traditional tales, homelier and less resonant than myth, but often

308 NOTES TO INTRODUCTION

more archaic and thus more accessible and more disregarded, were a kind of cellar of plot and imagery put down by the first teratological kids."

53. It is important to distinguish between moralizing in the sense of enforcing conventional morality, i.e. dominant social and religious values, which shaped the reception of the fairy tale in England, and the French moralist tradition represented by such seventeenth-century authors as La Bruyère and La Rochefoucault, who depicted the ways of the world in a matter-of-fact and ironic manner as a means to caution readers against naïveté and ignorance. My contention is that Carter aligned herself with the French moralist tradition. Aidan Day in *Angela Carter* notes Carter's interest in Perrault's *contes* for being "grounded in material reality" (132), unlike most fantasy literature.

54. Carter, "Company of Wolves," 20. In this interview Carter expresses her admiration for folklore. She mentions the evocative force and striking imagery of the tales collected by the Grimm brothers, grounded as they are in the harsh realities of peasant life. In the class notes collected in the "Miscellaneous Fairy Tale Material" file (Angela Carter Papers, British Library), Carter writes under "Roots of Narrative" that the folktale typically presents "simple systems of internal logic depending very largely on verbal ambiguities, puns, tricks with words, and very simple narrative structures in which one thing follows another in an orderly, if at times bizarre way" before moving on to the more complex narrative forms.

55. Rereading extended to her own work as a form of internal translation or rewriting. The Angela Carter archive confirms that writing involved important revisions, annotations, and even generic shifts that resulted in significant transformations of the original text, even in the later stages of the editorial process. To give a relatively straightforward example, the archive includes a typewritten draft, a heavily annotated version of what would eventually become "The Snow Child," with the title "The Sleeping Beauty"; a revised draft, with further annotations, titled "The Snow Child"; and a fair copy, unannotated, bearing the same title.

56. All quotations of Perrault's French *contes* are from Charles Perrault, *Contes*, edited by Jean-Pierre Collinet, and their English translation is Carter's translation, *The Fairy Tales of Charles Perrault* (shortened to *Fairy Tales* in citations), unless otherwise specified.

57. The tale was widely circulating during Perrault's time, notably in chapbook versions (see Bottigheimer, *Fairy Tales*). Perrault probably read it in the *Bibliothèque Bleue*, which reproduced Petrarch's somewhat more misogynistic version of the tale.

58. See Sage, "Angela Carter," especially fn 8. Carter also wrote *The Donkey Prince* (1970) for children. It does not seem to refer to Perrault's *conte* specifically but rather freely adapts and combines elements from "The Golden Ass" to magic apples, animal babies, and so on.

59. See Linkin, "Isn't It Romantic." See also Pedot, "Obscurs éclaircissements."

60. Clapp, *Card from Angela Carter*, 7.

61. See Velay-Vallantin, "Charles Perrault."

62. Benjamin, "The Storyteller," 83.

63. Spivak, "Politics of Translation," 370.

Chapter 1

1. See Hatim and Mason, *Translator as Communicator*, 11–12.
2. This chapter is based on materials in the Angela Carter Papers, British Library, London. The Gollancz archives at the University of Warwick apparently do not hold any correspondence with Carter.
3. The red coloring is reminiscent of the title of *The Bloody Chamber* collection and more specifically of the passage in "The Company of Wolves" where the girl undresses before the wolf, taking off "her scarlet shawl, the colour of poppies, the colour of sacrifices, the colour of her menses, and, since her fear did her no good, she ceased to be afraid" (*Bloody Chamber*, 117).
4. See "Penguin Modern Classics: The Complete List" at http://www.penguinclassics.co.uk/static/minisites/minimodernclassics/download/catalogue.pdf (accessed August 10, 2012).
5. Penguin also released a selection of seven tales translated by Carter in their Modern Classics small format series, with the title *Bluebeard* in 2011. This book contains "Bluebeard," "Little Red Riding Hood," "Puss in Boots," "The Sleeping Beauty in the Wood," "Cinderella: or, The Little Glass Slipper," "Ricky with the Tuft," and "The Foolish Wishes." The cover is silver gray, and the book contains no critical apparatus. The first moral of "Bluebeard" is used as an epigraph, and the blurb describes Carter's translation as "playful and subversive retellings of Charles Perrault's classic fairy tales," which "conjure up a world of resourceful women, black-hearted villains, wily animals and incredible transformations. In these seven stories, bristling with frank, earthy humour and gothic imagination, nothing is as it seems." Here again, the influence of *The Bloody Chamber* is perceptible in the choice of "Bluebeard" for the title of this edition, and the description of the content.
6. "With titles like *Splish Splash*, *Shit-Kicker*, and *Mudbath*, they were anything but; Minter had her models kick around three different pairs of gemmed shoes in dirty water while she photographed. The mud-spattered results stayed up in Chelsea the entire month. Soiled couture on New York City billboards . . . what did it mean? . . . 'I don't pass any moral judgment,' she says, waving away my questions. 'Who am I to tell people what to do? I love the idea of making a startling image just for fun. . . . From portraits of addiction to porno to Dior heels, Minter's paintings and photographs have embraced messiness, the accidental, sweat- and mud-covered moments when beauty is caught boiling in the sun or falling into a puddle. . . . As slick and sensual as her work looks, there is always a blemish, something unmistakably human pushing through the veneer, democratizing the glamour. The artist's philosophy is simple, summed up by her in an interview with artist Mary Heilmann: 'If you're dancing in a disco all night your feet get dirty,' she quips, 'even if you have the most expensive shoes on.'" Kim, "Marilyn Minter."
7. See Genette and Maclean, "Introduction to the Paratext," 261, based on Genette's *Seuils*.
8. For an overview of the reception of Perrault's tales in England, see G. Verdier, "De ma mère l'Oye à Mother Goose"; Malarte-Feldman, "Challenges of Translating"; and Lathey, *Role of Translators*. For a reassessment of the early reception of Perrault's *contes* in England from the perspective of book history, see Bottigheimer, "Misperceived Perceptions."

9. The emergence of the *conte de fées* as a literary institution has been well documented in recent decades, starting with Jacques Barchilon's critical edition of a newly discovered copy of Perrault's *Contes de ma Mère l'Oye* (*Perrault's Tales of Mother Goose: The Dedication Manuscript of 1695 Reproduced in Collotype Facsimile with Introduction and Critical Text by Jacques Barchilon*), followed by his groundbreaking study of the fashion for fairy tales in seventeenth-century France, *Le conte merveilleux en France*. Several studies documenting this literary movement have been written since, including Seifert, *Fairy Tales*; Mainil, *Madame d'Aulnoy*; Sermain, *Métafictions* and *Le conte de fées*; and Seifert and Stanton, *Enchanted Eloquence*.

10. Several contemporary witnesses believed that the young man collected the stories directly "from the mouth of his nanny." But contrary evidence (i.e., that Perrault authored the tales) is now considered more conclusive by contemporary scholars. The "posture of childhood," it is now widely admitted, was meant to establish the value of nonclassical literature and to produce an effect of freshness, naïveté, and innocence that gave no reason to suspect any sort of disguised criticism. In the January 1697 issue of *Mercure Gallant*, the upcoming publication of Perrault's *Contes* is mentioned with a side note that the authorship, instead of being attributed to a single author, is the work of "an infinite number of fathers, mothers, grandmothers, [and] governesses" who told and retold the stories. As Escola points out, this strategy was an effective means to avoid censorship while fueling the controversy of the Ancients and the Moderns.

11. The mythical storyteller is represented in the frontispiece of Perrault's dedication manuscript of 1695 and in the first published edition of 1697. For a discussion of the role and representation of the storyteller in the fairy-tale tradition, see Warner, *From the Beast*.

12. The concept has been coined and theorized by the historian of the book, Roger Chartier. On the role of the material form of a book as determining an "implicit reading experience," see the essay "Du livre au lire" in Chartier, *Pratiques* (62–88); and Chartier, *Lectures*.

13. Sermain, "La face cachée du conte."

14. See the Introduction for a discussion of Carter's interest in the fairy tale and the originality of her position in the debate about the politics of the genre in a period marked by the polarization of a valued oral folk tradition favorable to women and a written literary tradition seen as encoding a conservative ideology.

15. "Les moralités n'induisent . . . en rien une lecture moralisante, mais un jeu distancé—un jeu de la lecture lettrée avec elle-même et non pas directement de la morale avec la fiction." Escola, *Commentaires*, 124.

16. See Noël, *La fable*. See also the issue of *Féeries* on *Le conte et la fable*, guest-edited by Aurélia Gaillard and Jean-Paul Sermain.

17. Robert Samber's *Histories or Tales of Past Times, with Morals* (1729), had already introduced a floral motif between the tale and its moral.

18. The phrase "politics of experience" comes from Ronald David Laing's widely influential study *The Politics of Experience*, which formulated a critique of conventional psychiatry. Laing saw madness as symptomatic of a constitutive alienation of the self that could be treated independently of psychiatric institutions. I am grateful to Neil Forsyth for drawing my attention to this book, which Carter apparently disapproved of.

19. For a discussion of the long history and popularity of "Little Red Riding Hood" in Western culture, see Zipes, *Trials and Tribulations*. The predominance of the tale may also have to do with its assimilation to children's literature, because its young heroine facilitates identification with the child reader. The selection of tales (and exclusion of "Griselidis"), the shift from verse to prose, and the reorganization of their sequence are all characteristic of the reception of Perrault's *contes*. Carter places the chronologically older verse tales at the end of the volume.
20. Perrault, *Histories or Tales of Past Times Told by Mother Goose*. The book includes a frontispiece and woodcuts. This edition is a reprint of an older edition allegedly predating Samber's translation (*Histories or Tales of Past Times with Morals*). Carter's signature figures to the front free endpaper. For a discussion of the phenomenon of wrong attribution, see Palmer and Palmer, "English Editions."
21. "Grisélidis," "Peau d'Ane," and "Les Souhaits ridicules" appeared in verse over the period 1691–1695, whereas the prose tales appeared in manuscript form in 1695 and in expanded form in 1697. Some tales, such as "La Belle au bois dormant," first appeared individually in the *Mercure Galant*.
22. Sermain observes that the pedagogical scene represented in the frontispiece is modeled on Aesop's fables. Published as a book, Perrault's collection of tales self-consciously introduces a reading practice that is markedly different from the live interaction between the storyteller and his or her audience (see Sermain, "La face cachée du conte," 13).
23. Ware's unusual visual representation of the wealthy ogre in "Puss in Boots" is reminiscent of Carter's masked beast in "The Tiger's Bride."
24. Ware's orange Puss on the cover anticipates Carter's description of the "marmalade" tomcat in "Puss-in-Boots."
25. Ware represented his wife as one of the female characters, although he did not say which one (personal communication, November 2, 2010).
26. See G. Verdier, "Comment l'auteur des fées."
27. From the outset Lang describes Perrault as a benefactor of children "borne on the wings of the fabulous Goose, notre Mère L'Oye" (*Perrault's Popular Tales*, vii). He goes on to portray him as a rebellious if respectable figure: "Though a man of unimpeached respectability of conduct, Charles Perrault was a born Irregular" (vii). Lang concludes his biographical sketch with a warm eulogy of Perrault: "Charles Perrault was a good man, a good father, a good Christian, and a good fellow. He was astonishingly clever and versatile in little things, honest, courteous, and witty, and an undaunted amateur. The little thing in which he excelled most was telling fairy tales. Every generation listens in its turn to this old family friend of all the world. No nation owes him so much as we of England, who, south of the Scottish, and east of the Welsh marches, have scarce any popular tales of our own save Jack the Giant Killer, and who have given the full fairy citizenship to Perrault's Petit Poucet and La Barbe Bleue" (xvi). Tellingly, the previous owner of my (original) edition added an exclamation mark in the margin, as though Lang's recognition of the influence of Perrault (and French literature in general) were resisted or resented, then as now.
28. This echoes Lang's description of Perrault as "an architect without professional training, a man of letters by inclination, a rebel against the tyranny of the classics, and immortal by a kind of accident" (*Perrault's Popular Tales*, vi). Carter also saw herself

as a maverick who, as she comically put it in a dedication to a 1968 copy of *The Magic Toyshop*, was turned down from an art school for not having had formal schooling. The inscription by the author on the front free endpaper with a sketch of a rose read, "To Joe from Angela, and they wouldn't let me into art school, the bastards. They said I was a dilettante."

29. See Velay-Vallantin, "Le miroir des contes."
30. Carter's notion of a shift from early simplicity to increasing sophistication in fairy-tale aesthetics is questionable, as an examination of Marie-Catherine d'Aulnoy's *contes de fées* of 1697 and 1698 confirms. In turn, Carter will match the moral perversity of the decadent Marquis in "The Bloody Chamber" with the "monstrous excesses" of her style, possibly in homage to d'Aulnoy.
31. The question of the French *conteurs* and *conteuses*' access to the Italian collections of Giovanni Francesco Straparola and Giambattista Basile is debated. See Bottigheimer's argument in favor of a direct transmission through the circulation of books in *Fairy Tales*.
32. This idea probably comes from Iona and Peter Opie's *Classic Fairy Tales*. The Opies' description of the origins of the tale seems to be based on Paul Delarue's discovery of a folk version allegedly predating Perrault's. See Delarue, "Story of Grandmother." See also Zipes, *Trials and Tribulations*. Zipes's book is dedicated to Angela Carter.
33. "Mae West: My Old Flame," http://www.youtube.com/watch?v=jW6BgNK-OAU&feature=related (accessed August 20, 2011).
34. For a critique of the mythologizing of Carter as a Fairy Godmother figure after her death, see Makinen, "Angela Carter and Decolonization." See also G. Verdier, "Figures de la conteuse"; and Marina Warner's classic study, *From the Beast to the Blonde*.
35. Ware confirms that he received "many flattering reviews" after the publication of *The Fairy Tales of Charles Perrault*, although "an extremely nasty one" was such an unpleasant experience that he "didn't actively pursue a career as an illustrator afterwards, though [he] received various commissions as a result" (personal communication, November 2, 2011).
36. For an overview of children's literature in context, see Moss, "The Seventies." Moss outlines the effects of social, economic, and cultural changes on children's books in Britain during the period. She argues that "what is a children's book was the question being asked throughout the seventies when adults were gradually discovering that the genre so described could be the repository of fine writing as well as of the coarser bran that is part of the stuff of children's reading" (8). This revaluation of children's literature went with a growing interest in teenage readers (she singles out Gollancz's "outstanding list of American teenage novels" on page 9), a thematic concern with social issues such as "educational thinking, sex-politics and race relations" (15), an increasing internationalization of the book market, and "the growth of a strong literary establishment of children's books early in the decade" (15) with children's books being reviewed in the major newspapers.
37. See Zipes, *Fairy Tales and the Art of Subversion*.
38. Andrea Dworkin's condemnation of fairy tales in *Woman Hating* started a veritable trend in feminist criticism in the 1970s and 1980s. After Beauvoir, Dworkin argues that the representation of gender roles in classic fairy tales influences real-life attitudes,

behavior, and expectations, pointing out, for example, that passive females are particularly desirable (as in "Snow White" and "Sleeping Beauty").

39. See a review of Krailsheimer's *Three Sixteenth Century Conteurs* at http://fs.oxfordjournals.org/content/XXI/4/343-a.extract (accessed June 22, 2012).

40. Michael Foreman is best known for his soft watercolors that emphasize childhood imagination, adventure, and sense of wonder. In his own words, his aim in illustration is to make the created worlds "emotionally real," "telling a story by capturing the essence of the situation, giving it some meaning" (Wikipedia, http://en.wikipedia.org/wiki/Michael_Foreman_%28author/illustrator%29, accessed June 22, 2012). In contrast to Ware, landscapes play an important role in Foreman's dreamlike watercolors. Foreman was awarded the Kurt Maschler Award and the Kate Greenaway Medal for *Sleeping Beauty and Other Favourite Fairy Tales*.

41. The reorganized order is "The Sleeping Beauty in the Wood," "Little Red Riding Hood," "Puss in Boots," "Bluebeard," "The Foolish Wishes," "Beauty and the Beast," "The Fairies," "Hop o' my Thumb," "Donkey-Skin," "Ricky with the Tuft," "Cinderella: or, The Little Glass Slipper," "Sweetheart," and finally "About the Stories."

42. For a discussion of the assimilation of the French and German versions of the tale to the English context in the nineteenth century, see Seago, "Nursery Politics."

43. As Hélène Cixous observed in the 1970s: "Beauties slept in their woods, waiting for princes to come and wake them up. In their beds, in their glass coffins, in their childhood forests like dead women. Beautiful, but passive: hence desirable: all mystery emanates from them" ("Sorties," 65–66). Closer to our time, Mieke Bal refers to the stereotypical image of Sleeping Beauty as "waiting for princes on white horses" (Sparagana and Bal, *Sleeping Beauty*, 95). This iconic image and other chivalric motifs are a staple feature of nineteenth- and twentieth-century fairy-tale illustrations.

44. The golden coach evokes the pumpkin magically transformed into a coach by Cinderella's godmother but also and more disquietingly the golden coaches owned by Bluebeard.

45. *L'Enfant et la vie familiale sous l'ancien régime* by the self-styled "historien du dimanche" Philippe Ariès became successful only when the book was translated into English in 1962 and widely read in the United States and England, where it was heralded as an important study arguing for a shift in perceptions of childhood between the seventeenth and eighteenth centuries. Although the central argument of Ariès's book has been challenged since, it met with considerable acclaim in Anglophone countries and influenced Carter's understanding of changing perceptions of childhood in history. Ariès's book is premised on the idea that parents' attachment to their children and awareness of childhood as a distinct period of life and form of consciousness came with birth control and a fall in child mortality at the end of the eighteenth century. Before then, children were considered "adultes en devenir" and child mortality prevented too strong an attachment on the part of mothers and fathers. For a review of Ariès's book, see Wilson, "Infancy."

46. Carter's selective use of information from the Opies' *Classic Fairy Tales* is interesting. The Opies contrast d'Aulnoy's "Le mouton" (The Ram) to "La Belle et la Bête," although Carter makes no mention of this literary connection. She retains that Madame de Beaumont emigrated to England after an unhappy marriage and repeats almost verbatim that "writers who were interested in education . . . were beginning to see

that children could confidently be addressed as people who would remain children for some years, rather than as small adults who were only momentarily disguised as young people" (Opie and Opie, *Classic Fairy Tales*, 24–25). Carter, however, significantly departs from the Opies' judgment of Beaumont's style as "plain" and "colloquial" (25), emphasizing instead its elegance and psychological and emotional subtlety.

47. Showalter, *Literature of Their Own*. Carter took an active part in reviving scholarly interest in women's fiction. She edited two volumes of fairy tales for Virago, a feminist press that notoriously reissued many long-out-of-print texts by women writers who had been pushed to the margins of the canon. Carter's *Sleeping Beauty and Other Favourite Fairy Tales* already reflects her growing interest in a female literary tradition.

48. Sandra M. Gilbert and Susan Gubar open their influential study of nineteenth-century fiction by women, *The Madwoman in the Attic: The Woman Writer and the Nineteenth-Century Literary Imagination* (1979), with a famous chapter on "Snow White" as a paradigmatic tale of patriarchy. Carter draws attention to the continuity between the fairy tales and classic realist fiction, and as she does so, she traces a hidden genealogy between Beaumont and the female Victorian authors. Another important difference is that Carter stresses the literariness of Beaumont's text rather than the exploitation of the fairy tale as a cultural myth. Carter pursued her critical and creative dialogue with Gilbert and Gubar in "Ashputtle *or* The Mother's Ghost."

Chapter 2

1. Beckett, *Red Riding Hood*.
2. See Carter's provisional plan for her new Mother Goose tales in the Angela Carter Papers, British Library, MS 88899/1/96, cited in the Introduction.
3. Perrault's collection *Histoires ou contes du temps passé, avec des moralités* (1697) opens with "La Belle au bois dormant," followed by "Le Petit Chaperon rouge." Both tales figure in the 1695 collection, with slight variations. "The Little Red Riding-Hood. Tale I" is placed in initial position in Robert Samber's 1729 translation of *Stories or Tales of Past Times*. The French translator of *The Bloody Chamber*, Jacqueline Huet, moved the Red Riding Hood–inspired stories to the beginning and even changed the title of the book accordingly (*La compagnie des loups*, 1985), probably under the influence of Neil Jordan's film, *The Company of Wolves* (1984). See Bianchi and Nannoni, "Back to the Future." The popularity of the tale is reflected in the wealth of retellings and critical studies devoted to it, including Zipes, *Trials and Tribulations*; Dundes, *Little Red Riding Hood*; Orenstein, *Little Red Riding Hood Uncloaked*; Beckett, *Recycling Red Riding Hood*; and Beckett, *Red Riding Hood for All Ages*.
4. *The Bloody Chamber* collection is composed of interlinked tales structured around a basic confrontation that develops and is resolved in different ways. The fact that the two classic versions of "Little Red Riding Hood" present radically different endings shows that variability is built into the history of the tale. The moral of Perrault's *conte* already suggests that the story can be read literally ("Je dis le loup . . .") and metaphorically ("Mais hélas! Qui ne sait que ces Loups douceureux, De tous les Loups sont les plus dangereux," *Contes*, 145). The Grimms' *Märchen* is followed by an appendix or sequel in which the girl and her grandmother trick the wolf into drowning in a big trough without the help of a hunter.
5. Carter, *Curious Room*, 507.

6. Angela Carter Papers, British Library, MS 88899/1/82 (1984).
7. In an interview with John Haffenden, Carter states that "some of the stories in *The Bloody Chamber* are the result of quarreling furiously with Bettelheim" (Haffenden, "Angela Carter," 83).
8. Goldsworthy, "Angela Carter," 10. In this interview, Carter declared: "I was taking the latent image—the latent content of those traditional stories and using that; and the latent content is violently sexual. And because I am a woman, I read it that way."
9. Jack Zipes contends in *Trials and Tribulations* that rape has always been the underlying meaning of the story. Anne Sexton also alludes to Fromm's interpretation of the wolf's mock-pregnancy in her own take on "Little Red Riding Hood" in *Transformations* (1971).
10. See Robert Darnton's discussion of "Little Red Riding Hood" in the chapter "Peasants Tell Tales: The Meaning of Mother Goose" in his *Great Cat Massacre*. Carter mentions Darnton in her interview with Haffenden (Haffenden, "Angela Carter," 84). It is noteworthy that Carter includes her own translation of Perrault's "Le Petit Chaperon rouge" as the first story in the "Moral Tales" section of *The Virago Book of Fairy Tales* (1990). In her scholarly notes, she repeats the anecdote of hearing the story as a child and also recommends Jack Zipes's *The Trial and Tribulations of Little Red Riding Hood* (1983) for "an in-depth sociological, historical and psychological discussion of this story." She notes that "Jack Zipes thinks that 'The Story of Grandmother' is part of a 'Red Riding Hood' tradition of a thoroughly emancipated kind" (*Angela Carter's Book of Fairy Tales*, 464) and goes on to reproduce the folktale in the same footnote.
11. For a useful survey of feminist studies of fairy tales from the 1970s to the 1990s, see Haase, "Feminist Fairy-Tale Scholarship."
12. Orenstein, *Little Red Riding Hood Uncloaked*, 4.
13. Walker, *Disobedient Writer*, 6.
14. Simon, *Gender in Translation*, 23.
15. Similarly, La Fontaine saw his fables as childlike stories that served to wrap up important truths.
16. Perrault's recognition of the role played by the reader's *pénétration* in the construction of meaning is quite modern in its focus on reception and variable understanding of a text depending on various factors (age, intelligence, perceptiveness, etc.).
17. Carter's "Peter and the Wolf," included in *Black Venus* (1985), pursues the idea of the wolf-child who challenges social rules. The story reads like a continuation of "Wolf-Alice" reframed through another wolf tale for children originating in Prokofiev's musical piece. See Moss, "Desire."
18. The twofold purpose of literature as *docere et delectare* is as old as Horace's *De arte poetica*. The genre of the poetical literary treatise reflecting on the form, effect, and purpose of literature was particularly fashionable at the time of Perrault (e.g., Boileau's *Art poétique* or Pope's *Essay on Criticism*). Horace, we remember, also upheld the Moderns against the Ancients (i.e., the Greeks).
19. The wolf thus takes on biblical resonances, echoing "Beware of false prophets, which come to you in sheep's clothing, but inwardly they are ravening wolves" (Matthew 7:15) and "Behold, I send you forth as sheep amidst the wolves" (Matthew 10:16).

Carter's critique of animal symbolism in Judeo-Christian culture is forcefully expressed in "Little Lamb, Get Lost."

20. Several critics have commented on Carter's fictional engagement with theory, which in turn makes her "popular with critics because she gives them so much to work with," to quote Sarah Gamble in *The Fiction of Angela Carter* (8). Carter was familiar with Roland Barthes's work, which she referred to in her review of Georges Bataille's *Story of the Eye* (1979), and she subsequently reviewed the publication of *The Fashion System* in English in 1985; she was also probably familiar with Vladimir Propp's *Morphology of the Folktale* (first published in Russian in 1928; translated 1958).

21. *The Classic Fairy Tales* is mentioned in Carter's 1977 journal and included among the recommended reading for her 1984 class on fairy tales. Carter refers to the Opies' *Oxford Dictionary of Nursery Rhymes* as early as her BA thesis (1965).

22. Dundes, *Little Red Riding Hood*, 13–20. After Delarue, Dundes argues in his introduction that "modern scholarship has established that Perrault did not invent the tale, but rather he adapted one that was already popular in French oral tradition," claiming that "authentic oral tales almost never have a didactic or cloying moral attached" (3).

23. Dundes, *Little Red Riding Hood*, 19.

24. See also Y. Verdier, "Grand-mères si vous saviez." Verdier reads the folktale ethnographically as a reflection on female destiny (puberty, maternity, menopause).

25. Dundes, *Little Red Riding Hood*, 20.

26. Bacchilega mentions this connection in *Postmodern Fairy Tales*. See also Kimberly J. Lau's subtle analysis in "Erotic Infidelities."

27. In her journal for 1977, Carter mentions *The Wild Boy: The Savage of Aveyron*. The story was adapted to the screen by Werner Herzog in *The Enigma of Kaspar Hauser* in 1974. See http://en.wikipedia.org/wiki/The_Enigma_of_Kaspar_Hauser (accessed September 7, 2012).

28. Carter made extensive notes on wolves in her 1977 journal (life, habits, etc.).

29. Crofts, *Anagrams of Desire*, 179.

30. See Escola, *Commentaires*, especially the sections on gallant allegory and playful reading ("jeux de lecture").

31. In her interview with John Haffenden, Carter retells the personal anecdote about being told "Little Red Riding Hood" by her grandmother, adding that "like all small children, I loved being tickled and nuzzled: I found it bliss, and I'd beg her to reiterate the story to me just for the sake of this ecstatic moment. When I was researching the story I looked at a facsimile of Perrault's manuscript, and I found that when he comes to the bit about the wolf jumping on Little Red Riding Hood, it says in the margin 'The storyteller should do likewise'—so that acting out the story has always been part of the story, traditionally" (Haffenden, "Angela Carter," 83).

32. In this sense the tale itself is like the wolf, available in multiple guises and taking every renewed role and identity in Carter's work through generic, structural, stylistic, and thematic transformations.

33. Carter would stress the dark side of mother-daughter relationships in "Ashputtle *or* The Mother's Ghost," included in *American Ghosts and Old World Wonders* (1987).

34. The original title of Perrault's *conte* is "Le Petit Chaperon rouge." Robert Samber

keeps the article in the first English translation (1729), unlike "G. M." in the 1802 reprint owned by Carter ("Little Red Riding-Hood"). The girl's characteristic feature soon crystallized into a proper name. We find the same process at work in the shift from Perrault's "La Barbe bleue" to Samber's "The Blue Beard," G. M.'s "Blue Beard," and Carter's "Bluebeard."

35. The narrative strategy that casts the text as a wolflike predator that lures, catches, and engulfs the guileless reader is also thematized and enacted in "The Erl-King," although this time it is the forest that acts as the entrapping presence.

36. The word *doucereux* is used by Perrault in the figurative sense. See *Dictionnaire de l'Académie française* (1694): "Il se dit fig. des personnes, & des choses qui sont particulierement propres aux personnes, & signifie, Qui paroist trop doux & trop affecté. *C'est un homme doucereux. il a l'air doucereux, la mine doucereuse. il fait le doucereux*. On dit, *Faire le doucereux auprés d'une femme*, pour dire, Affecter par ses façons de luy faire croire que l'on est amoureux d'elle. On dit aussi dans ce mesme sens, *Des vers doucereux, une lettre doucereuse. dire des choses doucereuses*." Carter, however, spontaneously associates its literal meaning of sweet with the smoothness of tongue and the softness of fur. The sensual attraction of the wolf's speech, or voice, and pelt is explored in "The Company of Wolves" and is encapsulated in the recurrent image of the "hairy on the inside"—that is, an invisible fur that is revealed only through metamorphosis.

37. Carter similarly plays down both the horror and the erotic subtext of "Bluebeard," unlike the rewriting that presents the relationship between the Bluebeard figure and his bride as a sadomasochistic one in "The Bloody Chamber." In this sense "The Bloody Chamber" is the exact reverse of "Little Red Riding Hood": "The wolf consumes Red Riding Hood; what else do you expect if you talk to strange men, comments Perrault briskly. Let's not bother our heads with the mysteries of sado-masochistic attraction" (Carter, "The Better To Eat You With," 453).

38. See Crofts's excellent chapters on "The Company of Wolves" as radio play, film script, and screen adaptation in *Anagrams of Desire*.

39. Zipes, "Remaking of Charles Perrault," xxii.

40. Zipes, "Remaking of Charles Perrault," xx.

41. In a similar fashion, though at the expense of the wolf this time, Roald Dahl's version of the tale in *Revolting Rhymes* (1982) and Stephen Sondheim's musical *Into the Woods* have Red Riding Hood overcome the wolf and later appear wearing a fur coat made of the wolf's fur. In James Thurber's "The Little Girl and the Wolf" Red Riding Hood is not fooled by the wolf but takes a gun from her basket and shoots him. The narrator comments: "It is not so easy to fool little girls nowadays as it used to be." The humor of Carter's moral is taken up and developed in the burlesque treatment of the macabre aspects of the tale in "Wolf-Alice."

42. The experience of reading as analogous to taking a walk and getting lost in the woods is thematized (and enacted) in "The Erl-King," which is in part a revisiting of "Little Red Riding Hood" from the perspective of the girl entrapped by an enchanter who embodies the spirit of the forest.

43. Eco, *Six Walks*, 3.

44. Eco, *Six Walks*, 6, 8.

45. Eco, *Six Walks*, 12.

46. Martin Ware's unconventional illustrations depict the heroine as a serious-looking prepubescent girl. The lifelike characters are placed on a stylized background that evokes the idea of distance and perspective. The first full-page illustration of "Little Red Riding Hood" (*Fairy Tales of Charles Perrault*, 25) presents a geometric, flat, triangular ground with a small girl playing with butterflies; she is seen from a distance, and from behind, and in the foreground a wolfish dog looks in the opposite direction.

47. Ware's emphasis on frames and enclosures (rooms, doors, windows, etc.) suggests the multiple meanings of the word "to frame" as an apt visual image for "Little Red Riding Hood" and "Bluebeard," in the sense of to compose or to conceive but also in the sense of to enclose with a frame and hence to contrive the dishonest outcome of a contest. The body of the wolf itself functions as a frame that incorporates other characters.

48. Angela Carter Papers, British Library, "The Bloody Chamber and Other Short Stories," 1, MS 88899/1/33. The file includes autograph notes and drafts of "The Bloody Chamber," three annotated typewritten drafts, and one incomplete manuscript. Carter declares that she wants to read to an anonymous addressee "a nursery suite that's the result of 6 months work on fairy tales. It is all derived from Perrault's classic exposition of the story of 'Little red Riding Hood.'"

49. On the same worksheet, Carter also quotes the opening lines of Rossetti's poem "The Dead City," about a girl wandering in an enchanting forest. The poem inspired "The Erl-King," but it can also be seen as a variation on "Little Red Riding Hood." For the text of the poem, see http://www.unc.edu/courses/2006spring/engl/021/006/PDFs/TheDeadCity.pdf (accessed September 7, 2012).

50. Bacchilega, *Postmodern Fairy Tales*, 58.

51. Bacchilega, *Postmodern Fairy Tales*, 59.

52. Bacchilega, *Postmodern Fairy Tales*, 60.

53. Bacchilega, *Postmodern Fairy Tales*, 61.

54. In an interview with Lorna Sage, Angela Carter declared: "We [my brother and I] speculate on this point. We often say to one another, How is it possible such camp little flowers as ourselves emanated from Balham via Wath-upon Dearne and the places my father comes from, north Aberdeenshire, stark, bleak and apparently lugubriously Calvinistic, witch-burning country?" (Sage, "Savage Sideshow," 53).

55. Bacchilega, *Postmodern Fairy Tales*, 64. For a discussion of the productivity of "unfaithful readings" that challenge "the authorities of both feminist theory and patriarchal culture," see Lau, "Erotic Infidelities" (85). Although I disagree with the claim that Perrault's *conte* is a "patriarchal 'Little Red Riding Hood'" (78), Lau's point about Carter's restoring of "women's sexual agency by calling attention to their/our positioning within a culture that fetishizes young girls as objects of sexual desire" (79) captures Carter's project in her translation for children and hints at a continuity with her rewritings in *The Bloody Chamber*.

56. See Bacchilega, *Postmodern Fairy Tales*, ch. 3.

57. Dundes, *Little Red Riding Hood*, 15.

58. Bacchilega, *Postmodern Fairy Tales*, 64.

59. Bacchilega, *Postmodern Fairy Tales*, 56.

60. The recurrent image of the wolf being "hairy on the inside" presumably comes from John Webster's *Duchess of Malfi* (1612–1613), where the cruel Duke is a lycanthrope.

The doctor informs Pescara (and the audience) that lycanthropes run about "churchyards in the dead of night" to "dig dead bodies up" (5.2.11–12). Ferdinand has been seen at midnight behind a church, "with the leg of a man / Upon his shoulder" (5.2.14–15) and howling. When approached during this particular incident, Ferdinand "said he was a wolf" and that while "a wolf's skin was hairy on the outside," his was hairy "on the inside" (5.2.16–18). This diagnosis reveals that Ferdinand's lycanthropia is a "very pestilent disease" (5.2.5) and a "madness" (5.2.26). "Wolf-Alice" self-consciously references this macabre tragedy, albeit in a parodic mode.

61. The first draft of the screenplay, which differs somewhat from the finished film, has been published in *The Curious Room* (1996). See also Rose, "The Dreaming."
62. Jacques Lacan developed his theory of the mirror stage in the 1950s. According to Lacan, the moment a child recognizes her body image in the mirror as herself is a crucial turning point in the development of the child's sense of self that also opens up the possibility of articulate speech. Carter's imaginative exploration of the psyche of this human "other" who has been brought up as a wolf draws on Lacan's connection of the mirror as a precondition for self-recognition and access to language but also modifies it by stressing smell and touch rather than vision and inhabiting an intermediary state that resists categorization: "This habitual, at last boring, fidelity to her every movement finally woke her up to the regretful possibility that her companion was, in fact, no more than a particularly ingenious variety of the shadow she cast on sunlit grass. . . . yet her relation with the mirror was now far more intimate since she knew she saw herself within it" ("Wolf-Alice," *Bloody Chamber*, 147).
63. This echoes Marina Warner's tracing of cultural changes in the perception and representation of bears in *From the Beast*.
64. Angela Carter Papers, British Library, "The Bloody Chamber and Other Short Stories," 2. The "tour ténébreuse" could be a reference to Marie-Jeanne L'Héritier de Villandon's *La Tour ténébreuse et les jours lumineux: contes anglois* (1705).
65. Duncker, "Re-Imagining," 6.
66. Stone, "Misuses of Enchantment," 229.

Chapter 3

1. Haffenden, "Angela Carter," 96.
2. Note the use of capital letters, which endows the room with almost mythical resonances. The quotation is from Carter's inscribed copy of the book. In her course notes (a loose sheet titled "Bluebeard" collected in the "Miscellaneous Fairy Tale Material" file, Angela Carter Papers, British Library, MS 88899/1/82), Carter declares that she is going to "look at a story, or, rather the constellation of stories and ballads that assemble themselves around the story, Fitcher's Bird . . . in the edition of my childhood and try to extract some of what I believe to be the *latent* meaning out of a story that is already so haunting and so explicitly about itself—a young girl falls in with some kind of sex maniac and triumphantly turns the tables on him." Further on, Carter notes that Perrault's "Bluebeard" "has been almost completely purged of supernatural elements—the husband is a psychopathic murderer, a type who rarely intrudes into fairy tales. But if the husband is an ogrish wizard, as he is in 'Fowler's Fowl,' then his activities are normalised; comfortably, he is only behaving in a way which is natural to him.

He is not a psychopath. He is acting according to types." In "The Bloody Chamber" Carter emulates Perrault's realistic treatment of the criminal husband, but she also draws on alternative versions that emphasize the agency of the female characters.

3. "Das Mordschloss" is found in Appendix 14 of the Grimms' *Kinder- und Hausmärchen* (2007 ed., 2: 477–79). In this variation on "Bluebeard" ("Blaubart" also figures as Appendix 9), a shoemaker's daughter marries a rich nobleman for money. When they are on the way to his castle, he asks her if she repents, and she cannot help feeling uneasy. An important difference with Perrault's text is the absence of a prohibition. The bride explores the castle when her husband is away and discovers a cellar (*Keller*) where an old woman is scraping intestines. The old woman warns her that she will be scraping hers soon, and when the bride drops the key in the blood in horror, the old woman advises her to hide in a cart full of hay that is about to leave the castle. When the nobleman comes back, the old woman pretends that she has slaughtered the girl, and so enables her to escape unscathed. The bride finds refuge in the nearest castle. The murderous Count is eventually confounded with his bloody deeds over dinner when the disguised survivor tells her tale. He tries to escape but is checked. His castle is burned down, and all his possessions are handed over to the bride, who ends up marrying the son of the house where she found shelter. The motivation of the young woman to marry a rich nobleman, the presence of an older woman acting as a helper figure, and the role of (female) storytelling as a means to restore truth and justice are also found in Carter's "Bloody Chamber."

4. Haffenden, "Angela Carter," 86.

5. Quoted in Roemer and Bacchilega, "Introduction," 7.

6. Haffenden, "Angela Carter," 86.

7. As mentioned in the Introduction, for the early translations of Perrault's *conte*, I have used the translation by "G. M.," *Histories, or Tales of Past Times Told by Mother Goose* (1802), (*Histories* in the text), although I also occasionally refer to Robert Samber's translation of "Bluebeard" reproduced in the Opies' *Classic Fairy Tales*.

8. *Cabinet*: "lieu dans une maison où sont les tableaux de prix" (Richelet, *Dictionnaire français*, 1680, cited by Jean-Pierre Collinet in Perrault, *Contes*, 327). The *cabinets de curiosités* popular in the seventeenth and eighteenth centuries typically included *artificiala* (art objects and paintings), *erotica, exotica, naturalia*, and *scientifica*. Because the word *cabinet* is no longer used in that sense, it surely aroused Carter's curiosity when she translated Perrault's *conte* into English. Her choice of the word *chamber* (derived from the French word for "bedroom") for the title of her collection testifies to Carter's lexicographical interests and cross-linguistic borrowings.

9. Lang, *Perrault's Popular Tales*, lxi.

10. In the "Miscellaneous Fairy Tale Material" file (Angela Carter Papers, British Library), Carter contrasts Perrault's "Bluebeard" with "Fitcher's Bird," suggesting that the egg is "the one which eventually hatches out the heroine in her new career as a bird." Carter hatched her own Fevvers, the magical aerialist heroine of *Nights at the Circus* (1984), from that fictional egg. In the same file Carter also quarrels with Bettelheim's interpretation, which ignores the survival of the bride.

11. The Opies also recount an anecdote of the discovery of paintings in a chapel dedicated to St. Tryphine depicting "six scenes from Perrault's story of Bluebeard" (*Classic Fairy Tales*, 105).

12. Carter's understanding of Sade was apparently mediated by Pierre Klossowski's writings, which she briefly refers to in her notes for "The Bloody Chamber." The translator, writer, and artist was responsible for a new publication of Sade's violently pornographic and long censored *120 Days of Sodom & Other Writings* in 1964, and he authored two studies, *Sade mon prochain* (1947) and *Le philosophe scélérat* (1967).

13. The telepathic communication between the bride and her mother is reminiscent of a similar episode in *Jane Eyre*. This discrepancy in the otherwise realistic treatment of events in Brontë's novel notoriously bothered some readers, and Carter seems to be poking fun at the Opies for faulting Perrault with a similar breach of verisimilitude. We remember that Carter, who wrote an introduction to the Virago edition of *Jane Eyre* (published in 1990), was planning to write a sequel to the novel from the perspective of Adèle.

14. During the first decade of the twentieth century, Paul Poiret initiated a fashion sea change when he declared the wasp-waisted (corseted) silhouette outmoded and designed flowing gowns liberating women's bodies. Nicknamed the Sultan of Paris, Poiret was fascinated by Orientalism, and some of his most extravagant creations were inspired by *The Thousand and One Nights*. See Roemer, "Contextualization." The year 1922 was also when Henri Désiré Landru was sentenced to death for murdering several women and beheaded by guillotine. "The Bloody Chamber" also nods toward surrealism (Cocteau, Breton) through the literalization of the famous collective creative technique of the *cadavre exquis*.

15. Renfroe, "Initiation and Disobedience," 99.

16. Zipes, "Remaking of Charles Perrault," xxii.

17. Heidmann, "La Barbe bleue palimpseste."

18. Bettelheim, *Uses of Enchantment*, 301.

19. See the illustration at http://www.surlalunefairytales.com/illustrations/bluebeard/craneblue2.html (accessed September 11, 2012) from Crane, *Bluebeard Picture Book*.

20. The idea of killing women for art is also centrally explored in Gilbert and Gubar, *Madwoman in the Attic*.

21. The egglike doorknob and the skulls are reminiscent of the Grimms' "Fitchers Vogel," where female transgression is revealed by a stained egg; the last bride not only takes care to put the egg in a safe place before opening the door but she also puts her sisters' chopped limbs back together and revives them, before tricking the wizard with a decorated skull. Carter was to return to the vanitas pictorial tradition and the interplay of text and image in "Impressions: The Wrightsman's Magdalene" (1992), published in *American Ghosts and Old World Wonders* (1993).

22. In her analysis of the illustrations of the 1695 and 1697 editions of Perrault's *contes*, Ségolène Le Men observes that "in each case it is the imminent danger and not the crime itself which is pictured, as baroque pictorial conventions would dictate. As Lessing later explained in his 1766 work, Laokoon, which draws parallels between literature and the visual arts, the climactic effect is better achieved when not the climax itself, but the instant before it, is represented, leaving the imagination to remain free" ("Mother Goose Illustrated," 32). Le Men goes on to argue that the splitting of the illustration for "Bluebeard" to represent two simultaneous actions as well as the childlike iconography (flat characters and disregard of the rules of perspective, with flat

23. "Fin de siècle" first appeared in the journal *New Society* in 1972.
24. Tatar, *Hard Facts*, 158.
25. Berger, *Ways of Seeing*, 45 and 47.
26. Berger, *Ways of Seeing*, 49.
27. Berger, *Ways of Seeing*, 52.
28. Berger, *Ways of Seeing*, 56. See Maggie Tonkin's recent discussion of this critical intertext in *Angela Carter and Decadence*.
29. One of the most significant feminist interventions in the debate about the politics of representation in the late 1970s and 1980s was in film theory, notably Laura Mulvey's "Visual Pleasure and Narrative Cinema" and its response by E. Ann Kaplan, "Is the Gaze Male?" Andrea Dworkin in *Woman Hating* (1974) and Susanne Kappeler in *The Pornography of Representation* (1986) made polemical contributions to this debate. In the "Miscellaneous Fairy Tale Material" file (Angela Carter Papers, British Library, MS 88899/1/82), Carter quotes Mulvey on a loose sheet titled "Bluebeard": "The image of women in patriarchal representation refers more readily to its connotations within the male unconscious, to its fears and fantasies, than to the working-through of the female Oedipus complex, confrontation with castration & sexual difference."
30. See Sheets, "Pornography." Carter's treatment of fin de siècle visual and literary art reflects her questioning of the distinction between eroticism and pornography, although from a position that is radically different from the kind of feminist puritanism found in Dworkin or Kappeler.
31. My understanding of postmodernism is based on Linda Hutcheon's *Politics of Postmodernism*, which demonstrates the "undeniable political import" (3) of postmodern art as a paradoxical "complicitous critique" (9) of "the ideological values and interests that inform any representation" (7).
32. Cyril Edwin Mitchinson Joad defines "the decadent in art and literature (and by extension in every human area) [as] whatever rejects classical values and the fixed relation of the moral—more narrowly the ethical—to the aesthetic or to the philosophic and psychological as well" (*Decadence*, 117). Although challenged for its moralistic bias in recent years, this definition nevertheless points to Carter's own strictures against the decadent aesthetics and its implications for women. John R. Reed identifies certain themes and motifs that figure prominently in Carter's story, such as "sexual irregularity, sadomasochism, diabolism, occultism, and exoticism. A taste for decoration in the arts and artificiality in designs, implements, and behavior. . . . Certain human types prevail in the arts, from effete aesthetes and destructive women to decaying aristocratic families" (*Decadent Style*, 7). Reed rightly observes, however, that although this constitutes the material of most fin de siècle art, it does not provide a workable definition because it ignores style as an essential "aspect of statement" (8).
33. Showalter, *Daughters of Decadence*, vii.
34. Showalter, *Daughters of Decadence*, x.
35. The first chapter of Huysmans's *A rebours* begins with a detailed description of the boudoir of des Esseintes's Fontenay mansion, where he attracts girls who enjoy looking at their own reflections multiplied in the many mirrors which cover its walls.

36. In 1864 Edmond and Jules Goncourt declared in their *Journal*, "Nous avons à peu près remplacé la femme, autrement dit le prétexte de l'amour, et la nature par le tableau. Tout ce qui n'est pas traduit par l'art est pour nous comme de la viande crue" (1: 1120). (We have gradually replaced woman, as a mere pretext for love, and nature, by painting. Whatever is not transmuted [literally, translated] by art is for us like raw meat" [translation mine].)

37. Félicien Rops (1833–1898) was one of the most daring artists of the second half of the nineteenth century. He was the main illustrator of the decadents, and worked in close collaboration with Baudelaire and Huysmans among others. He is famous for his transgressive and sexually explicit engravings of depraved and demonic women (as in the series titled *Les sataniques*). The voyeuristic dimension of Rops's paintings is highlighted by the panels that hid some of them from view. Like other artists of the period, Rops treated the mythological theme of Salomé, which links eroticism and the macabre through the motif of the severed head. In her adaptation of "Bluebeard" to the context of the fin de siècle, Carter deliberately reverses gender roles so that the cruel femme fatale becomes the victim of the perverse husband who wants to behead her.

38. Huysmans's *Là-bas* traces the progress of Durtal's biography of Gilles de Rais, an endeavor that purports to rehabilitate him as a decadent artist *avant la lettre*. The scholar Durtal entertains his friends with detailed accounts of Gilles de Rais's lavishly furnished Tiffauges Castle in Brittany, his refined tastes, exacerbated religiosity, sexual perversions, and criminal career. Durtal is morbidly attracted to his subject, whom he introduces in superlative terms as "the most artist-like and the most exquisite, the most cruel and the most criminal of men" (Huysmans, *Là-bas*, 47). Devoting all his time and energy to "this Bluebeard [who] interests him more than the greengrocer round the corner" (41; translations mine), he strives to escape from the present, and nostalgically laments the loss of what he sees as the "golden age" of medieval decadence.

39. The Orientalization of Bluebeard runs through the iconographic tradition, including the three pictures chosen by the Opies to illustrate the tale in their *Classic Fairy Tales*. In her notes for Bluebeard, Carter refers to *The Arabian Nights*, even identifying herself with Scheherazade, although she wittily admits that "there was a sharper edge to it for her, told tales to keep herself alive" (Angela Carter Papers, British Library, MS 88899/1/33).

40. In the short story "Black Venus," Carter creates the imaginary portrait of Baudelaire's mulatto mistress, Jeanne Duval, who is believed to have been the model for "Les Bijoux." The object of some of Baudelaire's most famous poems becomes a subject in her own right, and as Hutcheon notes, "Carter's text consistently contrasts the language of Baudelaire's decadent male eroticism with the stark social reality of Jeanne Duval's position as a colonial, a black, and a kept woman. Male erotic iconography of women seems to have two poles: the romantic/decadent fantasist (like Baudelaire's) and the realist (the woman as sexual partner), but in neither case is the woman anything but a mediating sign for the male" (*Politics of Postmodernism*, 145).

41. Showalter, *Sexual Anarchy*, 10.

42. Besides their conventional grouping as decadent painters, these artists illustrate the intense and mutual influence of pictorial art and literature at the turn of the century. Although the titles of the pictures seem to be fictional, the female model described by the Marquis may be inspired by Susanne Valadon, a beautiful circus performer who haunted the sleazy bars of Montmartre and modeled for Degas, Toulouse-Lautrec,

Renoir, and Puvis de Chavannes. This reference would be ironic, because Valadon became a painter in her own right and was famous for her female nudes, which challenge pictorial conventions because they represent women as individuals rather than as sexualized objects.

43. The reference to *Sacrificial Victim* is fictional. The Marquis perhaps means to deliberately mislead the bride (and the reader?) in order to arouse her curiosity while of course alluding to her fate. The portrait that the Marquis describes is more reminiscent of Gustave Moreau's *La nuit* (1880), an oval watercolor representing a female nude decorated with fine and sophisticated jewelry whose weblike structure sets off her nakedness. She is crowned with a bright star, and her pale flesh is set in sharp contrast to the dark background. In her journal for 1977 (Angela Carter Papers, British Library, MS 88899/1/96), however, Carter indicates that "the Moreau painting in the castle is 'Iphigenia.'" She refers to Philippe Julian's *Symbolists* (1973) and mentions Doré, Baudelaire, and Huysmans, noting that "Des Esseintes dabbled in vice. 'Les Fleurs du Mal' bound in the form of a sumptuous missal." See Evanghélia Stead's recent study of bibliophily at the fin de siècle in *Chair du livre*.

44. The bride's musical abilities will indirectly contribute to her rescue, because the blind piano tuner hired at the request of the bride will take her side and collaborate with the mother to neutralize the Marquis before setting up a music school with the young widow at the end. It is interesting to note that although Gustave Moreau is famous for his paintings of femmes fatales such as Salomé, his other favorite subject was female martyrs, including Saint Cecilia.

45. Carter's work reflects a lifelong interest in circuses, fairgrounds, peep shows, and music halls—places associated with the carnivalesque, in which established hierarchies and the symbolic order of patriarchy are provisionally overturned and made fun of. In this passage the bride refers to the rich popular imagery surrounding Bluebeard, which she implicitly opposes to the treatment of the story in decadent art and "high" culture.

46. The mythological figure of Medusa was a central motif in fin de siècle culture, particularly in literature and painting. Like Salomé, who is also associated with decapitation, Medusa crystallized masculine obsessions with powerful and malevolent females embodying male fears of castration, as Freud famously argued in his essay "Medusa's Head." In their introduction to *The Medusa Reader*, Garber and Vickers draw attention to the "tension between the beautiful Medusa and the monstrous one [that] is intrinsic to the story, to the figure of Medusa herself, and to the twin strands of feminism and misogyny that have attached themselves to retellings of the Medusa myth throughout the ages" (1). The central ambivalence of the Medusa figure is also reflected in "the double power and danger of poetic as well as visual representation" (5).

Chapter 4

1. "Whittington and His Cat," first recorded in 1605, was included in Joseph Jacobs's *English Fairy Tales* (1890).
2. Carter intended "Puss-in-Boots" as a counterpart to her work on Sade. See Katsavos, "Interview," 15. Maria Sofia Pimentel analyzes Carter's "Puss-in-Boots" in light of Bakhtin's theory of "grotesque realism" ("Angela Carter's 'Puss-in-Boots,'" 2) in *Rabelais and His World*. Bakhtin accounts for the spread of the commedia dell'arte in Europe and the taste for the grotesque (caricature, broad humor) as a reaction against

classicism. Pimentel also notes that Carter's "Puss-in-Boots" mirrors and inverts "The Bloody Chamber." A short but suggestive reading of Carter's story as a rewriting of Basile's "Cagliuso" and Disney's short 1922 film is proposed in the introduction to Roemer and Bacchilega's *Angela Carter and the Fairy Tale* (13–15). Margaret Atwood makes a passing reference to the tale in "Running with the Tigers" (126–27), and Merja Makinen mentions it in "Angela Carter's 'The Bloody Chamber.'" A possible explanation for this relative disinterest is that the comic, lighthearted, and bawdy tone is not seen as typical of Carter's style in *The Bloody Chamber* (although she would exploit it later in *Wise Children* [1991], for example). Another possible reason is that the story is retold from the perspective of the lecherous tomcat, with a strong emphasis on his (and his master's) sexual exploits, although Carter takes care to celebrate female desire and agency as well.

3. The smiling cat of course evokes Lewis Carroll's mysterious Cheshire Cat.

4. Carter explicitly pays homage to the carnival spirit of the English pantomime tradition in "In Pantoland" (1991), reprinted in *American Ghosts and Old World Wonders* (1993). See Ryan-Sautour, "Carnaval." On the reception of "Puss in Boots" in England, see Velay-Vallantin, "Le Chat Botté."

5. In the radio play the murder of the old and miserly husband (Pantaleone slips over Tabs and falls down the stairs, breaking his neck) is elided, although his dead body is the occasion for some situation comedy in the mock consultation scene with the hero disguised as a doctor (*Yellow Sands*, 153–54).

6. As mentioned in the Introduction, I use the "G. M." translation, *Histories, or Tales of Past Times Told by Mother Goose* (*Histories* in the citations), unless specified otherwise.

7. Charlotte Crofts, in *Anagrams of Desire*, pays only marginal attention to "Puss in Boots," as she acknowledges herself in the introduction. Her comment on Carter's use of the recent technology of stereophonic sound to "maximis[e] radio's temporal and spatial agility" to "choreograph the feline acrobatics" (25) is particularly apt. The radio adaptations of "Puss in Boots" and "The Company of Wolves," she observes, "deserve to be studied in their own right, not least because of the skills with which Carter . . . tak[es] the new medium into account" (27).

8. Carter possibly also alludes to Marie-Catherine d'Aulnoy's "La Chatte blanche," which pays homage to Perrault's tale and the fabulistic tradition. D'Aulnoy tells the story of an aging king who sends his three sons on a quest for a little dog. The youngest son visits an enchanted castle whose walls are decorated with visual representation of fairy tales, including "l'histoire des plus fameux chats, Rodilardus pendu par les pieds au conseil des rats, Chat botté, marquis de Carabas, le Chat qui écrit, la Chatte devenue femme, les sorciers devenus chats, le sabbat et toutes ses cérémonies; enfin, rien n'était plus singulier que ces tableaux." The young prince is so pleased with the company of its owner, a white cat, that "il ne pensa plus qu'à miauler avec Chatte Blanche c'est-à-dire, à lui tenir bonne et fidèle compagnie." The tale also includes a (mock epic) battle between cats and rats. Another possible echo is the black veil that the unhappily married woman has to wear in Carter's prose "Puss-in-Boots," just like the white Cat in d'Aulnoy's fairy tale.

9. We remember that Angela Carter wrote the draft of a libretto for an opera based on Virginia Woolf's *Orlando*, which is included in *The Curious Room*.

10. Puss appears in the third act of Tchaikovsky's ballet *The Sleeping Beauty* in a *pas de caractère* with d'Aulnoy's White Cat.
11. The moral to "The Master Cat: or Puss in Boots" is not reproduced in the Opies' *Classic Fairy Tales*.
12. The "Miscellaneous Fairy Tale Material" file (Angela Carter Papers, British Library) contains a loose sheet titled "Puss in Boots." The prose rewriting was first published in *The Straw and the Gold*, edited by Emma Tennant (1979), before being included in *The Bloody Chamber*.
13. Pierre de Larivey's French translation of "Costantin Fortuné" was apparently known to Perrault's contemporaries, as Ruth Bottigheimer notes in *Fairy Godfather*, e.g., 126. In this version, as in the Italian sources, the cat is female.
14. When the Cat gives the rabbit to the king on behalf of his master, the narrator steps in to gloss the name invented by the Cat in a parenthetical explanation: "Voilà, Sire, un Lapin de Garenne que Monsieur le Marquis de Carabas (c'était le nom qu'il lui prit en gré de donner à son Maître) m'a chargé de vous présenter de sa part" (*Contes*, 158). Carter integrates the parenthetical statement in the main narrative: "Without his master's knowledge or consent, the cat had decided the miller's son should adopt the name of the Marquis of Carabas" (*Fairy Tales*, 12). Carter characteristically suppresses Perrault's parentheses and inserts the explanations directly into the text to make the narrative more fluid, but this act alters the tone of confidentiality and secrecy established between the narrator and the readers, encouraged as they are to become willing accomplices of the deception and to admire the cat's ingenuity, boldness, and linguistic inventiveness. Likewise, the parenthetical description of the physical qualities of the young man at the moment of rescue by the king's party is integrated into the main text.
15. Perrault had referred to these episodes in *Le labyrinthe de Versailles* (Aesop) and in his *Traduction des fables de Faërne* (Phaedrus). These two *tours de souplesse* are brought together in La Fontaine's fable, to which Perrault pays homage in his *conte*.
16. Interestingly, Beatrix Potter's children's books are not unrelated to the tales of Antiquity. Potter studied mythology and the classic fairy tales of Western Europe, and she chose for her first illustrations traditional rhymes and stories, including "Cinderella," "Sleeping Beauty," "Ali Baba and the Forty Thieves," "Puss-in-Boots," and "Little Red Riding Hood." Although her fantasies feature her own pets (mice, rabbits, kittens, and guinea pigs), stories involving talking animals belong to an age-old fabulistic tradition that Potter was familiar with.
17. See Barchilon and Pettit, *Authentic Mother Goose*.
18. The Littré dictionary gives the following definitions of the phrase: "Tours de souplesse, tours des saltimbanques qui demandent un corps souple." "*Fig*. Tours de souplesse, moyens subtils, artificieux pour en arriver à ses fins."
19. See the bibliographical repertory of the English editions of the tale established by Denise Dupont-Escarpit in *Histoire d'un conte*.
20. Carter may also be paying homage to T. S. Eliot's *Old Possum's Book of Practical Cats*, a collection of comic poems about feline psychology and sociology first published by Faber & Faber in 1939. The poems were written during the 1930s, and Eliot, using his assumed name "Old Possum," mentioned them in letters to his godchildren. The col-

lection has also been published in reillustrated versions by Edward Gorey (1982) and Axel Scheffler (2009).

21. Several critics, including Dupont-Escarpit in *Histoire d'un conte* and, more recently, Heidmann and Adam in *Textualité*, have drawn attention to the importance of capitalization in the original edition of Perrault's volume. A close look at the 1697 edition shows a striking use of capitals to designate the human and animal protagonists (down to the "Rats" caught by the Cat), but also the "Château," the "Appartement de sa Majesté," and even his "Carrosse." Capitals abound, even though Perrault himself had recommended to limit their use in official documents in 1673, qualifying them as "incommode ornement." This apparent contradiction reinforces still further the satirical dimension of Perrault's *conte*, which puts cats and kings, millers and marquis, rabbits and princesses, ogres and flies on the same level. This strategy seems quite deliberate, because in the passage where the "Ogre" is tricked into changing into a mouse, the Cat's challenge is formulated as follows: "On m'a assuré encore, dit le Chat . . . que vous aviez aussi le pouvoir de prendre la forme des plus petits Animaux, par exemple, de vous changer en un Rat, en une souris" (*Contes*, 160). Significantly, the absence of a capital in *souris* mimics the small size of the animals that will enable the Cat to destroy his powerful opponent, a big and powerful ogre, and appropriate his many possessions. The play with the materiality of the text foregrounds its nature as *writing* that needs to be carefully deciphered, in keeping with the "pact of reading" formulated in the preface of Perrault's collection. This confirms Louis Marin's classic interpretation of Perrault's *conte* as a playful but profound reflection on the deceptiveness of signs. The typographical changes that take place between Perrault's original text and its subsequent translations, including Carter's, reflect significant shifts in conventions but also shifts in genre and audience. Perrault's use of capital letters is part of a deliberate strategy: He capitalizes the names of important characters as well as the things that belong to them, including the Cat's characteristic attribute, his "Bottes," or the "Lapin de Garenne" that enables him to win the king's trust. Perrault's use of capital letters also clearly alludes to the Jean de La Fontaine and Aesop fables that inspired them. By contrast, Carter chooses to keep the capital letter only for titles signaling status, as in "Sire" and "Marquis of Carabas," either because she chooses to comply with the typographical conventions of her time or because she considers that the complex irony and intertextual references introduced by Perrault will be lost on her young readers (who may not even be reading the tale on their own). Carter seems to be alert to the significance of capital letters for titles (either genuine or usurped) that orient the social critique of her translation toward class divisions and snobbery.

22. Carter explicitly refers to Dick Whittington in "In Pantoland" as one of the heroes of pantomime (in *Shaking a Leg*, 393).

23. The entry on *honnestement* in the *Dictionnaire de l'Académie française* (1694) gives the two meanings of "d'une mannière honneste" and "suffisamment, passablement, & par ironie, extremement." http://portail.atilf.fr/cgi-bin/dicollook.pl?stripped hw=honnestement (accessed November 14, 2011).

24. Another possible Dickensian echo in Carter's text is the cat's groveling politeness when he offers the rabbit he has poached to the king "with his humblest compliments," which the translator adds to signal the cat's dishonest intentions. This echoes Uriah Heep's obsequiousness and insincerity in *David Copperfield*, captured in his repeated

claims of being "'umble.'" Like a negative and creepy version of Perrault's Cat, Uriah Heep strives to appropriate his master's estate as well as his daughter, but his plans are thwarted in the end.

25. What makes Perrault's tale comic, among other things, is the fact that the Cat is fastidious about his costume: He asks for boots and even wears "handsome boots" in Carter's translation. This added emphasis on the beautiful boots is also found in Gustave Doré's famous image of an extravagantly booted cat, dressed as a musketeer and adopting histrionic postures. The boots are comically referred to again when the Cat, frightened by the lion, jumps onto the roof. In Carter's translation he almost slips "because his boots weren't made for walking on tiles"—a comic echo of Nancy Sinatra's pop song "These Boots Are Made for Walkin'" (1966), which was seen as a symbol of female power and emancipation. The theme of self-transformation is treated positively in the tale, but it also provokes the death of the Proteus-like ogre, who is provoked into changing into a mouse and is eaten by the cat, just like "Le Petit Chaperon rouge," which Carter echoes in "gobbled him up."

26. See Louis Marin's classic study *Le récit est un piège*, ch. 4, "A la conquête du pouvoir" (124–27): "Il nous faut nous attarder un moment sur la ruse du chat, double en vérité et qui provoque une transformation essentielle dans l'état des choses. Sa ruse est de discours: elle consiste, de la part du chat, à nommer librement son maître. . . . Le nom du maître . . . est non seulement un pseudonyme—un faux nom—mais il est une usurpation d'une appellation—un faux titre. . . . [Le chat] détourne la force du pouvoir (de 'nommer') dans son usage public à son usage particulier, tout en rendant, par la répétition, cet usage particulier acceptable par celui qui détient le pouvoir de nommer."

27. The musical quality of the tale is also anticipated by Carter's translation choices when she associates the repeated phrase imposed by the cat with a refrain: "'C'est à Monsieur le Marquis de Carabas,' dirent-ils tous ensemble" (*Contes*, 159); "They had been so intimidated by the cat, that they dutifully *chorused*" (*Fairy Tales*, 48; italics mine). Similarly, in her prose rewriting, the cats sing "their raucous choruses" at night (*Bloody Chamber*, 68).

28. "Habileté, industrie pour réussir ce qu'on entreprend" (P. Richelet, *Dictionnaire françois*, 1680, quoted by Jean-Pierre Collinet in Perrault, *Contes*, 333n21).

29. Because it activates pre-Perrault connections with the Italian tradition and post-Perrault connections with Enlightenment comedy, Carter's densely intertextual fiction is indeed "a kind of literary criticism," to quote Carter herself (Haffenden, "Angela Carter," 79).

30. *Puss in Boots* was broadcast on BBC Radio 3 in 1982, starring Andrew Sachs in the title role. The script was published in Carter's *Come unto These Yellow Sands* and later in the posthumous collection *The Curious Room*, which also included production notes.

31. Carter pays homage to the irreverent, carnivalesque spirit of street theater while drawing attention to its interplay of repetition of the same old plots and types and improvisation (which makes every performance unique), which is analogous to her own intervention in the fairy-tale tradition.

32. Beaumarchais's life and career suggest that he was very much a Puss in Boots figure himself. The Wikipedia entry describes him as a French watchmaker, inventor, musician, diplomat, fugitive, spy, publisher, arms dealer, financier, and revolutionary best known for his three Figaro plays. Curiously, he also wrote a number of short plays

(called parades), including the fairy-tale-based farce "Les Bottes de sept lieues." Admittedly, Beaumarchais's plays were semi-autobiographical, including caricatures of his real-life enemies and sexual exploits. *Le Mariage de Figaro* was initially passed by the censor in 1781 but banned from performance by Louis XVI after a private reading. Queen Marie-Antoinette lamented the ban, as did various influential members of her entourage. Nonetheless, the king was unhappy with the play's satire on the aristocracy and overruled the queen's entreaties to allow its performance. Over the next three years Beaumarchais gave many private readings of the play and made numerous revisions to try to pass the censor. The king finally relented and lifted the ban in 1784. The play premiered that year and was enormously popular, even with aristocratic audiences. Mozart's opera premiered just two years later.

33. This is how Carter describes Bataille's "Story of the Eye" in her review of the text and its English translation ("Georges Bataille, Story of the Eye"). The scatological elements in Carter's "Puss-in-Boots" are more limited and playful; they include the old hag's loose bowels and the cat's repeated licking of his "hinder parts" (*Bloody Chamber*, 80).
34. Carter married Paul Carter in 1960 and not too happily either. She later married Mark Pearce, with whom she had a son, Alexander, in 1982.
35. Calinescu, *Rereading*, 1, quoted in Falconer's introduction to *Rereading*.
36. See Dupont-Escarpit, *Histoire d'un conte*.

Chapter 5

1. The photograph is titled "Where Romance Is Celebrated." It was part of the 2009 "What Will You Celebrate?" ad campaign for Disney Parks.
2. http://www.nt2099.com/J-ENT/news/asian-entertainment/japanese-entertainmentnews/mariya-yamada-and-toru-kusano-promote-disneys-sleeping-beauty-bluray-anddvd/ (accessed September 17, 2009). On Disney movies and culture in relation to the fairy-tale tradition, see Kay Stone's early essay "Things Walt Disney Never Told Us" and the more elaborate "Fairytales for Adults"; see also Jack Zipes's critical assessment of Disney's appropriations of the genre in "Breaking the Disney Spell" and "Once Upon a Time" as well as his more recent discussion of Disney's films in *The Enchanted Screen*.
3. Lieberman, "Some Day My Prince Will Come," 187.
4. Lieberman, "Some Day My Prince Will Come," 198.
5. Lieberman, "Some Day My Prince Will Come," 199.
6. See also Madonna Kolbenschlag's *Kiss Sleeping Beauty Good-Bye*, a feminist study rejecting feminine myths and models identified with Sleeping Beauty.
7. Even Andrew Lang refers to the tale as "The Sleeping Beauty" in *Perrault's Popular Tales*, li.
8. "The Snow Child" is titled "The Sleeping Beauty" in Carter's autograph and first typewritten draft. Typically, Carter heavily annotates her drafts, often adding quotes in English, French, or German. Here, she glosses in French: "snow: la blancheur invincible immaculée." In one of the drafts the first sentence of the text, "There are many ways of beginning this sto[ry]" (subsequently crossed out), hints at the Grimms' alternative beginning for "Schneewitchen." Carter annotates: "The dominant elements

in this brief and allusory narrative are: Cold; cruelty; the ominous presence of the raven; the flower that stings. Abstraction of desire. No love." The absence of love sets it against "The Lady of the House of Love." The motto is given as "If you love, or if you want to love, do not dream" (Robert Desnos). In the next draft Carter writes, "The countess can bear no children"; "All contain the same elements: snow, invincible, immaculate, desire, sterility."

9. The scene represents "the old fairy ill-wishing the infant princess, illustration, probably by J. D. Watson, from Routledge's Shilling Toy Book *The Sleeping Beauty in the Wood*, 1872" Reproduced in Opie and Opie, *Classic Fairy Tales*, 84.

10. The first occurrence of the word *ogre* in the *Oxford English Dictionary* has a short definition of a "man-eating giant" (1713), which originates from a translation of a French version of *The Arabian Nights*. The word was first used in Perrault's *Contes* (1697), and it probably derived from the Italian *orco*, meaning "demon" or "monster," from the Latin *Orcus* (god of the infernal regions), possibly by way of an Italian dialect. The footnote is also found in a slightly different form in the reprint of the edition of *Histories, or Tales of Past Times* "Englished by G. M. Gent.," which Carter also owned.

11. A creature of the night, the shape-shifting villain is also endowed with a peculiar sense of humor: Maleficent imagines an ironic alternative to Disney's fairy-tale romance ending in her crystal ball, where she keeps Prince Charming under lock and key, only to be released when he has become a decrepit old man who miserably drags himself to Sleeping Beauty's bedside. This undoubtedly influenced Gilbert and Gubar's revaluation of the character as a master plotter and artist figure in *The Madwoman in the Attic*.

12. Unlike pictures representing Venus in bed, naked and asleep, the curtains mentioned in Perrault's text function as a kind of teaser, both hiding and revealing. The first time curtains are mentioned is when the prince discovers the princess. The curtains are open to reveal the wonderful sight of the sleeping princess, who is fully dressed ("Elle était toute habillée," *Contes*, 136). The second time is when the prince and the princess go to bed together ("la Dame d'honneur leur tira le rideau," *Contes*, 136), when the possibility arises that she may not be so fully dressed or may soon come to be undressed, as the narrator hints at a night of lovemaking. Thus in the first instance Perrault is careful to suppress the erotic implications of the scene (which also distinguishes his own version of the tale from Basile's), and yet he subtly reintroduces the erotic element associated with the curtain the second time.

13. In contrast to the French medieval romance of *Perceforest* or the Italian *Pentamerone*, there is no sexual violence in Perrault's *conte* but only mutual love and desire expressed upon the awakening of the princess.

14. As mentioned in the Introduction, I use the G. M. translation, *Histories, or Tales of Past Times Told by Mother Goose* (*Histories* in the citations), unless specified otherwise.

15. The guardian dogs ("les gros mâtins de basse-cour," *Contes*, 134) disappear from the long list of the people, animals, and things put to sleep by the fairy. Likewise, the narrator's wry comment about the king's unnecessary measures to publish bans to protect his daughter's sleep ("Ces défenses n'étaient pas nécessaires," 134) is eliminated. Apart from avoiding redundant information (the word *défenses* is repeated twice in two consecutive sentences), Carter's translation tones down the king's ineffectual efforts to protect his daughter, which, as Van Elslande argues in "Parole d'enfant," turns "La Belle au bois dormant" into an allegory of the fragility of monarchic power.

16. Likewise, the parenthetical gloss on the magical boots of the dwarf who helps the good fairy, "c'était des bottes avec lesquelles on faisait sept lieues d'une seule enjambée" (*Contes*, 133), is eliminated, possibly because the explanation has become unnecessary for modern children familiar with "Puss in Boots." Further, the narrator's appreciative comment on the old pieces of music ("vieilles pièces," *Contes*, 136) played at dinner after the princess's awakening ("mais excellentes, quoiqu'il y eût près de cent ans qu'on ne les jouât plus," *Contes*, 136) is changed in Carter's translation to "the court orchestra played old tunes on violins and oboes they had not touched for a hundred years" (*Fairy Tales*, 66). As a result, the narrator's humorous comment on art and fashion (which is similar to that made previously about the heroine's high-collared dress like *his* grandmother's) is eliminated, because these asides are directed at the refined and fashion-conscious members of the salons but would be lost on modern-day children.

17. By eliminating the speculations of Perrault's narrator on the princess's sleep and actions, Carter's translation also tends to reduce the discrepancy between story and telling, seeming and being, appearances and reality, make-believe and truth, that is central to Perrault's text. Cutting the humorous metatextual parenthetical comment that raises the issue of the generic status of the text and its source exemplifies the simplification of the text for a new audience. In "The Lady of the House of Love" Carter (like Anne Sexton, Joyce Carol Oates, and Francesca Lia Block, among others) explores the possibility of a nightmarish or traumatic sleep.

18. Likewise, Carter's set phrase "dinner [is] ready" (*Fairy Tales*, 66) ("la viande était servie," *Contes*, 136) is reminiscent of family life, which emphasizes the familiarity and homeyness of the story. It is possible that Carter also understood *viande* (food) in the more contemporary sense of "meat" (even "flesh").

19. The idea of the ineffectual cure is taken up in "The Lady of the House of Love" when the naive and rational (or simply unimaginative) young man visiting Dracula's country plans to take the lady vampire he encounters to the ophthalmologist to cure her oversensitivity to light and to the dentist to arrange her teeth.

20. References to time past include the opening formula ("Il était une fois," *Contes*, 131; Carter's "Once upon a time," *Fairy Tales*, 57) and the association of fairies with a bygone era ("comme c'était la coutume des Fées en ce temps-là," *Contes*, 131; "according of the custom of those times," *Fairy Tales*, 57).

21. The disgruntled fairy stayed in her tower for "cinquante ans" (fifty years) (*Contes*, 131), but only for "fifteen years" (*Fairy Tales*, 58) in Carter's translation, which suggests that the old fairy is in fact the old woman in the tower, as in Martin Ware's illustration of the old spinner as a winged being. This fairy/old woman dichotomy probably reflects the pressure of the Grimms' tale, which conflates the two magical beings. See François, "Fées et *weise Frauen*," 268–69. As in her "Cinderella; or, The Little Glass Slipper," Carter (mis)translates the young fairy's "baguette" (magic wand) (*Contes*, 134) as "magic ring" (*Fairy Tales*, 62), perhaps because the French word indeed contains another word, *bague* (ring), in it. In light of the moral the magic ring of the fairy reinforces the ironic association of magic transformation with marriage in Carter's translation. It may also reflect the influence of folktales and Norse mythology as well as Richard Wagner's *Der Ring des Nibelungen* (which features a sleeping virgin, Brünnhilde, awakened by a courageous knight, Siegfried), W. M. Thackeray's *Rose*

and the Ring, and J. R. R. Tolkien's epic fantasy *The Lord of the Rings*, which was quite popular between the 1960s and 1980s.

22. The softening of the curse is visible in Carter's translation of "terrible don" (*Contes*, 132) as "unpleasant present" (*Fairy Tales*, 58). The ambivalent aspect of the alleviated curse retains only its positive side in Carter's truncated translation: "La bonne Fée qui lui avait sauvé la vie, *en la condamnant à dormir cent ans*" (*Contes*, 133; italics mine) becomes "the good fairy who saved her life" (*Fairy Tales*, 61). Although the king's measures to protect his daughter are inspired by fear of the old fairy's curse ("le *malheur* annoncé par la vieille," *Contes*, 132; italics mine), Carter's translation stresses the "comfort" (*Fairy Tales*, 60) brought by the intervention of the good fairy. The stress on happiness at the end of Carter's translation confirms the positive inflection given to the tale.

23. Carter's radio play *Vampirella* was first broadcast on BBC Radio 3 in 1976, and "The Lady of the House of Love" was originally published in the *Iowa Review* in 1975 (summer/autumn issue), although we know from Carter herself that the radio play came first. The Carter papers include a cutout of a voluptuous Vampirella by José Gonzalez, reproduced in Figure 5.3 (from the cover of the 1977 *Vampirella* special issue).

24. Angela Carter Papers, British Library, "The Bloody Chamber and Other Short Stories," 2 (MS 88999/1/34), creation date 1975–1979. The file contains two heavily annotated typewritten drafts and a lightly annotated fair copy, marked "For Chris" (n.d.).

25. Crofts, *Anagrams of Desire*, 40.

26. The performative power of language is a theme that runs through the history of the fairy tale. On the tension between spoken and written language and the metafictional potential of the story, see Haase, "Kiss and Tell." Carter also picks up on "the course of romance and redemption lying at the heart of the Sleeping Beauty tale" (Haase, "Kiss and Tell," 286).

27. The association of the two stereotypes of seductive femininity (passive vs. dangerous) is already present in fin de siècle fairy-tale-inspired literature. In her review of Pabst's *Pandora's Box* and von Sternberg's *Blue Angel*, titled "Femmes Fatales" (*New Society*, 1978), Carter reads this powerful myth of the twentieth century as a misogynistic fantasy that construes female sexual desire and independence as destructiveness, encapsulated in the statement of "the spineless sponger" in Wedekind's play, that "[a] woman blossoms for us precisely at the right moment to plunge a man into everlasting ruin; such is her natural destiny" (quoted by Carter, "Femmes Fatales," 353).

28. Already in Carter's *Infernal Desire Machines of Doctor Hoffman* (1972), the mayor's daughter Mary Anne is "a beautiful somnambulist" (56) living in a mansion surrounded by a garden overgrown with roses that sting and lash at Desiderio as he approaches the house. Mary Anne, "the beauty in the dreaming wood" (57) sleeps with the hero but does not wake from her slumber, and she mysteriously drowns like Ophelia. Michael Foreman's cover illustration for *Sleeping Beauty and Other Favourite Fairy Tales* (1982) also plays on this ambiguity as it depicts a fairy-tale knight on a white horse with a backdrop of forests shaped like a woman's profile (see Figure 1.4).

29. David Punter devotes a few perceptive pages to Carter as a modern Gothic writer in his classical study *The Literature of Terror*. He notes that "one of the epigraphs to

Carter's *Heroes and Villains*, which also has strong, and malevolent, connections with fairy-tale, is from Fiedler's *Love and Death in the American Novel*: 'The Gothic mode is essentially a form of parody, a way of assailing clichés by exaggerating them to the limit of grotesqueness'" (139).

30. See Punter, *Literature of Terror*, 100.

31. Symbolic birds abound in the romance tradition, representing the association of text and music and its metafictional implications. Another possible echo in Carter's text is to Ibsen's *Doll's House*, when Torvald Helmer affectionately (and somewhat patronizingly) calls Nora "my own little skylark." Like Nora, who disavows her prescribed role in patriarchal, bourgeois society, Vampirella and the Countess escape from their own cages, never to return. In *Nights at the Circus* (1984), Carter's unconventional heroine Fevvers is another avatar of the bird woman who works as an aerialist in a traveling circus, but this time she is gloriously fleshy, fleshly, strong, and independent.

32. For a discussion of Carter's reappropriation of horror writing from a feminist perspective, see Wisker, "Revenge of the Living Doll." In *Vampirella* the erotic appeal of a woman's corpse is celebrated by the necrophiliac Henri Blot, whose intervention serves as an ironic comment on the topos of the *belle endormie* embodied by the Sleeping Beauty figure. For a discussion of the persistence of the motif in contemporary art and its voyeuristic implications, see Wanning Harries's "Old Men and Comatose Virgins."

33. For a nuanced discussion of the significance of the medium of radio for a feminist poetics, see Crofts, *Anagrams of Desire*.

34. See Sceats, "Oral Sex," 110.

35. The Countess recovers the childlike innocence associated with fairy tales as children's stories when she experiences death as a soft and gentle falling asleep in the Hero's arms.

36. *Der Struwwelpeter* (1845) is a popular German children's book by Dr. Heinrich Hoffmann. It comprises ten illustrated and rhymed stories, mostly about children, that contain clear morals demonstrating the disastrous consequences of misbehavior typical of nineteenth-century pedagogy, although the comic side of the book should not be underestimated.

37. In "The Lady of the House of Love" the situation is even more ironic because the traditional roles of female vampire and male victim are reversed when the young hero kisses the finger of the Countess, who has cut herself on broken glass, and she bleeds to death. The conflation of the familiar motif of the deathly pricking of the finger with the life-giving kiss of the prince draws attention to the presence of horrific elements arousing a mixture of fear and fascination in traditional versions of the fairy tale.

38. Warner, *No Go the Bogeyman*, 33. The Scottish governess hired by Count Dracula to take care of his daughter comes from a family condemned for anthropophagy and necrophilia, and she ominously (and humorously) quotes the Ogre's lines from "Jack and the Beanstalk" when the naive Hero arrives at the castle: "Fee fi fo fum. I smell the blood of an Englishman" (Carter, *Yellow Sands*, 90).

39. See Brown, "Fairy Tales," 349.

40. The threatening atmosphere, violence, and transgressive behavior present in earlier versions of the tale known as "Sleeping Beauty" were considerably toned down over

the course of time, to the point of being reduced to the stereotype of a sleeping girl waiting for Prince Charming to kiss her awake.

41. "Au bout de cent ans, le Fils du Roi . . . étant allé à la chasse de ce côté là, demanda ce que c'était que ces Tours qu'il voyait au-dessus d'un grand bois fort épais; chacun lui répondit selon qu'il en avait *ouï parler*. Les uns disaient que c'était un vieux Château où il revenait des Esprits; les autres que tous les Sorciers de la contrée y faisaient leur sabbat. La plus commune opinion était qu'un Ogre y demeurait, et que là il emportait tous les enfants qu'il pouvait attraper, pour les pouvoir manger à son aise, et sans qu'on le pût suivre, ayant seul le pouvoir de se faire un passage à travers le bois" (*Contes*, 134–35; italics mine). The stories within the story are marked as orally transmitted folktales and, literally, hearsay.

42. The ritual dinner at birth finds its source in ancient rituals, myths, and beliefs. See Ballestra-Puech, *Les Parques*, and Hennard Dutheil de la Rochère and Dasen, *Des Fata aux fées*.

43. The predatory queen clearly inspires Carter's hungry female vampires prowling around the castle (let alone the werewolves that haunt *The Bloody Chamber*): "On moonless nights, her keeper lets [the Countess] out into the garden. This garden, an exceedingly sombre place, bears a strong resemblance to a burial ground and all the roses her dead mother planted have grown up into a huge, spiked wall that incarcerates her in the castle of her inheritance. When the back door opens, the Countess will sniff the air and howl. She drops, now, on all fours. Crouching, quivering, she catches the scent of her prey" (*Bloody Chamber*, 95).

44. Fanzines are amateur-produced magazines written for a subculture of enthusiasts devoted to a particular interest. In this case of vampire stories, the fanzines are called horrorzines (or horror zines).

45. The cult comic-strip *Vampirella*, published by Warren Publishing, tells of the adventures of a sexy female vampire. This black-and-white magazine (except for the lurid covers), in the style of horror comics, ran from 1969 to 1983. See http://www.vampilore.co.uk/history01.html (accessed June 6, 2011).

46. 46. Carter surely had in mind Charles Baudelaire's poems "Le vampire" and "Les métamorphoses du vampire," one of the "pièces condamnées" from *Les fleurs du mal* (1857, 1861).

Chapter 6

1. Jeanne-Marie Leprince de Beaumont's "Le Prince Chéri" and "La Belle et la Bête" first appeared in *Le Magasin des enfants, ou Dialogues d'une sage gouvernante avec ses élèves de la première distinction*, published in London in 1756. As the full title indicates, the book includes biblical stories, elements of geography, fables, and moral tales framed by conversations between a governess and her female pupils. The fairy tales were anthologized in *Le Cabinet des fées*, edited by Charles-Joseph de Mayer. Because Jean Marie Robain's edition contains a biography of the author and useful historical documents apart from the fairy tales themselves, I have used his *Madame Leprince de Beaumont intime, avec ses principaux contes et des documents inédits* (*Beaumont* in the citations).

2. We can draw specific thematic, visual, and aesthetic parallels between Cocteau's *Beauty and the Beast* and Carter's "Tiger's Bride," including the embrace of a fantasy

NOTES TO CHAPTER 6   335

world to escape a mean and disappointing human reality; the depiction of the monster as a humanized figure with a tiger's head (stripes, snub nose) and his nature as a hunter, carnivore, and predator who can barely control his killer's instinct (hence the temple to Diana in the garden, the dead deer, and the Beast's urging Beauty to lock her door at night); the fusion between the fairy tale and the fantastic (the enchanted palace open to the winds, with no clear boundary between inside and outside); the presence of animated objects, such as the living bedcover, which is not unlike the fur collar that turns back to sables in Carter's text, and Beauty's earrings, which turn to water, inverting the motif of the tear turning into a diamond in Cocteau's film; and desire depicted as a complex mix of attraction, fear, and repulsion, which Carter also explores in "The Bloody Chamber."

3. Carter's translations of Beaumont's *contes* appear to have been done immediately after Perrault's, if we consider the precise intertextual echoes found in the rewritings. Carter even corrects a mistake she had made in "Little Red Riding Hood," when the word *ruelle* appears again in "Beauty and the Beast": "Le marchand . . . fut bien étonné de le trouver [i.e. le coffre rempli d'or] à la ruelle de son lit" is translated as "In the space between the bed and the wall." "The Courtship of Mr. Lyon" first appeared in *Vogue* (U.K.) in 1979 before being included in *The Bloody Chamber*. Carter's 1977 journal contains a number of bibliographic references related to "Beauty and the Beast," including Madame de Villeneuve's *La jeune Amériquaine et les contes marins* (1740); *Le Cabinet des Fées: Magasin des enfants* (1756); Mary Elisabeth Storer's *La mode des contes de fées* (1928); *Le cabinet des fées*, edited by André Bay (1955), with the indication "very selective, in 2 volume, 17th c story-tellers only"; Todorov's *Fantastic* (1973); *Beauty and the Beast Anthology*, December 1878; and an article by Barchilon titled "Beauty and the Beast: From Myth to Fairy Tale," published in the *Psychoanalytic Review* in 1959.

4. Haffenden, "Angela Carter," 83.

5. Carter's mannerist aesthetics could even be said to build on Beaumont's style, filtered through Cocteau's fairy-tale film. Partly as a result of her early fascination with surrealism, Carter was familiar with the haunting visual images and creepy mix of the sensual and the sinister in Cocteau's movie, which openly relates the fairy tale to adaptations of Gothic literature (notably Poe) to the screen. The film barely hides the sexual subtext of the fairy tale (which hints at the complex nature of desire) and emphasizes the strange, threatening, and marvelous atmosphere of the palace with its disorienting sensory perceptions.

6. See Monnier, "Naissance et renaissance," which shows how Carter fuses the two intertexts in "The Courtship of Mr. Lyon."

7. For a history of the fairy tale focused on the literary tradition, see Wanning Harries, *Twice Upon a Time*; and for a broader cultural perspective on the role of female storytellers and writers on the development of the genre, see Marina Warner's classic *From the Beast to the Blonde*. Lewis Seifert has discussed Beaumont's "infantilization" of the French *conte merveilleux* for children in "Beaumont and the Infantilization of the Fairy Tale."

8. In *The Classic Fairy Tales* the Opies compare d'Aulnoy's "Le mouton" (The Ram) to "La Belle et la Bête." Carter makes no mention of this animal-groom tale, preferring the connection through feline characters. She also contradicts the Opies' negative as-

sessment of Beaumont's style as "plain" and "colloquial" and praises its elegance and psychological subtlety instead.

9. Connections with Charlotte Brontë's *Jane Eyre* are also suggested. We know that Carter admired Brontë, whom she described in the introduction to the Virago edition of *Jane Eyre* (1990) as "a young woman of genius" (v). In that introduction Carter also spells out the fairy-tale intertexts in the novel as indicating the continuing presence of the fairy tale in literary history. Carter was among the first critics to stress the pressure of the fairy-tale genre on a novel, which was long seen as a classic realist text with elements of the Gothic.

10. This depiction of Beaumont is very much in the spirit of what Virginia Woolf and later Elaine Showalter (and more generally second-wave feminists) recommended to women eager to create (or restore) a sense of continuity and literary genealogy with like-minded literary foremothers. Specifically, Carter's homage to a female predecessor is consistent with the stated mission of Virago Press, with whom Carter had a long-term collaboration. See Showalter, *Literature of Their Own*.

11. At the time, Beaumont was seen as a progressive writer promoting the rights of women: "Im 18. Jh war sie vor allem als Vorkämpferin für Frauenrechte in Frankreich und England sowie als Pädagogin bekannt" (Zipes, 1996, 922).

12. Quoted in Robain, *Beaumont*, 37. A complex and paradoxical character, Madame de Beaumont had a passionate love affair with a shady and opportunistic Frenchman known as Tyrrell during her stay in England, despite her moral and religious convictions and in contradiction to her repeated warnings against opportunistic seducers.

13. As Beaumont puts it in her *Magasin des adolescentes*: "Il ne faut jamais croire aucune chose parce qu'on l'a lue ou entendue, mais parce qu'elle est conforme à notre raison. Je prétends donc que vous examinerez tout ce que je vous dirai et que vous me contredirez quand vous croirez avoir de bonnes raisons pour le faire. Vous me les direz, ces raisons. J'aurai ainsi la liberté de vous représenter les miennes et l'on croira celle dont les raisons sont les meilleures" (quoted in Robain, *Beaumont*, 46). ("One should never believe something because one has read or heard it, but because it conforms to one's reason. I therefore encourage you to examine whatever I will say to you, and you will contradict me if you have good reason to do so. You will explain it to me, and I will then be at liberty to formulate mine, and we will believe the one who has presented the best argument.")

14. Carter fundamentally seeks to reclaim "subgenres" and trace their influence on more culturally valorized genres and traditions.

15. The connections between the fairy tale and Gothic fiction are also explored in "The Lady of the House of Love."

16. Carter parenthetically notes that Perrault's Ricky with the Tuft is *not* transformed at the end of the tale but remains "as ugly as he ever was"; the moral rationalizes fairy-tale magic through the transformative power of love on subjective perception.

17. Carter's translation of "Le Prince Chéri" seems to be based on the French text by Jeanne Marie Leprince de Beaumont anthologized in *Le Cabinet des fées* (41 vols., 1785–1789). The tale also appears in Andrew Lang's *Blue Fairy Book* (1889), with the title "Prince Darling."

18. A similar point is made in a more convoluted fashion in the French source: "On n'est

point innocent quand on refuse d'exécuter vos volontés, reprit le confident; mais je suppose que vous commettiez une injustice, il vaut bien mieux qu'on vous en accuse que d'apprendre qu'il est quelquefois permis de vous manquer de respect et de vous contredire" (Robain, *Beaumont*, 194).

19. Other allusions to the Grimms' *Märchen* include the girl's character, the rags-to-riches plot, and the magical ring (in Carter's translation of the tale). In "The Courtship of Mr. Lyon" birds of paradise reappear as decorative motifs on the wallpaper of Mr. Lyon's Palladian house.

20. Angela Carter Papers, British Library, MS 88899/1/33.

21. Note that wolves have already appeared in Beaumont's tale, in the forests surrounding the magic castle: "When night approached, he thought that either he would die of hunger and cold or else be eaten by the wolves he could hear howling all around him" (Carter, *Sleeping Beauty*, 47). Beauty is afraid to be eaten (and even fattened for that purpose) by the Beast when she arrives at the castle. Animals hold a special place in the Beast's enchanted world. For example, Beauty's father's horse is taken care of when they eventually get to the castle, and from then on knows exactly his way to and from the castle. Carter's translation even emphasizes this aspect by conveying "le pauvre animal, qui mourait de faim, se jeta dessus avec beaucoup d'avidité" by "the poor, famished animal at once began to munch hay and oats *that looked as though they might have been specially prepared for it*" (48; italics mine).

22. The Opies also note that Beaumont's tale was included in *Tabart's Collection of Popular Stories for the Nursery* (1804) and inspired Charles Lamb's "poetical *Beauty and the Beast; or, A Rough Outside with a Gentle Heart*, published on William Godwin's behalf in 1811" (*Classic Fairy Tales*, 138). They also draw attention to the reception of the tale in the popular theater and the pantomime tradition: "It has been the inspiration of numerous pantomimes and melodramas, such as *Beauty and the Beast; or, The Magic Rose*, produced at the Royal Coburg Theatre in 1819, and Planché's *Beauty and the Beast* at the Theatre Royal, Covent Garden, 1841" (138). The adaptation of the tale on the popular stage clearly inspires some of the illustrations included in *The Classic Fairy Tales*. In her notes Carter also lists James Robinson Planché's play version of "Beauty and the Beast." The prolific and popular playwright was famous for his productions of "fairy extravaganzas" drawing on comedy, pantomime, farce, melodrama, and opera.

23. *La Belle et la Bête* (1946) was directed by the poet and filmmaker Jean Cocteau; it starred Jean Marais as the Beast and Josette Day as Beauty. This version adds a subplot involving Belle's suitor Avenant, who schemes to kill the Beast and steal his riches. When Avenant enters the magic pavilion that is the source of Beast's power, he is struck by an arrow and turns into the dying Beast: the curse ends when Belle declares her love and Avenant returns as the Prince. The conflation of the Beast and his antagonist makes the happy ending particularly ambiguous, because the Beast ends up being the suitor Beauty had previously rejected in favor of the Beast. An added layer of irony is that the monstrous Beast was played by Cocteau's lover, the actor and sex symbol Jean Marais, reputed for his handsome looks. The film was praised for its surreal quality and its masterful use of existing movie technology to evoke a feeling of magic and enchantment. The association of the fairy-tale film with surrealism and the pathos of the lonely and melancholic Beast influenced Carter's appreciation of Beaumont's text.

24. Probably *Beauty Becomes the Beast*, a B-movie directed by Vivienne Dick; see http://www.imdb.com/title/tt0074193/ (accessed October 26, 2012).
25. Carter is referring to Betsey Hearne's *Beauty and the Beast: Visions and Revisions of an Old Tale*. The inclusion of post-1977 versions of the tale suggests that Carter used her journal as a notebook more than a diary.
26. Warner, *From the Beast*, 312.
27. On postmodern conceptions of the human-animal boundary, see Steiner, *Anthropocentrism*, esp. ch. 9. Jacques Derrida attempted to deconstruct the separation and hierarchical relation between human and animal by arguing that "any border between the animal and the *Dasein* of speaking man [is] unassignable" (quoted in Steiner, *Anthropocentrism*, 220). Carter's "Tiger's Bride" suggests an inner kinship between Beauty and Beast, which is partly cultural (women being assigned an inferior status under patriarchy) and partly a recovery of a primordial natural state underneath the veneer of civilization. Carter pursues these reflections in "Wolf-Alice."
28. The illustration alludes to the ancient fable of Cupid and Psyche in Apuleius's *Metamorphoses*, where Psyche's sisters claim that her invisible husband who comes to visit her during the night is in fact a monstrous serpent; in Villeneuve's version the sisters' lie comes true, as it were, because the Beast becomes a big scaly monster.
29. The sheer number of illustrations reproduced by the Opies' in their *Classic Fairy Tales* indicates a genuine fascination for the Beast: He is a larger-than-life hairy, chicken-legged, wolf-headed, and long-snouted animal standing upright and wearing a kind of dress in Gordon Browne's engraving (1886) (*Classic Fairy Tales*, 146) and a mix between a boar and a bear in an 1813 edition of the tale (144). Another illustration by Eleanor Vere Boyle (1875) represents a modest-looking Beauty at a table with a huge black sea lion (pun on the lion?), set in an Italian Renaissance mansion (149).
30. In "The Bloody Chamber" the bride's mother shoots a man-eating tiger during her "adventurous girlhood in Indo-China" (*Bloody Chamber*, 7) and is therefore well-equipped to defend her daughter against another predator who looks—and smells—like a beast: "I could see the dark, leonine shape of his head and my nostrils caught a whiff of the opulent male scent of leather and spice" (8). Framed by his silver-streaked "dark mane" (8), his face evokes a mask: "And sometimes that face ... with the heavy eyelids folded over the eyes that always disturbed me by their absolute absence of light, seemed to be like a mask, as if his real face ... lay underneath this mask" (9). The imprint of his "strangler's fingers" (28) is also found on the opera singer's neck. Conversely, the Beast in "The Tiger's Bride" is wearing a real mask to hide his animal face, and he disguises his pungent smell with perfume: "The Beast not much different from any other man, although he wears a mask with a man's face painted most beautifully on it. Oh, yes, a beautiful face; but one with too much formal symmetry of feature to be entirely human" (53).
31. Carter's 1977 journal, Angela Carter Papers, British Library, MS 88899/1/96.
32. The translation suppresses an allusion to sexuality as belonging to the animal side of humanity that needs to be controlled to achieve full human status. When Chéri is tempted to enter the "Palais de la Volupté," he resists and is rewarded by a metamorphosis that signals his progress toward humanity. The perversions of the sexual instinct under the guise of high culture are explored in "The Bloody Chamber." In her notes Carter also mentions Barchilon's "Beauty and the Beast." Barchilon reviews the

best-known versions of the tale from Apuleius to Basile, Melle Bernard's and Perrault's versions of "Riquet à la Houppe," and Villeneuve and Beaumont, noting the complex mix of realism and fantasy and arguing that the story serves to articulate concerns about sex because it "presents the humanization of the beast and the 'bestialization' of his female companion" (27).

33. The title of Carter's short story also echoes another tradition of monster-human interactions: *Frankenstein*, and its sequel *Frankenstein's Bride*, as the modern myth par excellence of tragic monsters aspiring to a recognition of their humanity.

34. Further on Carter translates, "Then, quite suddenly, the merchant lost everything. No money was left. All he possessed now was a little house far away in the country" (*Sleeping Beauty*, 46) ("Tout d'un coup le marchand perdit son bien, et il ne lui resta qu'une petite maison de campagne bien loin de la ville," Robain, *Beaumont*, 177). The familiar language register is perceptible in such lexical choices as "high-faluting" ("orgueil"), "gewgaws" ("bagatelles"), and "show off" ("se distinguer"). Markers of orality are found in the emphatic punctuation that anticipates oral delivery: "Still nobody to be seen!" ("Où il ne trouva personne"). The lexical choices also imply a child reader, as in "Now she's got Daddy into this awful fix and look at her, she's not even sorry!" ("Elle va causer la mort de notre père et elle ne pleure pas!"). The oralized style is also used by the narrator in addresses to the reader, as in the passage where she intervenes to explain why Beauty asks for a rose: "Don't think Beauty cared so much about roses" ("Ce n'est pas que la belle se souciât d'une rose"). The emphatic punctuation is another clear marker of orality, such as question marks, exclamation marks, and even onomatopoeia: "No!"; "Still nobody to be seen!"; "Whoosh!" The use of idiomatic phrases, such as "the high and mighty" or she "hid her light under a bushel," emphasize the familiar dimension of this favorite fairy tale.

35. The possibility arises that Beaumont's story, although based on Villeneuve's, also amalgamates elements from Perrault's "Cinderella" and "Bluebeard," with the important difference that unlike Bluebeard, the Beast is an *honnête homme* underneath his monstrous appearance. Verbal echoes include the Beast's threat to Beauty's father, which echoes Bluebeard's threat to his disobedient wife: "Je ne vous donne qu'un quart d'heure pour demander pardon à Dieu" ("I give you a quarter of an hour in which to prepare to meet your maker"). In "La Barbe bleue" the time for repentance is "un demi quart d'heure," often translated as "a quarter of an hour" (as in Carter's "Bluebeard"). Another intertext activated by Beaumont (and even more deliberately by Carter) is "Little Red Riding Hood": Beauty's sisters hope that the monster will devour her if she disobeys him ("peut-être qu'elle la dévorera"; "perhaps . . . he will gobble her up"). The association of "Beauty and the Beast" with "Bluebeard" is also found in the chapter "The Animal-Groom Cycle of Fairy Tales" in Bettelheim's *Uses of Enchantment* (277–310). Bettelheim's reading of the tales as variations on the theme of sexual initiation echoes Carter's explicit aim to foreground the sexual subtext of the fairy tales in her rewritings and their order of appearance in *The Bloody Chamber*. They even seem to respond more specifically to Bettelheim's observation that "we are left in the dark about the feelings of the heroine" (*Uses of Enchantment*, 277), although Carter clearly questions the Oedipal interpretation offered by the psychoanalyst. Bettelheim's mention of a Bantu folktale in which "a crocodile is restored to its human form by a maiden who licks its face" (285), however, may have inspired the substitution of licking for kissing in "The Tiger's Bride" and "Wolf-Alice."

NOTES TO CHAPTER 6

36. The reference to gambling in Carter's "Tiger's Bride" may nod to Beaumont's marriage to a compulsive gambler, whom she eventually divorced (Robain, *Beaumont*, 34–35).
37. The stress on Beauty's generosity in Carter's translation ties in with a modern discourse on values and alertness to social and gender inequality. The class-conscious sisters are contrasted with Beauty's indifference to social status and material possessions. The laziness of the privileged classes is contrasted with the peasants' "till[ing] the soil with their own hands to scratch a living."
38. *Le dictionnaire de l'Académie française* (1694) defines *vertu* as "une habitude de l'âme, qui la porte à faire le bien, et à fuir le mal. Vertu chrétienne, vertu morale, vertu intellectuelle, vertus naturelles, vertus acquises," and so on. The modern meaning retains the idea of virtue as the disposition to do good and avoid evil, and chastity for a woman. Although Carter avoids the word and its rather dated associations with chastity and religious dogma, she keeps the ideas of "being good" in the sense of loving (parents, animals) and strength of character as a key moral quality (i.e., moral courage and the ability to confront hardship with calm and determination).
39. These are the twin motivations of the Marquis's bride in "The Bloody Chamber."
40. This is what Bruno Bettelheim responds to in his interpretation of "Beauty and the Beast" as a tale about Oedipal attachment and the need to grow up in order to confront the sexuality embodied by the Beast. Carter clearly takes another direction in her reading of the tale.
41. Note the shift from "château" to "palace," which announces Mr. Lyon's Palladian house, and the grand but decaying Italian palazzo of "The Tiger's Bride."
42. Note that Robinson's illustration is taken from a collection of fairy tales attributed to Perrault that also includes "Beauty and the Beast": Perrault, *Old-Time Stories*.
43. This reflects Beaumont's ambivalence toward the *mondain* world and its reception dinners, which she depended on for her living and reputation but whose *faux-semblants* she described in an image reminiscent of Perrault's metaphor of the arcane book of spells that one must learn to decipher (in his moral to "La Barbe bleue"). Beaumont declared that she did not have much taste for "this country of illusions and enchantments" (Robain, *Beaumont*, 49; translation mine).
44. The same thing happens in "Bluebeard" with more dramatic consequences, when the bride changes her mind about the monstrosity of Bluebeard after being entertained at one of his country houses; the master's beard, she reflects, is not so blue after all. Another, even more obvious, analogue is with Perrault's ugly Prince in "Ricky with the Tuft."
45. Madame de Villeneuve's Beast is less shy about the sexual implications of their union: He asks Beauty if she is willing to sleep with him.
46. Here again, Carter translates the fairy's wand (*baguette*) as "ring."
47. Carter's translation suggests that the Prince Charming figure is banal and expected at the end of the twentieth century, whereas Beaumont nods at her classic source, namely, Apuleius's *Metamorphoses*, which contains the tale of Amor and Psyche.
48. I am indebted to Marie Emilie Walz for the title of this subsection, which pays homage to Marina Warner's landmark study *From the Beast to the Blonde*.
49. The Marquis tellingly quotes Baudelaire, who famously declared in *Mon coeur mis à nu:*

journal intime, that woman is abominable because she belongs to nature: "La femme est le contraire du Dandy. Donc elle doit faire horreur. / La femme a faim, et elle veut manger; soif, et elle veut boire. / Elle est en rut, et elle veut être f. . . Le beau mérite! / La femme est *naturelle*, c'est-à-dire abominable. / Aussi est-elle toujours vulgaire, c'est-à-dire le contraire du Dandy."

50. Tigers, literary and otherwise, roam in Carter's fiction. They are a source of awe and fascination as an embodiment of the wild forces of nature, and they often give rise to a reflection on the nature-culture, prey-predator divide (rather than on good and evil, as in Blake's "The Tyger," which Carter greatly admired). As she puts it in "The Tiger's Bride": "The tiger will never lie down with the lamb; he acknowledges no pact that is not reciprocal. The lamb must learn to run with the tigers" (*Bloody Chamber*, 64). The tiger is usually an occasion to reflect "on the tigerness" of human beings and the "humanity" of tigers (see Almansi, "Alchemist's Cave," 220). See also Atwood, "Running with the Tigers." Almansi notes that tigers also feature in Carter's *Nights at the Circus* and in "Lizzie with the Tiger" in Carter's *American Ghosts* (Almansi, "Alchemist's Cave").

51. See Crunelle-Vanrigh, "Logic"; and Bacchilega, *Postmodern Fairy Tales*, 89–102.

52. In her 1977 journal, Carter lists "The Blue Bird," "Beauty & the Beast," "The White Cat," "The Yellow Dwarf," and "The Wonderful Sheep" (with a question mark), as potential tales to be included in a second book of fairy tales.

53. "The Tiger's Bride," formerly titled "La Bestia" and also "The Lion's Bride (Venetian version)" was written circa 1978 (Angela Carter Papers, British Library, MS 88899/1/34).

54. This idea had already been explored in Carter's *Infernal Desire Machines of Doctor Hoffman*.

Chapter 7

1. This hybrid collection contains seven texts that Angela Carter completed before her death, including an unfinished draft for a screenplay, essays, and short stories. As Susannah Clapp observes in the introduction to *American Ghosts*, "These stories, written late in Angela's life," navigate the "divide between old and new ways of story-telling and celebration" (ix), like the ships of Christmas in "The Ghost Ships." All explore "the infinite intercouplings of possible texts" and genres, to borrow Carter's own description of pantomime in "In Pantoland" (103).

2. Carter, *Shaking a Leg*, 465. "The German Legends of the Brothers Grimm" was originally published in *The Guardian* in 1981.

3. In her notes for "Ashputtle *or* The Mother's Ghost," Carter mentions a photocopy of "Ashputtle" from Ralph Manheim's *Grimms' Tales for Young and Old* (83–89).

4. Karen Seago, in "Nursery Politics," sees this merging of the French and German traditions in the course of the nineteenth century as "one of the most important features of the tale's reception in England" (180).

5. It is tempting to see in Angela Carter's first retelling, "The Burned Child," a shift (even a pun?) from the scarfed portrait of Cinderella to the scar-faced Ashputtle, "charred, like a stick half burned and picked off the fire" (*American Ghosts*, 117).

6. See Aarne, *Types of the Folktale*. Stith Thompson published an influential study, *The*

Folktale, in 1977. See also Dundes, *Cinderella*, which contains the most popular versions of the Cinderella tale by Basile, Perrault, and Grimm but also a number of classic essays on the tale, including R. D. Jameson's "Cinderella in China," Paul Delarue's "From Perrault to Walt Disney: The Slipper of Cinderella," and Anna Birgitta Rooth's' "Tradition Areas in Eurasia."

7. Carter cites Andrew Lang's *Perrault's Popular Tales* in *The Fairy Tales of Charles Perrault* (1977). In his abundant notes Lang refers to the ritual of bodily mutilation to fit beauty standards in the Chinese custom of binding young girls' feet. In her introduction to *The Virago Book of Fairy Tales* Carter highlights the multiple versions of the tale: "The basic plot elements of the story we know as 'Cinderella' occur everywhere from China to Northern England" (xv).

8. On a more personal note, we recall that Carter described herself as a tall, big-boned woman with large feet and saw herself as a "Glumdalclitch" in Japan (Carter, "A Souvenir of Japan" repr. in *Burning your Boats*, 31). In another essay, she relates her poor body image to her anorexia during adolescence (see Carter, "Fat Is Ugly").

9. Like Conrad in *Heart of Darkness* or James George Frazer in *The Golden Bough* (1890–1906/1915), Andrew Lang reads into folklore survival of our "savage" past. For Carter, however, "there's no core, or point of origin, or ur-story 'underneath,' just a continuous interweaving of texts" (Sage, "Angela Carter: The Fairy Tale," 74). Stephen Benson also observes that it is this complex, ongoing interweaving that troubles any genealogical approach to deciphering the palimpsestic relationships in Carter's texts (*Contemporary Fiction*, 34).

10. The Opies observe about Cinderella that "in these deeply-penetrating tales, fairy godmothers do not suddenly materialize, waving wands that make everything come right. The power of godmothers is limited. Sometimes all they are able to offer is advice. They are never able, it seems, to change a worldly situation, or alter a wicked heart" (*Classic Fairy Tales*, 14).

11. Some degree of plotting is required in the seduction strategy engineered by the Fairy Godmother. Cinderella's mysterious identity and her leaving the ball unexpectedly add to the suspense but also to the romance element of the story and hence enhance the heroine's desirability. Cinderella's desirability is also linked to the dissimulation of her identity as a source of comedy with her stepsisters.

12. Furetière's *Dictionnaire universel* (1690) simply indicates that the figurative sense is to instruct: "Se dit figurément en Morale, et signifie, instruire et disposer à faire quelque chose. Ce précepteur a bien *dressé* cet écolier. . . . On le dit par extension des animaux."

13. See Haase, "Feminist Fairy Tale Scholarship."

14. The mutilation of the girls seems to activate verbal echoes of "Three Blind Mice," an old (and equally cruel) nursery rhyme where the farmer's wife cuts off the tails of the blind mice "with a carving knife."

15. According to Marc Escola, Perrault's second moral cautions against the truth value of all morals (*Commentaires*, 128).

16. Following Samber, Newbery, and Barchilon, Carter associates Perrault's *conte* with English nursery tales, an editorial phenomenon that characterizes the reception of Perrault's collection.

17. In her journal for 1977 (Angela Carter Papers, British Library, MS 88899/1/96),

Carter notes under "cosmetics" that "the idea of concealment suggests that there is something to conceal"; she lists various ointments used in the seventeenth and eighteenth centuries, including lethal ones like arsenic and white lead. Under "patches," often used to conceal blemishes and smallpox scars, she writes: "The wearers of these patches must have appeared as perpetual participants in a fancy-dress ball."

18. Cinderella's charm ties in with dominant feminist opinion encapsulated in Adorno's statement, quoted by Carter, that "the feminine character, and the idea of femininity on which it is modelled, are products of masculine society" ("Wound in the Face," 110) and with Carter's personal interest in fashion as reflected in her cultural criticism. See, in particular, Carter's 1975 article "The Wound in the Face" for *New Society*, where she reflects on "the nature of the imagery of cosmetics" (109) and observes that "the face of the seventies matches the fashion in clothes that have dictated some of its features, and is directly related to the social environment which produces it" (109). "Designers," she observes, "are trying to make us cripple our feet again with high-heeled shoes and make us trail long skirts in dogshit. The re-introduction of rouge is part of this regression" (109–10). Carter goes on to argue that "the basic theory of cosmetics is that they make a woman beautiful," so that the fleeting fashion for red eyeshadow and black lipstick seems to suggest a possible form of liberation "from the burden of having to look beautiful" (111). See also Carter's review of David Kunzle's "Fashion and Fetishisms" (1982) and "Roland Barthes: The Fashion System" (1985) collected in *Shaking a Leg*.

19. In her preparatory notes Carter comments on the namelessness of the Grimms' heroine. She observes that at the beginning of the story, "Ashputtle has no name; she is her mother's daughter and that is all. It is the stepmother who gives her the name, Ashputtle, removes her status as a daughter." Bettelheim disapproves of the English equivalent of the French Cendrillon as Cinderella because it loses the reference to ash and mourning.

20. As in earlier chapters, I have used the translation by G. M., *Histories, or Tales of Past Times Told by Mother Goose* (1802) (*Histories* in the text).

21. In Perrault's *conte* the nasty stepsister is "malhonnête" (i.e., not in keeping with the rules of civility and probity) in spite of her noble birth; that is, she is lacking in education and the proper behavior that goes with it (politeness, courtesy, and virtue).

22. In the "Miscellaneous Fairy Tale Material" file (Angela Carter Papers, British Library, MS 88899/1/82), Carter muses on the strangeness of the Grimms' version of the Cinderella story. She mentions Ralph Manheim's translation "based on the original ms" of the Grimms' *Kinder-und Hausmärchen, Tales for Young and Old*, in the Gollancz edition of 1978, which she quotes verbatim in her own rewriting. In her notes Carter adds, "Distinction between *lit.* products—Hans Anderson [sic], Oscar Wilde; and folklore." This echoes Manheim's understanding of the German tales in the preface to his volume, where he insists on their being "faithful" to their oral sources. In his turn, Manheim describes his attempt to restore the strange, irrational, and unseemly elements that were "cleaned up" when the tales were adapted for the nursery and to convey the many tones and voices of the individual storytellers, whether "mysterious, elegiac, hushed-and-frightening, poetic, whimsical, rowdy, solemnly or mock-solemnly moralizing, and so on" (*Grimms' Tales*, 1). Manheim also muses on the inadequacy of the term *fairy tale* to designate the Grimms' *Märchen*, hence his preference for "tales"

in the title of his own translation and his choice of "Ashputtle" as the title for the tale in translation.

23. The first retelling reads like a follow-up to Sandra Gilbert and Susan Gubar's classic analysis of Snow White in *The Madwoman in the Attic* (1979). The absent father is equally at issue, but Carter shifts from a symbolic reading of the mirror as ruling over female beauty to women's actual access to wealth, in keeping with her feminist and materialist sensibility.

24. Gilbert and Gubar's *Madwoman in the Attic* famously begins with a critique of "Snow White" that arguably informs Carter's own response to "Ashputtle." Gilbert and Gubar's reading of "Snow White" as a paradigmatic text of patriarchy constitutes a sort of prelude to the rest of the book, which shows how Victorian literature by women negotiates dominant representations reducing them to domestic "angels" or wicked witches. Note that in her interview with John Haffenden, Carter observes that her "fiction is very often a kind of literary criticism, which is something I've started to worry about quite a lot" (Haffenden, "Angela Carter," 79).

25. "An angel in the house of myth, Snow White is not only a child but (as female angels always are) childlike, docile, submissive, the heroine of a life that has *no story*" (Gilbert and Gubar, *Madwoman in the Attic*, 39). Carter literalizes the figure of Snow White in "The Snow Child," which is set "in midwinter" and replays the motifs of "sewing, snow, blood, enclosure associated with key themes in female lives (hence in female writing)" (37).

26. The idea of "sharing" a man across two generations of women is also present in "Donkey-Skin," although in this case it is the king who lusts after his own daughter, raising the taboo of incest. This connection is made by most commentators on the tale (including Bettelheim), and we remember that Carter also translated "Peau d'Âne" (its prose version) into English.

27. In the introduction to the second edition of *The Madwoman in the Attic*, Gilbert notes that "mothering, motherhood, and mothers: as I look back on the years when we were researching and writing *The Madwoman*, I realize that maternity was always somehow central to our project" (Gilbert and Gubar, *Madwoman in the Attic*, xxii). Sage perceptively notes that Carter "wanted to *secularise* the art of writing, in the last analysis, and for her this was bound up with the demystification of motherhood which she undertook with such cruel gusto in the 1970s. . . . Demystify motherhood, and you abolish the last hiding-place for eternity" (*Flesh and the Mirror*, 18). See also Nicole Ward Jouve's essay "Mother Is a Figure of Speech" in the same collection.

28. See Verdier, "De ma mère l'Oye à Mother Goose," 185–86.

29. Carter's strategy therefore distinguishes itself both from Perrault's *conte* and from the moralizing reception of the genre in England. Like Perrault's female contemporaries, Carter liked to posture as a modern fairy drawing from personal experience to advise and "instruct" the young girls to whom she addressed her translations and the older women for whom she destined her rewritings. Sage and Benson have commented on Carter's posture as fairy godmother/Mother Goose figure. Benson observes, "If the adoption of the role of Mother Goose was in part a deliberate siding with the non-Bloomian territories of literature (and with a distinctly un-Bloomian conception of literary tradition and influence) and, concomitantly, with a performative, even pantomimic notion of authorship, it was also an unequivocally feminist strategy, dem-

onstrated in Carter's editing of the two Virago books of fairy tales" (*Contemporary Fiction*, 47).

30. Ware also plays a game with the reader in *The Fairy Tales of Charles Perrault*. In the preceding tale, "The Fairies," the bad sister spits frogs and snakes (79). The visual echoes are therefore deliberate, suggesting the conjuring power of language, where words turn into things and images.

31. Literary motherhood and female genealogies were first theorized by Virginia Woolf and were taken up again in the work of feminist critics of Carter's generation, such as Elaine Showalter in *A Literature of Their Own* (1977) and Sandra Gilbert and Susan Gubar in *The Madwoman in the Attic* (1979).

32. Gamble, "Penetrating to the Heart," 27.

33. Carter's rewriting of the Cinderella tale has been relatively neglected, with the notable exceptions of Cristina Bacchilega's and Michelle Ryan-Sautour's insightful analyses of intertextuality and strategies of interpellation, in keeping with the narrator's encouragement of the reader to "construct her own text." Ryan-Sautour notes that "Ashputtle" "in its open juxtaposition of three renditions, weaves together the genealogy of the Cinderella tale with questions of motherhood and ultimately generates allegory about culture and authorship" ("Authorial Ghosts"). The juxtaposition of "three versions of one story" can even be seen as a strategy of "slippage" (pun on slipper) that shifts the meaning of the tale. Ryan-Sautour recalls that "in her introduction to *The Virago Book of Fairy Tales* (1990) Angela Carter comments on the status of the authorial figure in relation to the collective, oral tradition of the fairy tale: 'Ours is a highly individualised culture, with a great faith in the work of art as a unique one-off, and the artist as an original, godlike and inspired creator of unique one-offs. But fairy tales are not like that, nor are their makers' (x). This collective dimension is clearly at the heart of Carter's attraction to 'fairy tales, folk tales, stories from the oral tradition,' such narratives reflecting 'the most vital connection we have with the imaginations of the ordinary men and women whose labour created our world' (ix)" ("Authorial Ghosts").

34. A cognate of the word *kin* also appears at the beginning of "Wolf-Alice," when her "foster kindred" (*Bloody Chamber*, 119) respond to her wolflike howls. The wolf-child feels dread for her human kin but a close connection with her foster animal kin.

35. For Carter the kitchen is a laboratory of fiction where individual contributions and anonymous collective creation are articulated in the metaphor of cooking: "Who first invented meatballs? In what country? Is there a definitive recipe for potato soup? Think in terms of the domestic arts. 'This is how *I* make potato soup'" (*Virago Book of Fairy Tales*, x).

36. This echoes Virginia Woolf's idea of women writers thinking back through their literary mothers.

37. See Shuli Barzilai's insightful analysis of "Snow White" in "Reading 'Snow White.'"

38. "Of course, the real problem here is that it is Baron Hardup of Hardup Hall, father of Cinderella, stepfather of the Ugly Sisters who, these barren days, all too often occupies the post of minister of finance in Pantoland" (Carter, "In Pantoland," 393).

39. Interestingly, Perrault himself plays on words in the scene of transformation. When the six mice are transformed into horses, they form "un beau attelage de six chevaux,

d'un beau gris de souris pommelé" (*Contes*, 173) ("six dappled greys," *Fairy Tales*, 87). Literalizing metaphors as a strategy of "magicking" (to quote Carter from Haffenden, "Angela Carter") is something that Carter shared with her predecessor.

40. Sage, *Angela Carter*, 12.
41. The following discussion is indebted to Mercedes Gulin's master's thesis, "La Fille des Cendres."
42. Bacchilega, in Zipes, *Oxford Companion to Fairy Tales*, 90.
43. Carter expressed concern about the hybrid nature of her fiction: "But my fiction is very often a kind of literary criticism, which is something I've started to worry about quite a lot" (Haffenden, "Angela Carter," 79).
44. The kind of analysis practiced in this first section evokes the structuralist criticism characteristic of the period.
45. Gilbert and Gubar, *Madwoman in the Attic*, 38.
46. Gilbert and Gubar, *Madwoman in the Attic*, 38–39.
47. Gilbert and Gubar, *Madwoman in the Attic*, 42, 43.
48. See Aarne and Thompson's index, referred to in Dundes, *Cinderella*.
49. The legend of Oochigeas is a version of the Cinderella tale told by New England Abénaquis. It may or may not predate the arrival of European colonizers. Oochigeas (i.e., the girl marked by fire) is the youngest of three sisters, and she is in charge of fire, which has burnt her hair and face. The "prince" is a hunter with the power of invisibility; the beautiful dress is made by the girl herself out of bark. Oochigeas marries the hunter after seeing him, and her burns are magically healed. http://cacouna.net/legendeOochigeas_e.htm.
50. Armitt, "Fragile Frames." See also Sarah Gamble's perceptive discussion of the "bloody chamber trope" in "Penetrating to the Heart" (38).
51. Bettelheim, *Uses of Enchantment*, 264–65.
52. Carter's linking of the tiny shoe with the Chinese tradition of foot binding is an allusion to the story of Yeh-hsien recorded in the ninth century.
53. Carter seems to nod at Sexton's ironic similes in "Cinderella." The storyteller stresses the horror of the bloody shoe before describing Cinderella's slipping her foot into it through a romantic simile that starkly contrasts with the actual circumstances: "This time Cinderella fit into the shoe / like a love letter into its envelope" (Sexton, *Transformations*, 56).
54. Gamble, *Fiction of Angela Carter*, ch. 8.
55. Benson, "Angela Carter," 47. See also Ryan-Sautour, "Authorial Ghosts."
56. The three-partite structure of "Ashputtle *or* The Mother's Ghost" itself foregrounds the effects of cotextuality. As Bacchilega points out, Carter paid particular attention to framing devices and subtitles in her editorial work (*Postmodern Fairy Tales*, 21). To quote Ryan–Sautour, "Carter's 'Ashputtle,' with its hybrid status as story/framed narrative, foregrounds a meta-editorial/fictional self-consciousness of the role of framing in the multiple individual performances that make up the genealogy of the fairy tale as 'stories without known originators that can be remade again and again by every person who tells them' (Carter, 1990, ix)" ("Authorial Ghosts").
57. The play is the tragedy, "Man / And its hero, the Conqueror Worm." Edgar Allan Poe

includes these lines in "Ligeia," (*Complete Tales*, 659), which tells about the return of the title character after her death through another woman's body.
58. The text was written during the same period as "Ashputtle *or* The Mother's Ghost."
59. Sage observes that in 1991 Carter "discovered she had lung cancer and died in less than a year" (*Angela Carter*, 58).
60. Bennett and Royle, *Introduction to Literature*, 135. They add that "literature is a place of ghosts, of what's unfinished, unhealed and even untellable" (135). Moreover, "Great works call to be read and reread while never ceasing to be strange, to resist reading, interpretation and translation" (136), and this haunting is both thematized and enacted in Carter's rewriting.

Conclusion

1. Thorpe, "Angela Carter's Unknown Poems"; Vasagar, "Angela Carter's Teenage Poetry."
2. Bassnett, *Translation Studies*, 10.
3. Atwood, "Magic Token," 61.

Bibliography

Primary Texts

Aulnoy, Marie-Catherine, d'. *Contes nouveaux, ou Les fées à la mode*, ed. Nadine Jasmin. Paris: Honoré Champion, 2004 (1698).

———. *The Fairy Tales of Madame d'Aulnoy*, trans. Annie Macdonell and Miss Lee; intro. Anne Thackeray Ritchie. London: Lawrence & Bullen, 1892.

Baudelaire, Charles. "Les métamorphoses du vampire." In *Les Fleurs du mal*, 167–68. Paris: Gallimard, 1972 (1857).

———. "Le vampire." In *Les Fleurs du mal*, 59–60. Paris: Gallimard, 1972.

Beaumarchais, Pierre-Augustin Caron de. *Le mariage de Figaro*. Paris: Gallimard, 1973 (1778).

Beaumont, Jeanne-Marie Leprince de. *Le Magasin des enfants, ou dialogues entre une sage gouvernante et plusieurs de ses élèves de la première distinction*, ed. J.-J. Lambert. Paris: Delarue, 1859 (1756).

Carter, Angela. *American Ghosts and Old World Wonders*. London: Vintage, 1994 (1993).

———, ed. *Angela Carter's Book of Fairy Tales*. London: Virago, 2005 (1990, 1992).

———. "Animals in the Nursery." In *Shaking a Leg*, 298–301.

———. "The Art of Horrorzines." In *Shaking a Leg*, 447–51.

———. "The Better to Eat You With." In *Shaking a Leg*, 451–55.

———. *Black Venus*. London: Vintage, 1996 (1985).

———. *The Bloody Chamber and Other Stories*. London: Penguin, 1979.

———. *Come unto These Yellow Sands*. Newcastle upon Tyne, UK: Bloodaxe Books, 1985 (1976).

———. *La compagnie des loups*, trans. Jacqueline Huet. Paris: Seuil, 1985.

———. "The Company of Wolves: Angela Carter, an Interview." *Marxism Today*, January 1985, 20–22.

———. *The Curious Room: Plays, Film Scripts, and an Opera*, ed. Mark Bell. London: Chatto & Windus, 1996.

———. "Fat Is Ugly." In *Shaking a Leg*, 56–60.

———. "Femmes Fatales." In *Shaking a Leg*, 350–54.

———. "Fin-de-siècle." In *Shaking a Leg*, 153–57.

———. "Georges Bataille, Story of the Eye." In *Shaking a Leg*, 68–69.

———. *Heroes and Villains*. London: Penguin Classics, 2011 (1969).

———. "An I for Truth." In *Shaking a Leg*, 455–59.

———. *The Infernal Desire Machines of Doctor Hoffman*. London: Penguin, 2011 (1972).
———. "In Pantoland." In *Shaking a Leg*, 393–99. Also reprinted in *American Ghosts*, 98–109.
———. "Little Lamb, Get Lost." In *Shaking a Leg*, 305–9.
———. *The Magic Toyshop*. London: Heinemann, 1968.
———. *Nights at the Circus*. London: Vintage, 2006 (1984).
———. "Notes from the Front Line." In *Shaking a Leg*, 36–43.
———. *The Sadeian Woman: An Exercise in Cultural History*. London: Virago, 1979.
———, ed. *The Second Virago Book of Fairy Tales* (aka *Strange Things Still Sometimes Happen: Fairy Tales from Around the World*). London: Virago, 1993 (1992).
———. *Several Perceptions*. London: Virago, 1997 (1969).
———. *Shaking a Leg: Collected Journalism and Writings*. London: Vintage, 1998.
———, trans. *Sleeping Beauty and Other Favourite Fairy Tales*. London: Victor Gollancz, 1991 (1982).
———. "A Souvenir of Japan." In *Fireworks: Nine Profane Pieces*. London: Quartet Books, 1974. Repr. in *Burning your Boats: Collected Stories*. London: Vintage, 2006, 27–34.
———, ed. *The Virago Book of Fairy Tales* (aka *The Old Wives' Fairy Tale Book*). London: Virago, 1990.
———, ed. *Wayward Girls and Wicked Women: An Anthology of Subversive Stories*. London: Virago, 1986.
———. *Wise Children*. London: Vintage, 1992 (1991).
———. "The Wound in the Face." In *Shaking a Leg*, 109–13.
Dahl, Roald. "Little Red Riding Hood." In *Roald Dahl's Revolting Rhymes*, 36–40. New York: Puffin Books, 1995.
Delarue, Paul. "The Story of Grandmother." In *Little Red Riding Hood: A Casebook*, ed. Alan Dundes, 13–20. Madison: University of Wisconsin Press, 1989.
Grimm, Jacob, and Wilhelm Grimm. *The Complete Fairy Tales of the Brothers Grimm*, trans. Jack Zipes. New York: Bantam Books, 1987.
———. *Grimms' Tales for Young and Old: The Complete Stories*, trans. Ralph Manheim. New York: Anchor, 1983 (Doubleday, 1977; Gollancz, 1978).
———. *Kinder- und Hausmärchen*, 3 vols., ed. Heinz Rölleke. Frankfurt am Main: Reclam, 1980.
Huysmans, Joris-Karl. *A rebours*. Paris: Folio, 1977 (1884).
———. *Là-bas*. Paris: Gallimard, 1985 (1891).
Jacobs, Joseph, coll. *English Fairy Tales*. London: David Nutt, 1895 (1890).
La Fontaine, Jean de. *Fables*. Paris: Folio Classique, 1991 (1668–1694).
Lang, Andrew, ed. *The Blue Fairy Book*. New York: Dover, 1965 (1889).
———. *Perrault's Popular Tales*. Oxford: Clarendon, 1888.
Mayer, Charles-Joseph de. *Le cabinet des fées*. Amsterdam, 1785-1789.
Opie, Iona, and Peter Opie. *The Classic Fairy Tales*. London: Oxford University Press, 1974.
———, eds. *The Oxford Dictionary of Nursery Rhymes*. London: Oxford University Press, 1951.
Perrault, Charles. *Contes*, ed. Jean-Pierre Collinet. Paris: Gallimard (Folio classique), 1981.
———. *The Fairy Tales of Charles Perrault*, trans. Angela Carter. London: Victor Gollancz, 1977.
———. *The Fairy Tales of Charles Perrault*, trans. Angela Carter. London: Penguin (Modern Classics), 2008.

———. *Histoires ou contes du temps passé, avec des moralités.* Paris: Barbin, 1697.

———. *Histories or Tales of Past Times, Told by Mother Goose. With Morals. Written in French by Charles Perrault, and Englished by G. M. Gent.* London: Fortune Press, 1928 (1719 [1729?]).

———. *Histories or Tales of Past Times, with Morals,* trans. Robert Samber. London, 1729. Reprinted in *The Authentic Mother Goose Fairy Tales and Nursery Rhymes,* ed. Jacques Barchilon and Henry Pettit. Denver: A. Swallow, 1960.

———. *Little Red Riding Hood, Cinderella, and Other Classic Fairy Tales of Charles Perrault,* trans. Angela Carter. London: Penguin (Penguin Classics), 2008.

———. *Old-Time Stories,* trans. A. E. Johnson. New York: Dodd, Mead, 1921.

———. *Perrault's Tales of Mother Goose: The Dedication Manuscript of 1695 Reproduced in Collotype Facsimile with Introduction and Critical Text by Jacques Barchilon.* New York: Pierpont Morgan Library, 1956.

Poe, Edgar Allan. *The Complete Tales and Poems of Edgar Allan Poe.* London: Penguin, 1982 (1838).

Robain, Jean Marie. *Madame Leprince de Beaumont intime, avec ses principaux contes et des documents inédits.* Geneva: Slatkine Erudition, 2004.

Sexton, Anne. *Transformations.* Boston: Houghton Mifflin, 1971.

Shelley, Percy Bysshe. "To a Skylark." In *The Poetical Works of Percy Bysshe Shelley,* ed. Mary Wollstonecraft Shelley, v. 3, 323–28. London: Edward Moxon, 1866.

Webster, John. *The Duchess of Malfi* (originally published as *The Tragedy of the Dutchesse of Malfy*). Bristol, UK: Bristol Classical Press, 1989 (1623).

Critical Texts

Aarne, Antti. *The Types of the Folktale: A Classification and Bibliography.* Helsinki: Finnish Academy of Science and Letters, 1961.

Almansi, Guido. "In the Alchemist's Cave: Radio Plays." In *Flesh and the Mirror: Essays on the Art of Angela Carter,* ed. Lorna Sage, 216–29. London: Virago, 1994.

Ariès, Philippe. *L'enfant et la vie familiale sous l'ancien régime.* Paris: Plon, 1960.

Armitt, Lucie. "The Fragile Frames of *The Bloody Chamber.*" In *The Infernal Desires of Angela Carter: Fiction, Femininity, Feminism,* ed. Joseph Bristow and Trev Lynn Broughton, 88–99. London: Longman, 1997.

Atwood, Margaret. "Magic Token Through the Dark Forest." *The Observer,* 23 February 1992, 61.

———. "Running with the Tigers." In *Flesh and the Mirror: Essays on the Art of Angela Carter,* ed. Lorna Sage, 117–35. London: Virago, 1994.

Bacchilega, Cristina. *Postmodern Fairy Tales: Gender and Narrative Strategies.* Philadelphia: University of Pennsylvania Press, 1997.

Bakhtin, Mikhail M. *Rabelais and His World,* trans. Hélène Iswolsky. Bloomington: Indiana University Press, 1993.

Bal, Mieke. *A Mieke Bal Reader.* Chicago: University of Chicago Press, 2006.

Ballestra-Puech, Sylvie. *Les Parques: essai sur les figures féminines du destin dans la littérature occidentale.* Toulouse: Editions Universitaires du Sud (Études littéraires), 1999.

Barchilon, Jacques. "Beauty and the Beast: From Myth to Fairy Tale." *Psychoanalytic Review* 46.4 (1959): 19–29.

———. *Le conte merveilleux français de 1690 à 1790: Cent ans de féerie et de poésie ignorées de l'histoire littéraire.* Paris: Honoré Champion, 1975.

———, ed. *Nouveau cabinet des fées*, v. 15. Geneva: Slatkine Reprints, 1978.

———. "Remembering Angela Carter." In *Angela Carter and the Fairy Tale*, ed. Danielle M. Roemer and Cristina Bacchilega, 26–29. Detroit: Wayne State University Press, 2001.

Barchilon, Jacques, and Henry Pettit, eds. *The Authentic Mother Goose Fairy Tales and Nursery Rhymes*. Denver: Alan Swallow, 1960.

Barthes, Roland. *L'empire des signes*. Paris: Skira, 1970.

Barzilai, Shuli. "Reading 'Snow White': The Mother's Story." *Signs: Journal of Women in Culture and Society* 15.3 (1990): 515–34.

Basile, Giambattista. *The Tale of Tales, or Entertainment for Little Ones* (aka *Pentamerone*), trans. Nancy L. Canepa. Detroit: Wayne State University Press, 2007 (1634, 1636).

Bassnett, Susan. *Translation Studies*. London: Routledge, 2002 (reprinted 2010).

———. "Writing and Translating." In *The Translator as Writer*, ed. Susan Bassnett and Peter R. Bush, 173–83. London: Continuum, 2006.

Beckett, Sandra L. *Recycling Red Riding Hood*. London: Routledge, 2002.

———. *Red Riding Hood for All Ages: A Fairy-Tale Icon in Cross-Cultural Contexts*. Detroit: Wayne State University Press, 2008.

Benjamin, Walter. "The Storyteller," trans. Harry Zohn. In *Illuminations: Essays and Reflections*, ed. Hannah Arendt, 83–110. New York: Schocken Books, 2007 (1969).

———. "The Task of the Translator," trans. Harry Zohn. In *The Translation Studies Reader*, ed. Lawrence Venuti, 15–25. London: Routledge, 2005.

Bennett, Andrew, and Nicholas Royle. *An Introduction to Literature, Criticism, and Theory*. Hemel Hempstead, UK: Prentice Hall, 1999 (1995).

Benson, Stephen. "Angela Carter and the Literary Märchen: A Review Essay." In *Angela Carter and the Fairy Tale*, ed. Danielle M. Roemer and Cristina Bacchilega, 30–58. Detroit: Wayne State University Press, 2001.

———, ed. *Contemporary Fiction and the Fairy Tale*. Detroit: Wayne State University Press, 2008.

———. *Cycles of Influence: Fiction, Folktale, Theory*. Detroit: Wayne State University Press, 2003.

Benson, Stephen, and Andrew Teverson, eds. Special issue on the Fairy Tale After Angela Carter. *Marvels & Tales* 24.1 (2010).

Berger, John. *Ways of Seeing*. London: Penguin, 2008 (1972).

Berman, Antoine. *The Experience of the Foreign: Culture and Translation in Romantic Germany*, trans. S. Heyvaert. Albany: State University of New York Press, 1992.

Bettelheim, Bruno. *The Uses of Enchantment: The Meaning and Importance of Fairy Tales*. New York: Vintage, 1976.

Bhabha, Homi K. *The Location of Culture*. London: Routledge, 1994.

Bianchi, Diana, and Catia Nannoni. "Back to the Future: The Journey of *The Bloody Chamber* in Italy and France." *Marvels & Tales* 25.1 (2011): 51–69.

Blom, J. M. "The Life and Works of Robert Samber (1682–c. 1745)." *English Studies* 70.6 (1989): 507–50.

Bottigheimer, Ruth B. *Fairy Godfather: Straparola, Venice, and the Fairy Tale Tradition*. Philadelphia: University of Pennsylvania Press, 2002.

———. *Fairy Tales: A New History*. Albany, NY: Excelsior, 2009.

———. "Misperceived Perceptions: Perrault's Fairy Tales and English Children's Literature." *Children's Literature* 30 (2002): 1–18.

Bristow, Joseph, and Trev Lynn Broughton, eds. *The Infernal Desires of Angela Carter: Fiction, Femininity, Feminism.* London: Longman, 1997.

Brown, Penelope. "Fairy Tales, Fables, and Children's Literature." In *The Oxford History of Literary Translation in English*, v. 3, *1660–1790*, ed. Stuart Gillespie and David Hopkins, 349–60. Oxford: Oxford University Press, 2005.

Calinescu, Matei. *Rereading.* New Haven, CT: Yale University Press, 1993.

Chartier, Roger. *Lectures et lecteurs dans la France d'ancien régime.* Paris: Seuil (L'Univers historique), 1987.

———. *Pratiques de la lecture.* Marseille: Rivages, 1985.

Cixous, Hélène. "The Laugh of the Medusa," trans. Keith Cohen and Paul Cohen. *Signs* 1.4 (1976): 875–93.

———. "Sorties: Out and Out—Attacks/Ways Out/Forays." In *The Logic of the Gift: Toward an Ethic of Generosity*, ed. Alan Schrift. London: Routledge, 1997. Reprinted from *The Newly-Born Woman*, ed. Hélène Cixous and Catherine Clément; trans. Betsy Wing (Minneapolis: University of Minnesota Press, 1986).

Clapp, Susannah. "Angela Carter: A Portrait in Postcards." *The Observer*, 21 January 2012. http://www.guardian.co.uk/books/2012/jan/22/angela-carter-postcards-susannah-clapp (accessed January 23, 2012).

———. *A Card from Angela Carter.* London: Bloomsbury, 2012.

———. "Introduction." In *American Ghosts and Old World Wonders*, by Angela Carter, ix–xi. London: Vintage, 1994.

Crane, Walter. *The Bluebeard Picture Book.* London: Routledge, 1875. http://www.surlalune-fairytales.com/illustrations/bluebeard/craneblue2.html (accessed July 2, 2012).

Crofts, Charlotte. *"Anagrams of Desire": Angela Carter's Writing for Radio, Film, and Television.* Manchester, UK: Manchester University Press, 2003.

Crunelle-Vanrigh, Annie. "The Logic of the Same and Difference: 'The Courtship of Mr. Lyon.'" In *Angela Carter and the Fairy Tale*, ed. Danielle M. Roemer and Cristina Bacchilega, 128–44. Detroit: Wayne State University Press, 2001.

Darnton, Robert. *The Great Cat Massacre and Other Episodes in French Cultural History.* New York: Basic Books, 1984.

Day, Aidan. *Angela Carter: The Rational Glass.* Manchester, UK: Manchester University Press, 1998.

Derrida, Jacques. "La loi du genre." In *Parages*, 249–87. Paris: Galilée, 1986.

———. *Specters of Marx: The State of the Debt, the Work of Mourning, and the New International*, trans. Peggy Kamuf. London: Routledge, 1994 (1993).

———. "Les tours de Babel" (1985). In *Difference in Translation*, trans. and ed. Graham F. Joseph, 165–208. New York: Cornell University Press, 1985.

———. "What Is a 'Relevant' Translation?" trans. Lawrence Venuti. In *The Translation Studies Reader*, ed. Lawrence Venuti, 423–46. London: Routledge, 2005.

Didi-Huberman, Georges. *Ce que nous voyons, ce qui nous regarde.* Paris: Minuit (Critique), 1992.

Dollerup, Cay. *Tales and Translation: The Grimm Tales from Pan-Germanic Narratives to Shared International Fairytales.* Amsterdam: John Benjamins, 1999.

Duncker, Patricia. "Re-Imagining the Fairy Tale: Angela Carter's Bloody Chambers." *Literature and History* 10.1 (1984): 3–14.

Dundes, Alan, ed. *Cinderella: A Folklore Casebook.* New York: Garland, 1982.

———. *Little Red Riding Hood: A Casebook.* Madison: University of Wisconsin Press, 1989.

Dupont-Escarpit, Denise. *Histoire d'un conte: "Le Chat Botté" en France et en Angleterre*, 2 vols. Paris: Didier-Erudition, 1985.
Dworkin, Andrea. *Pornography: Men Possessing Women*. New York: Dutton, 1979.
———. *Woman Hating*. New York: Plume, 1991.
Eastman, Mary Huse. *Index to Fairy Tales, Myths, and Legends*. Boston: Boston Book Co., 1915.
Eco, Umberto. *Six Walks in the Fictional Woods*. Cambridge, MA: Harvard University Press, 1994.
Escola, Marc. *Commentaires des Contes de Perrault*. Paris: Gallimard (Foliothèque), 2005.
François, Cyrille. "Fées et *weise Frauen*: les faiseuses de dons chez Perrault et les Grimm, du merveilleux rationalisé au merveilleux naturalisé." In *Des Fata aux fées: regards croisés de l'Antiquité à nos jours*, ed. Martine Hennard Dutheil de la Rochère and Véronique Dasen. Special issue of *Etudes de Lettres* 289.3–4 (2011): 259–78.
Friday, Nancy. *My Mother, My Self: The Daughter's Search for Identity*. New York: Delacorte, 1977.
Fromm, Erich. *The Forgotten Language: An Introduction to the Understanding of Dreams, Fairy Tales, and Myths*. New York: Rinehart, 1951.
Gaillard, Aurélia, and Jean-Paul Sermain, eds. "Le conte et la fable." Special issue of *Féeries*, no. 7 (2010).
Gamble, Sarah. *Angela Carter: A Literary Life*. Basingstoke, UK: Palgrave Macmillan, 2005.
———. *Angela Carter: Writing from the Front Line*. Edinburgh: Edinburgh University Press, 1997.
———, ed. *The Fiction of Angela Carter*. Basingstoke, UK: Palgrave Macmillan, 2001.
——— "Penetrating to the Heart of the Bloody Chamber: Angela Carter and the Fairy Tale." In *Contemporary Fiction and the Fairy Tale*, ed. Stephen Benson, 20–46. Detroit: Wayne State University Press, 2008.
Garber, Marjorie, and Nancy J. Vickers, eds. *The Medusa Reader*. London: Routledge, 2003.
Genette, Gérard. *Seuils*. Paris: Seuil (Poétique), 1987.
Genette, Gérard, and Marie Maclean. "Introduction to the Paratext." *New Literary History* 22.2 (1991): 261–72.
Gilbert, Sandra M., and Susan Gubar. *The Madwoman in the Attic: The Woman Writer and the Nineteenth-Century Literary Imagination*. New Haven, CT: Yale University Press, 1980.
Goldsworthy, Kerryn. *"Angela Carter." Meanjin 44.1 (March 1985): 4–13*.
Goncourt, Edmond de, and Jules de Goncourt. *Journal: Mémoires de la vie littéraire, 1864–1867*. Monaco: Editions de l'imprimerie nationale de Monaco, 1956–1958.
Gulin, Mercedes. "La fille des cendres: étude comparative de deux réécritures de Cendrillon, 'Ashputtle *or* The Mother's Ghost' (1987) par Angela Carter et 'L'Exaucée' (1894) par Marcel Schwob." Master's thesis, University of Lausanne, 2006.
Haase, Donald, ed. *Fairy Tales and Feminism: New Approaches*. Detroit: Wayne State University Press, 2004.
———. "Feminist Fairy Tale Scholarship." In *Fairy Tales and Feminism: New Approaches*, ed. Donald Haase, 1–36. Detroit: Wayne State University Press, 2004.
———. "Kiss and Tell: Orality, Narrative, and the Power of Words in 'Sleeping Beauty.'" In *Des Fata aux fées: regards croisés de l'Antiquité à nos jours*, ed. Martine Hennard Dutheil de la Rochère and Véronique Dasen. Special issue of *Etudes de Lettres* 289.3–4 (2011): 279–96.

Haffenden, John. "Angela Carter." In *Novelists in Interview*, ed. John Haffenden, 76–96. London: Methuen, 1986.
Haraway, Donna. "Universal Donors in a Vampire Culture: It's All in the Family—Biological Kinship Categories in the Twentieth-Century United States." In *Uncommon Ground: Rethinking the Human Place in Nature*, ed. William Cronon, 321–66. New York: Norton, 1996.
Hatim, Basil, and Ian Mason. *The Translator as Communicator*. London: Routledge, 1997.
Hearne, Betsey. *Beauty and the Beast: Visions and Revisions of an Old Tale*. Chicago: University of Chicago Press, 1989.
Heidmann, Ute. "La Barbe bleue palimpseste: comment Perrault recourt à Virgile, Scarron et Apulée en réponse à Boileau." *Poétique: Revue de théorie et d'analyse littéraires* 154 (2008): 161–82.
Heidmann, Ute, and Jean-Michel Adam. "Text Linguistics and Comparative Literature: Towards an Interdisciplinary Approach to Written Tales—Angela Carter's Translations of Perrault." In *Language and Verbal Art Revisited: Linguistic Approaches to the Study of Literature*, ed. Donna R. Miller and Monica Turci, 181–96. London: Equinox, 2007.
———. *Textualité et intertextualité des contes: Perrault, Apulée, La Fontaine, Lhéritier, . . .* Paris: Classiques Garnier (Lire le XVIIe siècle), 2010.
Hennard Dutheil de la Rochère, Martine. "'But Marriage Itself Is No Party': Angela Carter's Translation of Charles Perrault's 'La Belle au bois dormant.'" *Marvels & Tales* 24.1 (2010): 131–51.
———. "Conjuring the Curse of Repetition or 'Sleeping Beauty' Revamped: Angela Carter's 'Vampirella' and 'The Lady of the House of Love.'" In *Des Fata aux fées: regards croisés de l'Antiquité à nos jours*, ed. Martine Hennard Dutheil de la Rochère and Véronique Dasen. Special issue of *Etudes de Lettres* 289.3–4 (2011): 333–54.
———. "From Translation to Rewriting: The Interplay of Text and Image in *The Fairy Tales of Charles Perrault* and *The Bloody Chamber and Other Stories*." *Journal of the Short Story in English* 56 (2011): 93–108.
———. "Les métamorphoses de Cendrillon: analyse comparée de deux traductions anglaises du conte de Perrault." In *Autour de la retraduction*, ed. Enrico Monti and Peter Schnyder, 157–79. Paris: Orizons, 2011.
———. "Modelling for Bluebeard: Visual and Narrative Art in Angela Carter's 'The Bloody Chamber.'" In *The Seeming and the Seen: Essays in Modern Visual and Literary Culture*, ed. Beverly Maeder, Jürg Schwyter, Ilona Sigrist, and Boris Vejdovsky, 183–208. Bern: Peter Lang, 2006.
———. "Updating the Politics of Experience: Angela Carter's Translation of Charles Perrault's 'Le Petit Chaperon Rouge.'" *Palimpsestes* 22 (2009): 187–204.
Hennard Dutheil de la Rochère, Martine, and Ute Heidmann. "New Wine in Old Bottles: Angela Carter's Translation of Charles Perrault's 'La Barbe bleue.'" *Marvels & Tales* 23.1 (2009): 40–58.
Hennard Dutheil de la Rochère, Martine, and Véronique Dasen, ed. *Des Fata aux fées: regards croisés de l'Antiquité à nos jours*. Special issue of *Etudes de Lettres* 289.3–4 Lausanne (2011).
Hoffman, Heinrich. *Struwwelpeter*. New York: Dover, 1995 (1845).
Hutcheon, Linda. *The Politics of Postmodernism*. London: Routledge, 1989.
Jakobson, Roman. "On Linguistic Aspects of Translation." In *On Translation*, ed. R. A. Brower, 232–39. Cambridge, MA: Harvard University Press, 1959.
Joad, Cyril Edwin Mitchinson. *Decadence: A Philosophical Inquiry*. London: Faber & Faber, 1948.

Joosen, Vanessa. *Critical and Creative Perspectives on Fairy Tales: An Intertextual Dialogue Between Fairy-Tale Scholarship and Postmodern Retellings*. Detroit: Wayne State University Press, 2011.

Kaplan, E. Ann. "Is the Gaze Male?" In *Women and Film: Both Sides of the Camera*, 23–35. New York: Methuen, 1983.

Kappeler, Susanne. *The Pornography of Representation*. Cambridge, UK: Polity Press, 1986.

Katsavos, Anna. "An Interview with Angela Carter." *Review of Contemporary Fiction: Angela Carter and Tadeusz Konwicki* 14.3 (1994): 11–17.

Kim, Dave. "Marilyn Minter." http://www.smylesandfish.com/lounge/marilyn-minter.php/ (accessed August 16, 2011).

Klossowski, Pierre. *Le philosophe scélérat*. Paris: Editions du Seuil, 1967.

———. *Sade mon prochain*. Paris: Editions du Seuil, 1947.

Kolbenschlag, Madonna. *Kiss Sleeping Beauty Good-Bye: Breaking the Spell of Feminine Myths and Models*. New York: Bantam Books, 1981 (1979).

Krailsheimer, A. J. *Three Sixteenth Century Conteurs*. Oxford, UK: Oxford University Press, 1966.

Lacan, Jacques. "Some Reflections on the Ego." *International Journal of Psychoanalysis* 34 (1953): 11–17.

Laing, Ronald David. *The Politics of Experience*. London: Routledge & Kegan Paul, 1967.

Lathey, Gillian. *The Role of Translators in Children's Literature: Invisible Storytellers*. London: Routledge, 2010.

———, ed. *The Translation of Children's Literature: A Reader*. Clevedon, UK: Multilingual Matters, 2006.

Lau, Kimberly J. "Erotic Infidelities: Angela Carter's Wolf Trilogy." *Marvels & Tales* 22.1 (2008): 77–94.

Lefevere, André. *Translation, Rewriting, and the Manipulation of Literary Fame*. London: Routledge, 1992.

Lefevere, André, and Susan Bassnett. *Constructing Cultures: Essays on Literary Translation*. London: Multilingual Matters, 1998.

Le Men, Ségolène. "Mother Goose Illustrated: From Perrault to Doré." *Poetics Today* 13.1 (1992): 17–39.

Le Men, Ségolène, and Isabelle Havelange. *Le magasin des enfants: la littérature pour la jeunesse (1750–1830)*. Montreuil, France: Bibliothèque Robert Desnos, 1988.

Lepaludier, Laurent, ed. *Métatextualité et métafiction: théorie et analyses*. Rennes, France: Presses Universitaires de Rennes, 2002.

Lieberman, Marcia K. "'Some Day My Prince Will Come': Female Acculturation Through the Fairy Tale." In *Don't Bet on the Prince: Contemporary Feminist Fairy Tales in North America and England*, ed. Jack Zipes, 185–200. Aldershot, UK: Gower, 1986.

Linkin, K. Harriet. "Isn't It Romantic: Carter's Bloody Revision of the Romantic Aesthetic in 'The Erl-King.'" *Contemporary Literature* 35 (1994): 305–23. Reprinted in *Critical Essays on Angela Carter*, ed. Lindsey Tucker, 119–33 (New York: G. K. Hall, 1998).

Louvel, Liliane. *L'oeil du texte: texte et image dans la literature de langue anglaise*. Toulouse, France: Presses universitaires du Mirail, 1998.

———. *Texte/Image: images à lire, textes à voir*. Rennes, France: Presse universitaire de Rennes (Interférences), 2002.

Mainil, Jean. *Madame d'Aulnoy et le rire des fées: essai sur la subversion féerique et le merveilleux comique sous l'ancien régime*. Paris: Kimé, 2001.

Makinen, Merja. "Angela Carter's 'The Bloody Chamber' and the Decolonization of Female Sexuality." *Feminist Review* 42 (autumn 1992): 2–15.
Malarte-Feldman, Claire-Lise. "The Challenges of Translating Perrault's *Contes* into English." *Marvels & Tales* 13.2 (1999): 184–97.
Marin, Louis. *Le récit est un piège*. Paris: Minuit, 1978.
Meschonnic, Henri. "Traduire: écrire ou désécrire." In *Ethique et politique du traduire*. Paris: Verdier, 2007.
Monnier, Magali. "Naissance et renaissance du conte de fées: de Marie-Catherine d'Aulnoy à Angela Carter." In *Des Fata aux fées: regards croisés de l'Antiquité à nos jours*, ed. Martine Hennard Dutheil de la Rochère and Véronique Dasen. Special issue of *Etudes de Lettres* 289.3–4 (2011): 243–58.
Moss, Betty. "Desire and the Female Grotesque in Angela Carter's 'Peter and the Wolf.'" In *Angela Carter and the Fairy Tale*, ed. Danielle M. Roemer and Cristina Bacchilega, 187–203. Detroit: Wayne State University Press, 2001.
Moss, Elaine. "The Seventies in British Children's Books." In *The Signal Approach to Children's Books*, ed. Nancy Chambers, 48–82. Harmondsworth, UK: Kestrel Books, 1980.
Mulvey, Laura. "Visual Pleasure and Narrative Cinema." *Screen* 16.3 (1975): 6–18.
Munford, Rebecca, ed. *Re-Visiting Angela Carter: Texts, Contexts, Intertexts*. Basingstoke, UK: Palgrave Macmillan, 2006.
Murai, Mayako. "Voicing Authenticities Through Translation: Framing Strategies in the Multicultural Fairy Tale Collections of Andrew Lang and Angela Carter." *Synthesis* 4 (summer 2012): 104–20. http://synthesis.enl.uoa.gr/fileadmin/synthesis.enl.uoa.gr/uploads/Issue4/Synthesis_4_7_Murai.pdf (accessed October 26, 2012).
Nicolajeva, Maria, and Carole Scott. *How Picturebooks Work*. New York: Garland, 2001.
Noël, Jean-Pascal. *La fable au siècle des Lumières: 1715–1815—Anthologie des successeurs de La Fontaine, de La Motte à Jauffret*. Saint-Etienne, France: Publications de l'Université de Saint-Etienne, 1991.
Oittinen, Riitta. *Translating for Children*. New York: Garland, 2000.
Orenstein, Catherine. *Little Red Riding Hood Uncloaked: Sex, Morality, and the Evolution of a Fairy Tale*. New York: Basic Books, 2002.
O'Sullivan, Emer. *Comparative Children's Literature*, trans. Anthea Bell. London: Routledge, 2005.
Palmer, Nancy, and Melvin Palmer. "English Editions of French *contes de fées* Attributed to Mme d'Aulnoy." *Studies in Bibliography* 27 (1974): 227–37.
Paz, Octavio. "Translation: Literature and Letters," trans. Irene del Corral. In *Theories of Translation: An Anthology of Essays from Dryden to Derrida*, ed. Rainer Schulte and John Biguenet, 152–62. Chicago: University of Chicago Press, 1992.
Pedot, Richard. "Obscurs éclaircissements et transparence impénétrable: 'The Erl-King.'" In *Métatextualité et métafiction: théorie et analyses*, ed. Laurent Lepaludier, 187–204. Rennes, France: Presses universitaires de Rennes, 2002.
Perrot, Jean. *Art baroque, art d'enfance*. Nancy, France: Presses universitaires de Nancy, 1991.
Pimentel, Maria Sofia. "Angela Carter's 'Puss-in-Boots': Commedia dell'Arte Meets the Bluebeard Story." *Forma breve* 2 (2004): 247–55.
Punter, David. *The Literature of Terror: A History of Gothic Fictions from 1765 to the Present Day*, v. 2, *The Modern Gothic*. London: Longman, 1996.
Ramanujan, A. K., ed. *Folktales from India: A Selection of Oral Tales from Twenty-Two languages*. New York: Pantheon, 1991.

Reed, John R. *Decadent Style.* Athens: Ohio University Press, 1985.
Renfroe, Cheryl. "Initiation and Disobedience: Liminal Experience in Angela Carter's 'The Bloody Chamber.'" In *Angela Carter and the Fairy Tale,* ed. Danielle M. Roemer and Cristina Bacchilega, 94–106. Detroit: Wayne State University Press, 2001.
Roemer, Danielle M. "The Contextualization of the Marquis in Angela Carter's 'The Bloody Chamber.'" In *Angela Carter and the Fairy Tale,* ed. Danielle M. Roemer and Cristina Bacchilega, 107–27. Detroit: Wayne State University Press, 2001.
Roemer, Danielle M., and Cristina Bacchilega, eds. *Angela Carter and the Fairy Tale.* Detroit: Wayne State University Press, 2001.
———. "Introduction." In *Angela Carter and the Fairy Tale,* ed. Danielle M. Roemer and Cristina Bacchilega, 7–25. Detroit: Wayne State University Press, 2001.
Rose, James. "The Dreaming and the Dreamt: A Lexicon of Neil Jordan's *The Company of Wolves.*" *Irish Journal of Gothic and Horror Studies* 2 (March 2007). http://irishgothichorrorjournal.homestead.com/CompanyofWolves.html (accessed July 2, 2012).
Rutherford, Jonathan. "The Third Space: Interview with Homi Bhabha." In *Identity: Community, Culture, Difference,* by Jonathan Rutherford, 207–21. London: Lawrence & Wishart, 1990.
Ryan-Sautour, Michelle. "Authorial Ghosts and Maternal Identity in Angela Carter's 'Ashputtle or the Mother's Ghost: Three Versions of One Story' (1987)." *Marvels & Tales* 25.1 (2011): 33–50.
———. "Carnaval et réflexion métatextuelle dans 'In Pantoland' d'Angela Carter." In *Métatextualité et métafiction: théorie et analyses,* ed. Laurent Lepaludier, 141–60. Rennes, France: Presses universitaires de Rennes, 2002.
Sage, Lorna. *Angela Carter.* Plymouth, UK: Northcote House, 1994.
———. "Angela Carter: The Fairy Tale." In *Angela Carter and the Fairy Tale,* ed. Danielle M. Roemer and Cristina Bacchilega, 65–81. Detroit: Wayne State University Press, 2001.
———, ed. *Flesh and the Mirror: Essays on the Art of Angela Carter.* London: Virago, 1994.
———. "Penetrating to the Heart of the Bloody Chamber: Angela Carter and the Fairy Tale." In *Contemporary Fiction and the Fairy Tale,* ed. Stephen Benson, 20–46. Detroit: Wayne State University Press, 2008.
———. "The Savage Sideshow: A Profile of Angela Carter." *New Review* 4.39–40 (1977): 51–57.
Said, Edward W. *Culture and Imperialism.* London: Vintage, 1994 (1993).
———. *The World, the Text, and the Critic.* Cambridge, MA: Harvard University Press, 1983.
Sceats, Sarah. "Oral Sex: Vampiric Transgression and the Writing of Angela Carter." *Tulsa Studies in Women's Literature* 20.1 (2001): 107–21.
Seago, Karen. "Nursery Politics: Sleeping Beauty and the Acculturation of a Tale." In *The Translation of Children's Literature: A Reader,* ed. Gillian Lathey, 175–89. Clevedon, UK: Multilingual Matters, 2006.
Seifert, Lewis C. *Fairy Tales, Sexuality, and Gender in France (1690–1715): Nostalgic Utopias.* Cambridge, UK: Cambridge University Press, 1996.
———. "Madame Leprince de Beaumont and the Infantilization of the Fairy Tale." In *The Child in French and Francophone Literature,* ed. Norman Buford, 25–39. Amsterdam: Rodopi, 2004.
Seifert, Lewis C., and Domna Stanton, eds. *Enchanted Eloquence: Fairy Tales by Seventeenth-*

Century French Women Writers. Toronto: Centre for Reformation and Renaissance Studies and Iter Inc., 2011.

Sermain, Jean-Paul. *Le conte de fées du classicisme aux Lumières*. Paris: Desjonquères, 2005.

———. "La face cachée du conte: le recueil et l'encadrement." *Féeries* 1 (2004): 11–26.

———. *Métafictions (1670–1730): la réflexivité dans la littérature d'imagination*. Paris: Honoré Champion, 2002.

Sheets, Robin Ann. "Pornography, Fairy Tales, and Feminism: Angela Carter's 'The Bloody Chamber.'" *Journal of the History of Sexuality* 1.4 (1991): 633–57. Reprinted in *Forbidden History: The State, Society, and the Regulation of Sexuality in Modern Europe*, ed. John C. Fout, 335–59 (Chicago: University of Chicago Press, 1992).

Showalter, Elaine, ed. *Daughters of Decadence: Women Writers of the Fin de Siècle*. London: Virago, 1993.

———. *A Literature of Their Own: British Women Novelists from Brontë to Lessing*. Princeton, NJ: Princeton University Press, 1977.

———. *Sexual Anarchy: Gender and Culture at the Fin de Siècle*. London: Bloomsbury, 1991.

Simon, Sherry. *Gender in Translation: Cultural Identity and the Politics of Transmission*. London: Routledge, 1996.

Simpson, Helen. "Femme Fatale." *The Guardian*, 23 June 2006. http://www.guardian.co.uk/books/2006/jun/24/classics.angelacarter (accessed December 24, 2011).

———. "Introduction." In *The Bloody Chamber and Other Stories*, by Angela Carter, vii–xix. London: Vintage, 2006.

Sparagana, John, and Mieke Bal. *Sleeping Beauty: A One-Artist Dictionary*. Chicago: University of Chicago Press, 2008.

Spivak, Gayatri Chakravorti. "The Politics of Translation." In *The Translation Studies Reader*, ed. Lawrence Venuti, 397–416. London: Routledge, 2000.

Stead, Evanghélia. La Chair du livre. *Matérialité, imaginaire et poétique du livre fin-de-siècle*. Paris: Presses Universitaires Paris-Sorbonne (coll. Histoire du livre), 2012.

Steiner, Gary. *Anthropocentrism and Its Discontents: The Moral Status of Animals in the History of Western Philosophy*. Pittsburgh, PA: University of Pittsburgh Press, 2005.

Stone, Kay F. "Fairytales for Adults: Walt Disney's Americanization of the *Märchen*." In *Some Day Your Witch Will Come*, 24–35. Detroit: Wayne State University Press, 2008.

———. "The Misuses of Enchantment: Controversies on the Significance of Fairy Tales." In *Women's Folklore, Women's Culture*, ed. Rosan A. Jordan and Susan J. Kalcik, 125–44. Philadelphia: University of Pennsylvania Press, 1985.

———. "Things Walt Disney Never Told Us." In *Some Day Your Witch Will Come*, 813–23. Detroit: Wayne State University Press, 2008.

Tatar, Maria. *The Hard Facts of the Grimms' Fairy Tales*. Princeton, NJ: Princeton University Press, 1987.

Tennant, Emma, ed. *The Straw and the Gold*. London: Pierrot Books, 1979.

Thompson, Stith. *The Folktale*. Berkeley: University of California Press, 1977 (1946).

Thorpe, Vanessa. "Angela Carter's Unknown Poems Reveal the Celebrated Writer's Passion for Verse." *The Observer*, 12 March 2011.

Tonkin, Maggie. *Angela Carter and Decadence: Critical Fictions/Fictional Critiques*. Basingstoke, UK: Palgrave Macmillan, 2012.

Toury, Gideon. "Interlanguage and Its Manifestations in Translation." *Meta: Translator's Journal* 24.2 (June 1979): 223–31.

Travers, P. L. *About the Sleeping Beauty*. New York: McGraw-Hill, 1975.

van Coillie, J., and W. Verschueren, eds. *Children's Literature in Translation: Challenges and Strategies*. Manchester, UK: St. Jerome, 2006.

Van Elslande, Jean-Pierre. "Parole d'enfant: Perrault au déclin du grand siècle." *Papers on French Seventeenth Century Literature* 26.51 (1999): 439–54.

Vasagar, Jeevan. "Angela Carter's Teenage Poetry Unearthed at Old School." *The Guardian*, 30 March 2012.

Velay-Vallantin, Catherine. "Charles Perrault, la conteuse et la fabuliste: 'l'image dans le tapis.'" *Féeries* 7 (2010): 95–121. http://feeries.revues.org/index759.html?file=1 (accessed June 22, 2012).

———. "Le Chat Botté dans l'Angleterre du XVIIIe siècle: 'The infinite cat project' des Lumières." *Féeries* 8 (2011): 135–54.

———. "Le miroir des contes: Perrault dans les Bibliothèques bleues." In *Les Usages de l'imprimé*, ed. Roger Chartier, 129–85. Paris: Fayard, 1987.

Venuti, Lawrence. *The Scandals of Translation: Towards an Ethics of Difference*. London: Routledge, 1998.

———. *The Translator's Invisibility: A History of Translation*. London: Routledge, 1995.

Verdier, Gabrielle. "Comment l'auteur des fées à la mode devint 'Mother Bunch': métamorphoses de la Comtesse d'Aulnoy en Angleterre." *Marvels & Tales* 10.2 (1996): 285–309.

———. "De ma mère l'Oye à Mother Goose: la fortune des contes de fées littéraires français en Angleterre." In *Contacts culturels et échanges linguistiques au XVIIe siècle en France: actes du 3e Colloque du Centre international de rencontres sur le XVIIe siècle, Université de Fribourg (Suisse) 1996*, ed. Yves Giraud, 185–202. Seattle: Papers on French Seventeenth Century Literature, 1997.

———. "Figures de la conteuse dans les contes de fées féminins." *Dix-septième siècle* 180 (1993): 481–99.

Verdier, Yvonne. "Grand-mères si vous saviez . . .: le Petit Chaperon rouge dans la tradition orale." *Cahiers de Littérature Orale* 4 (1978): 17–55.

Walker, Nancy A. *The Disobedient Writer: Women and Narrative Tradition*. Austin: University of Texas Press, 1995.

Wanning Harries, Elizabeth. "Old Men and Comatose Virgins: Nobel Prize Winners Rewrite 'Sleeping Beauty.'" In *Des Fata aux fées: regards croisés de l'Antiquité à nos jours*, ed. Martine Hennard Dutheil de la Rochère and Véronique Dasen. Special issue of *Etudes de Lettres* 289.3–4 (2011): 359–78.

———. *Twice Upon a Time: Women Writers and the History of the Fairy Tale*. Princeton, NJ: Princeton University Press, 2001.

Ward Jouve, Nicole. "Mother Is a Figure of Speech." In *Flesh and the Mirror: Essays on the Art of Angela Carter*, ed. Lorna Sage, 136–70. London: Virago, 1994.

Warner, Marina. *From the Beast to the Blonde: On Fairy Tales and Their Tellers*. London: Chatto & Windus, 1994.

———. *No Go the Bogeyman: Scaring, Lulling, and Making Mock*. London: Chatto & Windus, 1998.

Watz, Anna. "Angela Carter and Xavière Gauthier's *Surréalisme et Sexualité*." *Contemporary Women's Writing* 4.2 (2010): 114–33.

Wilson, Adrian. "The Infancy of the History of Childhood: An Appraisal of Philippe Ariès." *History and Theory* 19.2 (1980): 132–53. http://www.jstor.org/pss/2504795 (accessed July 14, 2012).

Wisker, Gina. "Revenge of the Living Doll: Angela Carter's Horror Writing." In *The Infernal*

Desires of Angela Carter: Fiction, Femininity, Feminism, ed. Joseph Bristow and Trev Lynn Broughton, 116–31. London: Longman, 1997.

Zipes, Jack. "Breaking the Disney Spell." In *From Mouse to Mermaid: The Politics of Film, Gender, and Culture*, ed. Elizabeth Bell, Lynda Haas, and Laura Sells, 21–42. Bloomington: Indiana University Press, 1995.

———. "Crossing Boundaries with Wise Girls: Angela Carter's Fairy Tales for Children." In *Angela Carter and the Fairy Tale*, ed. C. Bacchilega and D. Roemer, 159–66. Detroit: Wayne State University Press, 2001.

———. *The Enchanted Screen: The Unknown History of Fairy-Tale Films*. London: Routledge, 2011.

———. *Fairy Tales and the Art of Subversion: The Classical Genre for Children and the Process of Civilization*. London: Methuen, 1988 (1983).

———. "Jeanne-Marie Le Prince de Beaumont" in *Enzyklopädie des Märchens. Handwörterbuch zur historischen und vergleichenden Erzählforschung*, ed. Rolf Wilhelm et al. Berlin: de Gruyter, 1996.

———. "Once Upon a Time Beyond Disney: Contemporary Fairy-Tale Films for Children." In *Happily Ever After: Fairy Tales, Children, and the Culture Industry*, 89–110. London: Routledge, 1997.

———, ed. *The Oxford Companion to Fairy Tales: The Western Fairy Tale Tradition from Medieval to Modern*. Oxford, UK: Oxford University Press, 2002 (2000).

———. "The Remaking of Charles Perrault and His Fairy Tales." In *Little Red Riding Hood, Cinderella, and Other Classic Fairy Tales of Charles Perrault*, by Charles Perrault, trans. Angela Carter, i–xxxiv. New York: Penguin, 2008.

———. *The Trials and Tribulations of Little Red Riding Hood*. London: Routledge, 2006 (1983).

Index

Note: Italicized page numbers indicate illustrations.

Ackerman, Forrest J., 223
adult fairy tales, 4, 11, 38
Adventures of Eulalie at the Harem of the Grand Turk (Carter), 148
American Ghosts and Old World Wonders (Carter), 263, 294–96
American Gothic, reception in France, 224–25
Angela Carter and the Fairy Tale (Roemer and Bacchilega), 12
"Animals in the Nursery" (Carter), 81
"Apologie des Femmes" (Perrault), 125–26
Armitt, Lucie, 293
art, as means of knowing the world, 20–21
"Art of Horrorzines, The" (Carter), 223–24
"Aschenputtel" (Grimm brothers), 265, 267, 274–75, 289, 292
"Ashputtle *or* The Mother's Ghost" (Carter): in *American Ghosts,* 284–85, 287–88, 294–96; analyses of, 345n33; "The Burned Child" in, 288–93, 297–98; caution against conformity to the norm, 293–94; complicity of female gender with circumstances of oppression, 285–86; as corrective to translation, 269–70; double focus on Ashputtle and her mother, 267–68, 285; father's absence in, 277; focus on women's obsession with marriage, 276, 278; influence of Grimm brothers' "Aschenputtel," 289; initial publication of, 263; "The Mutilated Girls" in, 275–76, 290–93; pumpkin-kin pun, 287; starting point for rewriting, 286–87; as three versions of one story, 263–64; "Travelling Clothes" in, 290, 292, 294, 297
Atwood, Margaret, 301
"Aufgabe des Übersetzers, Die" (Benjamin), 4
Authentic Mother Goose Fairy Tales and Nursery Rhymes, The (Barchilon), 14

Bacchilega, Cristina, 12, 97–98, 109, 289
"Barbe bleue, La" (Perrault), 111–13, 129, *134,* 135
Barber of Seville (Mozart), 163
Barchilon, Jacques, 11–14, 43, 78
Barrett Browning, Elizabeth, 264
Barthes, Roland, 1, 106
Bassnett, Susan, 4, 7, 300
Batten, John D., 46, 175–76
Baudelaire, Charles, 29, 149
Beast, literary and graphic representations of, 243–47, *244,* 252–54
beastliness, women's complex relations with, 228
Beast stories as transitional texts, 230–34

Beaumarchais, Pierre, 19, 162–63, 183–84, 328–29n32
Beaumont, Jeanne-Marie Leprince de: *contes* translated by Carter, 227–28, 335n3; contribution to fairy-tale literature, 66–68, 229–30; doubling and ambiguities in texts by, 228; on Eve as God's ultimate achievement, 231–32; "La Belle et la Bête," 249–50, 255; literary merits of prose by, 233–34; use of fairy tale by, 65; views on education, 231–32; women and power of metamorphosis in tales by, 257
Beauty (fairy-tale character), 68, 250–52
"Beauty and the Beast" (Beaumont, trans. by Carter): as beast-marriage story, 228; in *Bloody Chamber* collection, 18–19; characterization of Beauty in, 250–52; Christian moralizing replaced by ability to develop a generous heart, 254–55; context for, 65–68; metamorphosis of Beast into Prince Charming, 255; modernization of cultural references to education, 248–49; moral rectified in, 229; as occasion to question man-made divisions, 258; in *Sleeping Beauty* collection, 250; stories inspired by, 227; text simplification in, 248
Beauty and the Beast (Lamb), 241
Beauty and the Beast story: early reception in England, 232, 241–42
beauty-surprised-in her-sleep motif, 194
Beckett, Sandra, 71
"Belle au bois dormant, La" (Perrault), 190, 194–95, 200, 205–7, 219–20, 222–24
"Belle et la Bête, La" (Beaumont), 227–28, 249–50, 255
Belle et la Bête, La (Cocteau film), 227, 242, 337n23
Benjamin, Walter, 4, 30
Benson, Stephen, 12, 294, 306n29, 344n29
Berger, John, 137–38
Bettelheim, Bruno, 73, 270–71, 288, 293, 339n35

"The Better to Eat You With" (Carter), 25, 41, 44, 76, 85–86, 161–62, 272
Bhabha, Homi K., 7, 299
"Black Venus" (Carter short story), 297, 323n40
blood motif, 71–77, 81, 101–2, 109, 111, 278–79
"Bloody Chamber, The" (Carter short story): Bluebeard character in, 123, 139; bride as subject and object, 154–55; bride's appropriation of narrative and visual power, 141–42; bride's conditioning to submit to power of husband, 137, 151; bride's sexual initiation, 146–47; bride's visit to bloody chamber, 152–53; critique of mythologies in, 155; fairy-tale archaeology in, 110; femininity myths questioned, 136–37; fin de siècle culture in, 139–40; idea of physical repulsion and sexuality, 124; investigation of dominant representational modes in European culture, 138; key motif of, 29; Marquis's art gallery and library, 147–51; Medusa reference, 135–36; mirror motif, 112–13, 142–43; misogynistic bias critiqued in, 140; reading experience created in, 110–11; sociopolitical subtext exploration, 128; symbolic killing of women into art, 140–41; symbolist art and ekphrastic passages referenced in, 132–35; undressing of the bride, 143–44; Ware's illustrations for, 128–36
Bloody Chamber and Other Stories, The (Carter): background for and counterpoint to fairy-tale rewritings, 1; beastly men and manly beasts in, 228; Carter's plan for, 18; composition and structure of, 314n4; as continuation and counterpoint to *The Fairy Tales of Charles Perrault*, 3; experiments in, 73; the fairy tale and, 30–31; feminist critics' objections to use of fairy tale in, 106; idea of tale as generative

matrix, 286; as literary endeavor and tribute to folklore, 42–43; origins of, 13; planned sequel to, 18–19; revival of fairy tale as genre for adults, 4, 11; sexual subtext of fairy tales explored in, 17; translational poetics in, 8; variations on Little Red Riding Hood story, 71, 95–96

bloody shoe motif, 270–71, 292–93

"Bluebeard" (Perrault, trans. by Carter): meaning clarified for young readers, 119–20; morals of, 125–27; narrative voice, 118–19; opening of forbidden door, 129–31, *131;* scene of attempted beheading, 131–32, *133*, 135–36; shift of focus in, 120–23; textual and thematic connections between "Sleeping Beauty in the Wood" and, 204; use of word "attic," 124–25; Ware's illustrations for 1977 edition, *133*

Bluebeard-figure-as-God motif, 131

Bluebeard portrayed by Harry Clarke, in *The Classic Fairy Tales,* 117

Bluebeard story: Carter's sources and background reading on, 114–18; emancipatory potential in act of rewriting, 154; theme of female curiosity in, 113; variations on, 110; as version of decadent misogyny, 142; vision as central concern of, 128. *See also* "Barbe bleue, La"; "Bloody Chamber, The"

Blue Fairy Book (Lang), 190

Boëhme, Jacob, 29

Boileau, Nicolas, 53, 126

Borges, Jorge Luis, 92

bottle metaphor, 74–75, 111, 225, 304n5, 307–8n52

Burdick, Angela, 57–58

"Burned Child, The" (Carter short story), 263, 288–93, 297–98

butterfly motif, 49

Cabinet des fées, Le (de Mayer), 54

Carter, Angela: adaptations for radio, 160; in chain of transmitters, 10; commission to retranslate Perrault's *Histoires ou contes du temps passé,* 2; on confession magazines targeted at women, 207; connection of individual projects, 299–300; creative strategies, 223; dynamics of creation in work of, 213; eclectic sources used by, 19; emphasis on formal aspect of tale, 80; fairy-tale archaeology of, 97–99; as feminist writer, 74; human-animal divide and condition of women under patriarchy, 257; impending death and thoughts on afterlife as writer, 287–88; Japan experience, 1; as key figure in translation studies, 4; literary testament of, 296–98; personal library of, 13–14, 44–45; rewriting inspirations, 55; rewritings by, as counterpoint to translations, 76; on short fiction, 16; social consciousness of, 54; as storyteller and fairy-tale author, 106–7; text for *Martin Leman's Comic and Curious Cats,* 174; translational dynamics in writing of, 29–30; translational poetics of, 7–11; translations of, 27–28; as translator of moral tales for children, 9; valuing of folklore and of literary tradition, 230–31; view of interrelationship between reading, translating, and (re)writing, 75; views on education, 232; work of, as critique of myth, 106; as worldly-wise fairy godmother, 208; writing for radio, 103

"Castle of Murder" (Grimm brothers), 110, 339n35

Cecilia, Saint, 142, 151

"Cendrillon ou la petite pantoufle de verre" (Perrault), 263, 269, 271–73, 278–80

"Chatte blanche, La" (d'Aulnoy), 260

Chavannes, Puvis de, 150

children's literature, Carter's criticism of, 81

Cinderella (Disney film), 269

"Cinderella: or, The Little Glass Slipper" (Perrault, trans. by Carter): Carter's adaptations for young readers, 272; comparisons to Perrault's text, 276–77; concern with women in, 277; conflict between families in, 277–78; context for translation, 270; critique of beauty myth, 269; focus on mother-daughter relationship, 270–71; influence of Grimm brothers, 263; as matter-of-fact message to young girls, 264; morals in, 280–81; possibility of self-transformation in, 273; prose style in, 274–75; title and double thematic focus, 271; Ware's illustrations for, 281–84, *282, 284*

Cinderella story, 36–38, *37*, 267, 269. *See also* "Aschenputtel"; "Ashputtle *or* The Mother's Ghost"

Cixous, Hélène, 136, 313n43

Clapp, Susannah, 29, 174, 294

Classic Fairy Tales (Opie and Opie): Carter's selective use of information from, 313–14n46; color wood engraving by Evans, *246;* frontispiece to Hodgson's edition of "Puss in Boots," *170;* illustrations for Cinderella story, 264–65, *266;* illustrations for Sleeping Beauty story, 192; illustrations reproduced in, 242–43, 338n29; introduction to "Little Red Riding Hood," 80; omission of morals in, 21, 43

Cocteau, Jean, 227, 242

coffin motif, 294, 297

Collinet, Jean-Pierre, 194

Come unto These Yellow Sands (Carter), 6

comic book subculture, 223–25

commedia dell'arte traditions, 157–58, 160–65, 182–83

"Company of Wolves, The" (Carter short story): baroque style of, 86–88; blood motif, 101–2; exploration of reconciling (wo)man and beast, 82; Perrault's *conte* and, 76; preparatory notes, 96; sexuality and strong-mindedness of girl, 102; sexual subtext in, 74; structure and adaptations of, 72–73; transformation of flesh into meat, 101–2

contes by Perrault: audience for, 39, 45; Carter on style and spirit of, 53–54; Carter's assumptions about, 51–52; children's editions, 46–47; context and levels of, 14, 55; as cultural productions, 19; *en vers, 26,* 46, 53–56, 73, 75–76; false naïveté of, 83–84; intertextual echoes of, in Beaumont's "Belle et la Bête, La," 249–50; late 17th century, 7; lessons in, 44–45, 271; morals in, 43, 89–90; origin of, 65, 310n10; purported aim in, 307n51; reception of, 41–42; satirical dimension of, 327n21

contes de fées, 42, 232, 280

Contes de ma Mère l'Oye (Perrault), 13, 78

contes merveilleux, as genre, 41–42

Coover, Robert L., 36

counterpoint idea, 15

"Courtship of Mr. Lyon, The" (Carter short story), 227–29, 234, 242, 247, 258–61

Craik, D. M., 192

Crane, Walter, 245, *246*

Cruikshank, George, 166

curiosity, as moral function, 109–13, 128

Curious Room, The (radio play), 103

Dadd, Richard, 6

"Dark Corners of Childhood" (Mayes), 59–60

Darmancour, P., 42

d'Aulnoy, Marie-Catherine, 41, 230, 234–35, 260

"Dead City, The" (Rossetti), 29

Decadentism, 140–42, 149–52, 322n32, 323n37

de la Mare, Walter, 19

Delarue, Paul, 73, 81

"Der Erlkönig" (Goethe), 28–29

Derrida, Jacques, 5, 284

Dickens, Charles, 82, 166, 210

Dickinson, Emily, 7
Didi-Huberman, G., 128
Disney, Walt, 9, 189–90
"Donkey-Skin" (Perrault, trans. by Carter), 17, 47–48, 53, 61
Doré, Gustave, 94, *95*, 132, *134*
"Dornröschen" (Grimm brothers), 59, 190–91, 193, 210–12
duetto buffo di due gatti (Rossini), 163
Dulac, Edmund, 242
Duncker, Patricia, 106
Dworkin, Andrea, 207, 312–13n38

Eco, Umberto, 91
education: Beaumont's views on, 231; Carter's views on, 9, 232; foregrounded in *Sleeping Beauty* collection, 250; modernization of cultural references to, 248–49; theme of, as counterbalance to corrupting power, 258–59
English Fairy Tales (Jacobs), 46, 175–76
"Erl-King, The" (Carter), 8, 28
Escola, Marc, 19, 43
Evans, Edmund, *246*
Evening Standard review of *Fairy Tales of Charles Perrault*, 58–59
Express & News review of *Fairy Tales of Charles Perrault*, 62

fable genre, 43
fabulist tradition, 24, 80, 172
"Fairies, The" (Carter), 28, 50
"Fairies and Ogres" (Lang), 51
Fairy Book (Craik), 192
Fairy Candida (fairy-tale character), 68
fairy godmothers, 106, 208
fairy tales: authorship of, 47, 53–54, 79–80; as carriers of practical knowledge, 22–23, 208–9; Carter on, as vehicles for moral instruction, 21–22; Carter's archaeology of, 97–99, 104–5, 110; Carter's experiments with, in radio plays, 14; Carter's exploration of sexual subtext in, 17; Carter's use of, with radical intent, 9; Carter's use of term, 11–12; circulation between France and England, 19, 54; contrasted with French *conte* tradition, 25; educational role, 8, 231; emergence of canon of, 66; female tradition in, 17–18; French fashion for, 78; as genre for adults, 4, 11, 38; genre's potential for Carter, 107; international tradition, 7; objections to, as sexist genre, 20, 190; as open, ever-changing tradition, 207–8, 301; role of paratext in collections of, 41–42
Fairy Tales and the Art of Subversion (Zipes), 38, 305n27
Fairy Tales of Charles Perrault, The (Carter): 1977 edition, 14–15, 34; 2008 edition, 3, 12–13, 16, 33–34; audience for, 77; biographical sketch of Perrault, 51–52; Carter's account of Perrault's *contes en vers*, 53–56; Carter's aims for, 21–24; Carter's preparation for, 14; concluding words of, 17–18; didactic mode in, 22–23, 31; dust cover for, 47–50; early reception of, 56–62; foreword to, 50–51, 106, 118; in history of translation and reception of fairy tales, 9; introduction to, 43, 45–46; paratext of, 42–43; reviews of, 57–62; unification of Perrault's *contes en vers* and *contes en prose*, 46; Ware's illustrations for 1977 edition, 44–46, *48*, 50, *93*, *131*, *133*, *141*
fairy-tale studies, 11, 14
female fairy tale tradition, 17–18
feminist critics, 73, 106, 190, 270
"Fin de Siècle" (Carter), 139
"Fitchers Vogel" (Grimm brothers), 110
flesh-eating motif, 74–75, 81, 101–2, 222–23
folklore and folk heritage: Lang's view on Perrault and, 79–80; modern technology and, 217–19; as origin of Perrault's *contes*, 65; references to, in Perrault's "La Belle au bois dormant,"

folklore and folk heritage (*cont.*) 220–21; tensions and traffic between literary tradition and, 12, 54, 230–31; tradition of orally communicated texts, 266–67; valuing of, 230–31
folktale-myth connection, 79–80
folktales, role in Carter's writing, 11–12
"Foolish Wishes, The" (Carter), 28, 47–48
Foreman, Michael, 30, 63, *64*, 246–47, 313n40
Four and Twenty Fairy Tales (Planché), 192
French *moraliste* tradition, 23–24, 308n53
Freud, Sigmund, 96
Fromm, Erich, 73
fugues, 105, 163–64, 307n40

Gamble, Sarah, 20, 23, 285, 303n1
Gauthier, Théophile, 210
Gauthier, Xavière, 1, 36, 303n2
Genette, Gérard, 41
German *Märchen*, 77, 80, 85, 87–88, 97, 193, 212, 253
Gilbert, Sandra M., 124–25, 285, 289–90, 314n48, 344n24, 344n27
G. M., 22, 120, 122–24, 271
"Goblin Market" (Rossetti), 29
Godard, Barbara, 75
Goethe, Johann Wolfgang von, 28–29
Gollancz, Victor, 2, 63
"Goose Girl" (Grimm brothers), 78–79
Gothic motifs, in "The Lady of the House of Love," 218
Great Expectations (Dickens), 210
Grimm, Jacob and Wilhelm: "Aschenputtel," 265, 267, 274–75, 289, 292; "Dornröschen," 59, 190–91, 193, 210–12; "Fitchers Vogel," 110; "Goose Girl," 78–79; *Kinder-und Hausmärchen*, 10; "Mordschloss," 110, 339n35; "Schneewittchen," 211; "Singende, Springende Löweneckerchen," 240. *See also* "Rotkäppchen"
"Griselidis" (Perrault), 26–27, 46, 53

Gubar, Susan, 125, 285, 289–90, 314n48, 344n24, 344n27
Guichon, Marie, 52
Gulin, Mercedes, 294, 297

Haffenden, John, interview with Carter, 23, 26, 109, 111, 229, 316n31
Hampstead & Highgate Express (periodical), 62
"Happy Prince, The" (Wilde), 236
Haraway, Donna, 219
Hassal, John, 34–35
Hauser, Kaspar, 81
Hearne, Betsey, 242
Heidmann, Ute, 12
Heroes and Villains (Carter), 36
Hibernia (periodical), 62
Histoires ou contes du temps passé, avec des Moralités (Perrault), 2, 33, 47
Histories, or Tales of Past Times, With Morals (Samber), 22, 46
Histories, or Tales of Past Times told by Mother Goose, with Morals (G. M.), 22
Hodgson, Orlando, 169, *170*
Holy Family Album (Carter), 83
Hop o' My Thumb (fairy-tale character), 47, 59, 162
"Hop o' My Thumb" (Perrault, trans. by Carter), 28, 56, 60
Huysmans, Joris-Karl, 136, 143–44, 147

illustrators, as rewriters, 94. *See also* Ware, Martin
"Impressions: The Wrightsman Magdalene" (Carter), 296
Infernal Desire Machines of Doctor Hoffman, The (Carter), 36
"In Pantoland" (Carter), 294–96
intermedial and intersemiotic transposition, 5–6

Jacobs, Joseph, 46
Jakobson, Roman, 5
Jeune Américaine et les contes marins, La (Villeneuve), 233

Jordan, Neil, 72

Kinder- und Hausmärchen (Grimm brothers), 10
Krailsheimer, A. J., 60–61

Là-bas (Huysmans), 147, 151, 323n38
"Lady of the House of Love, The" (Carter short story): birdsong leitmotif, 215; disenchantment of the fairy tale in, 196–97; language in, 8; preparatory notes for, 210; sexual subtext of, 206; *Vampirella* and, 218–19; *Vampirella* script as raw material for, 212; vampire lore in, 191
La Fontaine, Jean de, 23, 28, 85
Lamb, Charles, 241
Lang, Andrew: *Blue Fairy Book*, 190; as Carter influence, 73; on documenting the history of "Puss in Boots," 165–66; editorialized translation of Beauty and the Beast, 241; "Fairies and Ogres," 51; on Perrault and folk tradition, 79–80, 311n27; Perrault's Cinderella *conte* contrasted with Grimm brothers' Ashputtle *Märchen*, 267–68; on Perrault's "La Belle au bois dormant," 191; *Perrault's Popular Tales*, 43, 45, 51, 78–80
language-music interplay in Carter's work, 15, 99–100, 105, 163–64, 307n40
L'apparition (Moreau), 152
Lathey, Gillian, 8–9
Leavis, F. R., 225
Lector in Fabula (Eco), 91
Lefevere, André, 7
Les enfants sauvages (Malson), 81
"Les Fées" (Perrault), 28
"Les Souhaits ridicules" (Perrault), 28
Levi, Eliphas, 147
Lieberman, Marcia K., 190
Lilac Fairy (fairy-tale character), 49, 56
literary and folk heritage, tensions and traffic between, 12, 54, 230–31
literature, and social change, 9
"Little Lamb, Get Lost" (Carter), 104–5
"Little Red Riding Hood" (Hassal), 34
"Little Red Riding Hood" (Perrault, trans. by Carter): accessibility to young readers, 84; Carter's modernization of, 77; influences in Carter's translation for children, 84–91; modern morals in, 88–91; palimpsestic history of tale, 71, 73; Ware's illustration for, 92–94, *93*
Little Red Riding Hood, Cinderella, and Other Classic Fairy Tales of Charles Perrault (Carter): Penguin's 2008 edition, 33–34, *35, 37;* Zipes's introduction, 3, 12–13, 16
Little Red Riding Hood story: Carter's early childhood experience of, 84; Eco and, 91–92; Opies on, 80, 82; pop-up scene from, *83;* scholarly sources for, 78–83; variable age of heroine in Carter's translations and rewritings, 96–97. *See also* "Company of Wolves, The"; "Petit Chaperon rouge, Le"; "Werewolf, The"; "Wolf-Alice"
Location of Culture, The (Bhabha), 7
Loughlin, Gerard, 61–62
Louis XIV and court of Versailles, 50, 77–80, 163, 200, 269, 281
Louvel, Liliane, 5

Madwoman in the Attic (Gilbert and Gubar), 125, 289, 314n48, 344n24, 344n27
Ma fille, Monsieur Cabanel! (Rops), 144–45, *145*
Magasin des enfants, Le (Beaumont), 67, 228, 232, 234
"Maître Chat, ou le Chat botté, Le" (Perrault), 165–66, 169, 171–72, 173–74
male gaze, tyranny of, 140–43, 145
Malson, Lucien, 81
Manheim, Ralph, 210–11, 274, 276
Mariage de Figaro, Le (Beaumarchais), 162–63, 183–84

Martin Leman's Comic and Curious Cats (Leman), 174
Mary Magdalene, 296–97
Mayer, Charles-Joseph de, 54, 66
Mayes, Ian, 59–60
McKinley, Robin, 242
Medusa (mythological figure), 135–36, 161, 324n46, 332n46
Merveilles & Contes (Marvels & Tales), 11
Meschonnic, Henri, 299
Michel, Louise, 303n2
Miège, Guy, 22
Minter, Marilyn, 36–38, *37*, 309n6
mirror motif, 112–13, 136–38, 142–43, 151
Moon, Sarah, 91
moral function of curiosity, 109–13
moral function of the novel, 109–10
morals *(moralités)*: in "La Barbe bleue," 111, 127; in "Beauty and the Beast," 229; in "Bluebeard," 125–27; Carter's rediscovery of, 21; in "Cendrillon ou la petite pantoufle de verre," 269, 271, 278–80; in "Le Chat botté," 165–66; in "Cinderella: or, The Little Glass Slipper," 280–81; in "Courtship of Mr. Lyon," 242; French tradition of, 23–24; in "Little Red Riding Hood," 88–91; in Perrault's *contes*, 43, 89–90; in "Le Petit Chaperon rouge," 76–77; in "Le Prince Chéri," 236–37; problem of, 165–69; in "Puss in Boots," 166–67, 177–78, 180–81; in "Puss-in-Boots," 185–86; in "Sweetheart," 236–39; in "The Werewolf," 98
"Mordschloss" (Grimm brothers), 110, 339n35
Moreau, Gustave, 150–52
"Morte amoureuse, La" (Gauthier), 210
Mother Goose, 18, 50–51, 294–96
mothering, ambivalence of, 289–94
Mozart, Wolfgang Amadeus, 163
"Mr. Fox" (English folktale), 110
Mulvey, Laura, 154, 322n29
murderous-look motif, in Bluebeard story, 161

"Mutilated Girls, The" (Carter short story), 263, 275–76, 289–93
myth-folktale connection, 79–80
mythologies: critique of, in Carter's work, 106, 136–37, 155, 269; of femme fatale, 148–49; vampire, cultural inflections of, 224–25

necrophagy, in "Wolf-Alice," 103–4
"New Mother Goose Tales" (Carter), 243
"new wine in old bottles" analogy, 74–75, 111, 225, 304n5, 307–8n52
novels, moral function of, 109–10

ogres and ogresses, 47, *48*, 192–93, 220–21, 330n10
"On Linguistic Aspects of Translation" (Jakobson), 5
Opie, Iona and Peter: on "Beauty and the Beast," 68; on early reception of "Little Red Riding Hood," 82; on fairy godmothers, 208; on literary origins of Beauty and the Beast story, 230; problem of the moral in "Le Chat botté," 166; on Samber as translator of Perrault's tales, 22; textual approach to fairy-tale tradition, 266–67; on wisdom of fairy tales, 80. *See also Classic Fairy Tales* (Opie and Opie)

palimpsest texts and palimpsestic dimension: in fairy-tale tradition, 264; "Little Red Riding Hood" as, 71, 73, 75; pedagogical function of, 111
pantomime tradition: and early reception of fairy tales in England, 82, 294; inspiration for, 159, 164; and the kiss in "Sleeping Beauty," 191; perennial subjects for, 60; Ware's artwork for "The Sleeping Beauty in the Wood" and, 193–94, 196
paratext, role in fairy-tale collections, 41–42
Paz, Octavio, 1
"Peau d'Ane" (Perrault), 17, 47
Penguin's Modern Classics series, 3,

12–13, 16, 34–36, *37*, 38–40, 309n5
Perrault, Charles: analogy between Puss and, 68–69; Beaumont compared to, 66; Carter's biographical sketch of, 51–53; Carter's response to, 16–17; Carter's understanding of, 20; commonalities in worldviews of Carter and, 25; directness of tales recorded by, 86; as figure of identification for children, 57; and French *moraliste* tradition, 23; Lang on, 311n27; parables of experience, 88; pragmatic pedagogy of, 55–56; role in Carter's development as fairy-tale writer, 13, 39; shifts in modern authorial constructions of, 33; use of fairy tale by, 65, 230
Perrault, Charles, works by: "Apologie des Femmes," 125–26; "La Barbe bleue," 111–13, 127, 129, *134*, 135; "La Belle au bois dormant," 190, 194–95, 200, 205–7, 219–20, 222–24; "Cendrillon ou la petite pantoufle de verre," 263, 269, 271–73, 278–80; *Contes de ma Mère l'Oye*, 13, 78; "Les Fées," 28; "Griselidis," 26–27, 46, 53; *Histoires ou contes du temps passé, avec des Moralités*, 2, 33, 47; "Le Maître Chat, ou le Chat botté," 165–66, 169, 171–72, 173–74; "Peau d'Ane," 17, 47; "Le Petit Chaperon rouge," 71, 75–77, 79, 91–92, *95;* "Le Petit Poucet," 28; "Les Souhaits ridicules," 28. *See also contes* by Perrault
Perrault, Pierre, 53
Perrault's Popular Tales (Lang), 43, 45, 51, 78–80
Perrault's Tales of Mother Goose (Barchilon), 43, 45
"Petit Chaperon rouge, Le" (Perrault), 71, 75–77, 79, 91–92, *95*
"Petit Poucet, Le" (Perrault), 28
Picasso, Paloma, 211
pictorial conventions in European art, and economic dependency of women, 137–38
Pierrot, Jean, 140

Planché, J. R., 192
pornography: in "The Bloody Chamber," 141–44, 148; Carter and feminist debate on, 20, 138; consumers of, 144; of the elite, 146–52; Minter and, 36, 38; redefined by Carter, 207
Potter, Beatrix, 172–73, 326nn15–16
"Prince Chéri, Le" (Beaumont), 227, 229, 234–37, 239
"Princesse Belle Etoile et le Prince Chéri, La" (d'Aulnoy), 234–35
Puss in Boots (Carter radio play), 157–58, 163–65
"Puss-in-Boots" (Carter short story): influence of commedia dell'arte and French Enlightenment comedy, 182–83; language in, 8; mock moral of, 185–86; predecessors of Carter's reformulation, 158; prose style, 186–87; as scatological fairy-tale about desire, 184–85
"Puss in Boots" (Perrault, trans. by Carter), 47; Carter's understanding of the moral in, 166–67; as comic relief in *The Fairy Tales of Charles Perrault*, 157; explanations and clarifications in, 175; gender politics reoriented in, 178–79; meaning and associations of title, 173; moral justice and injustice in, 176–77; moral of, 177–78; opening paragraph, 174–75; question of suitability of the tale, 162; translation of morals, 180–81; Ware's illustrations of, *168*
"Puss in Boots" (trans. by Hodgson), *170*
Puss in Boots story: Carter on, 161–62; Carter's variations on, 158–60; pre-Perrault versions of, 167–69. *See also* "Maître Chat, ou le Chat botté, Le" (Perrault)

radio plays by Carter: *The Curious Room*, 103; experiments with fairy tales in, 14; mix of black comedy and bizarre pathos in, 212, 217–18; as three-dimensional storytelling, 217. *See also*

radio plays by Carter (*cont.*)
Puss in Boots; Vampirella
Ramanujan, A. K., 11
reading: active, and intersemiotic/intermedial translation, 5–6; creative dimension of, 25–26; as re-creation, 19–20; translation as most intimate act of, 30
reality principle, in Carter's translation of Perrault, 96
Redon, Odilon, 150
"Red Riding Hood Rides Again" (Krailsheimer), 60–61
rereading, as form of internal translation or rewriting, 308n55
rewriting: emancipatory potential in act of, 92, 154; in fairy-tale tradition, 55; as form of translation, 3–11, 15
"Ricky with the Tuft" (Perrault, trans. by Carter), 28
Robinson, W. Heath, 243, *244*
rococo style, 16, 158, 163, 187–88
Roemer, Danielle, 12
Role of Translators in Children's Literature, The (Lathey), 8–9
Rops, Félicien, 142, 144–45, *145*, 148, 323n37
Rossetti, Christina, 29
Rossini, Gioachino, 163
"Rotkäppchen" (Grimm brothers): and alternative endings to "Little Red Riding Hood," 82; death of wolf in, 98; happy ending in, 88–89; influence on Carter, 77, 85, 96; Lang on, 79–80
Rowe, Karen, 190

Sadeian Woman, The: An Exercise in Cultural History (Carter), 20–21
Sage, Lorna, 288, 303n1
Said, Edward, 3–4, 15
Salomé (Moreau), 151–52
Salzmann, Christian Gotthilf, 9
Samber, Robert: *Histories, or Tales of Past Times, With Morals*, 22, 46; influence on Carter, 271; "Sleeping Beauty" translation, 192–93; translation of "La Barbe bleue," 120, 122–24; translation of Perrault's "La Belle au bois dormant," 192
"Schneewittchen" (Grimm brothers), 211–12
screenplays by Carter, 72, 210
Sermain, Jean-Paul, 42, 46–47
Sexton, Anne, 207–8
Shelley, Percy Bysshe, 214
Showalter, Elaine, 140
Simon, Sherry, 9
Simpson, Helen, 9
"Singing, Springing Lark" (Grimm brothers), 240
Sleeping Beauty (Disney), 189–90, 193
"Sleeping Beauty" (trans. by Samber), 192–93
Sleeping Beauty and Other Favourite Fairy Tales (Carter), 34, 63–66, 227, 230, 234, 250
"Sleeping Beauty in the Wood, The" (Perrault, trans. by Carter): cautionary message about marriage in, 204–5; differences between Perrault's text and, 203–4; emancipatory potential uncovered in, 198; marital happiness in, 206–7; narrative voice in, 199–200; reviews of, 58–60; scene of discovery in, 195–96; textual and thematic connections between "Bluebeard" and, 204; title of, 191; Ware's illustrations for, 193–94, 196, *197*
Sleeping Beauty story: feminist critics of the male gaze and, 194; idea of suspended time in, 201–2; interplay of text and image in, 193–97; the kiss, 190–92; psychosexual interpretations in late 1970s, 198–99; revamping of, 189–93; Samber's translation, 192–93; sinister aspects of, 220; traditional fairy-tale script reversed by Carter, 215; as vampire story, 193. *See also* "Belle au bois dormant, La"; "Lady of the House of Love, The"; *Vampirella*

(Carter radio play)
Smith, Ali, 36
"Snow Child, The" (Carter), 28, 211
"Snow White," Gilbert and Gubar's interpretation of, 290
somersault *(tours de souplesse)*, in Carter's variations on "Puss in Boots," 160–61
Spivak, Gayatri Chakravorti, 30
"Stepping Up" (Minter), 36–38, *37*
Stone, Kay, 106
"Story of Grandmother, The" (folktale), 73, 74–75, 80–82
Suleiman, Susan Rubin, 303n2
sun, anthropomorphized, 47, *48,* 50
Surréalisme et sexualité (Gauthier), 1
"Sweetheart" (Beaumont, trans. by Carter), 229, 234, 236–41, 247, 250, 257
Swift, Jonathan, 91

Tale of Benjamin Bunny (Potter), 172–73
Tale of Peter Rabbit (Potter), 172–73
text-image interplay in fairy-tale books, 19
Theatrical Picture-book (c. 1870), 82, *83*
"The Marquise de Salusses, or the Patience of Griselda." *See* "Griselidis"
thresholds, in editorial presentation of text, 41
tiger-lilies motif, in "The Bloody Chamber," 29
"Tiger's Bride, The" (Carter short story): animality chosen over humanity, 247, 257–58, 261–62; audience for, 228; Byron association with Beast figure, 243–44; deviations from Beauty and Beast story, 82, 229, 234; female side of story explored in, 227; inquiry into psychology and moral philosophy, 242; language in, 8; translational dynamics in, 29; trappings of humanity discarded by Beast and Beauty, 255–56
Times Educational Supplement (periodical), 62

translation: brief for, 33; connections linking Carter's rewriting to, 25–26; as creative literary activity, 4–5; cultural, concept of, 7; defined, 304–5n16, 305n17; as generating principle of Carter's oeuvre, 11–15, 300–301; rewriting as form of, 3–11
translational poetics in Carter's work, 6–7
translation-rewriting dynamic, 10–12, 15, 23–24
transposition, intralingual, interlingual, and intersemiotic, 5–6
"Travelling Clothes" (Carter short story), 263, 290, 292, 294, 297
Travers, P. L., 209

Vampirella (Carter radio play): birdsong leitmotif in, 213–15; conventions shared with "Lady of the House of Love," 218–19; creation of, 217–19; first broadcast, 332n23; idea of replay in, 209–10; inspirations for Countess character, 225; the kiss in, 216; as mix of fairy tale and vampire story, 191–92; vampirism as metaphor in, 212
Vampirella (magazine), *224,* 224–25
vampire myth, cultural inflections of, 224–25
vampire-story motifs, 211–12
vampirism, as metaphor, 209–17, 220
Venuti, Lawrence, 5, 304n10
Versailles, Louis XIV and court of, 50, 77–80, 163, 200, 269, 281
Victorian novels, characteristics of, 233
Villeneuve, Gabrielle Susanne Barbot de Gallon de, 233, 241
Virago Book of Ghost Stories (1987), 263
visual representation, issue of limits and ethics of, 130–31, 152

Ware, Martin: Carter and etchings by, 30; illustration of the Lilac Fairy, 56; illustrations for "Bluebeard," 130, *131,* 131–32, *133;* illustrations for "Cinderella," 281–84, *282, 284;*

Ware, Martin (*cont.*)
    illustrations for *Fairy Tales of Charles Perrault*, 47–50, *48;* illustrations for "Little Red Riding Hood," 92–94, *93*, 318nn46–47; illustrations for "Puss in Boots," 167, *168;* illustrations for "Sleeping Beauty in the Wood," 193–94, 196, *197;* influence of illustrations on "The Bloody Chamber," 128–36; influence on other illustrators, 57; reviews of illustrations produced by, 57–59, 61–62
Warner, Marina, 10–11, 227, 242, 248, 285
Ways of Seeing (Berger), 137–38
"Werewolf, The" (Carter short story), 76, 96–101
West, Mae, 56, 57
Whistler, Rex, 264–65, *266*
"White Cat, The" (d'Aulnoy), 260
"Whittington and His Cat" (collected by Jacobs), 175–76

Wilde, Oscar, 236
"Wolf-Alice" (Carter short story): as exercise in genre, 103–5; fairy-tale archaeology in, 104–5; initial publication of, 96; language in, 8; as last tale of *Bloody Chamber* collection, 286; rewriting sequence as fugue, 105; translational dynamics in, 29; as wolf-child exploration, 81; women's complex relations with beastliness in, 228–29
Wollstonecraft, Mary, 9

Zipes, Jack: Carter and, 11; on Carter's translations and rewritings, 39–40; *Fairy Tales and the Art of Subversion*, 305n27; introduction to Penguin reissue of *Fairy Tales of Charles Perrault*, 3, 12–13, 16, 34, 38–40; on morals in "Little Red Riding Hood," 90–91; perplexity at Carter's decision to translate Perrault, 13

www.ingramcontent.com/pod-product-compliance
Lightning Source LLC
Chambersburg PA
CBHW071810230426
43670CB00013B/2417